HOW TO RENDER ATTRACTIVE CHARACTERS WITH

COPIC MARKERS

YASAIKO MIDORIHANA

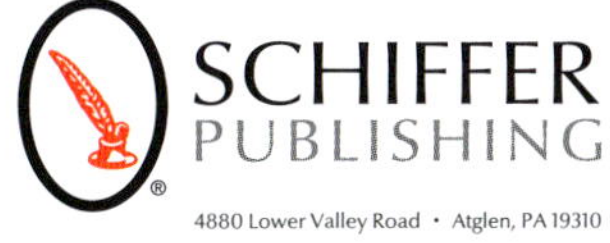

SCHIFFER PUBLISHING

4880 Lower Valley Road · Atglen, PA 19310

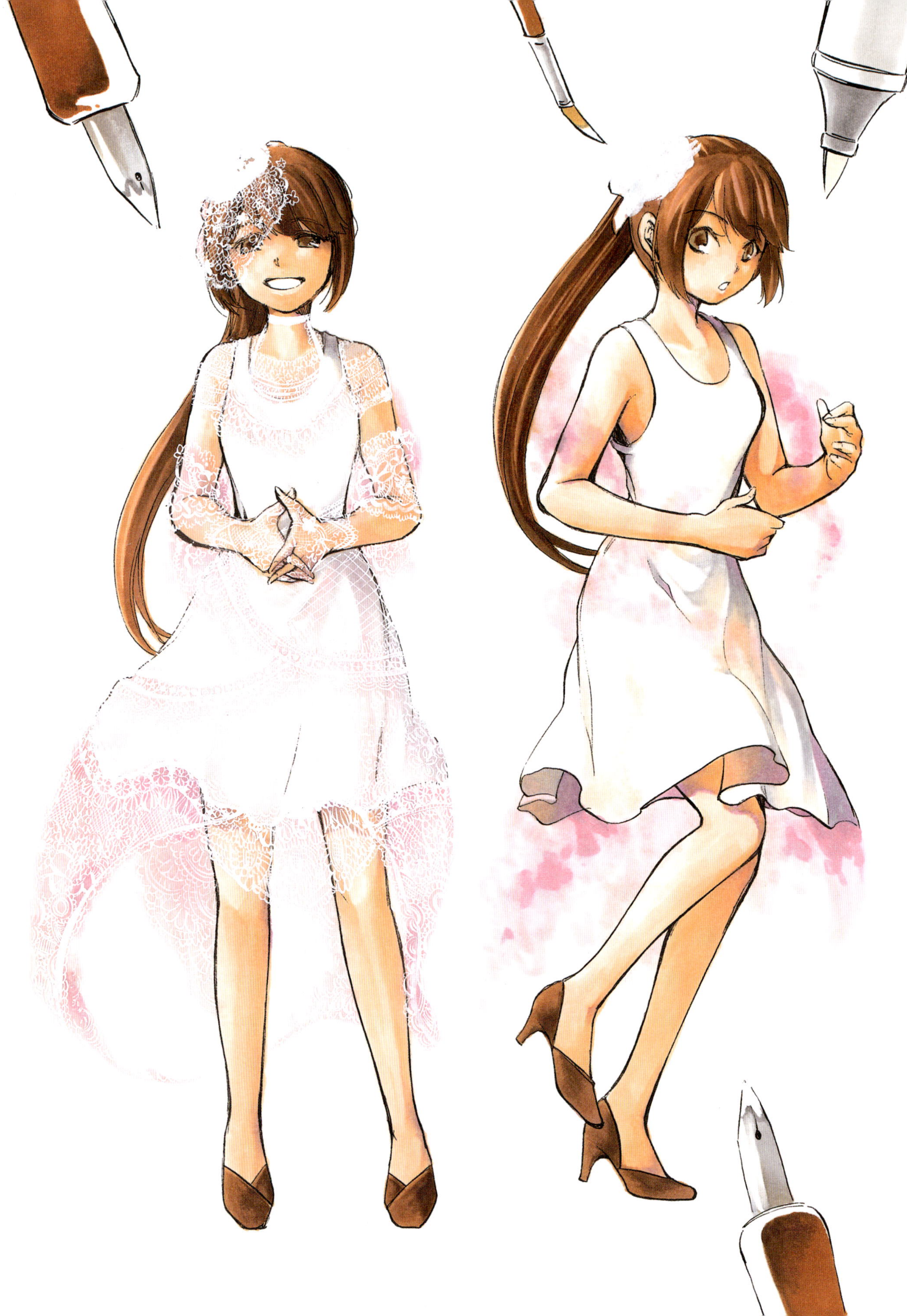

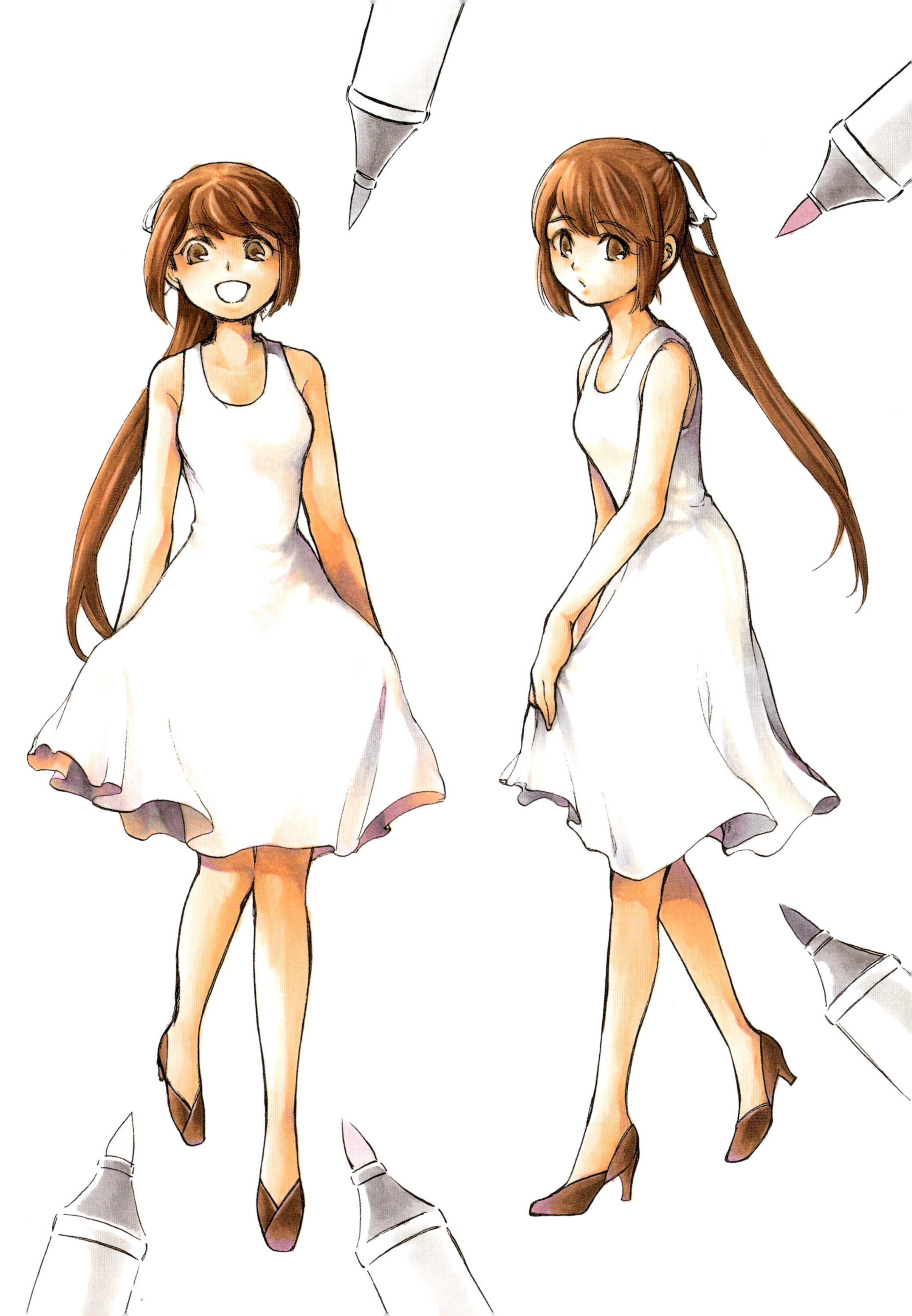

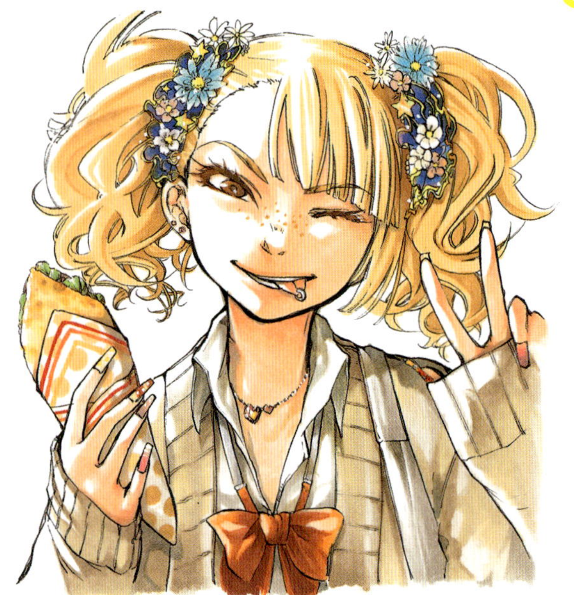

Contents

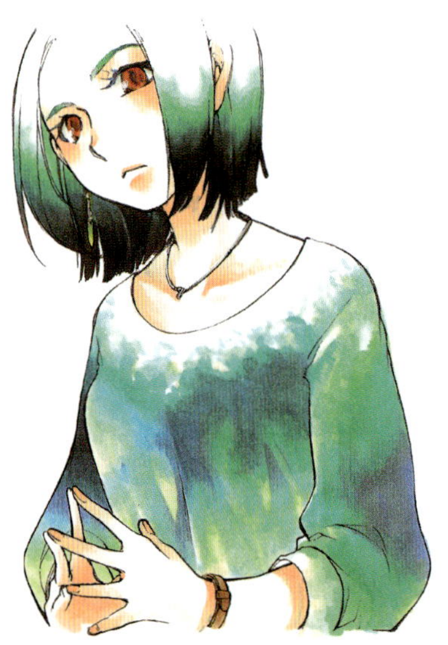

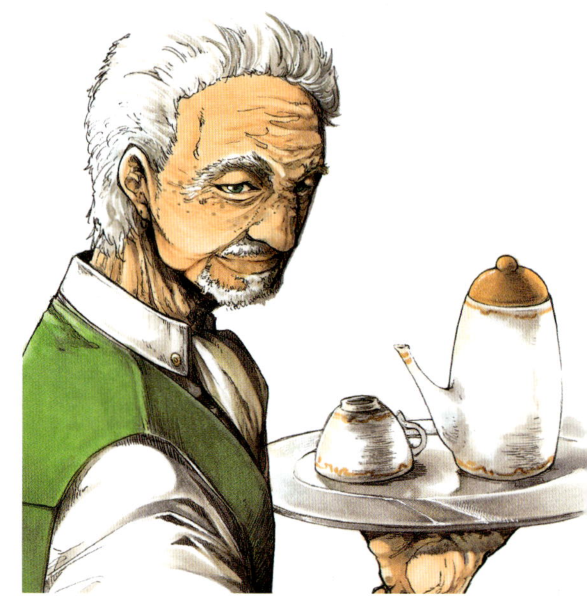

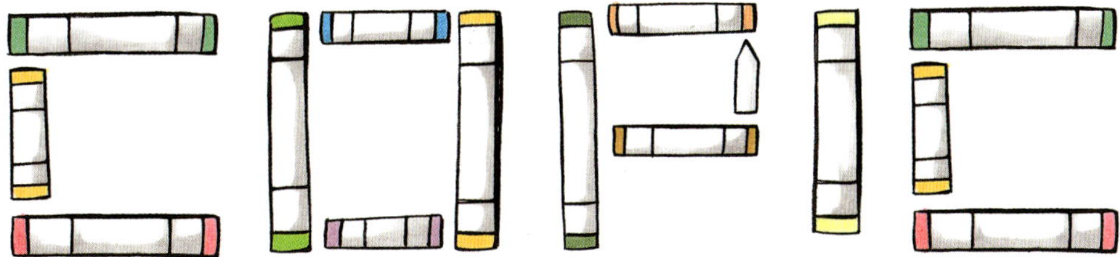

COPIC

Basic Lessons

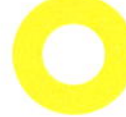

What Is a COPIC Marker?

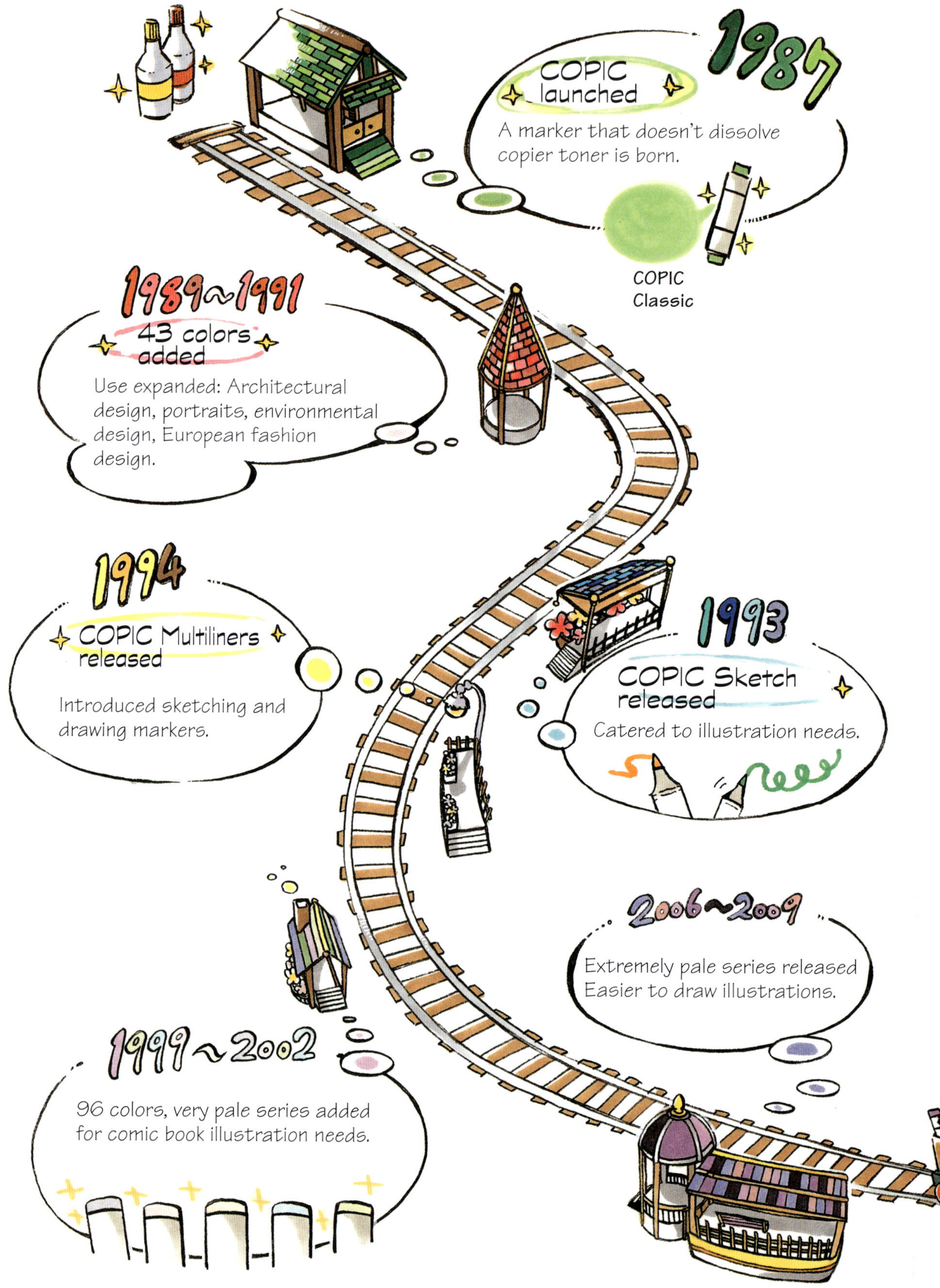

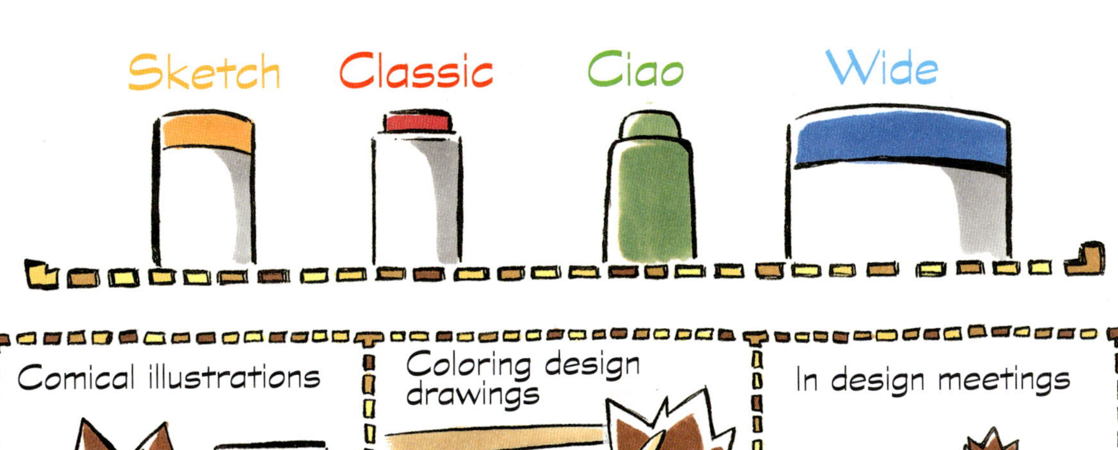

Sketch
Classic
Ciao
Wide

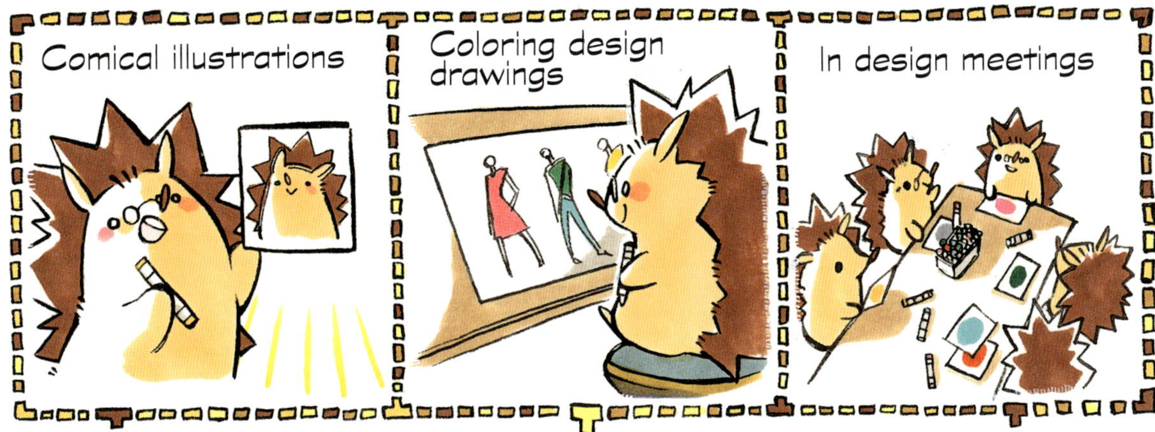

Comical illustrations
Coloring design drawings
In design meetings

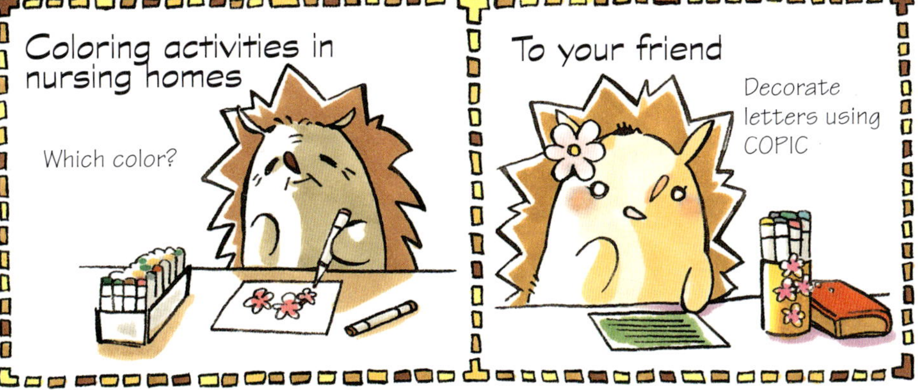

Coloring activities in nursing homes
Which color?
To your friend
Decorate letters using COPIC

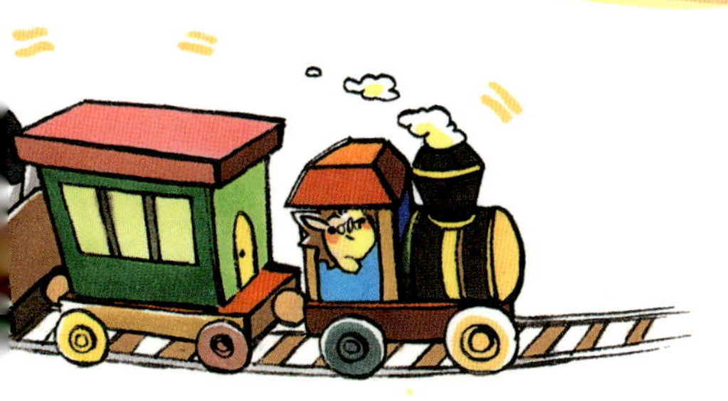

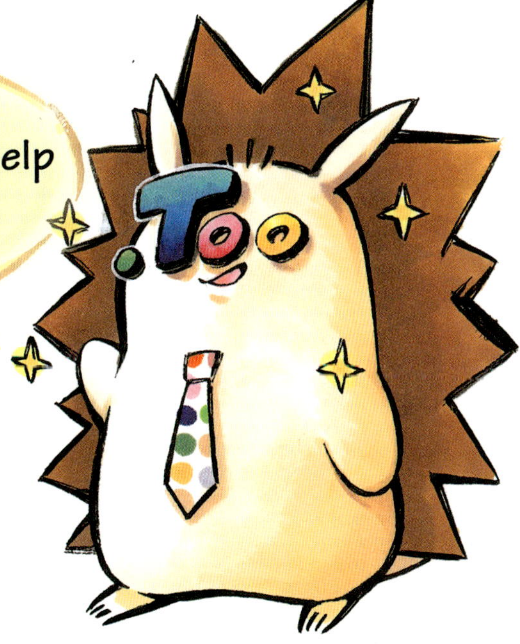

What is COPIC?
We want our products to help people be more creative!

Types of COPIC Marker

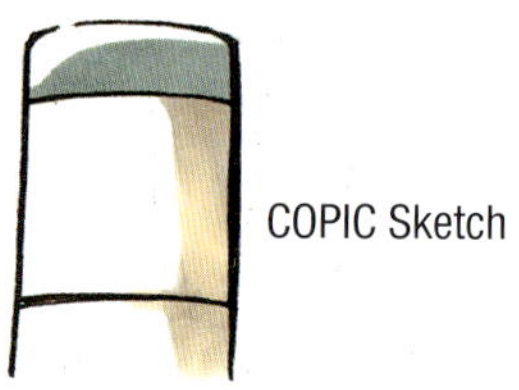

COPIC Sketch

COPIC Ciao

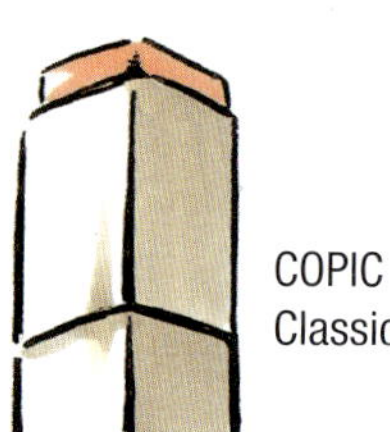

COPIC Classic

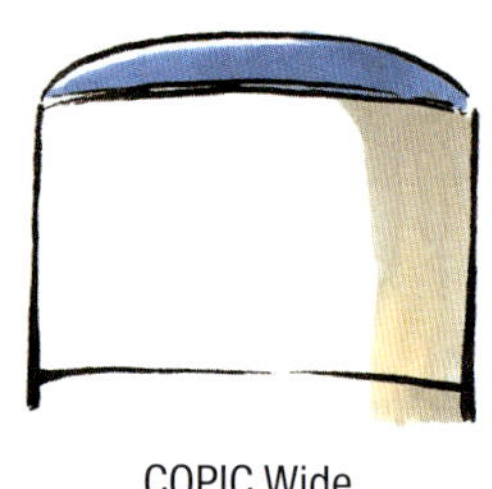

COPIC Wide

COPIC Ciao

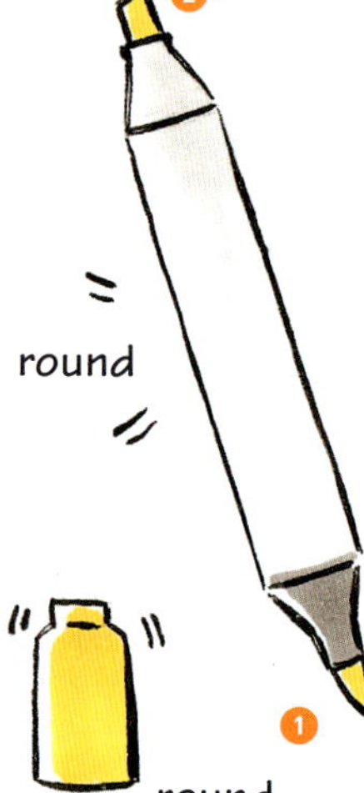

180 colors available

More economical choice. Fewer color variations and contains less ink than COPIC Sketch. Best option for COPIC beginners.

COPIC Sketch

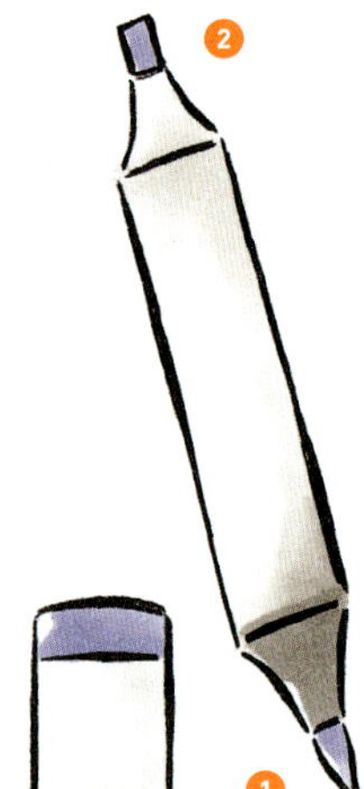

358 colors available

The standard COPIC marker.
One end (1) has a paintbrush-like nib, the other (2) has a hard, highlighter-like nib.

COPIC Classic

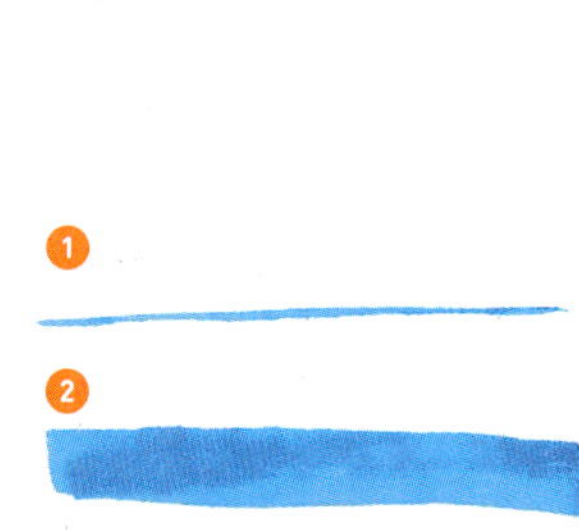

214 colors available.

1 is a fine nib and 2 is a hard, highlighter-like nib. Fewer colors than COPIC Sketch, but the fine nib 1 allows for intricate patterns and rendering. Contains more ink than COPIC Sketch.

COPIC Wide

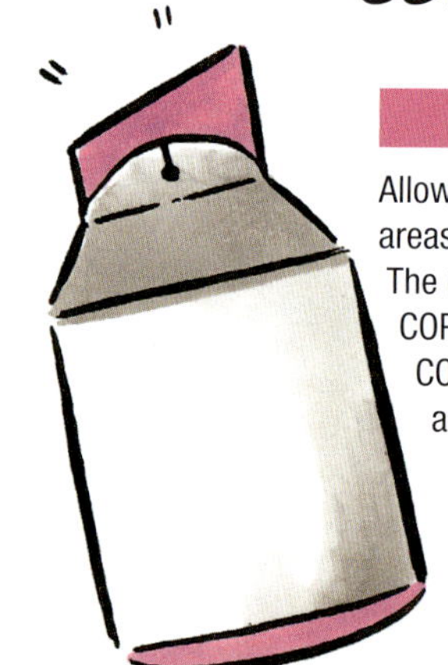

Fillable unit.

Allows for filling of large areas.
The unit is sold without COPIC ink. Purchase COPIC ink separately and fill the unit.

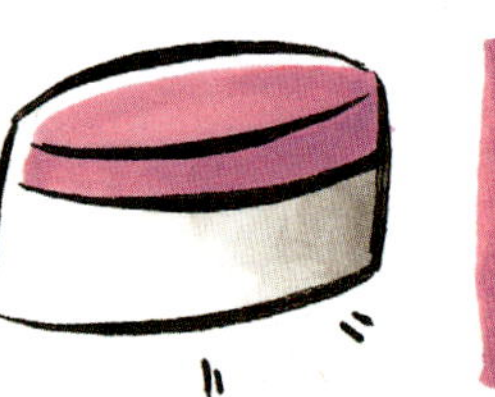

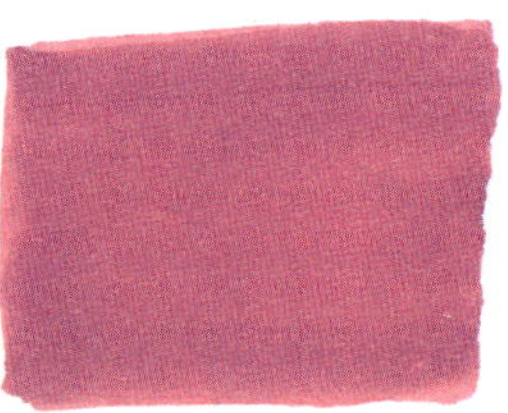

Maintenance Tool

COPIC Sketch, Ciao Replacement Nibs

There are replacement nibs for COPIC Sketch and COPIC Ciao.

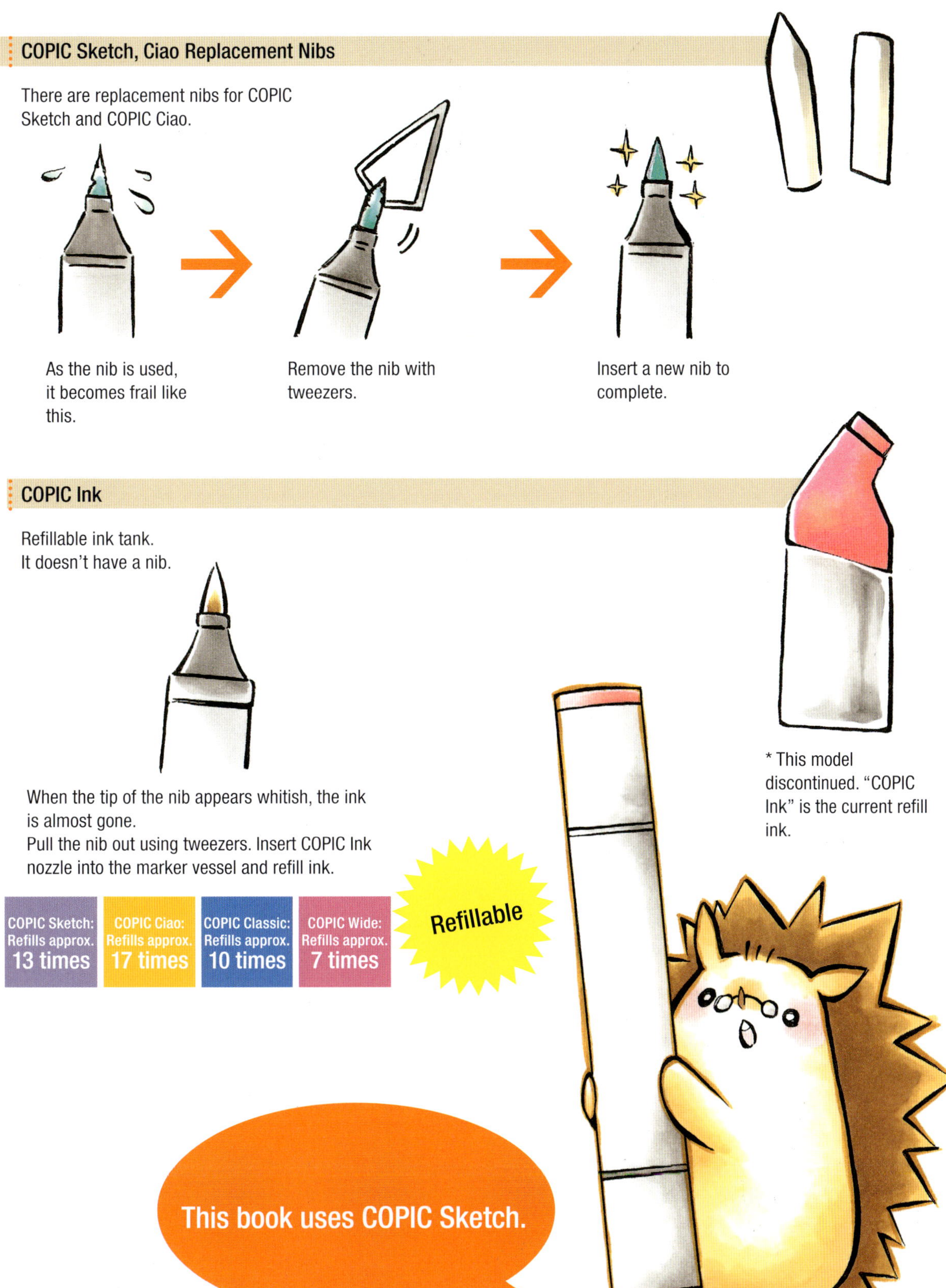

As the nib is used, it becomes frail like this.

Remove the nib with tweezers.

Insert a new nib to complete.

COPIC Ink

Refillable ink tank. It doesn't have a nib.

When the tip of the nib appears whitish, the ink is almost gone.
Pull the nib out using tweezers. Insert COPIC Ink nozzle into the marker vessel and refill ink.

* This model discontinued. "COPIC Ink" is the current refill ink.

⬤ Characteristics of COPIC Markers

The biggest advantage of COPIC markers is their excellent colors.
COPIC markers produce color in a manner similar to gouache. They have the advantage that you can make use of the texture of the paper in your work, like with watercolors.
Since COPIC markers are alcohol-based, they don't require any preparation – like setting up a palette, washing brushes, stretching paper. Also, the ink is quick to dry. Thus, COPIC markers are easier to handle in a precise way.

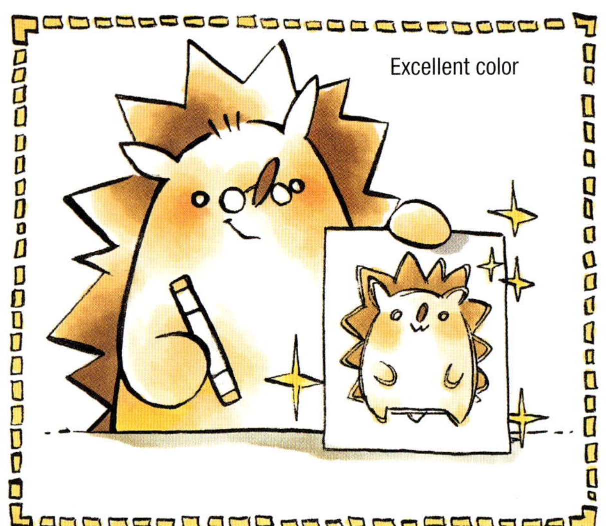

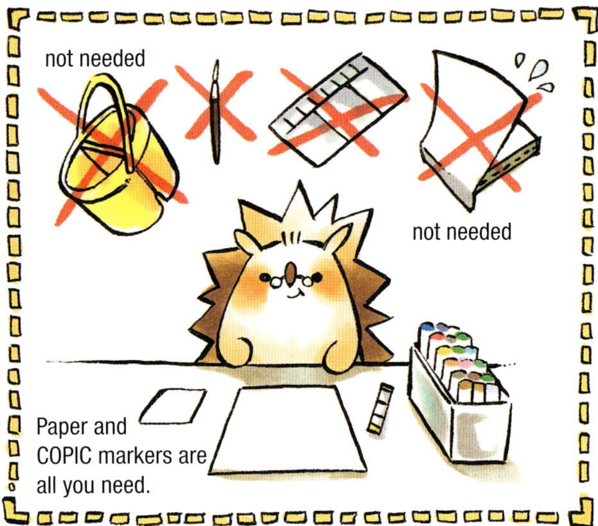

Take Care

COPIC markers use alcohol-based ink.
So, they will dry out if you leave the cap off.
Press the cap until you hear a clicking sound.
Avoid storing at high temperatures.

If the markers are left near a heater or in a sunny place for a long time, the ink may completely dry out.

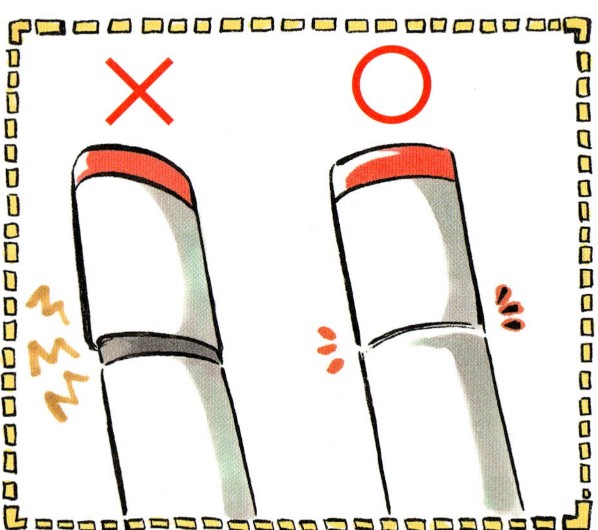

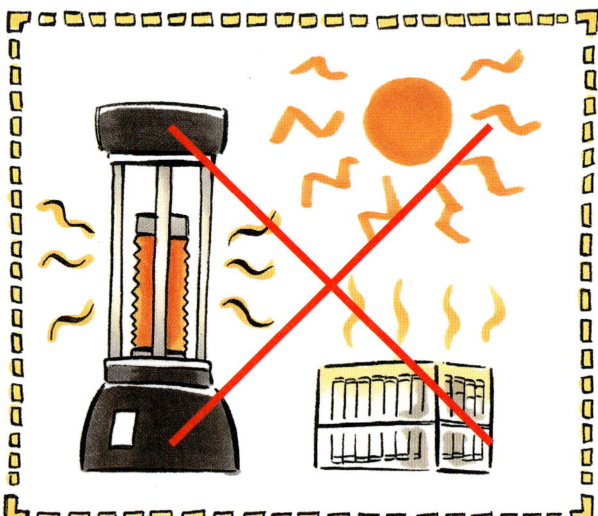

Life Span of COPIC Markers

If you pay attention to the "Take Care" notes on the previous page, you can maintain COPIC markers for about 8 years.
Ink evaporates slowly, even when the marker is not in use, so remember that your markers will have less ink in them than before. Even if they haven't been used for a while.

If the ink has dried completely, refill using COPIC Ink (see page 9).
Be careful: If the ink dries too quickly, the casing of the marker might crack.
If that happens, you need to replace the marker.

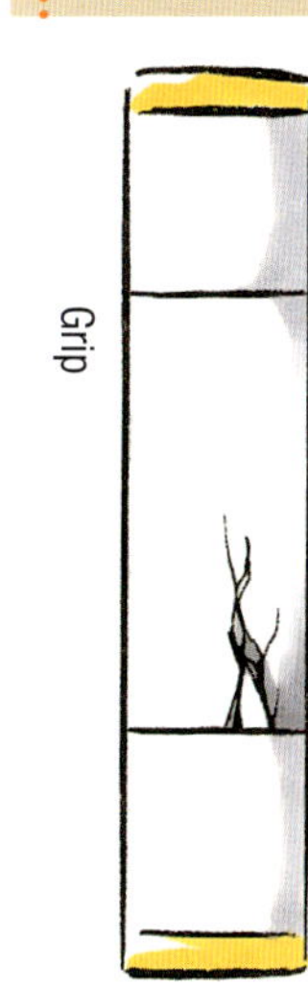
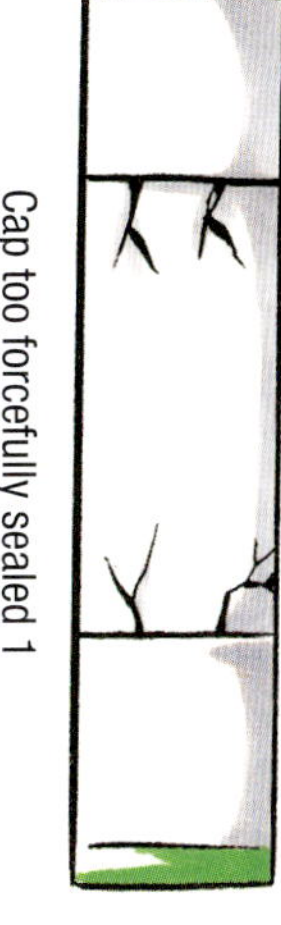

Storage Case

Since COPIC users often own several different types of markers, there are a variety of cases available. Some dedicated users even go so far as to make their own cases for convenience.

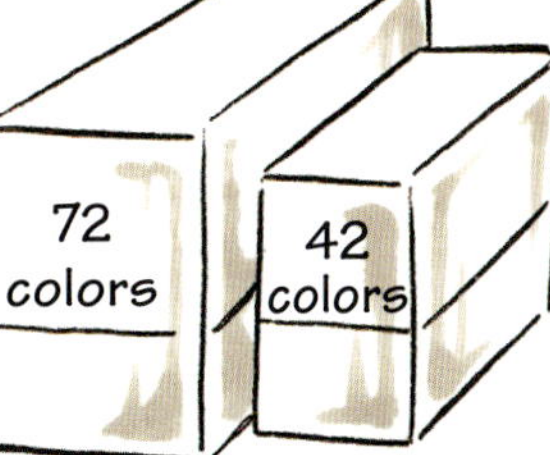

Plastic cases: Best storage capacity.

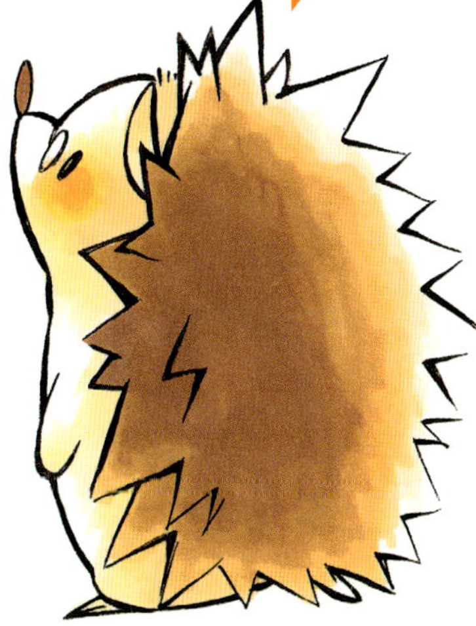

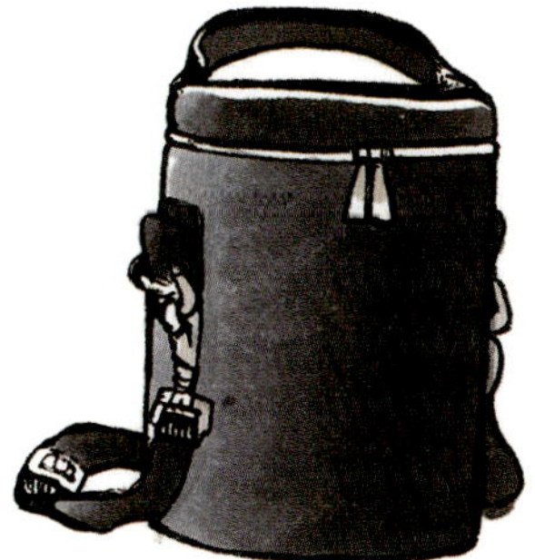

Pouch type: Convenient for carrying around. Good for sketching outdoors as well.

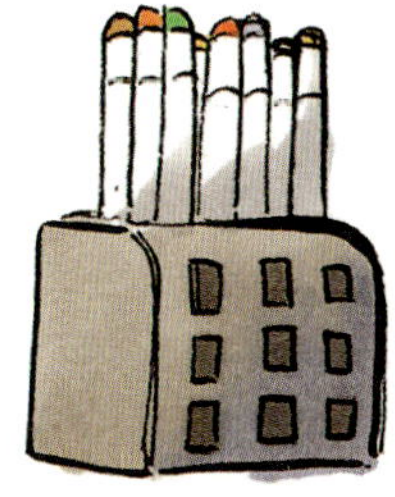

Block stand: Stylish

Characteristics of COPIC Markers

Color Family

The letter represents the color family. There are 16 categories.

Brightness Value

Color brightness is broken into 12 categories.

Color Saturation

Each color family is divided into 10 levels of color saturation, labeled 0 through 9.

Ciao

Color available in COPIC Ciao

Color Name

Individual name

These codes are printed on both COPIC Marker caps.

For COPIC Ciao these codes are printed on the casing side.

#0 marker doesn't have dyes in it. It's colorless and contains only alcohol. It is called "Colorless Blender" and is mainly used for blending and adding highlights.

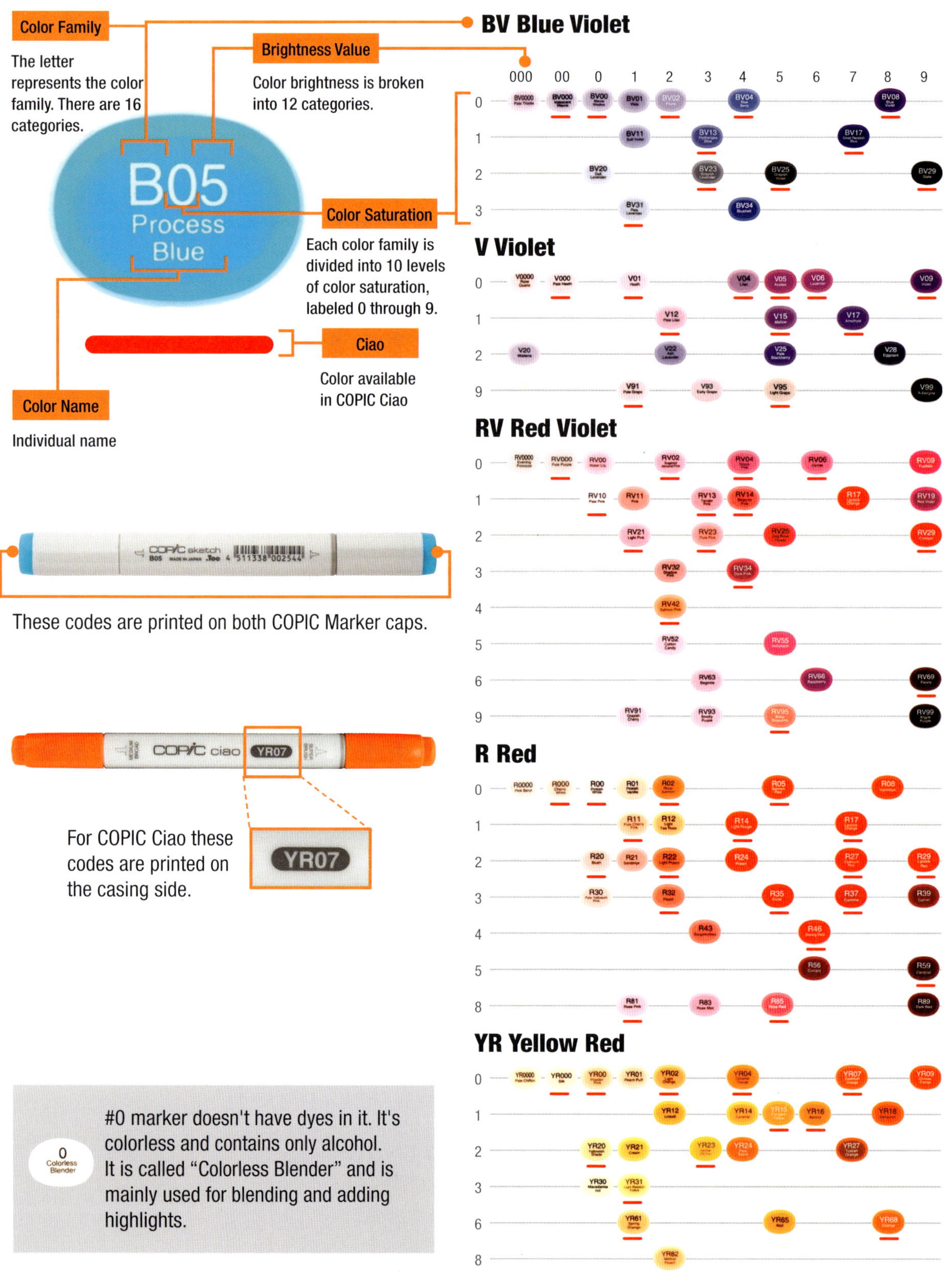

COPIC Markers offer 358 colors categorized into 16 color families. Each color is numbered by family, saturation, and brightness level. This makes it easier to figure out which color you want. This section provides a color chart for all 358 COPIC Sketch marker colors.

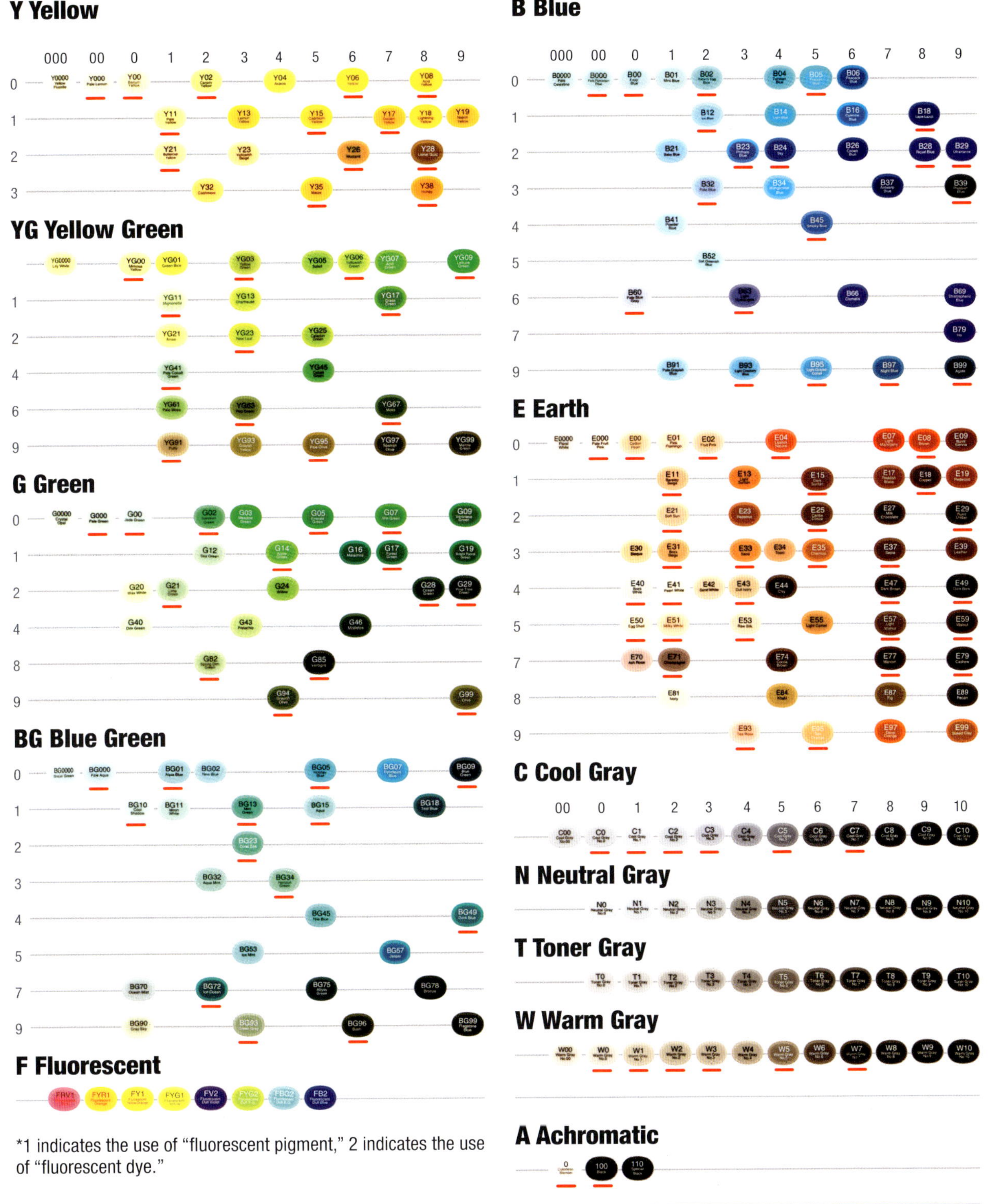

Y Yellow

YG Yellow Green

G Green

BG Blue Green

B Blue

E Earth

C Cool Gray

N Neutral Gray

T Toner Gray

W Warm Gray

F Fluorescent

A Achromatic

*1 indicates the use of "fluorescent pigment," 2 indicates the use of "fluorescent dye."

*Careful! The color of the plastic cap differs from the actual color of the ink in the marker.

Basic Coloring Tips

COPIC markers are not good for coloring large areas all at once. The reason is that the color tends to become darker when layered, resulting in unevenness. Here are some examples of how to apply colors evenly.

Three Basic Brush Strokes

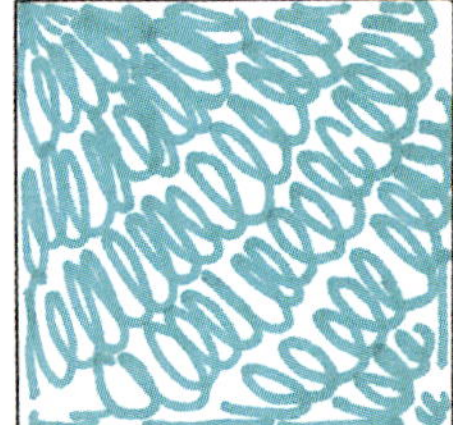

1 Spread Out Bit-by-bit from the Corner

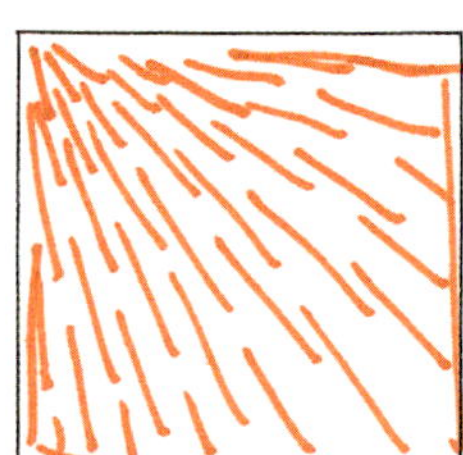

2 Applying Layers Inward from the Edge

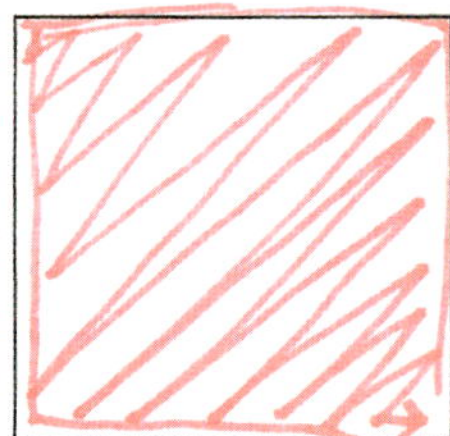

3 Overlapping Straight Lines

1 Spread Out Bit-by-bit from the Corner

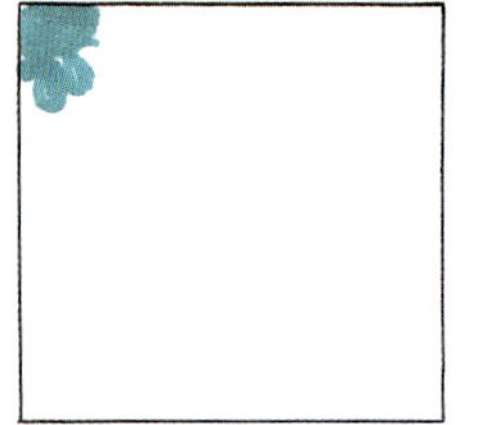
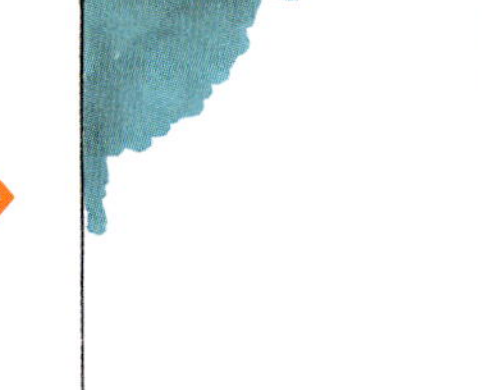
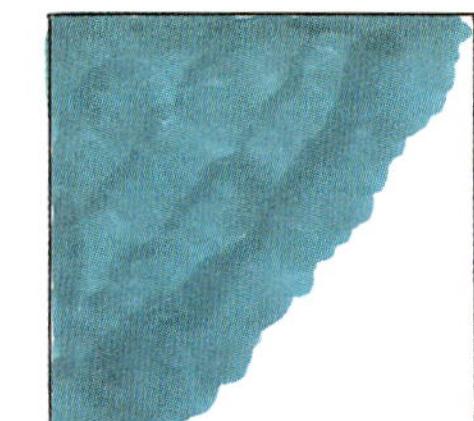

Moving diagonally from the corner is easiest.

Areas you don't want to jut out will be framed little-by-little.

If applied too quickly it will appear uneven, like above.

If applied slowly it should look like above.

2 Applying Layers Inward from the Edge

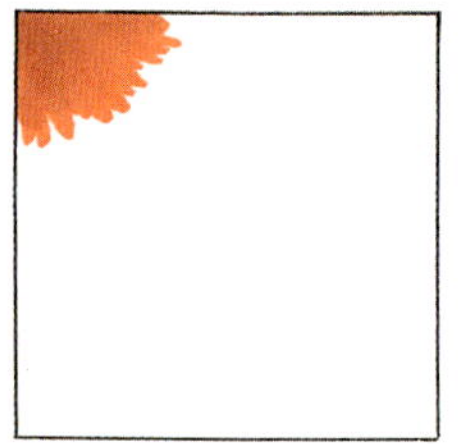
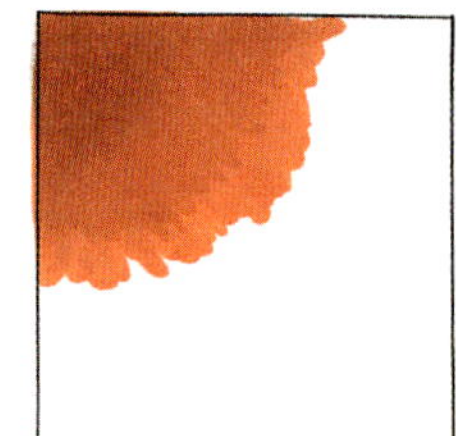

Begin as in 1 above.

Begin in the corner and spread out.

The initial area will be slightly darker, but at least it won't be uneven.

Two layered coats
Two coats will make things look better.

3 Overlapping Straight Lines

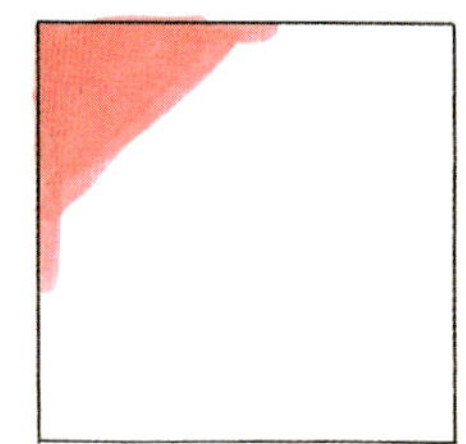
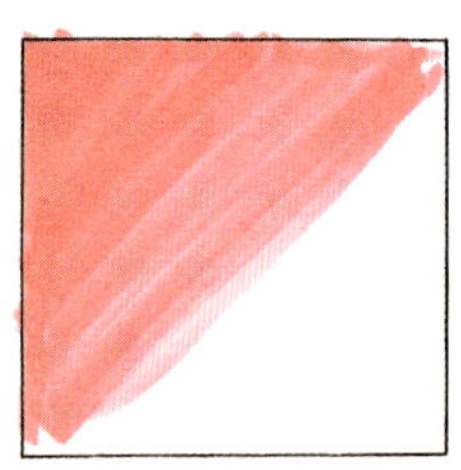
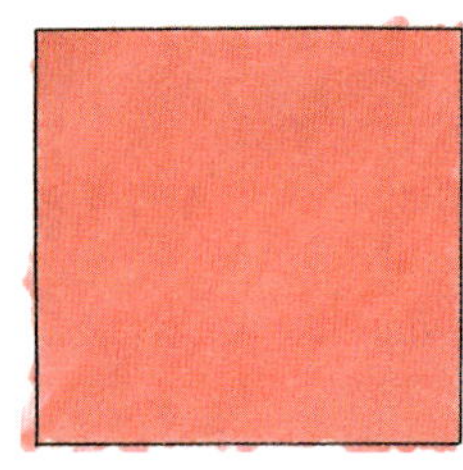

Simply move the brush back and forth.

We'll also frame the areas that we don't want to jut out.

If applied too fast, it will fade like above. So, apply slowly.

Once you get the hang of it, this is the easiest method. The trick is never lifting the nib of the marker from the paper while coloring.

4 Overlaying Colors

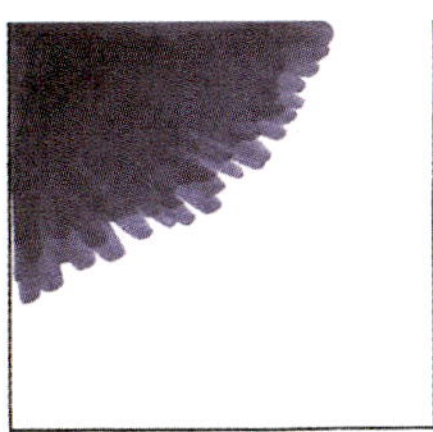

Blasting on a lot of color.

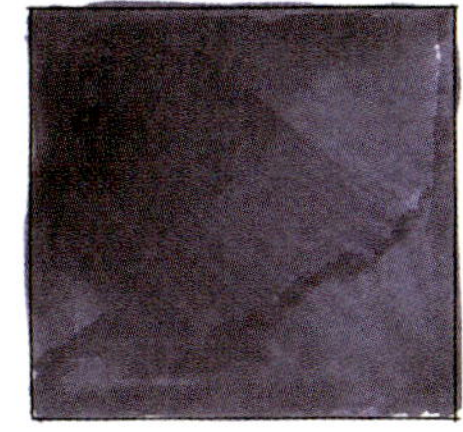

This will, of course, make it uneven.

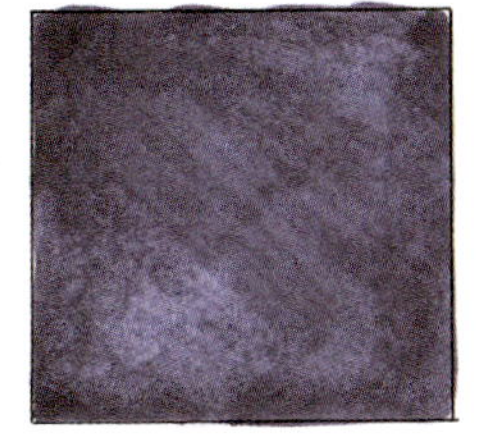

Lay down some #0 (colorless blender) on top.

Finish by adding another layer of color.

5 Using Two Colors

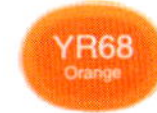

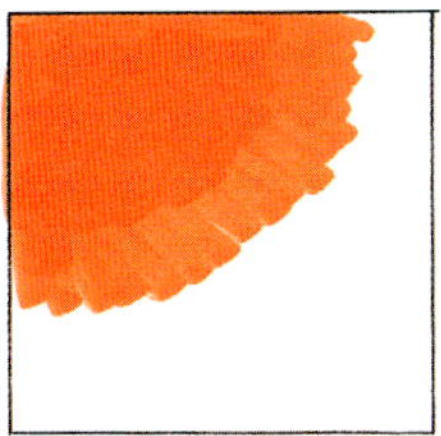

Blast on some color as in 4.

It will look something like this.

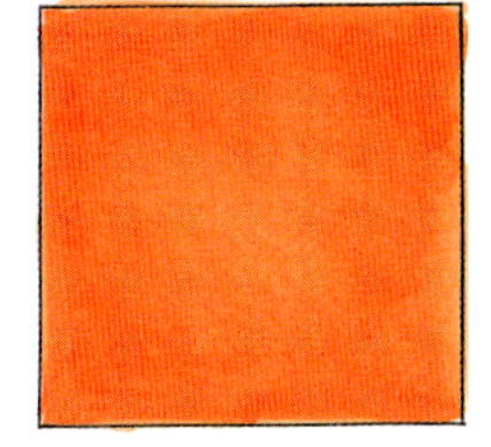

Add the second color on top. The colors are close enough to each other that the application will appear even.

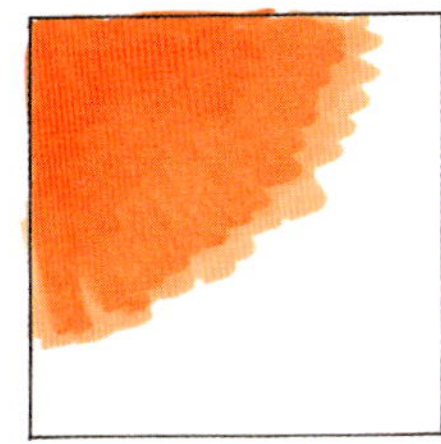

You can also apply color by alternating markers.

6 Mix to Create a Color

You can match dark and light colors together to make a completely different color.

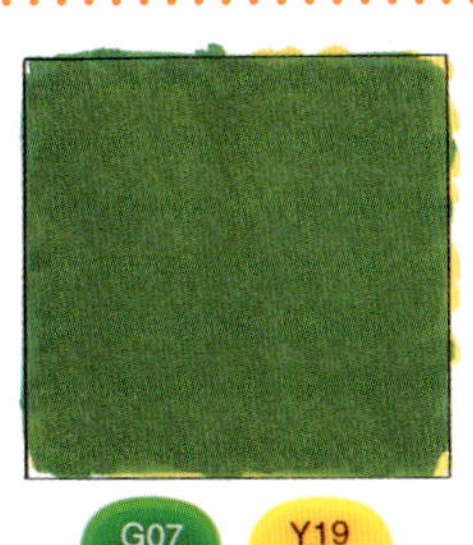

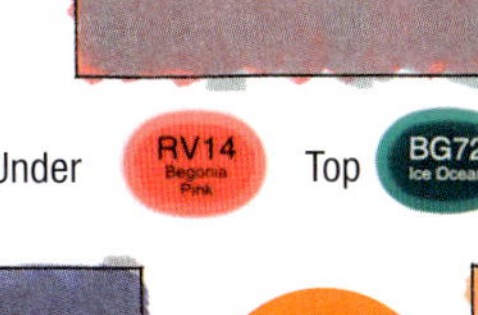

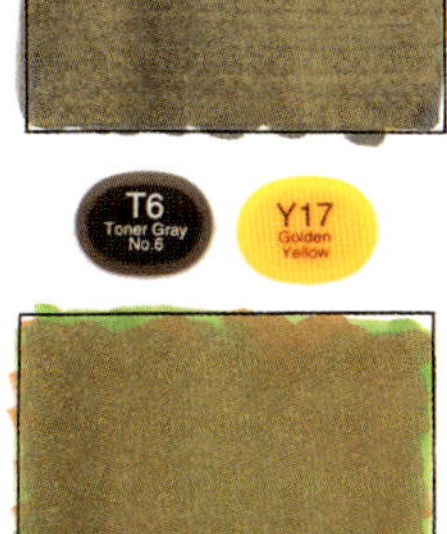

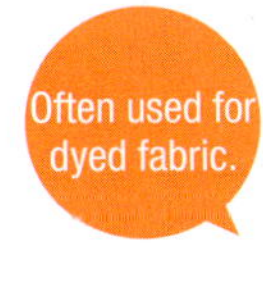

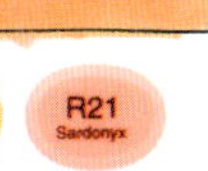

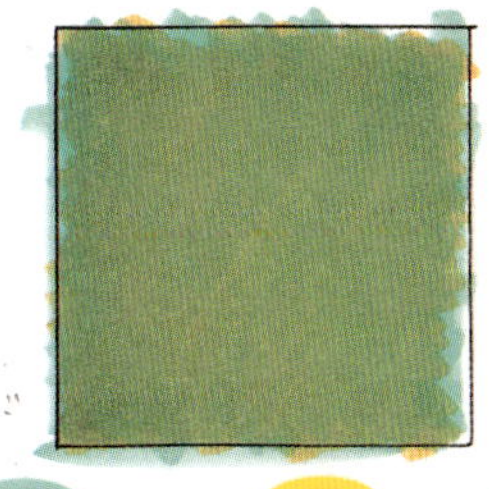
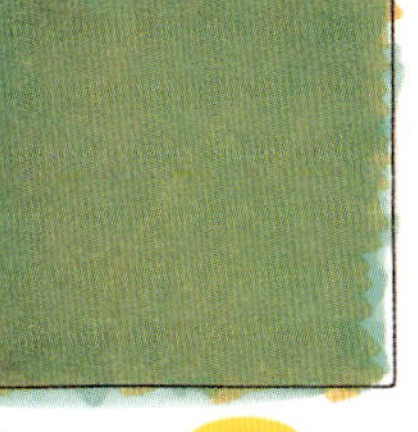

⭕ Using White Ink

Used to color things white. It can be layered to create a thicker white, and can used on a variety of media. In this book of course it is used for finishing (note that COPIC #0 is transparent, not white).

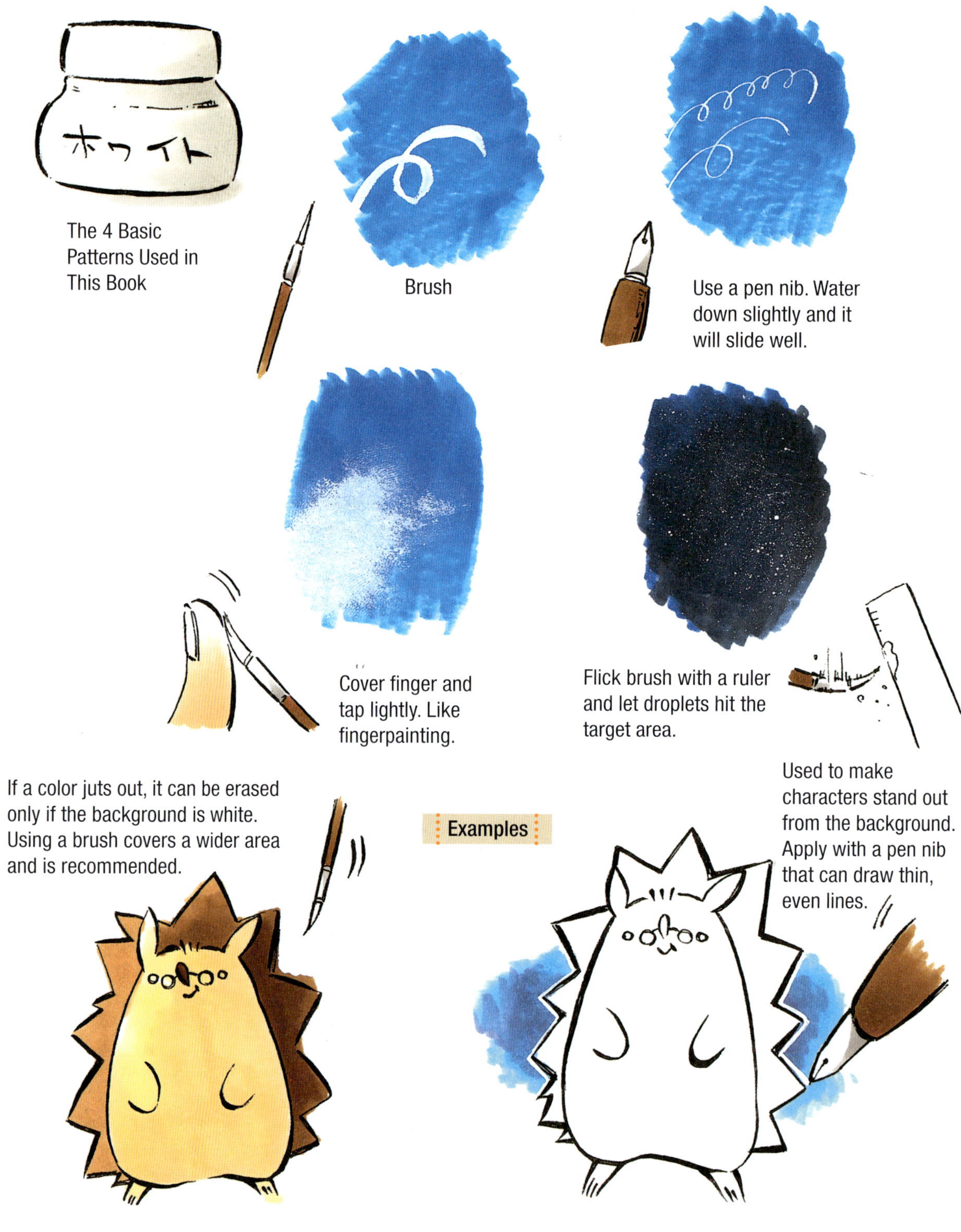

The 4 Basic Patterns Used in This Book

Brush

Use a pen nib. Water down slightly and it will slide well.

Cover finger and tap lightly. Like fingerpainting.

Flick brush with a ruler and let droplets hit the target area.

If a color juts out, it can be erased only if the background is white. Using a brush covers a wider area and is recommended.

Examples

Used to make characters stand out from the background. Apply with a pen nib that can draw thin, even lines.

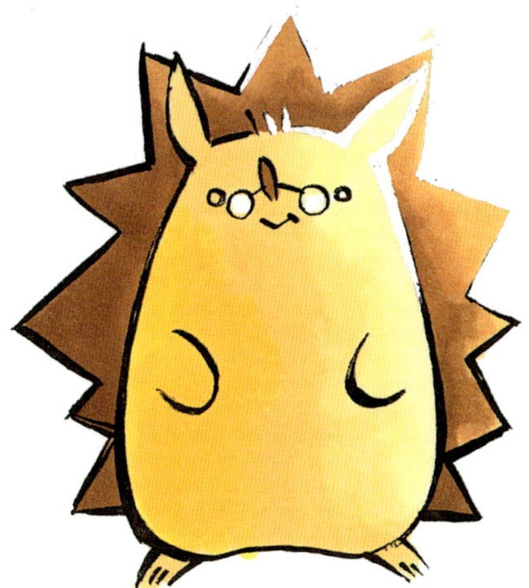

When drawing images under strong light, erase the main lines on the light side (a brush is best).

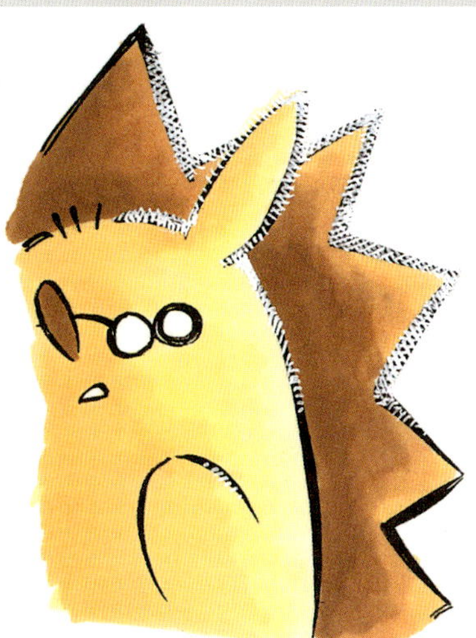

When drawing strong light itself, use crosshatching in the direction of the light (a pen nib is recommended).

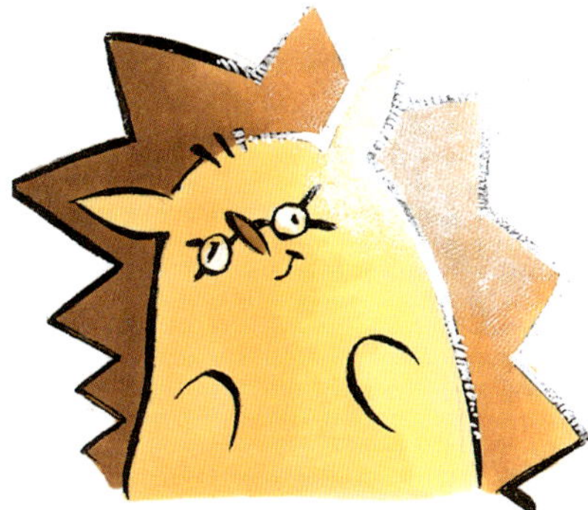

Press white onto the image with your finger; it will give the appearance of soft light.

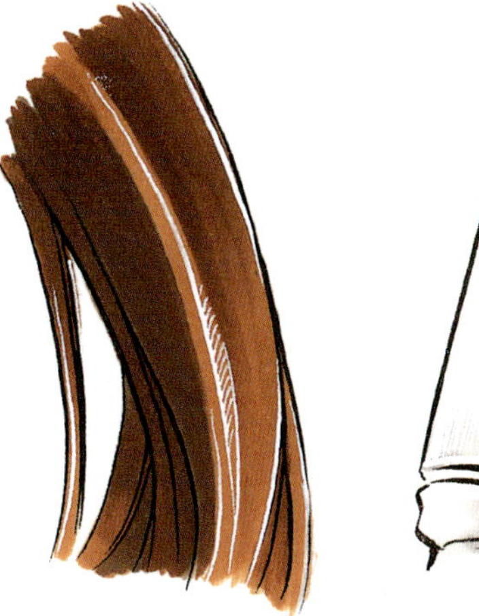

Also used to produce lustrous hair or metal.

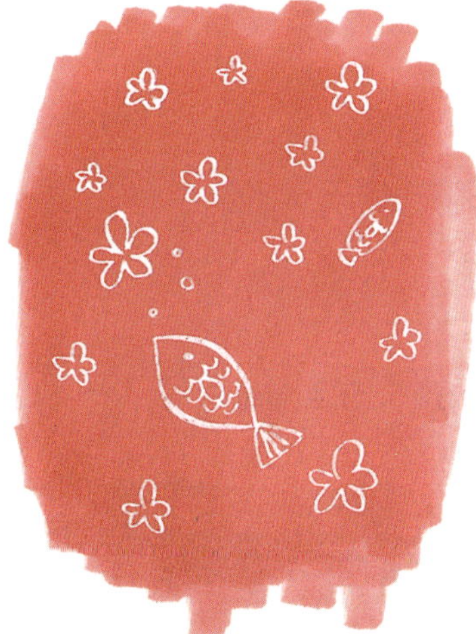

White ink isn't just to aid with light. It can also be used to create patterns or backgrounds.

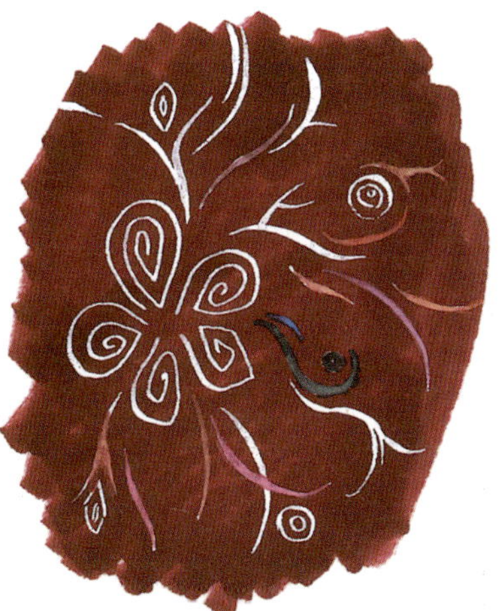

Use COPIC markers to add color to the patterns after they have dried. Don't apply too much because it will melt the white ink, thus making it practically impossible to create gradations. Use this method only when you want to add a tiny bit of color.

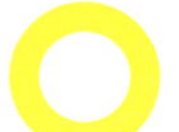 # Let's Color with COPIC Markers

After preparing a line drawing, decide on the base colors. Here all of the colors are specified in the example. However, in reality you can decide on the color of the "skin," "the top," "the accessories," etc., as you go.

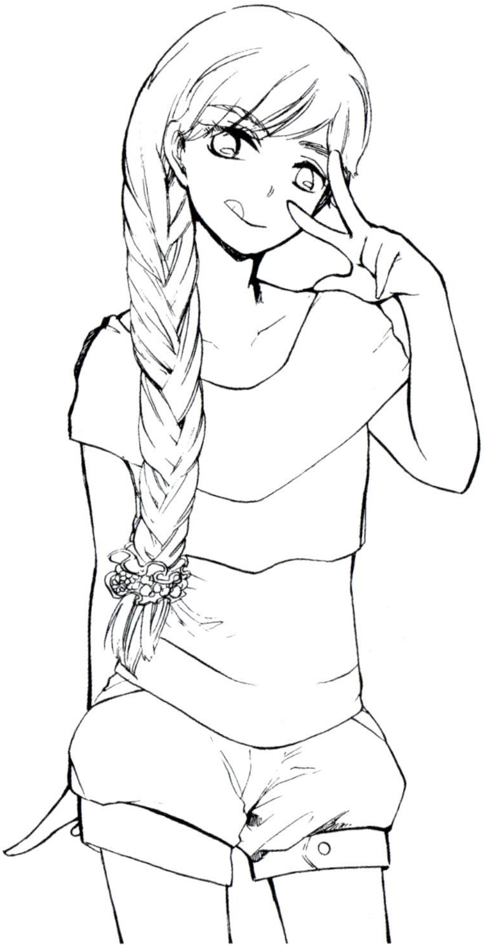

Line Drawing

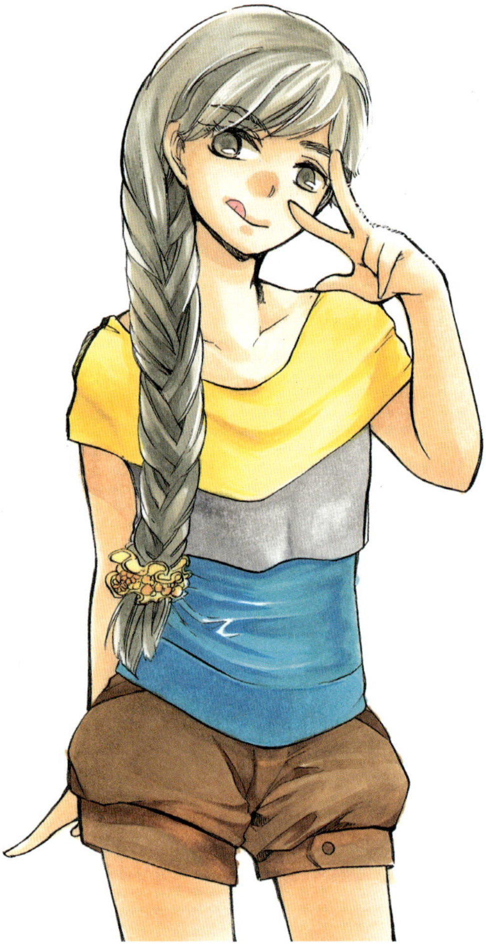

Base Colors

After deciding on the base colors, choose one lighter and one darker color. These will become the "light" and "shadow" that form the basis of all of the coloring.

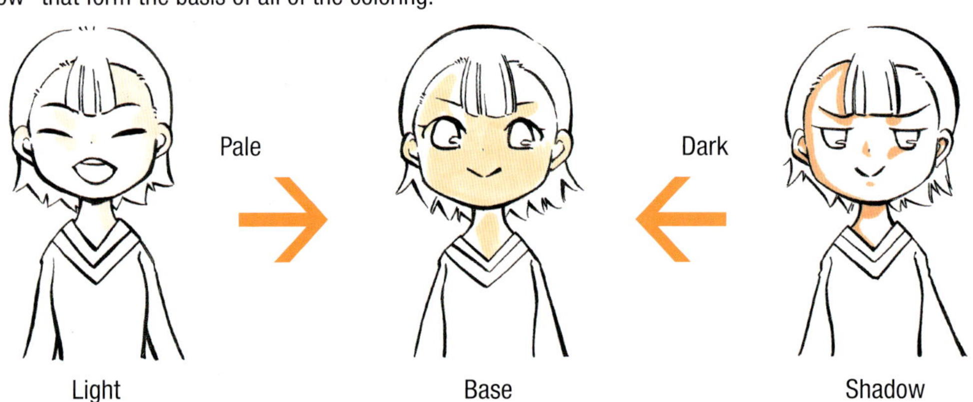

If it is difficult to decide on base colors for each area just print out copies of the line drawing and try coloring them. This is only to decide on the base colors so you can roughly add color.

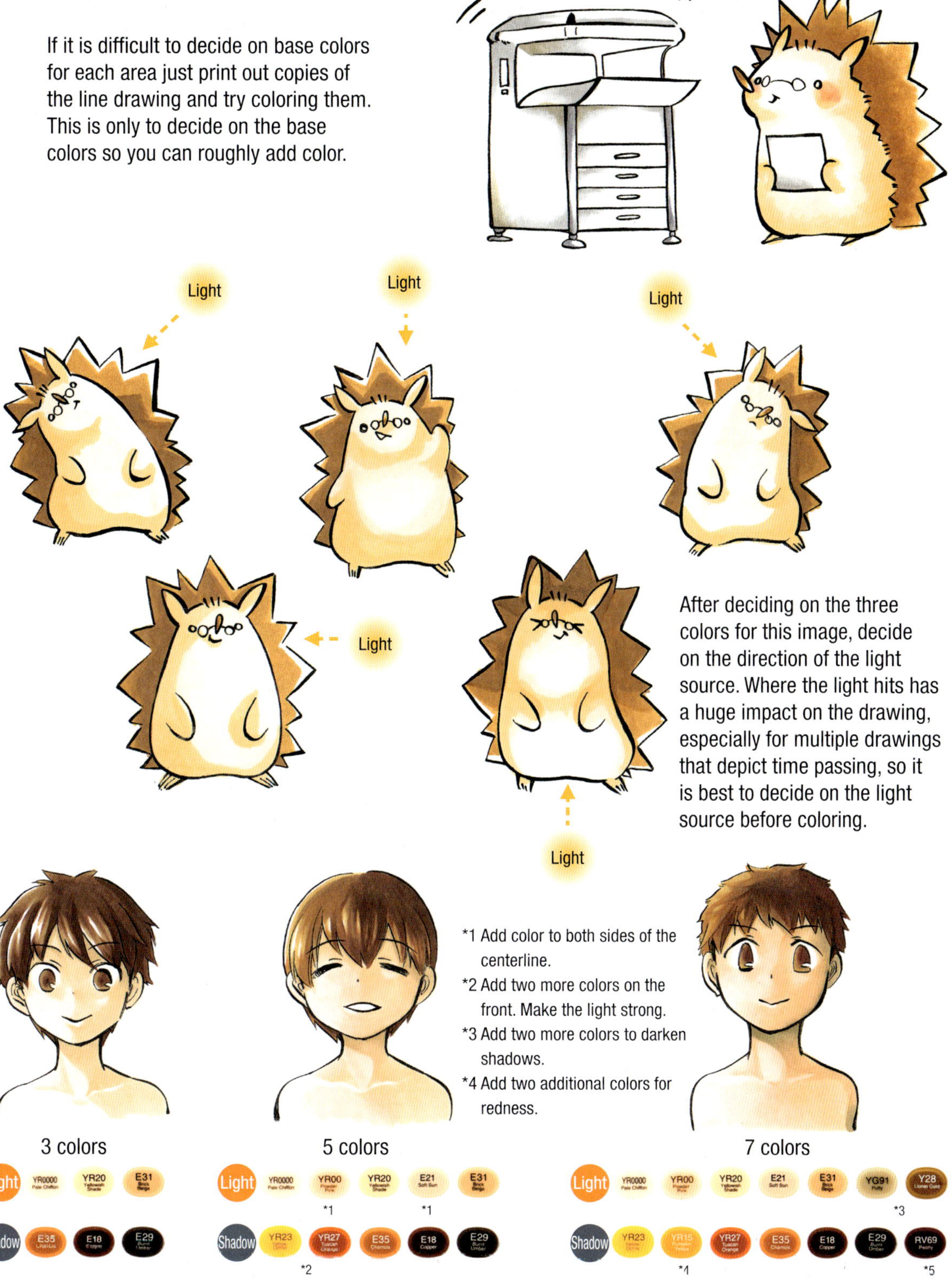

After deciding on the three colors for this image, decide on the direction of the light source. Where the light hits has a huge impact on the drawing, especially for multiple drawings that depict time passing, so it is best to decide on the light source before coloring.

*1 Add color to both sides of the centerline.
*2 Add two more colors on the front. Make the light strong.
*3 Add two more colors to darken shadows.
*4 Add two additional colors for redness.

After deciding on the light source, be sure to think about the three-dimensional effect of the object to be colored. Add light colors where the light will hit (areas that "bulge") and darken the shadows. Once you have mastered the basics, you can add more colors to your three basic colors and create more weight, lightness, or darkness. As shown above.

Color Order

Here are some things to keep in mind when coloring with multiple colors. Because of the natural tendency of COPIC markers to darken, it is most important to first decide on each initial color.

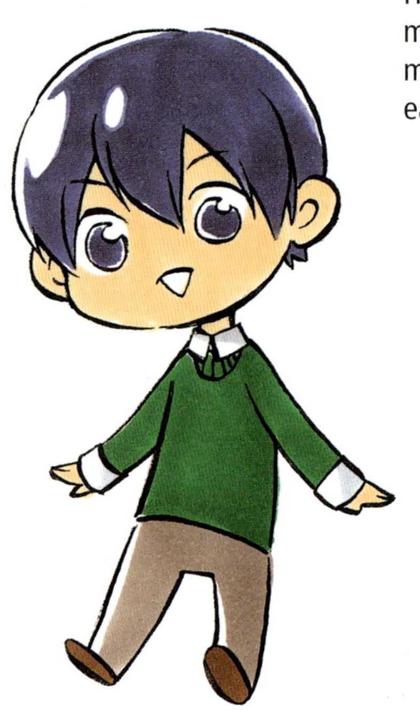

Head	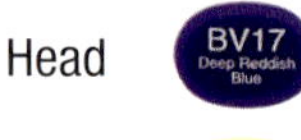 BV17 Deep Reddish Blue
Skin	YR20 Yellowish Shade
Shirt	C2 Cool Gray No.2
Top	G07 Nile Green
Pants	E71 Champagne
Shoes	E37 Sepia

Arrange these colors in your mind in order of lightest to darkest (or vice versa).

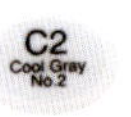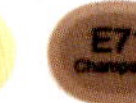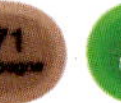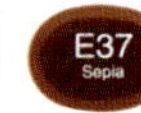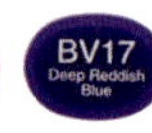

Light   Dark

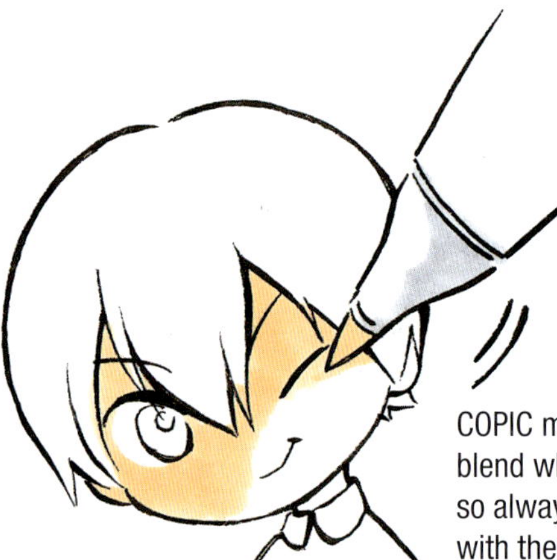

COPIC markers blend when layered, so always begin with the lighter colors.

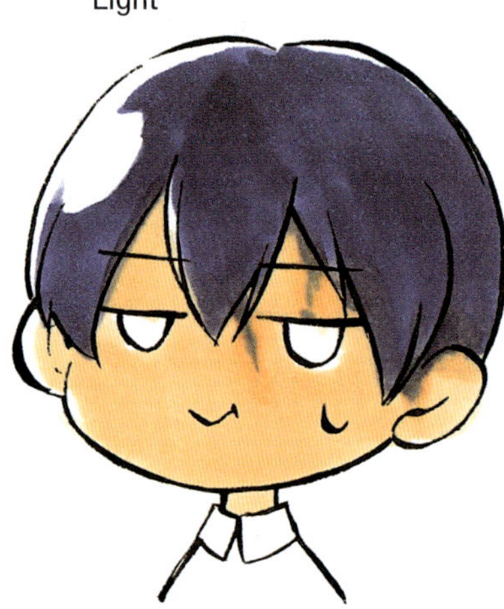

If you use a dark color first, even if you are careful, it can be dragged back over the lighter color by the nib (of the lighter color). As shown on the left.

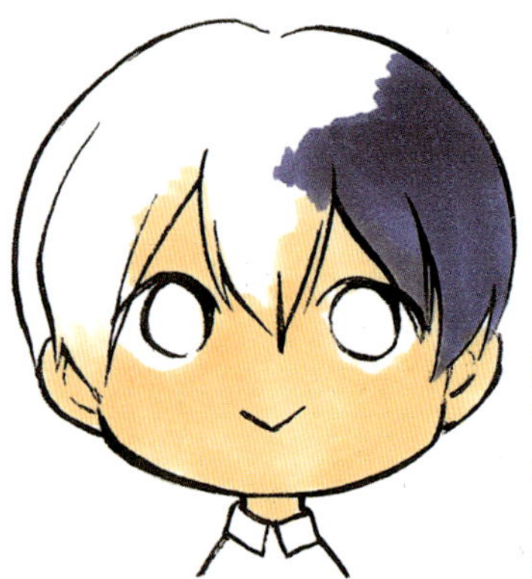

Dark colors can "erase" any overflowing light colors because they are more dense.

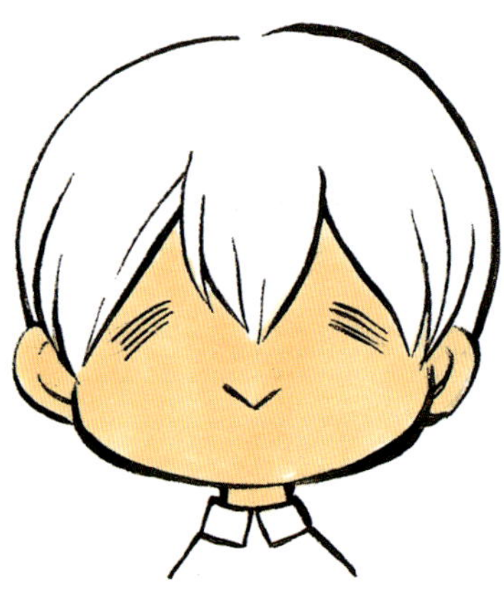

Be careful when using colors of the same density as they can't be erased by the other color.

Since we are only worried about adjacent colors, it's okay to apply the darkest colors quickly, as long as it's after you have colored the areas that are touched by the dark colors.
If you still feel "I'm worried that I just won't be able to decide which goes first," just start with the lightest color and work your way to the darkest.

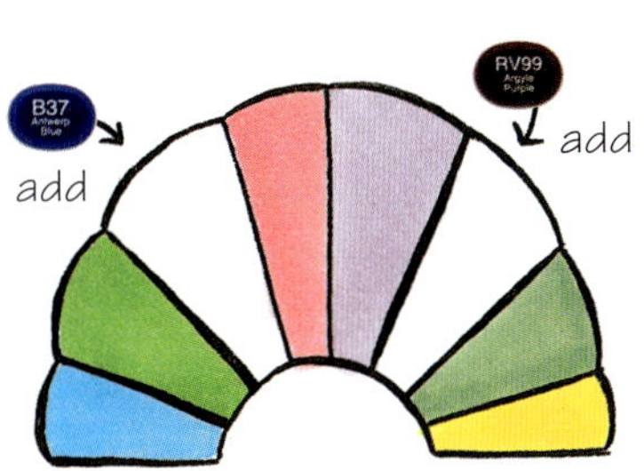

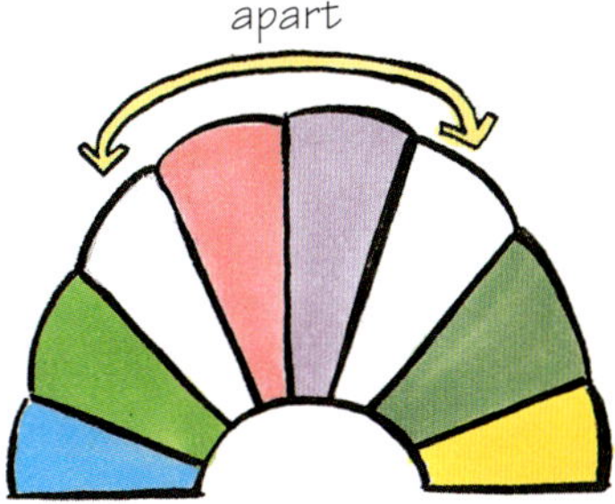

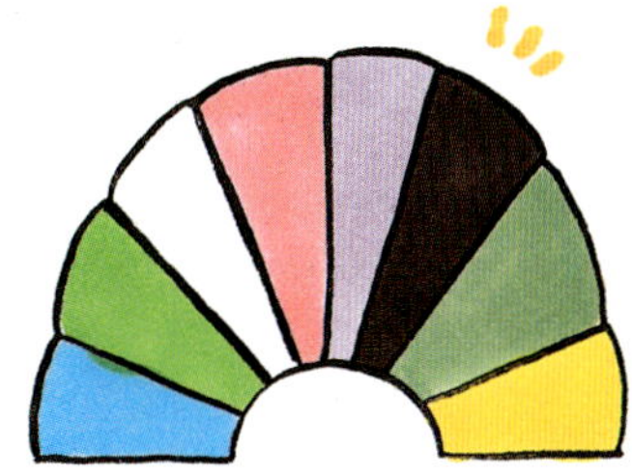

The darker colors are RV99 and B37. RV99 is darker but, given that the two colors are not touching, you can go ahead and use the RV99 first.

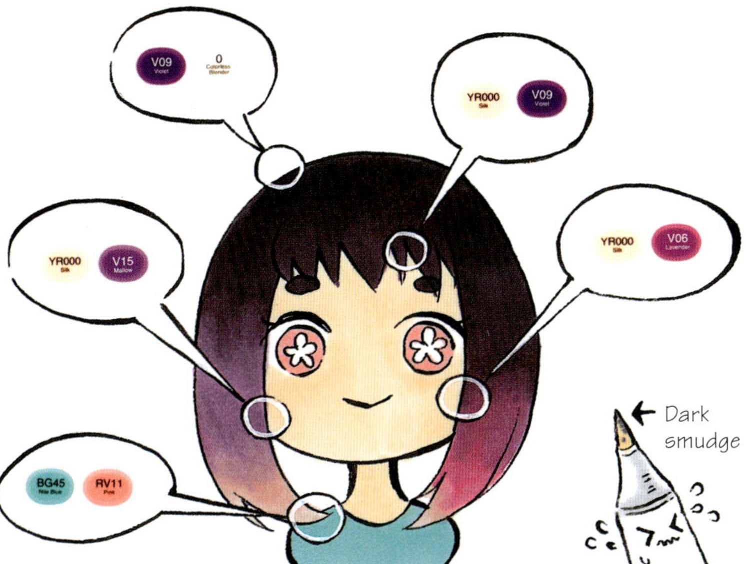

For the reasons noted above, the order will be different when producing gradations and shadows with lighter colors.
If you create gradations, as shown at left, the adjacent colors will be different depending on where they are located. For these areas, we must see the color on both sides (note the blobs with each color noted). Compare the colors and begin applying the lightest color. The hair ends are a part of the gradations inside the "block of hair," meaning that you need to color the hair block not just the ends.
In this case, I would color from the skin up/out (or from the ends of the hair if the skin is brown). Be careful not to smudge your COPIC nibs by misjudging.

Since the shadow is light in color and the border line will usually be the same color as that shadow, you can safely go darker or lighter than the shadow and overlay the two colors. Just think about whether you want to mix them or have them cancel each other out.
This technique is less difficult than gradation because you are making comparisons to a single color. However, the balance between shadows and colors is hard, so it can be extremely challenging in terms of coloring sense. That being said, once you are comfortable with COPIC marker colors and you have become familiar with them, you can feel free to challenge yourself.

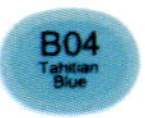

B04 Colored shadow

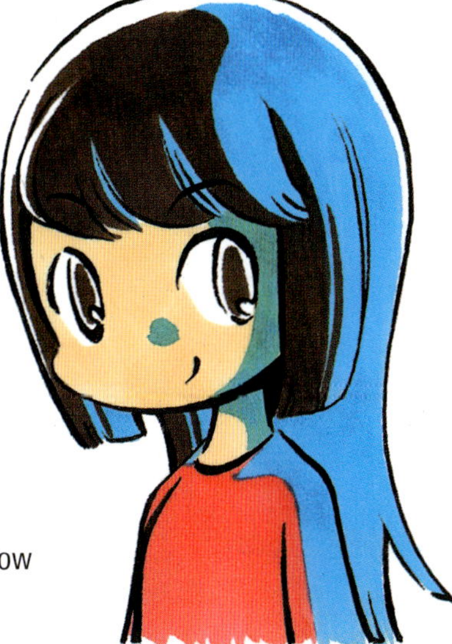

◯ About "Blocking"

COPIC markers are a difficult medium to apply over a large area. The wider the area, the more difficult it is to avoid unevenness with COPIC nibs, even if you are careful.
To make coloring easier, divide large areas into rough blocks in your mind and then color (if you can't see the divisions in your mind, print out a copy and make a draft).

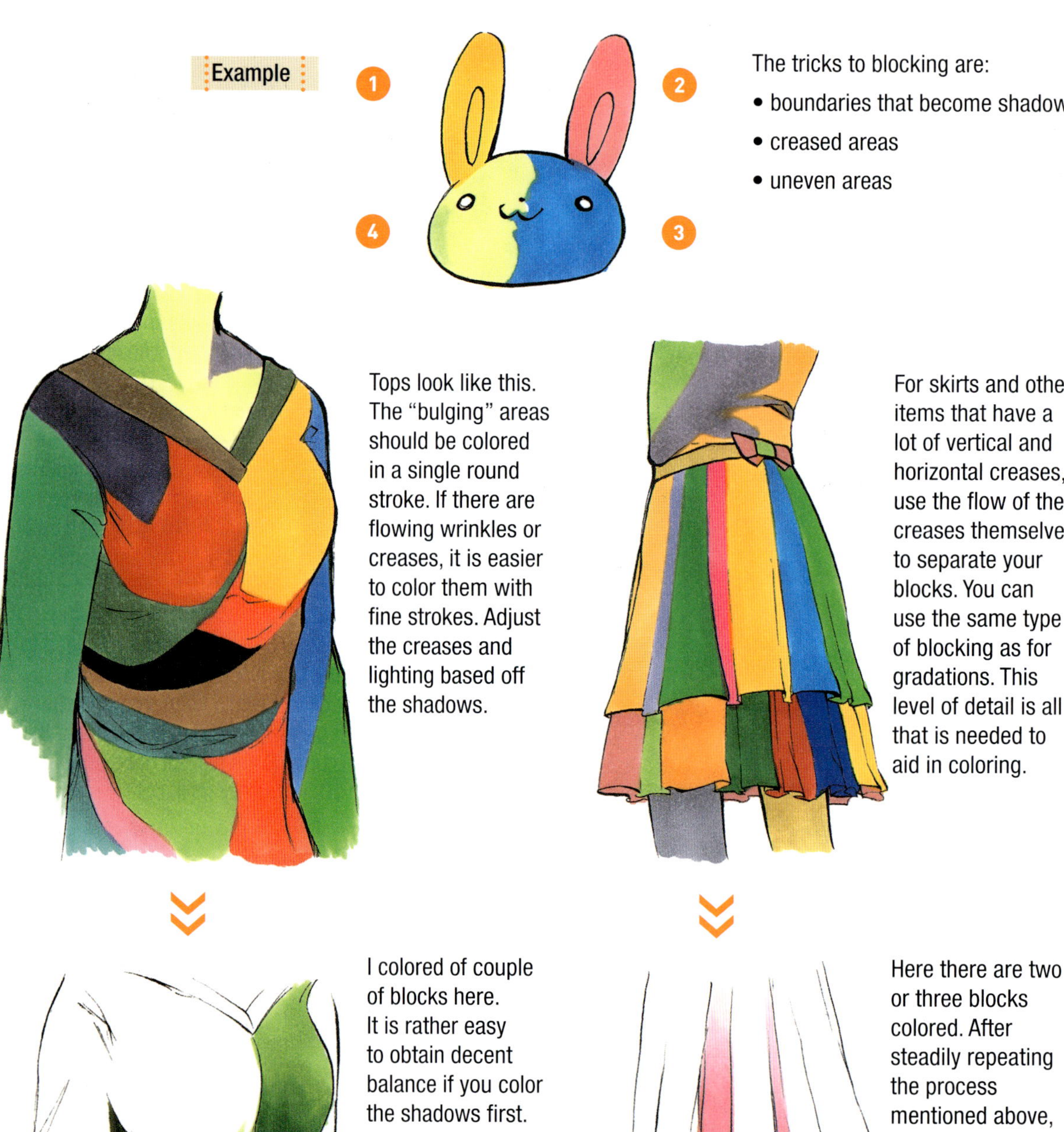

The tricks to blocking are:

- boundaries that become shadows
- creased areas
- uneven areas

Tops look like this. The "bulging" areas should be colored in a single round stroke. If there are flowing wrinkles or creases, it is easier to color them with fine strokes. Adjust the creases and lighting based off the shadows.

For skirts and other items that have a lot of vertical and horizontal creases, use the flow of the creases themselves to separate your blocks. You can use the same type of blocking as for gradations. This level of detail is all that is needed to aid in coloring.

I colored of couple of blocks here. It is rather easy to obtain decent balance if you color the shadows first.

Here there are two or three blocks colored. After steadily repeating the process mentioned above, proceed to fixing the overall balance.

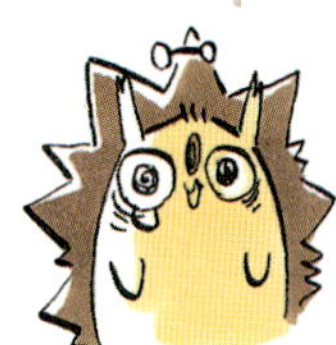

If you think this is a problem, you can draw the divisions in detail before beginning.

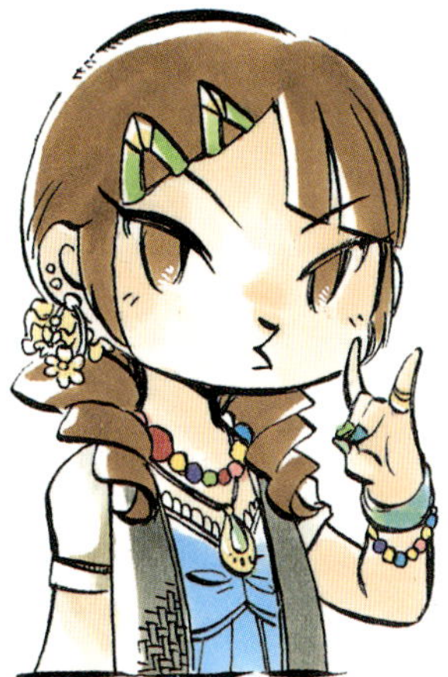

Draw accessories in detail.

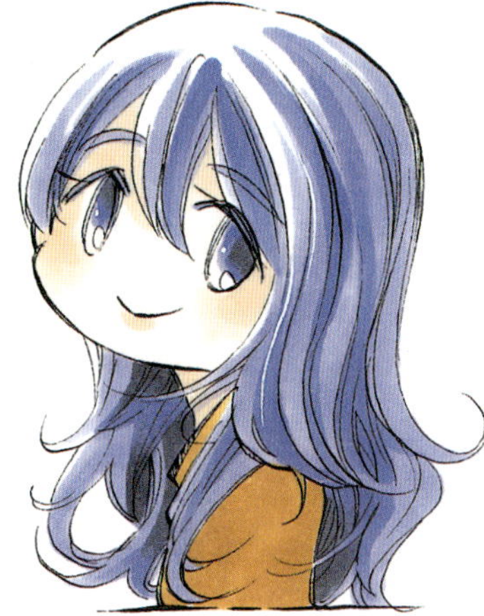

Add in the detail lines when drawing the main lines.

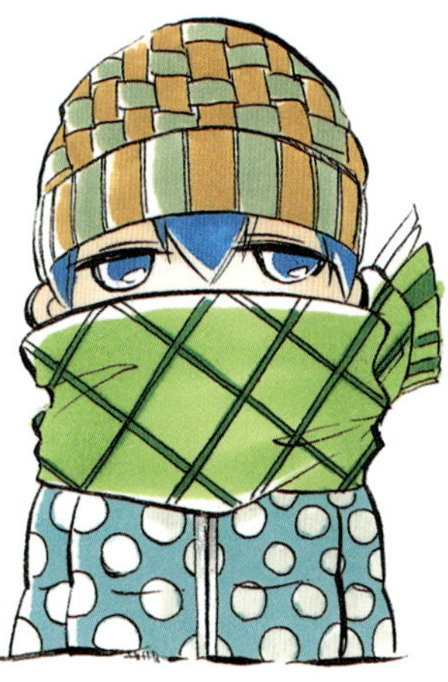

Draw the various patterns of the clothing items.

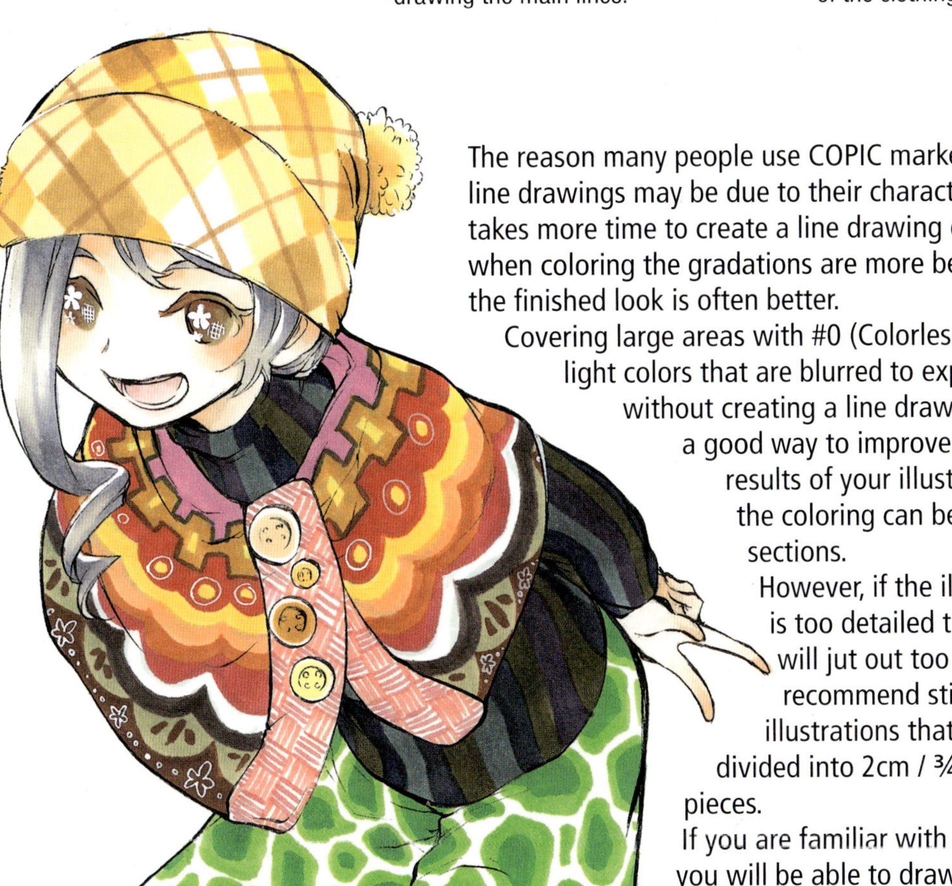

The reason many people use COPIC markers to do fine line drawings may be due to their characteristics. It takes more time to create a line drawing of course, but when coloring the gradations are more beautiful and the finished look is often better.

Covering large areas with #0 (Colorless Blender) or light colors that are blurred to express shading, without creating a line drawing, is also a good way to improve the overalls results of your illustration because the coloring can be done in small sections.

However, if the illustration is too detailed these details will jut out too much, so I recommend sticking with illustrations that can be divided into 2cm / ¾" x 3cm / ¼" pieces.

If you are familiar with blocking, you will be able to draw patterns and backgrounds without using line drawings. This will greatly expand your range of expression.

How to Think About Shadows

Shadows can look completely different depending on light direction. Here we will go over things to consider when there are overlapping shadows.

As Seen in These Examples

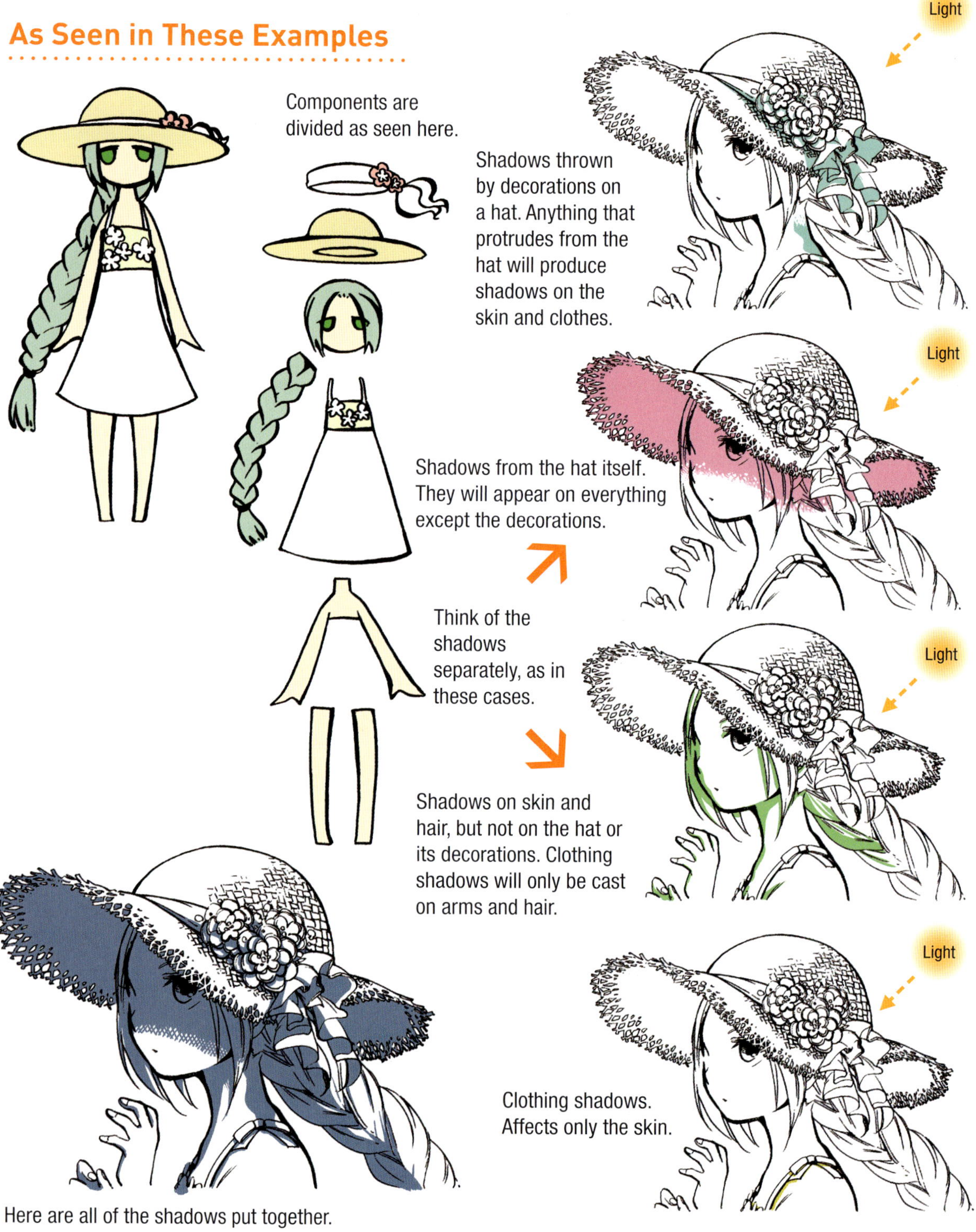

Components are divided as seen here.

Think of the shadows separately, as in these cases.

Here are all of the shadows put together.

Shadows thrown by decorations on a hat. Anything that protrudes from the hat will produce shadows on the skin and clothes.

Shadows from the hat itself. They will appear on everything except the decorations.

Shadows on skin and hair, but not on the hat or its decorations. Clothing shadows will only be cast on arms and hair.

Clothing shadows. Affects only the skin.

Next is the shadow's shape. Remember, even round hats have jagged edges, like this one. If you don't draw these jagged edges correctly, you'll end up with…

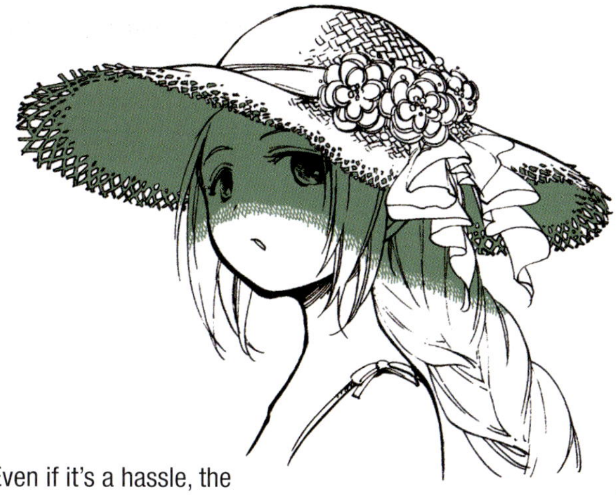

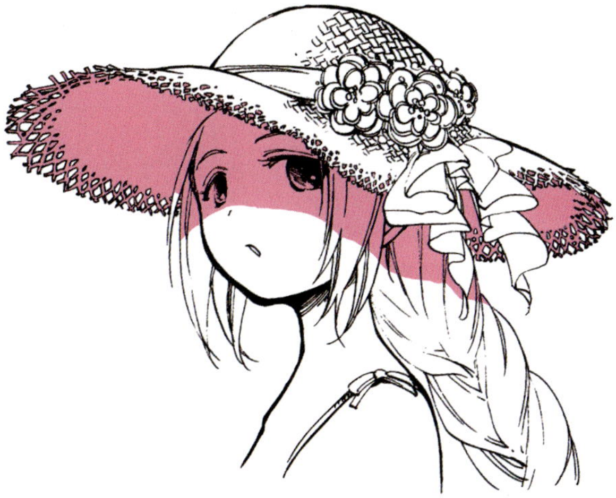

Even if it's a hassle, the illustration will be more convincing if the shadows of the hat are heavily detailed.

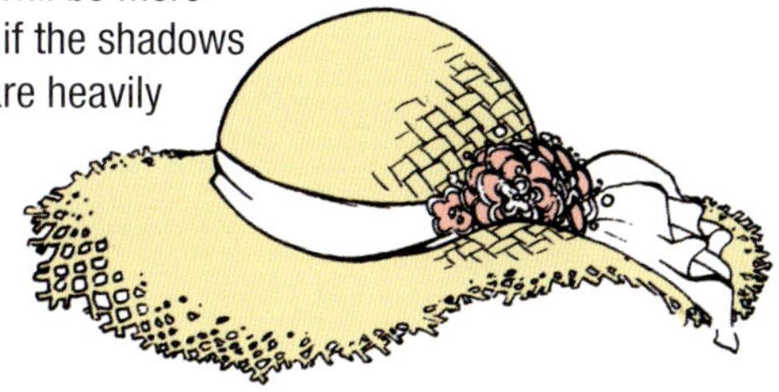

If you just make the hat round, the shape of the hat might look like this. Be careful when coloring.

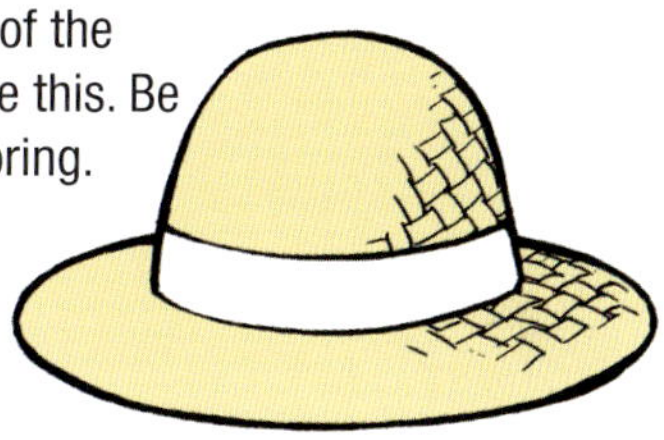

Shadows Cast by Different Types of Light

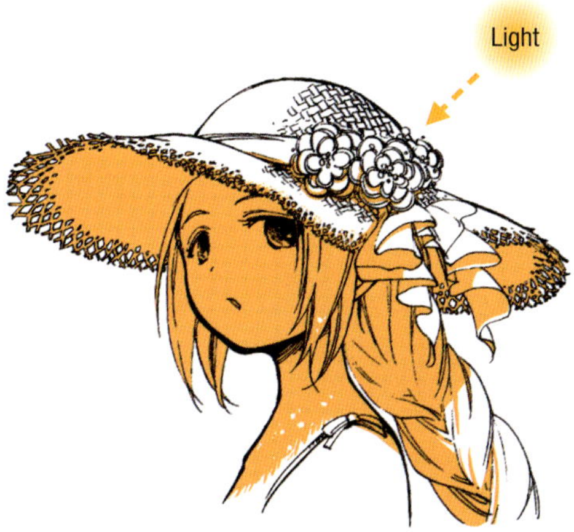

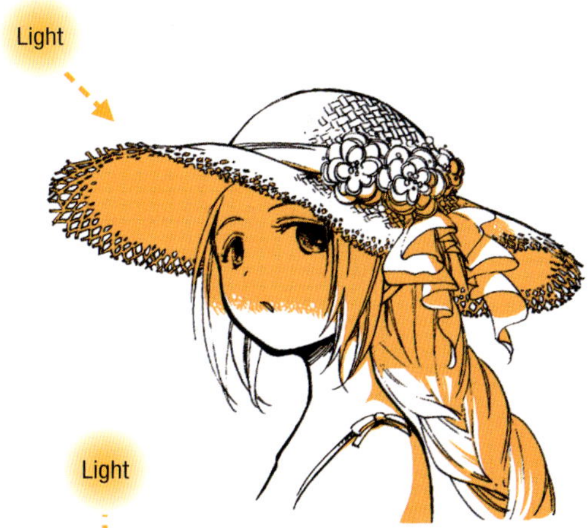

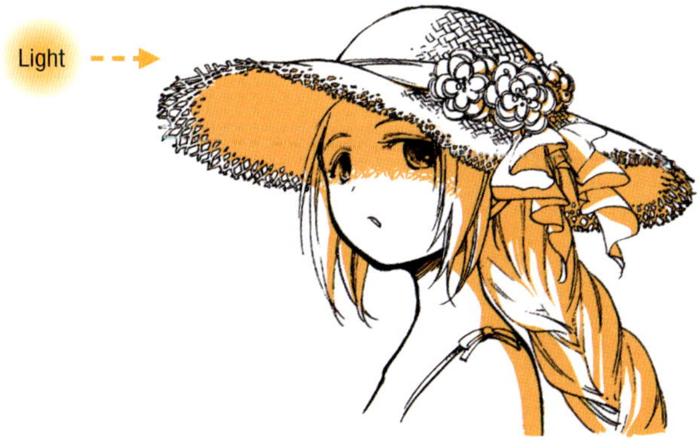

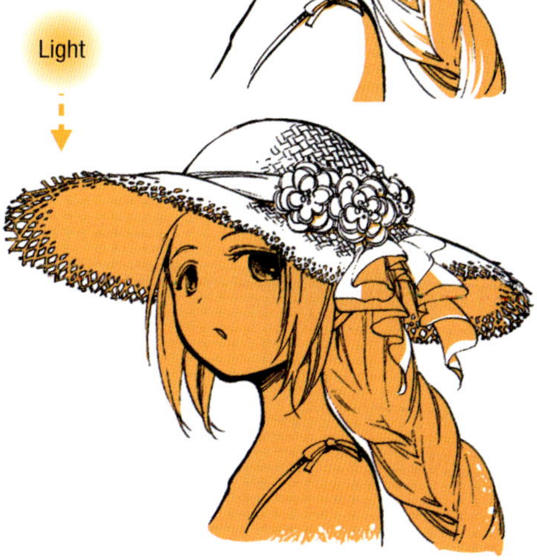

How Light Strikes Items

There are two types of light exposure: daylight and artificial light (as far as total illumination is concerned).

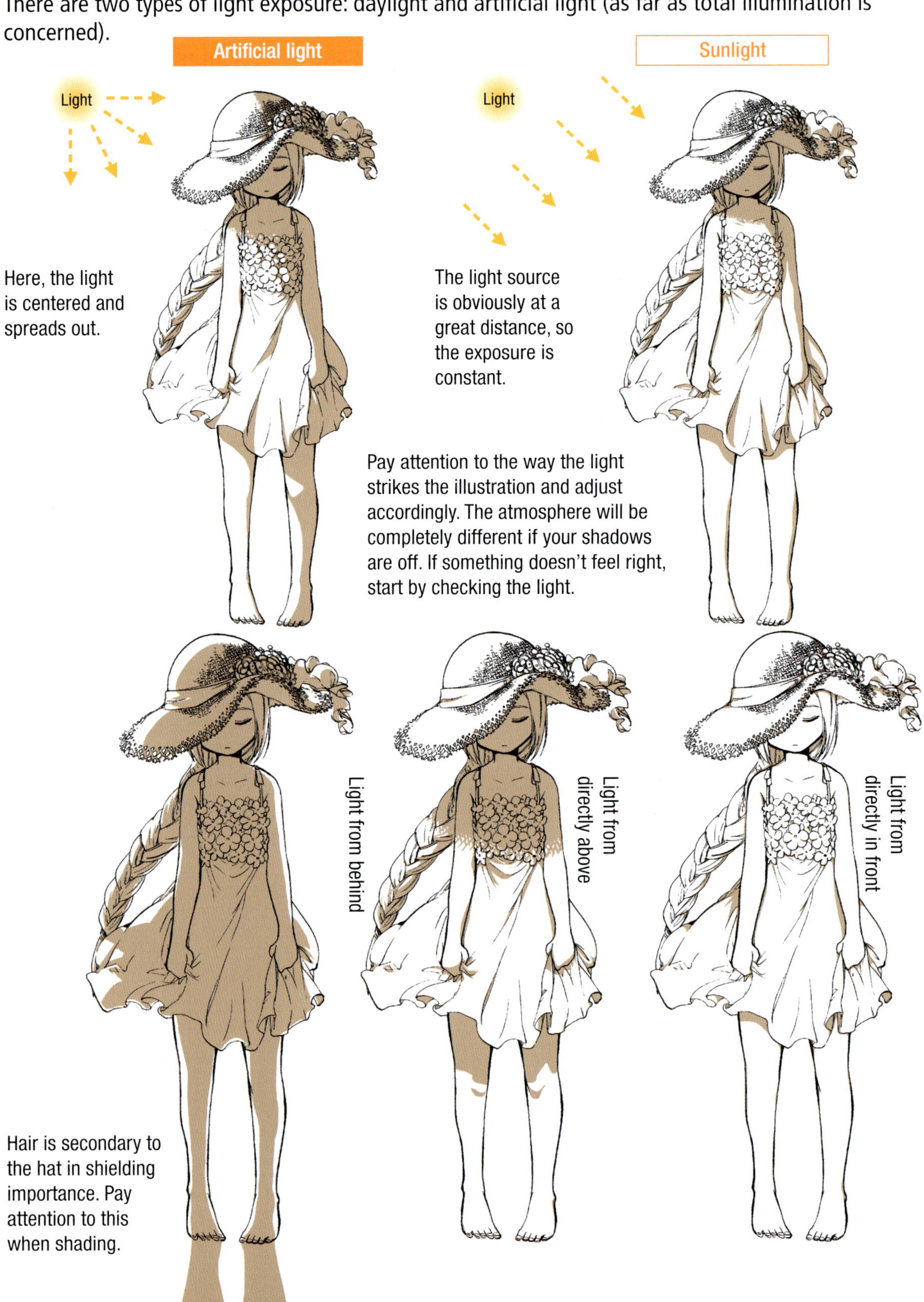

Here, the light is centered and spreads out.

The light source is obviously at a great distance, so the exposure is constant.

Pay attention to the way the light strikes the illustration and adjust accordingly. The atmosphere will be completely different if your shadows are off. If something doesn't feel right, start by checking the light.

Hair is secondary to the hat in shielding importance. Pay attention to this when shading.

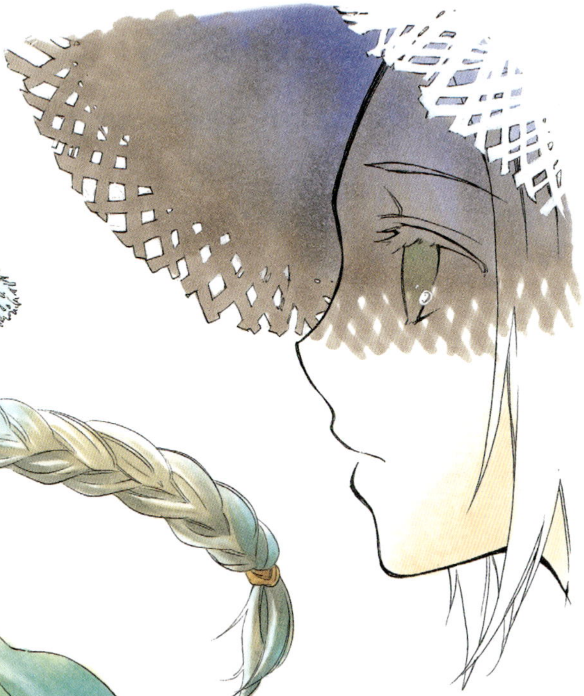

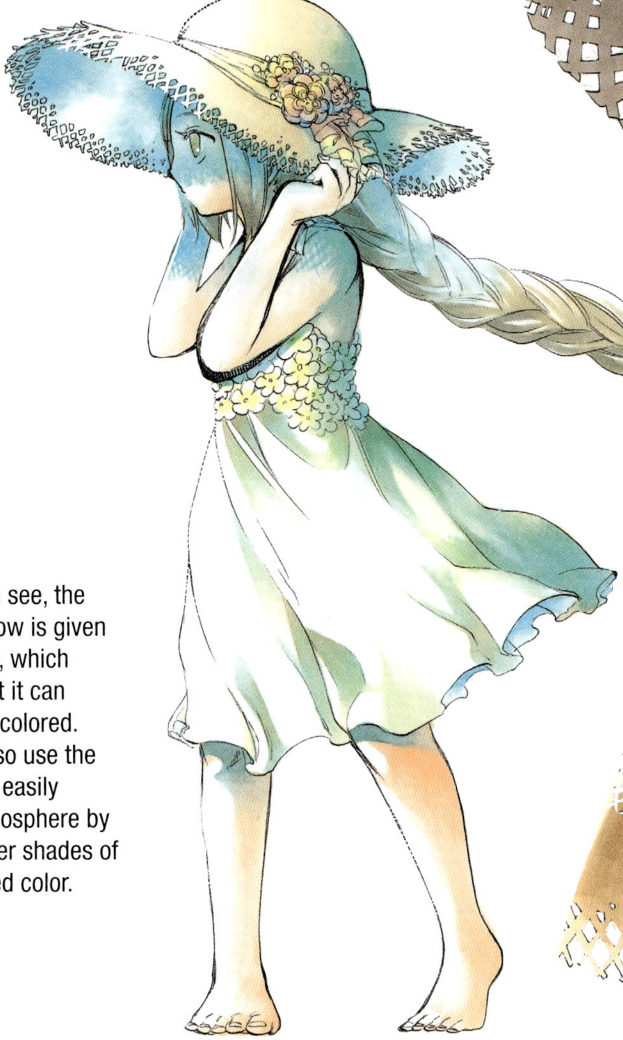

As you can see, the hat's shadow is given top priority, which means that it can be heavily colored. You can also use the shadow to easily create atmosphere by using lighter shades of the selected color.

Gradient shading from deep in the shadows

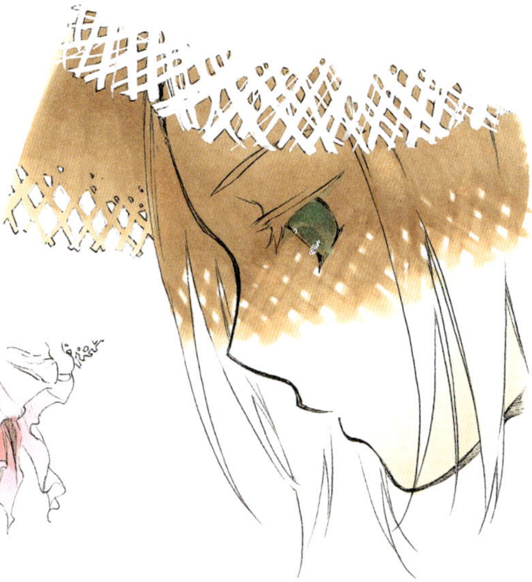

Shadows with softened edges

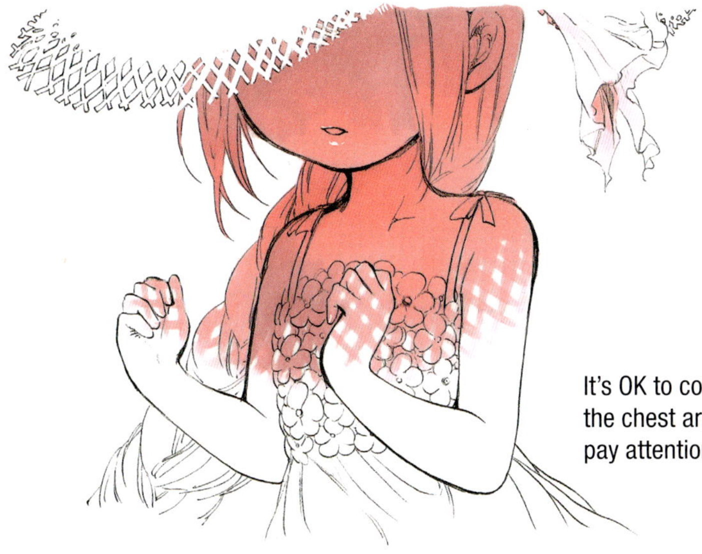

It's OK to color strongly down to the chest area. Just be careful to pay attention to where they end.

Regarding Gradations

Gradient is a technique that changes color from point x to point y, based on color A and color B.

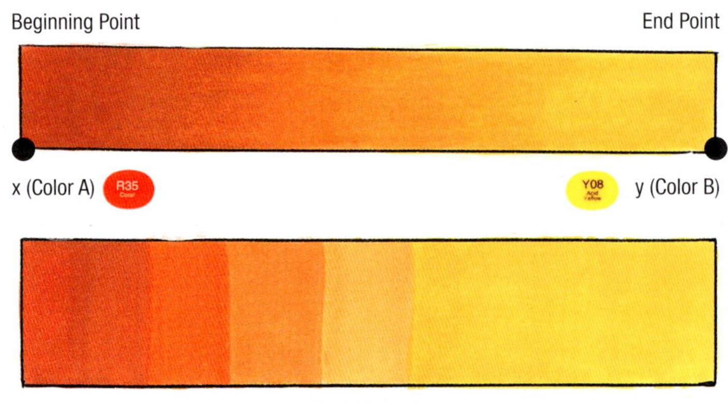

To put it simply, gradation is a technique that uses intermediate colors to create a gradual change in color from point x to point y so that color A becomes color B, as shown here. This technique uses a large number of colors, as shown at the left.

COPIC markers use alcohol ink so their colors will penetrate the paper, which means that gradations can be created through the use of "blending" or "bleeding" techniques.

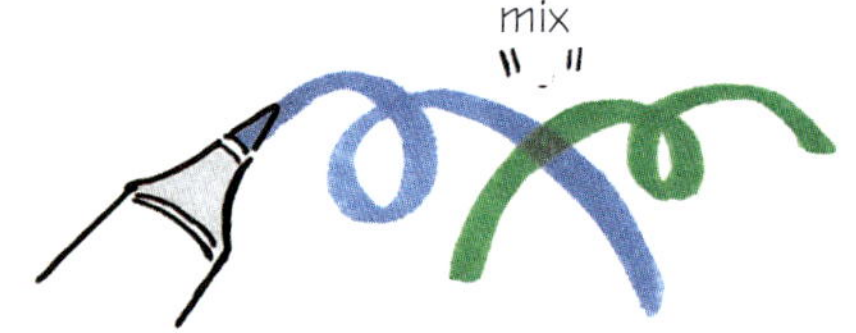

Blending

Bleeding

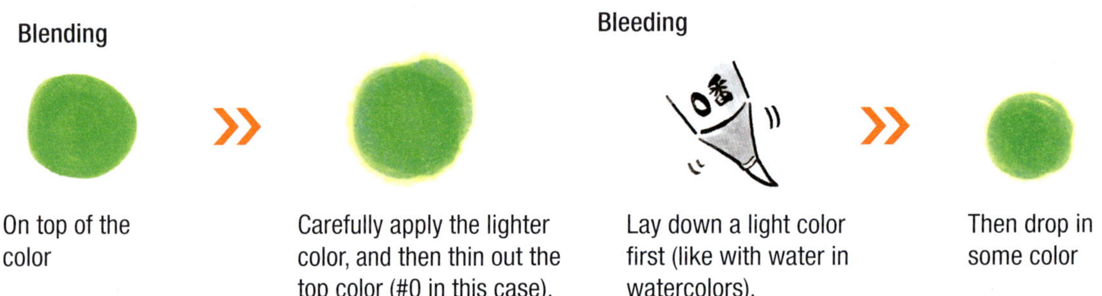

On top of the color

Carefully apply the lighter color, and then thin out the top color (#0 in this case).

Lay down a light color first (like with water in watercolors).

Then drop in some color

Single Color Gradation

To create a single color gradation, use the brush nib of the marker to "brush away" the color. If the color is too light, it will be difficult to make gradations. But, if the color is reasonably light, it is possible to create gradations from a "main" color out to the "background" color. This illustration consists of only intermediate colors and light, so just overlay the chosen colors to render shadows. Since only one color is used for each gradation, the number of colors to prepare is small.

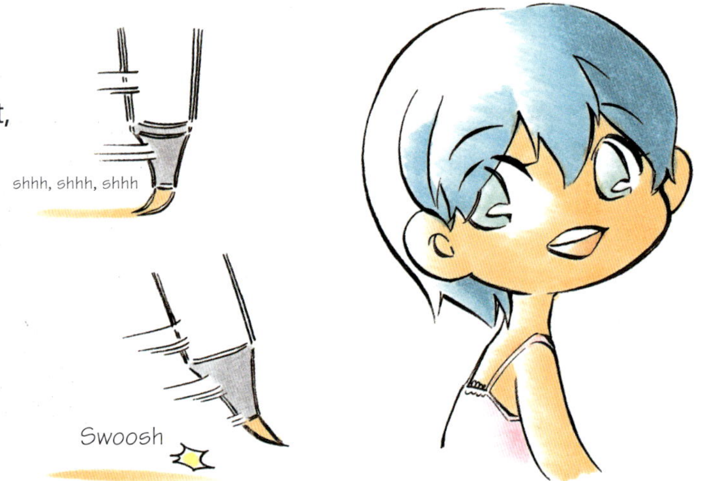

Two Color Gradation

 This is a gradation that uses 2 colors. We'll start with the most orthodox method, applying a color and then #0. COPIC #0 is a colorless, transparent ink that doesn't heavily affect colors it is applied over, and is seen to have a supporting role in the COPIC world. It can be used to remove color by applying a large number of coats on top of a certain color. This allows you to add patterns or even to correct irreversible overflow. If you want to use it for gradation, you will need to remove the target color at certain positions to create the gradation.

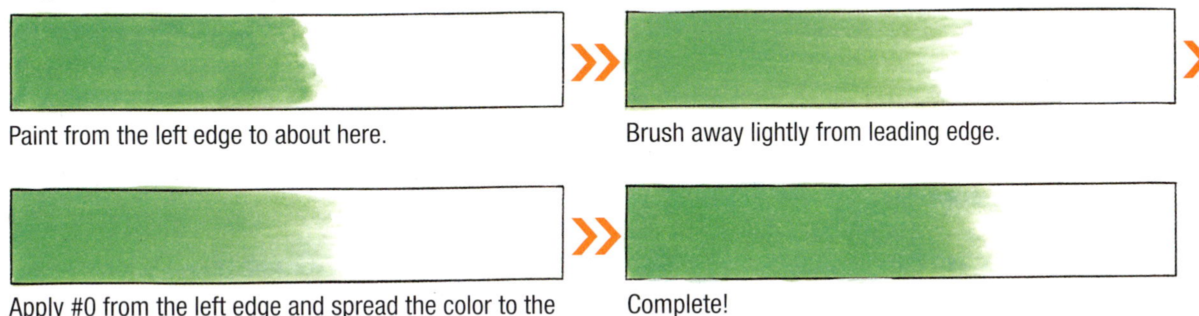

Paint from the left edge to about here.

Brush away lightly from leading edge.

Apply #0 from the left edge and spread the color to the right.

Complete!

The color > #0 gradation is likely to consume a large amount of alcohol ink in the #0 marker, depending of course on the color used. And since the #0 is used frequently, it is a good idea to have spares around when practicing.
If the nib gets dirty, you can clean the nib by rubbing it on a suitable piece of copy paper, as long as the nib isn't too shaggy. If the nib is stained from working with a previous color, it will stay stained during the gradation of another color, so clean it up immediately!

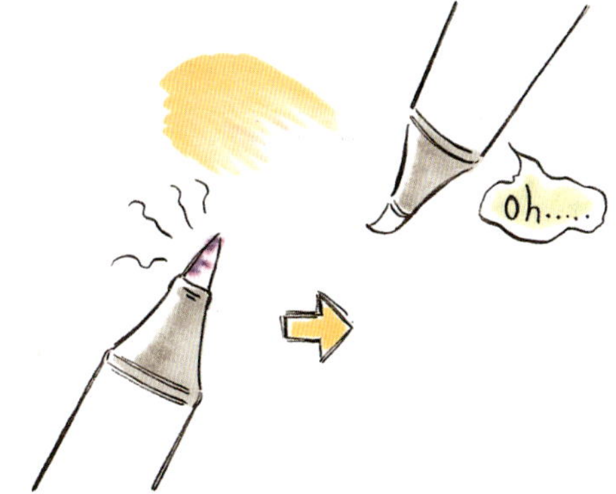

Color to Color Gradation

This technique begins with knowing the compatibility of colors. Colors have what is called a complementary relationship. Colors at opposite ends of the spectrum in the diagram below do not get along very well. If the complementary colors are the same, in terms of luminosity, a phenomenon called halation will occur. So, be careful.
When creating gradations, complementary colors are also very difficult to work with. Here's why.

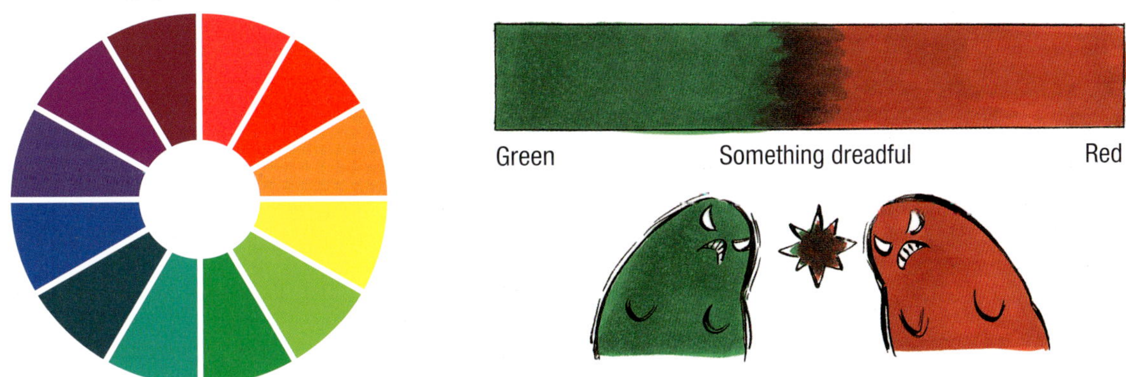

Examples of Two Color Gradation

So, let's start with similar colors. Here are a few patterns that are easy to gradate. Please refer to them in your own work.

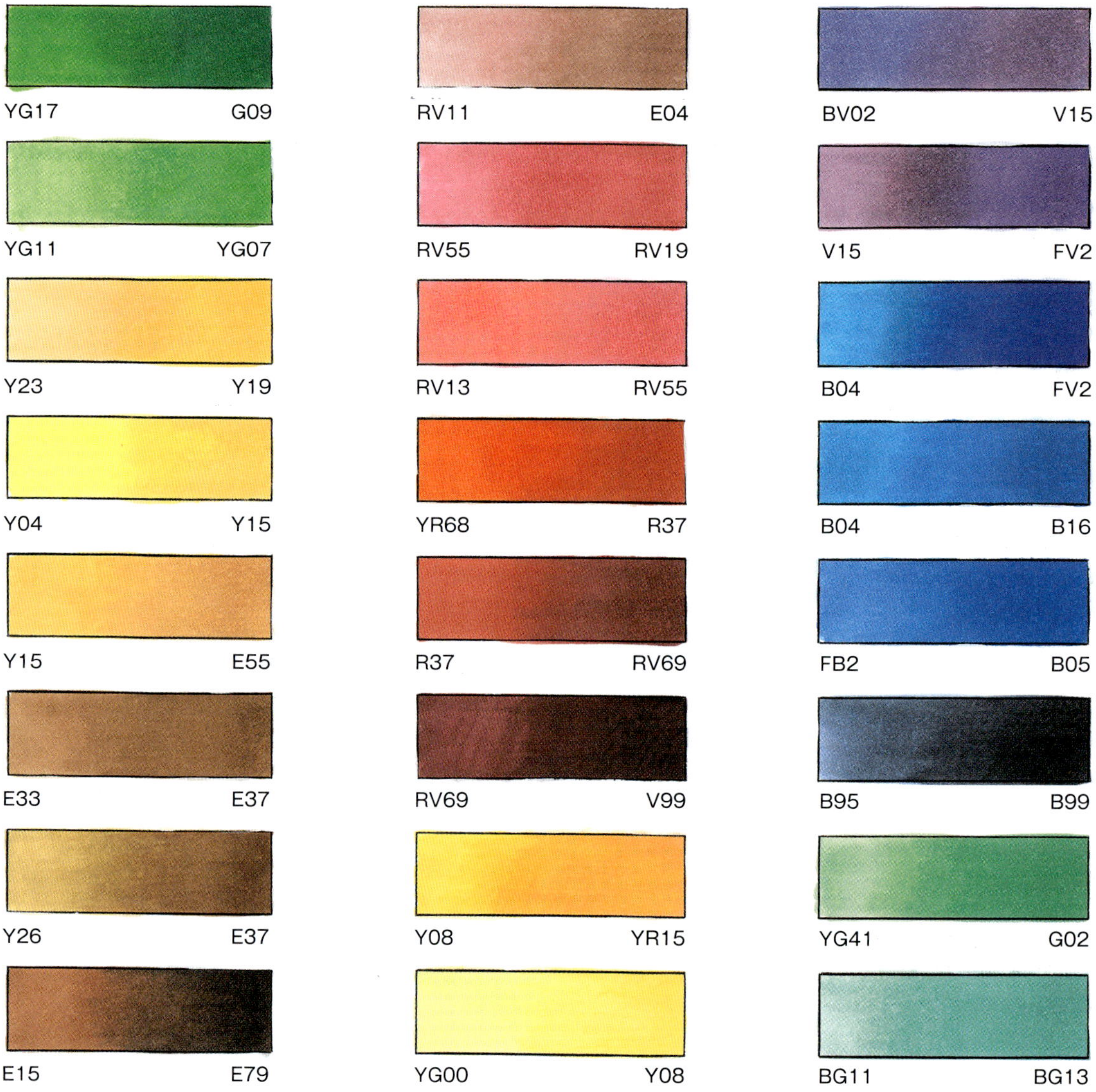

YG17	G09		RV11	E04		BV02	V15
YG11	YG07		RV55	RV19		V15	FV2
Y23	Y19		RV13	RV55		B04	FV2
Y04	Y15		YR68	R37		B04	B16
Y15	E55		R37	RV69		FB2	B05
E33	E37		RV69	V99		B95	B99
Y26	E37		Y08	YR15		YG41	G02
E15	E79		YG00	Y08		BG11	BG13

The gradation method is the same as when using #0. Note that the blended color is saturated, so it will get darker as you go over it. Be careful.

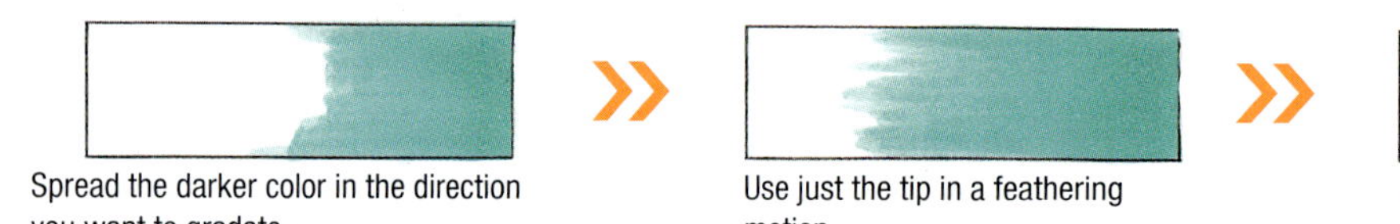

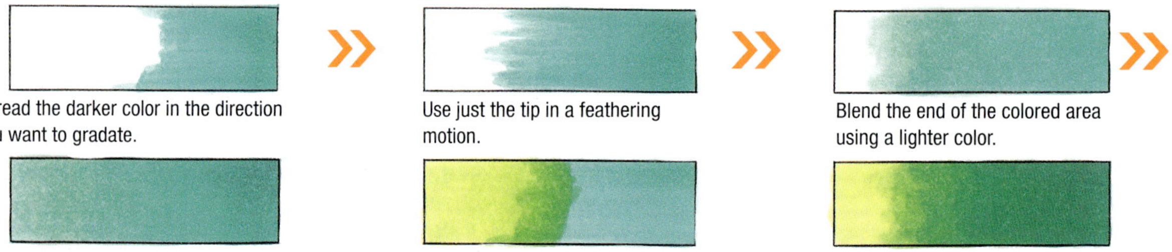

Spread the darker color in the direction you want to gradate.

Finish by coloring the entire area.

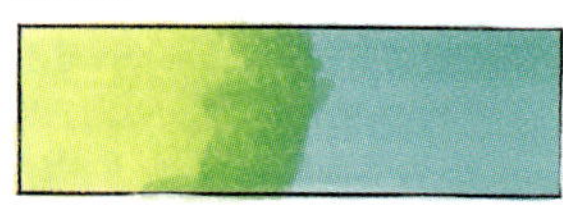

Use just the tip in a feathering motion.

If the colors are different, you can blend them by overlapping. But, it will look like this.

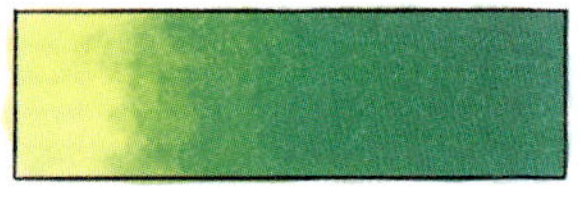

Blend the end of the colored area using a lighter color.

So, you can apply second color over the first color.

Gradate Evenly with Complementary Colors

How to gradate colors that are not compatible. The rough flow is shown in the figure below.

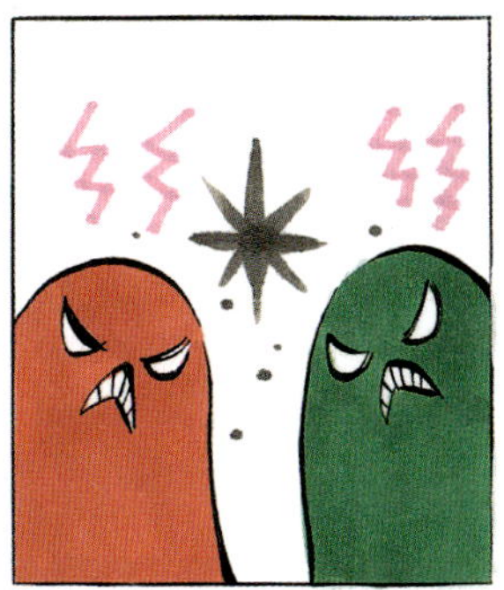

Complementary colors do not get along.

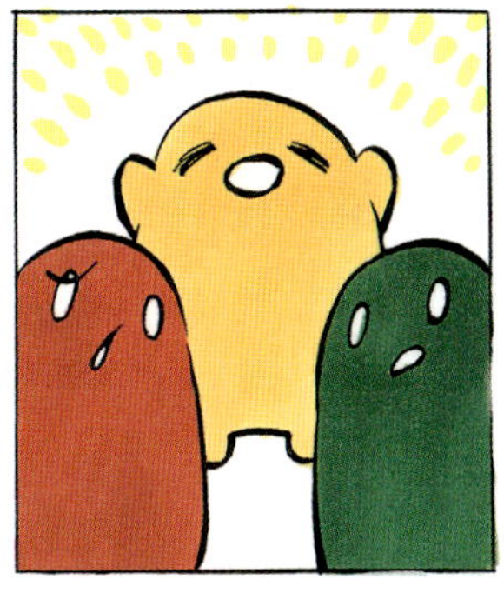

However, there should be another color that gets along well with both of those colors.

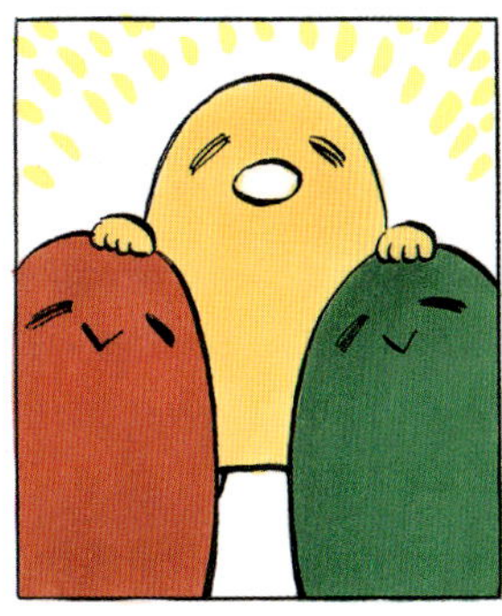

You can gradate through that color.

How to Find Color Transitions

Different colors mediate differently. When finding colors that match, think about the addition and subtraction of color.

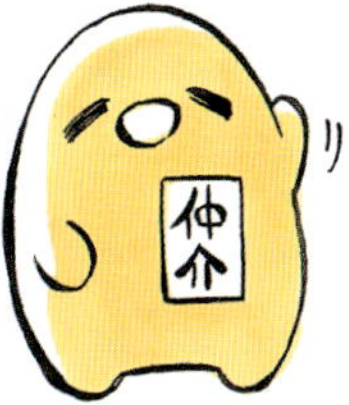

You can think of a simple combination of colors, leaving luminosity and other factors aside. This is a good way to learn and investigate addition and subtraction color relationships. How do you think it work for red, yellow, and green?

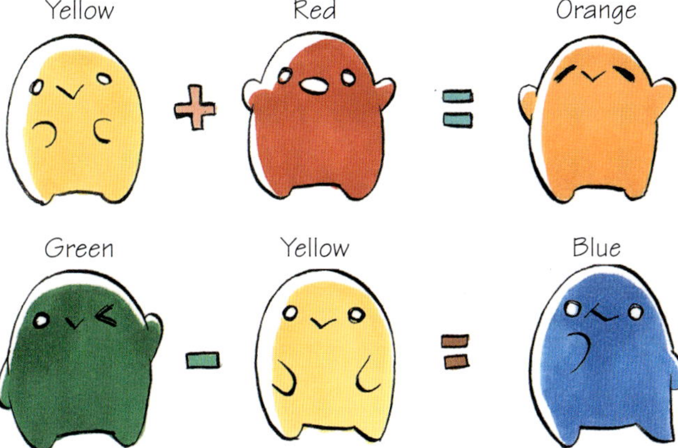

Addition

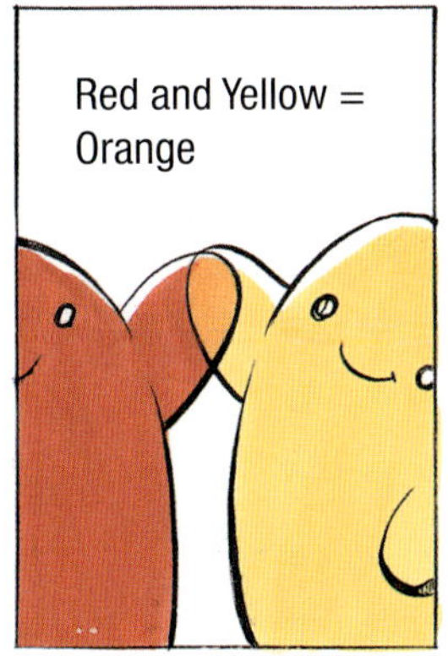

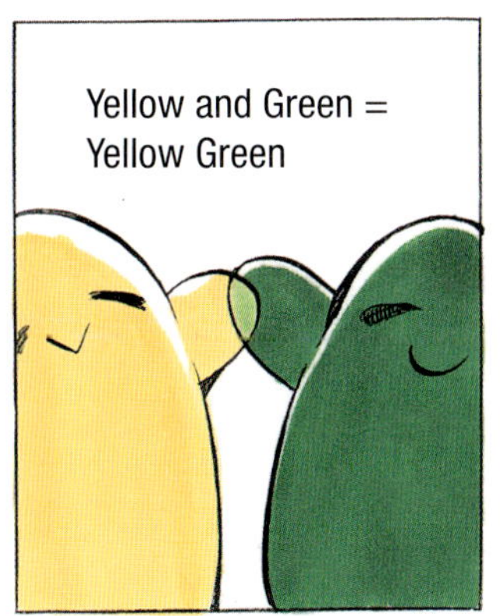

You can create this kind of gradation.

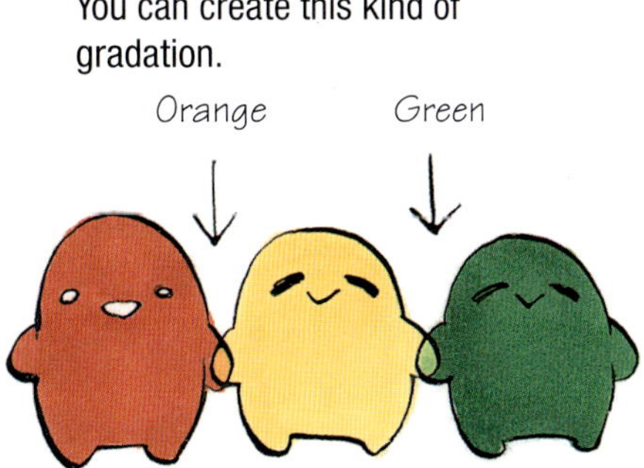

Examples of Complementary Color Gradation

The actual gradation of the three colors is shown in the figure below.

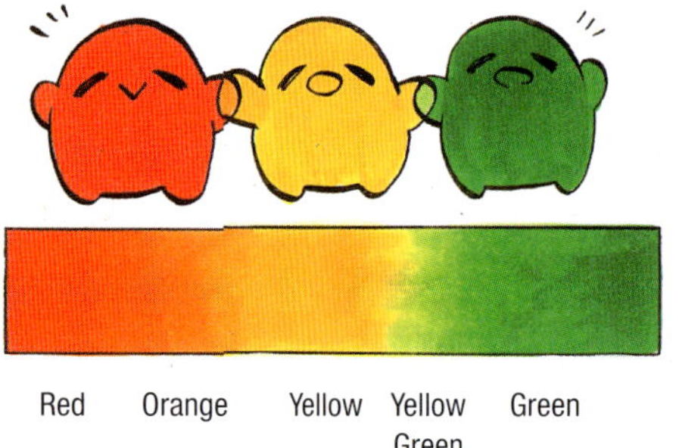

Red   Orange   Yellow   Yellow Green   Green

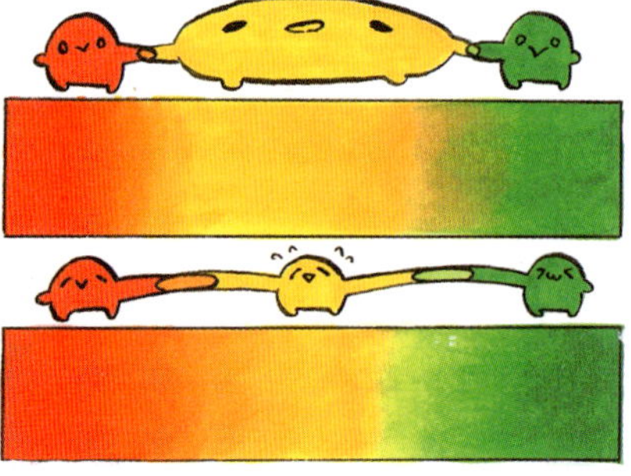

In this way, you can create the gradation of your choice with the ratio of these five colors.

Addition Summary

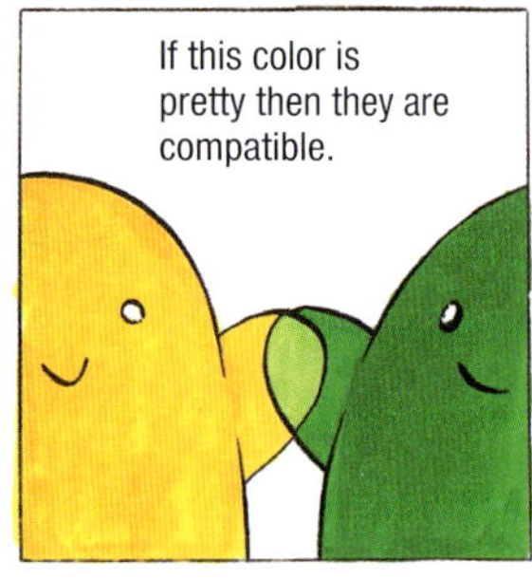

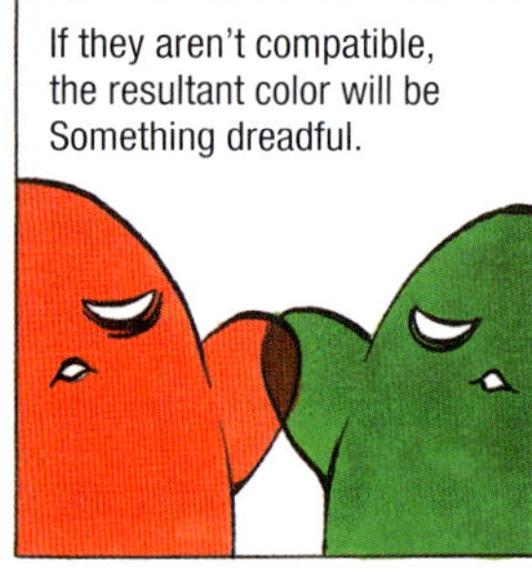

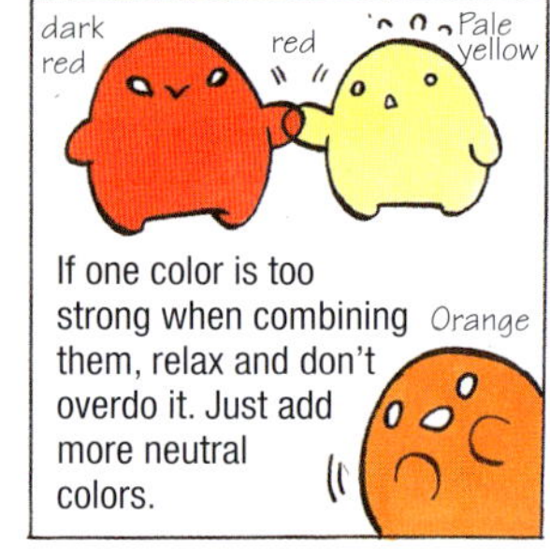

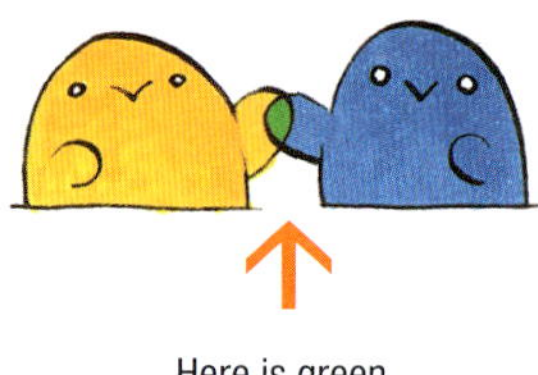

Here is green

The thing to keep in mind is that some colors cannot be made by mixing. They are red, yellow, and blue. So, these are the only three colors that cannot be subtracted. They can only be added, and in our example they can only be used to connect two complementary colors.

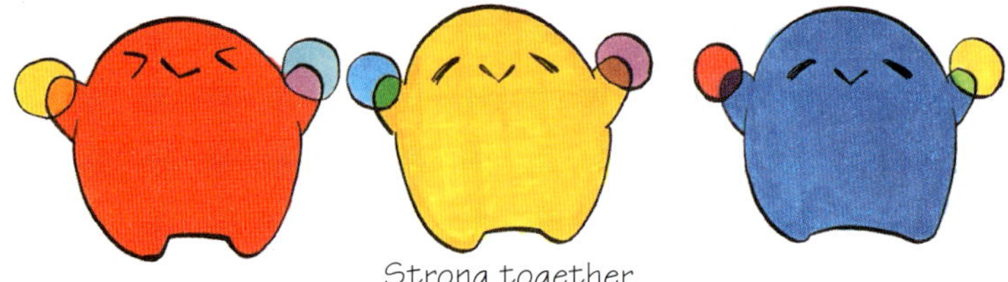

Strong together

Subtraction

With subtraction, you can look for colors that are compatible.

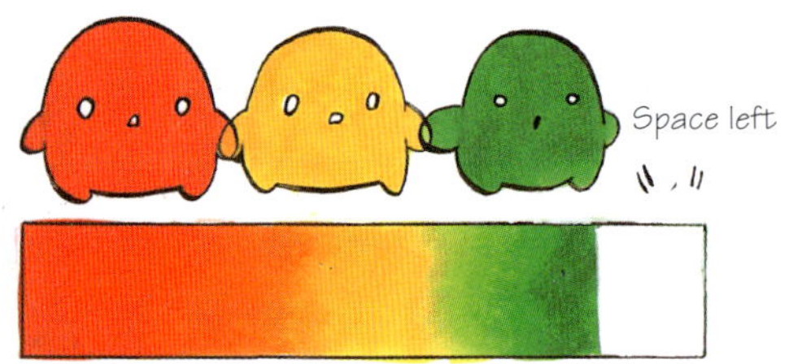

For example, when you need one more color like this.

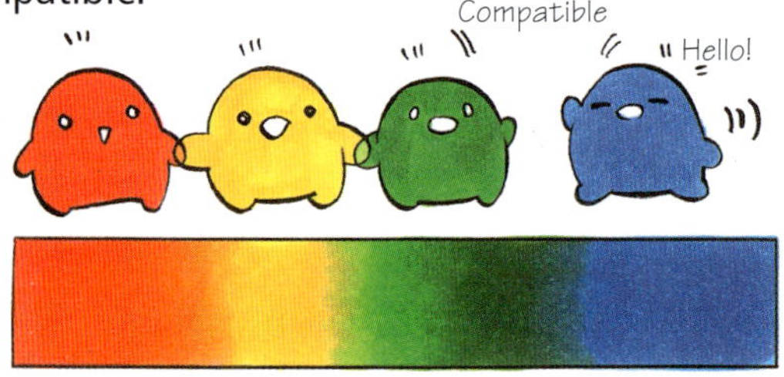

You can add blue to the green side naturally because they are compatible.

Luminosity and Saturation

This is how you create gradations. As mentioned in the addition section, colors have a "luminosity" and a "saturation."

For example, to make pink, you would normally mix red with white. But, if you use transparent ink instead of the white you will arrive at a COPIC type of pink.

If you mix complementary colors, you will get something dull. However, if the luminosity/saturation of the colors is different, the resultant color will be biased toward one of them. On the other hand, the lighter color could play the role of a COPIC #0, and in that way you can get a gradation from red to light green for example.

That being said, the colors are still incompatible. Still, it's not that they can't be used together, it's just that it is difficult to use them together. Keep in mind that explanations provided in the previous pages regarding producing gradation of complementary colors are given under an assumption the colors have similar luminosity and saturation.

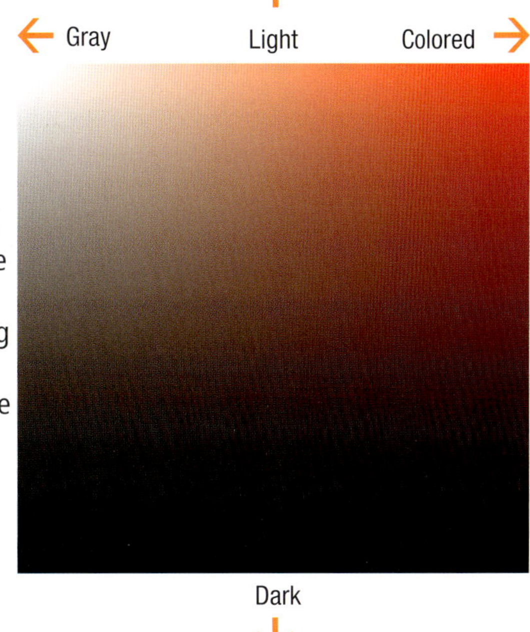

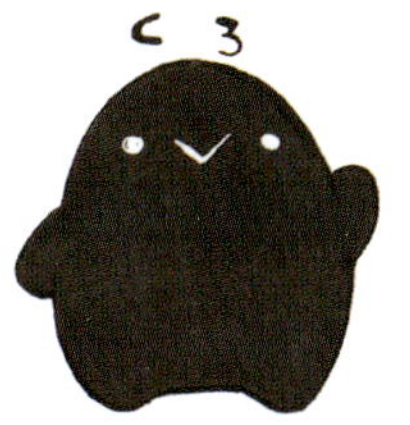
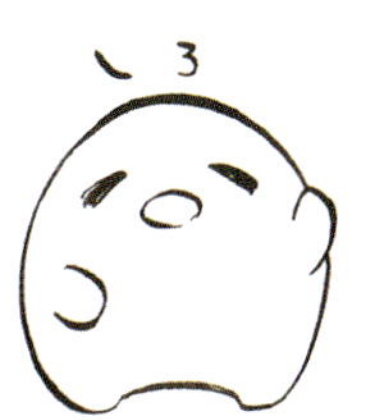

Black and white are called achromatic colors and have no saturation. Other colors are called chromatic colors, and their luminosity and saturation are determined by the ratio of achromatic to chromatic color.

Adding more black lowers the luminosity, and adding more white raises the luminosity and makes it lighter.

Saturation is literally the degree of vividness. The lower the saturation, the more gray it becomes, unlike luminosity.

Gradation

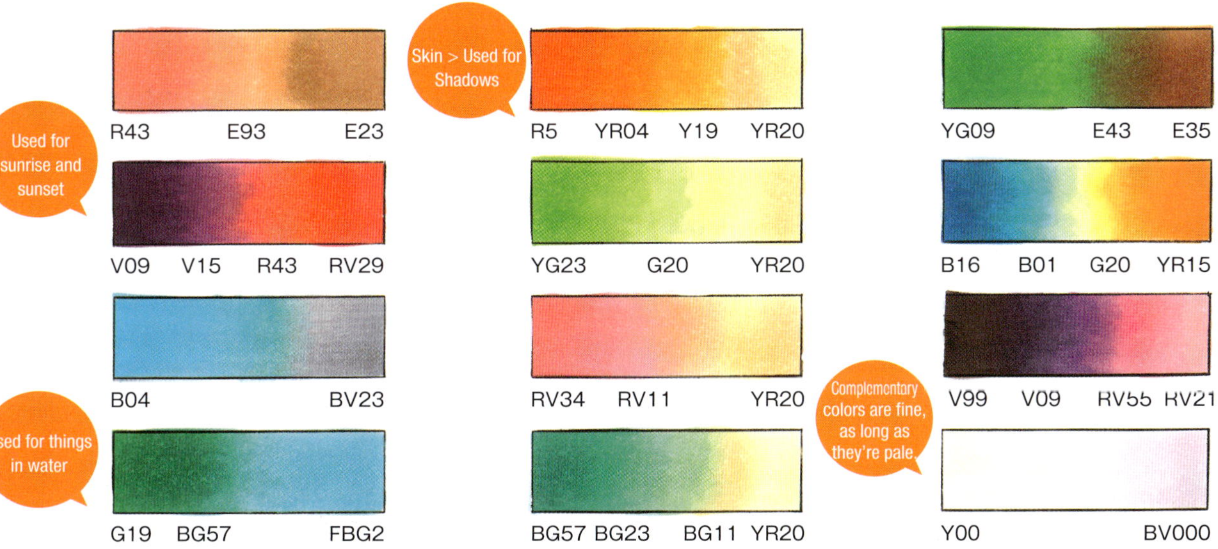

⭕ Softening Edges

This is a minor technique, but it will greatly expand your range of expression.

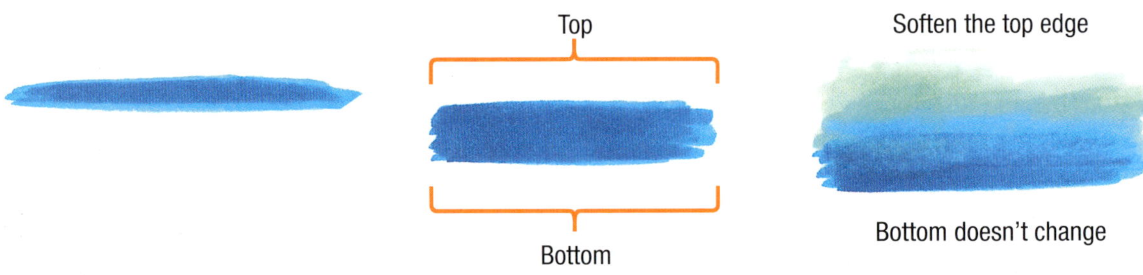

First, draw a normal line. If you are not familiar with this technique, make it a little thicker.

If you zoom in, it will look like this. Think of it as a rectangle with a top side and a bottom side.

The technique is to soften one side or the other.

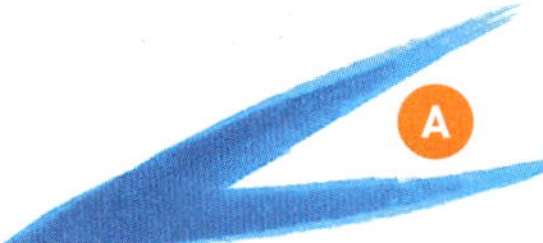

If you soften the edges of the A portion of this V-shaped drawing . . .

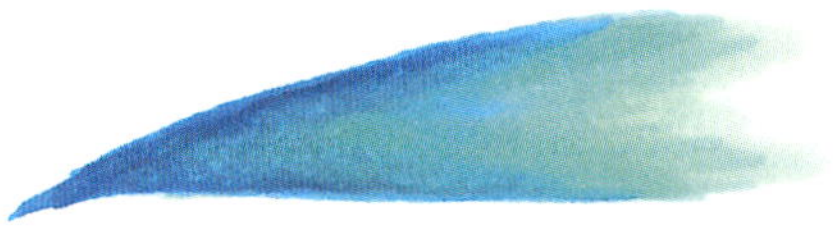

. . . you can create something like this.

Where to Use this Technique...

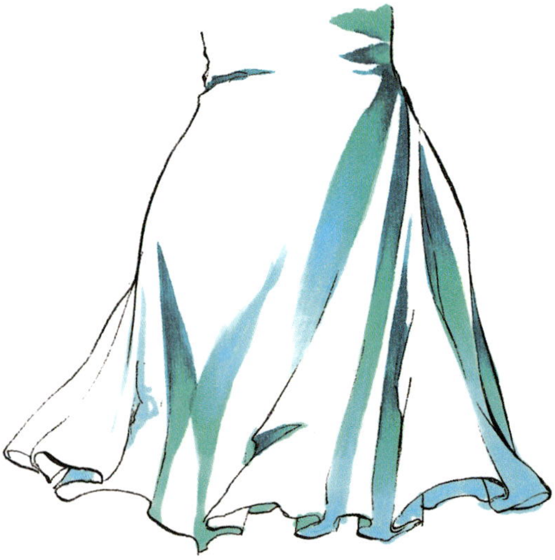

Creases in clothing

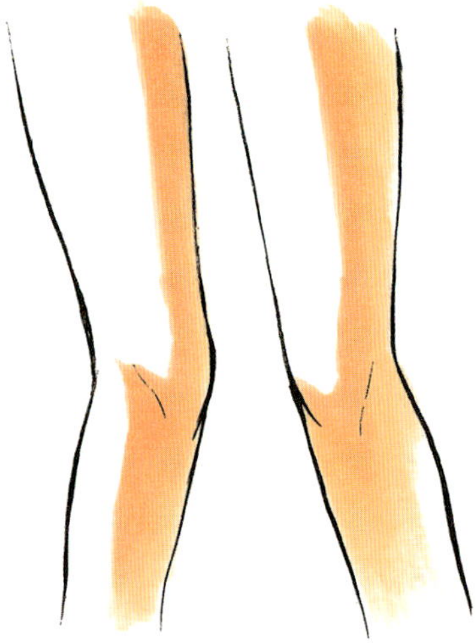

Distinct shadows

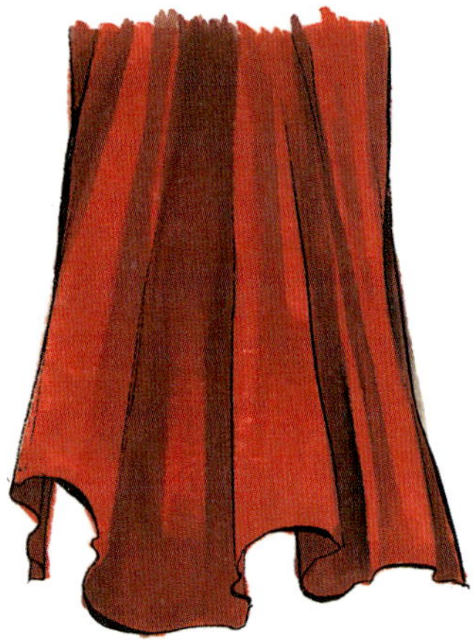

Use on dark-colored fabrics for a more realistic look.

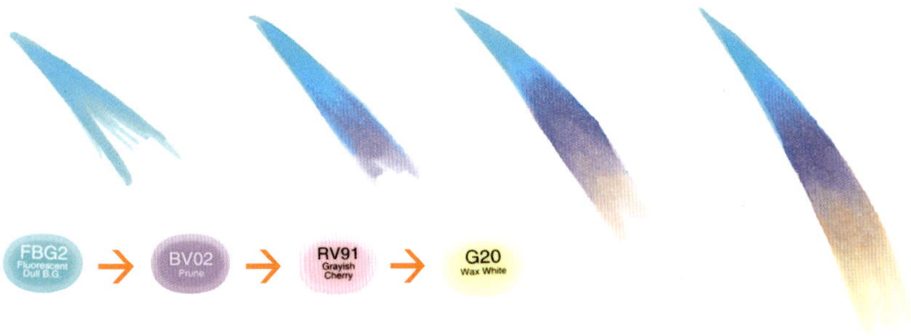

FBG2 Fluorescent Dull B.G. → BV02 Prune → RV91 Grayish Cherry → G20 Wax White

You can also use gradations like this. For morning and evening shadows, or to color dresses that change color in the light, like pearls.

Sample Patterns for Eyes and Lips

These are sample patterns for colors that can be used on eyes and lips. They can be expressed in a variety of ways depending on their shape.

Coloring to Match the Expression

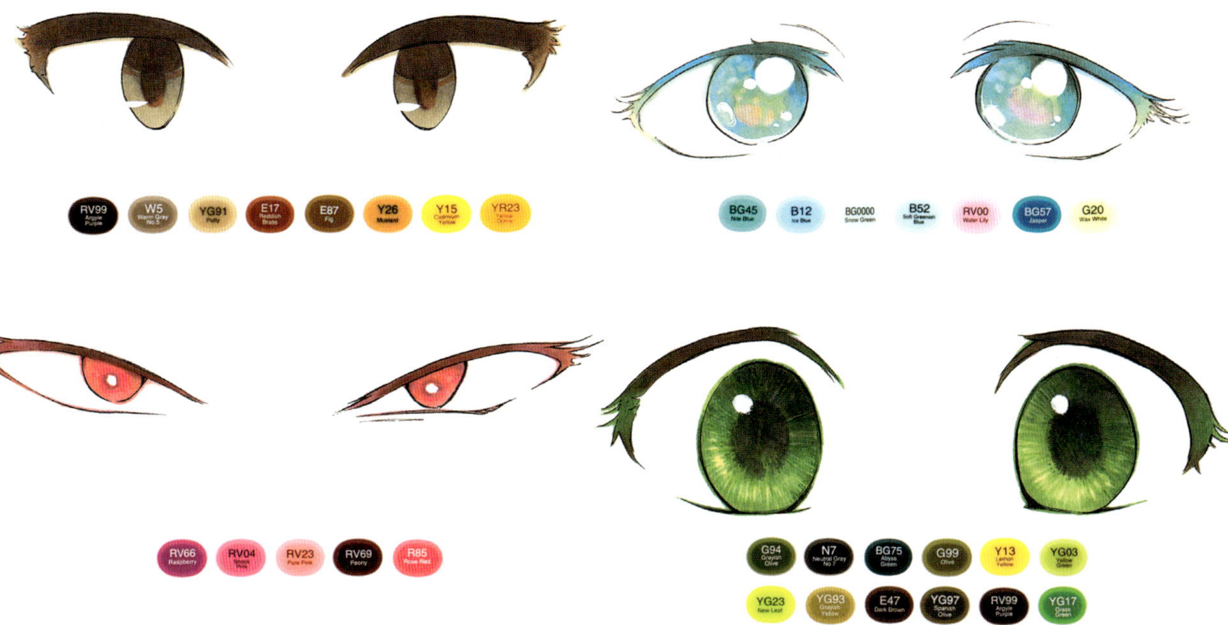

Different Types of Lips

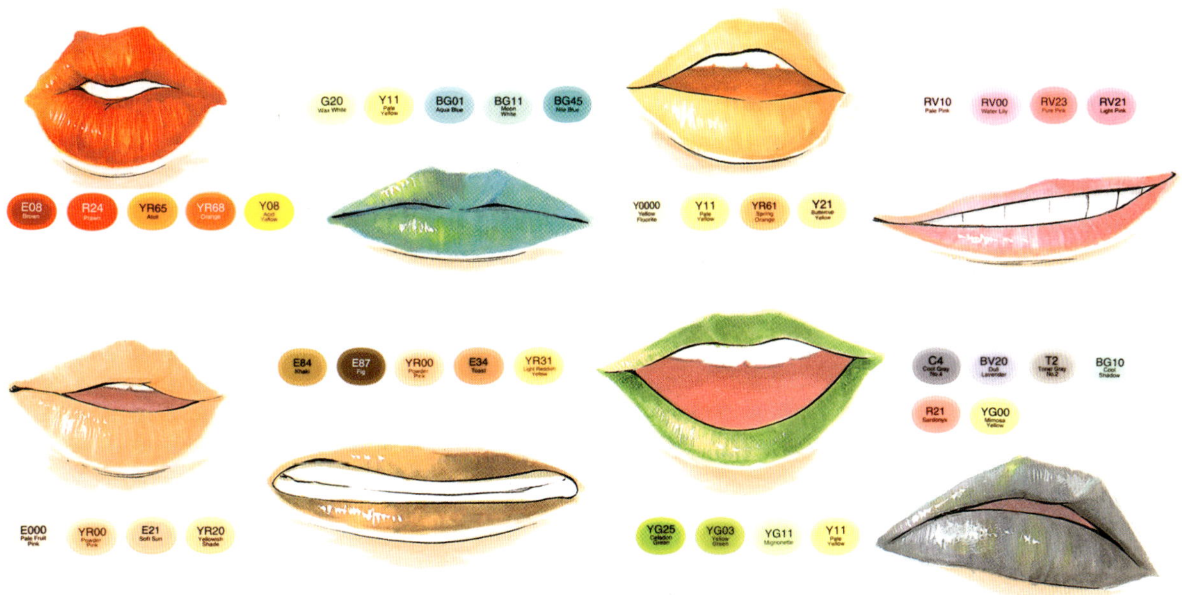

◯ Sample Patterns for Shoes

These are patterns for various styles of shoe. Here we have some with five colors and others with no color limit.

Five-Color Samples

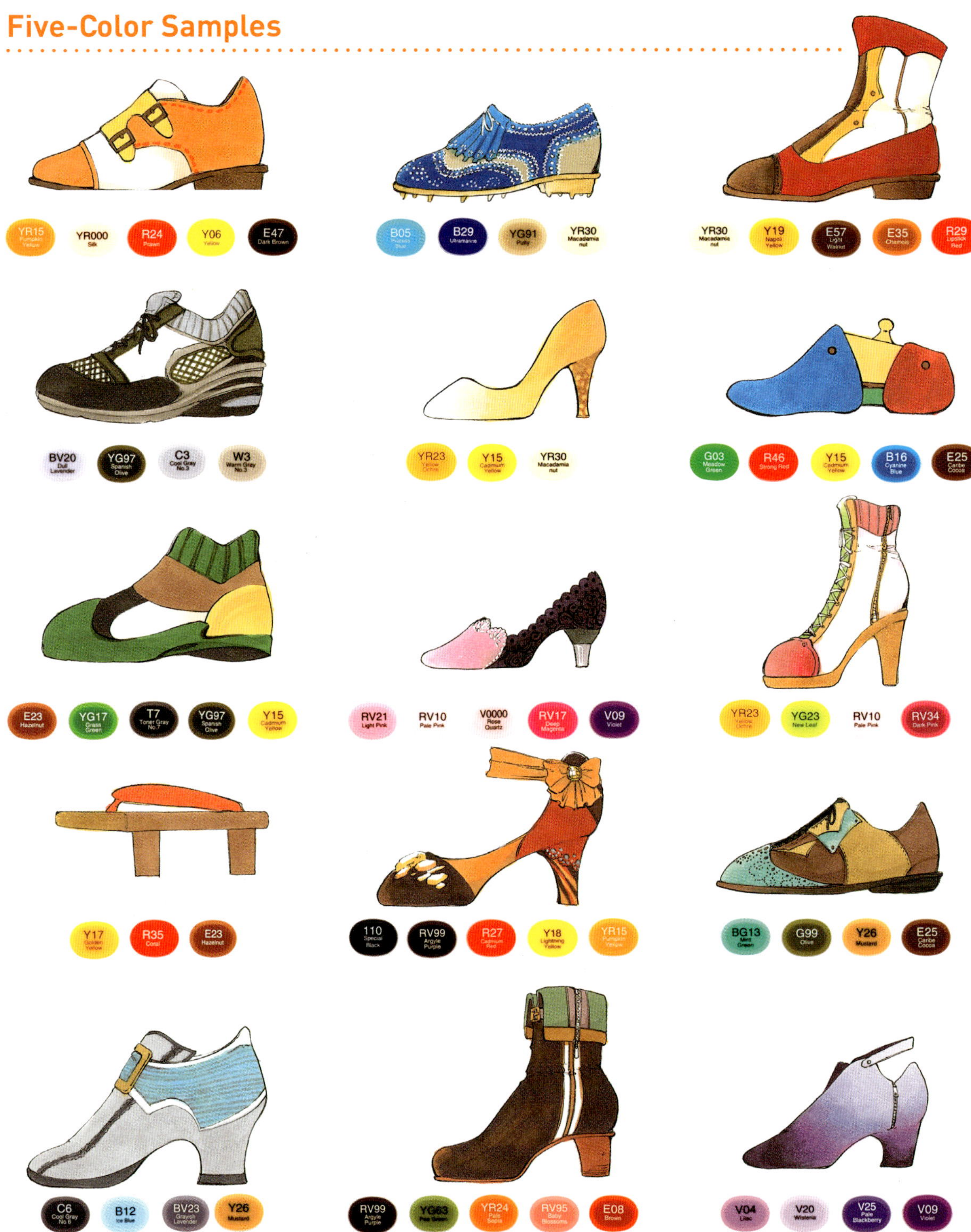

No Limit on Colors

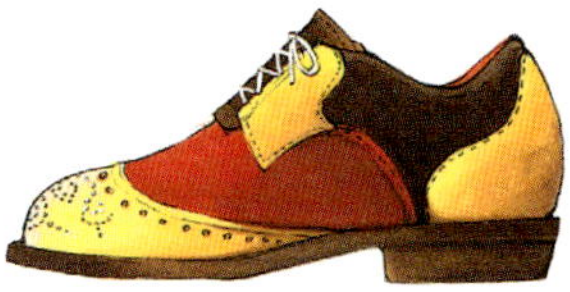

Shoe 1 (men's oxford)
- YR23 Yellow Ochre
- Y19 Napoli Yellow
- YR30 Macadamia nut
- Y06 Yellow
- E35 Chamois
- E08 Brown
- R29 Lipstick Red
- E47 Dark Brown
- RV99 Argyle Purple
- R17 Lipstick Orange
- RV55 Hollyhock

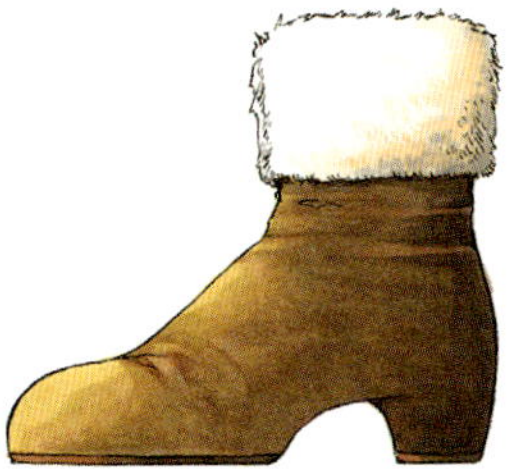

Shoe 2 (fur-trimmed boot)
- E000 Pale Fruit Pink
- E74 Cocoa Brown
- V0000 Rose Quartz
- E53 Raw Silk
- E35 Chamois
- YR30 Macadamia nut
- E79 Cashew
- Y26 Mustard
- E17 Reddish Brass
- BV02 Prune
- BV20 Dull Lavender

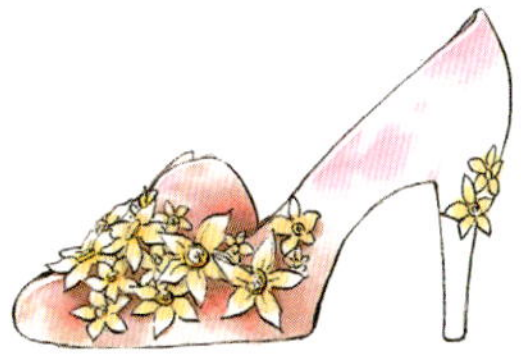

Shoe 3 (pink heel with flowers)
- R11 Pale Cherry Pink
- E0000 Floral White
- YR23 Yellow Ochre
- YG91 Putty
- RV52 Cotton Candy
- R20 Blush
- RV13 Tender Pink
- RV91 Grayish Cherry
- YG00 Mimosa Yellow
- RV11 Pink
- V0000 Rose Quartz
- YR31 Light Reddish Yellow
- E04 Lipstick Natural
- Y08 Acid Yellow

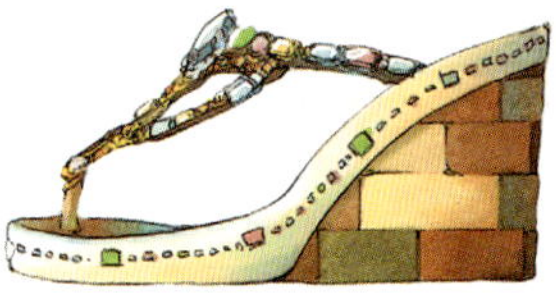

Shoe 4 (jeweled wedge sandal)
- YG25 Celadon Green
- BG10 Cool Shadow
- G20 Wax White
- E47 Dark Brown
- T1 Toner Gray No.1
- N4 Neutral Gray No.4
- B12 Ice Blue
- RV91 Grayish Cherry
- E84 Khaki
- RV95 Baby Blossoms
- B00 Frost Blue
- E35 Chamois
- RV34 Dark Pink
- Y11 Pale Yellow
- Y15 Cadmium Yellow
- YR23 Yellow Ochre

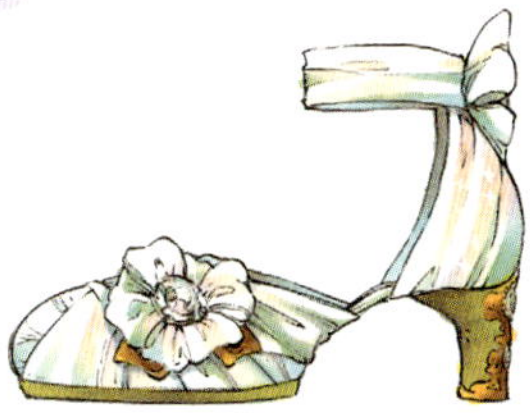

Shoe 5 (flower ankle-tie heel)
- YR30 Macadamia nut
- G12 Sea Green
- R0000 Pink Beryl
- Y19 Napoli Yellow
- BG10 Cool Shadow
- B00 Frost Blue
- E0000 Floral White
- RV10 Pale Pink
- BV20 Dull Lavender
- E37 Sepia
- W5 Warm Gray No.5

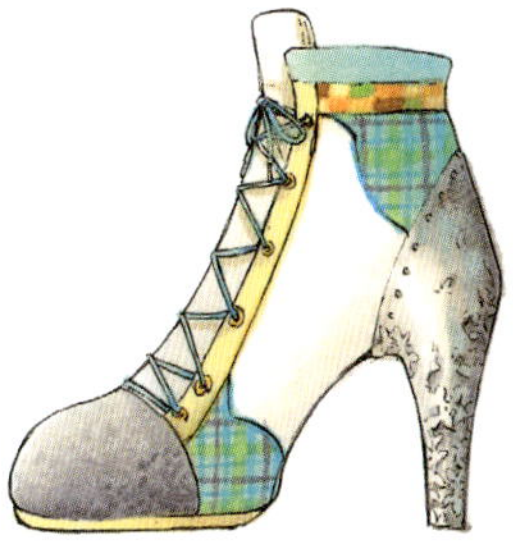

Shoe 6 (plaid laced boot)
- YG00 Mimosa Yellow
- BG53 Ice Mint
- B00 Frost Blue
- T4 Toner Gray No.4
- W2 Warm Gray No.2
- C3 Cool Gray No.3
- T1 Toner Gray No.1
- E53 Raw Silk
- BV23 Grayish Lavender
- BG53 Ice Mint
- E0000 Floral White
- B52 Soft Greenish Blue
- B05 Process Blue
- BG45 Nile Blue
- YG25 Celadon Green
- G00 Jade Green
- YG91 Putty
- Y35 Maize
- YR23 Yellow Ochre

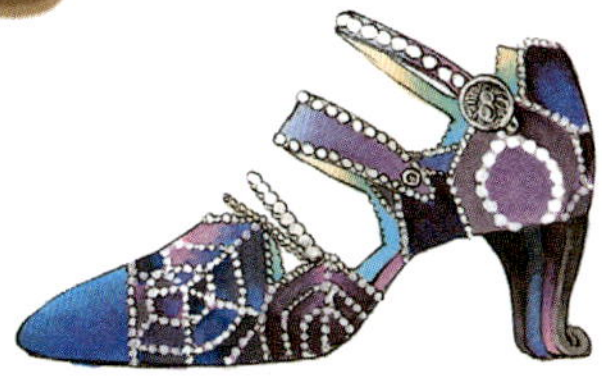

Shoe 7 (green strap heel sandal)
- E31 Brick Beige
- E35 Chamois
- YG03 Yellow Green
- E59 Walnut
- E84 Khaki
- YG06 Yellowish Green
- G94 Grayish Olive
- YG41 Pale Cobalt Green
- W5 Warm Gray No.5
- T2 Toner Gray No.2
- YG17 Grass Green
- Y19 Napoli Yellow
- Y08 Acid Yellow
- YR23 Yellow Ochre
- BG93 Green Gray

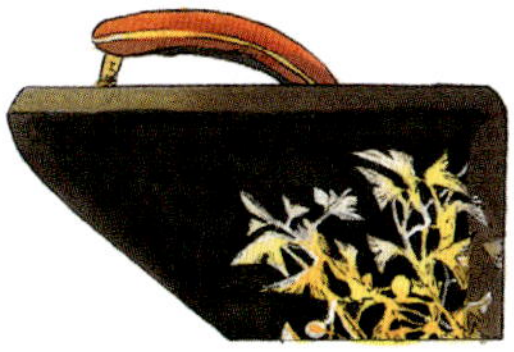

Shoe 8 (beaded pointed heel)
- T1 Toner Gray No.1
- T2 Toner Gray No.2
- N8 Neutral Gray No.8
- N4 Neutral Gray No.4
- N4 Neutral Gray No.4
- V22 Ash Lavender
- FBG2 Fluorescent Dull B.G.
- B93 Light Crockery Blue
- V04 Lilac
- B99 Agate
- E41 Pearl White
- V28 Eggplant
- V09 Violet
- B04 Tahitian Blue
- V04 Lilac
- B06 Peacock Blue
- B45 Smoky Blue
- BV17 Deep Reddish Blue
- V09 Violet
- B04 Tahitian Blue

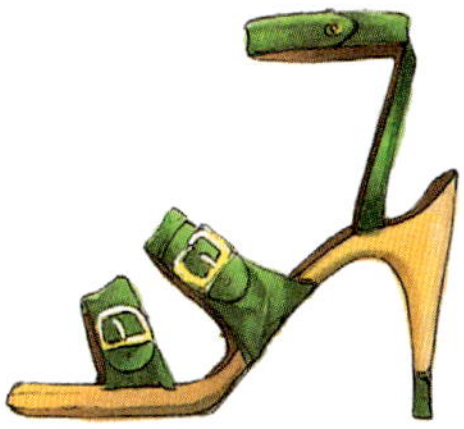

Shoe 9 (green embroidered bootie)
- G12 Sea Green
- YG95 Pale Olive
- G000 Pale Green
- N2 Neutral Gray No.2
- N4 Neutral Gray No.4
- BG11 Moon White
- B99 Agate
- YG45 Cobalt Green
- BG49 Duck Blue
- BG34 Horizon Green
- Y11 Pale Yellow
- Y06 Yellow

Shoe 10 (handbag)
- YR23 Yellow Ochre
- E41 Pearl White
- YR30 Macadamia nut
- YR15 Pumpkin Yellow
- Y26 Mustard
- R35 Coral
- R37 Carmine
- YR18 Sanguine
- E74 Cocoa Brown
- Y08 Acid Yellow
- 110 Special Black
- C8 Cool Gray No.8
- N4 Neutral Gray No.4
- W6 Warm Gray No.6
- V99 Aubergine

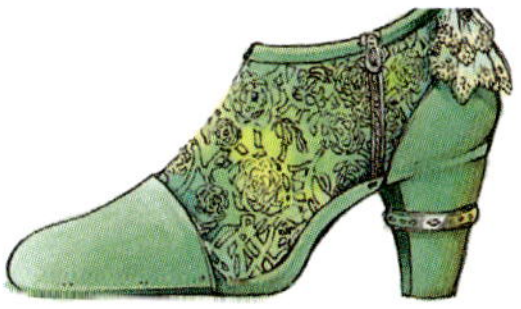

How to Draw Patterned Items

There are two methods when drawing patterns. 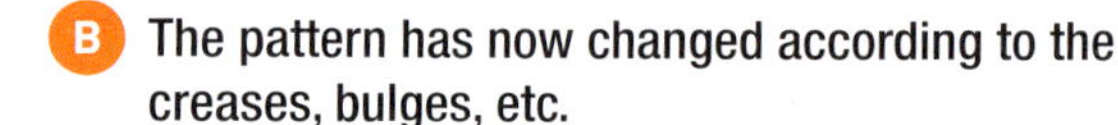 is a method that ignores creases, etc., and just adds patterns like pasting them on an item. Ⓑ is a method that changes the pattern to match the creases and bulges of the object.

It all depends on the style of the picture, but honestly the easiest way is to plaster the pattern on with Ⓐ. Ⓑ requires a lot more thinking and getting used to because you have to be careful around bulges, rounded edges, bumps, etc.

Ⓐ The pattern is just stuck on there, ignoring the creases.

Ⓑ The pattern has now changed according to the creases, bulges, etc.

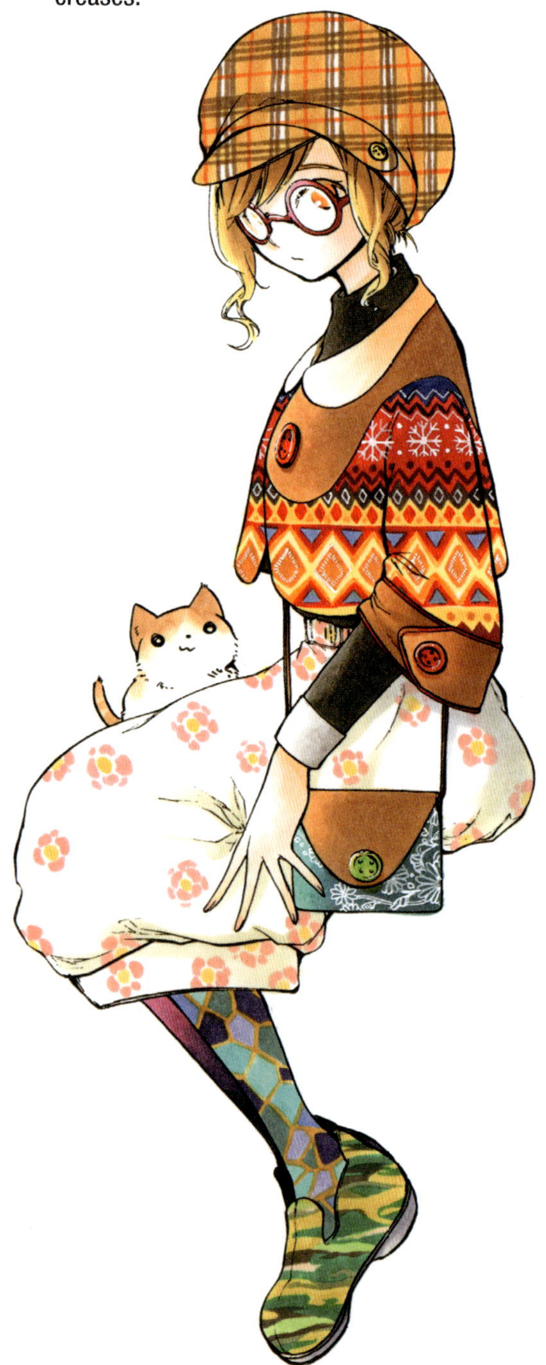

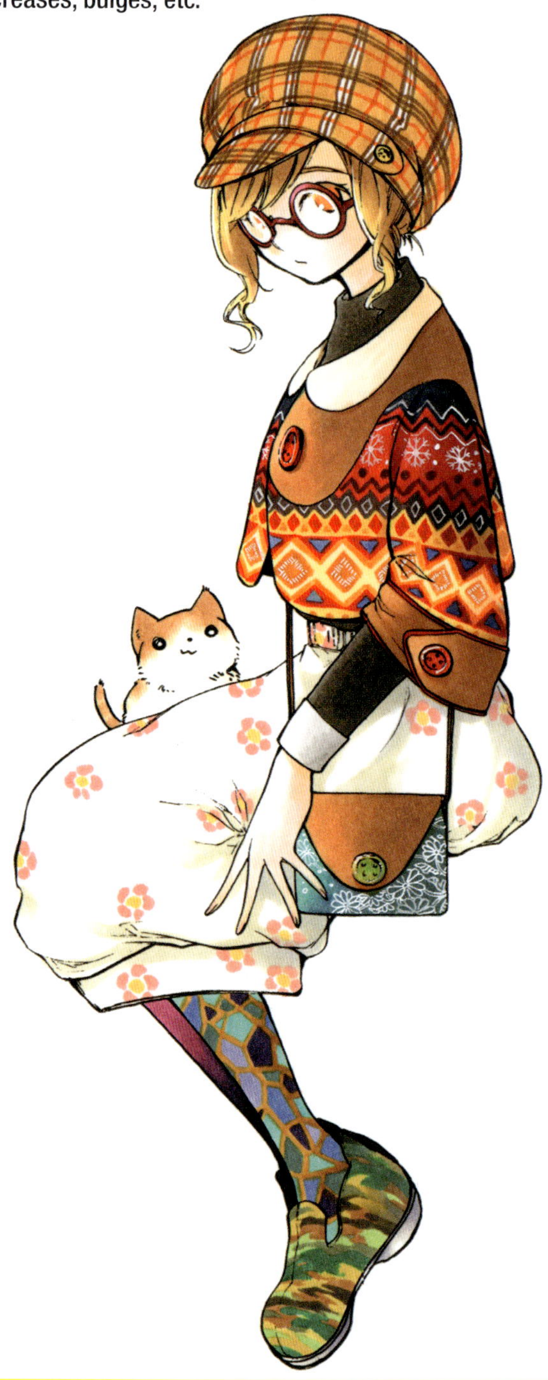

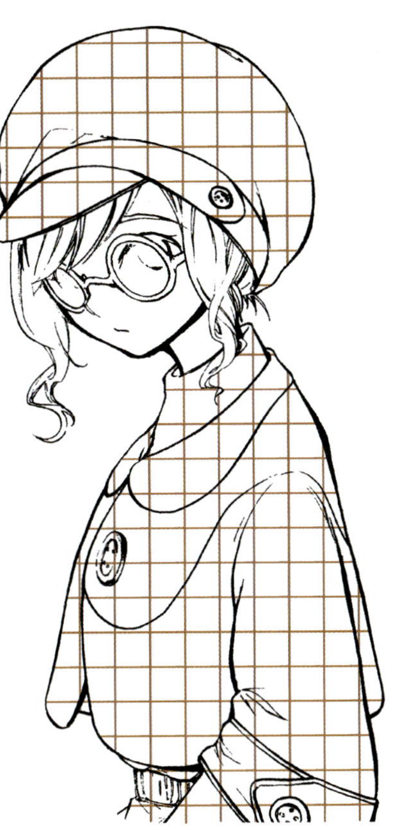

First, let's look at method A. This is how the squares would look without any distortion.

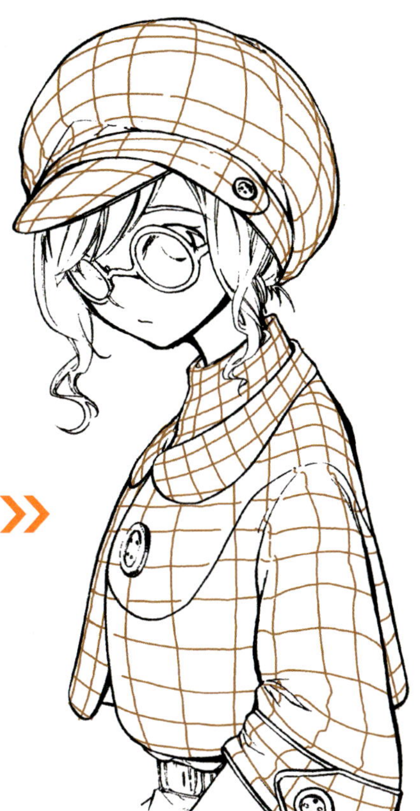

If we take into account the bulges using method B, we get this.

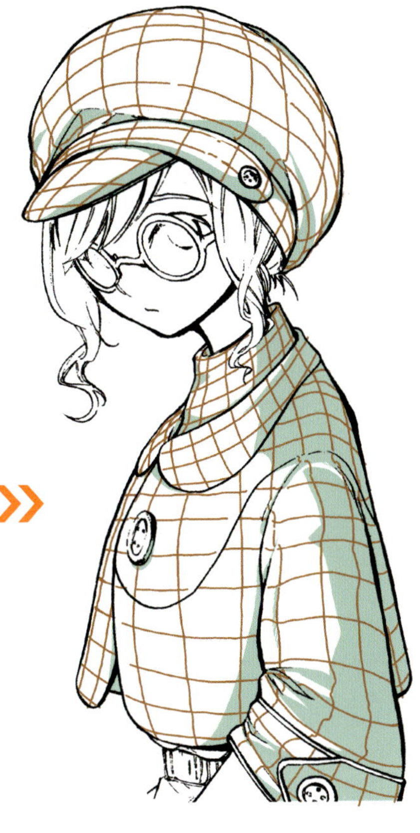

In addition to more fullness and roundness, be careful to add "layering" to the creases. If the pattern in the creased area is distorted, it will be much more convincing.

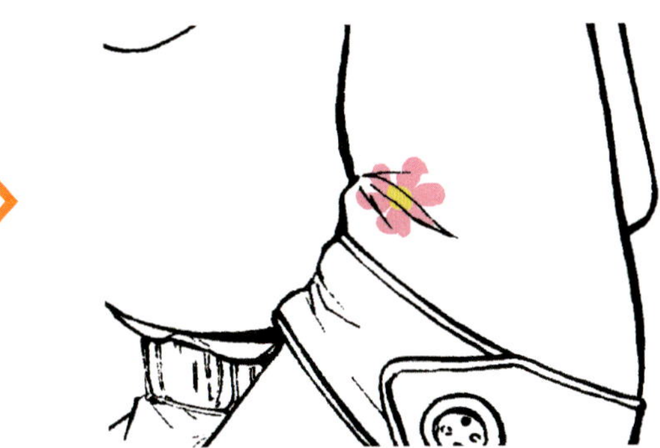

Use a darker color than the original for all the shadows. The same color can be used for all of them, but it is necessary to apply all colors separately. If you apply them all at once, the nib will drag the color you used for the pattern, making everything muddy.

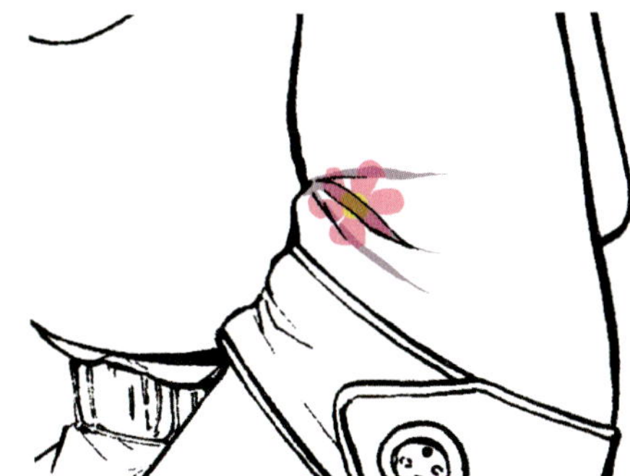

It can be colored like this. Color to match the shadows of the entire fabric.

Checkered Patterns (This is from the hat)

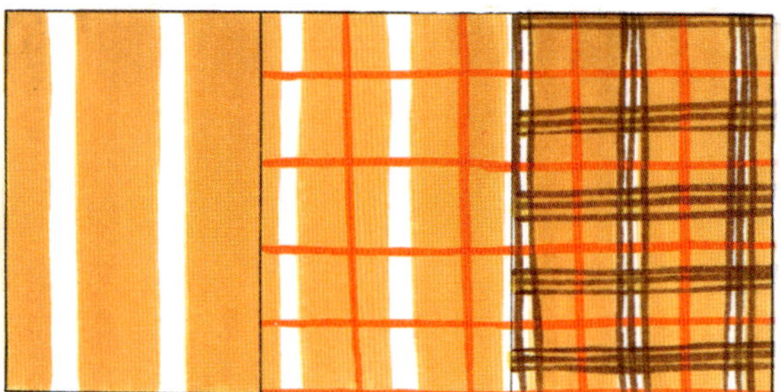

1 Make vertical lines with YR23.

2 Draw vertical lines and then some horizontal lines on top (1) with YR18. Make them as square as possible.

3 Draw three strips of E47 in the center and at the edges of the white area. Then three strips of YR23 horizontally to make small squares. Finally add Y15 at the intersections.

Diamond Checkers

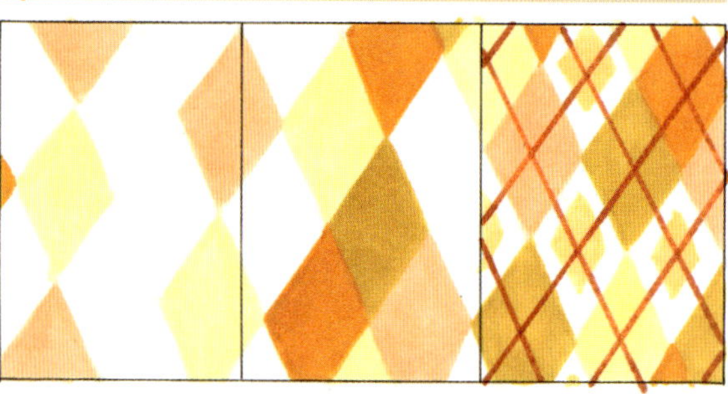

1 Use BG90 to create a diamond, and add E21 and Y11 so that they are not adjacent to each other.

2 Add Y26 and YR24 in the same manner.

3 Paint the white area with YR31 and add lines with E17. If E17 is too strong, change it or simply draw the broken lines using white space.

Patterns on the Jacket

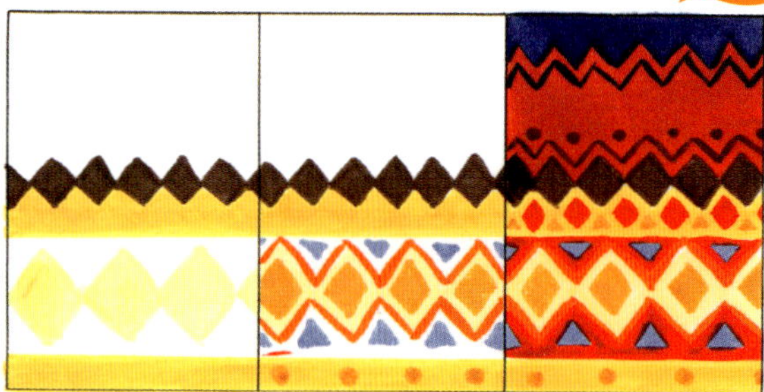

1 Use Y11 to draw the ◇ and Y08 to draw the patterns above and below. The trick is to add jagged edges.

2 Add ◇ using V99 and YR24. Add △ using B24.

3 Complete the patterns using B37, R46, and white ink.

Skirt Patterns

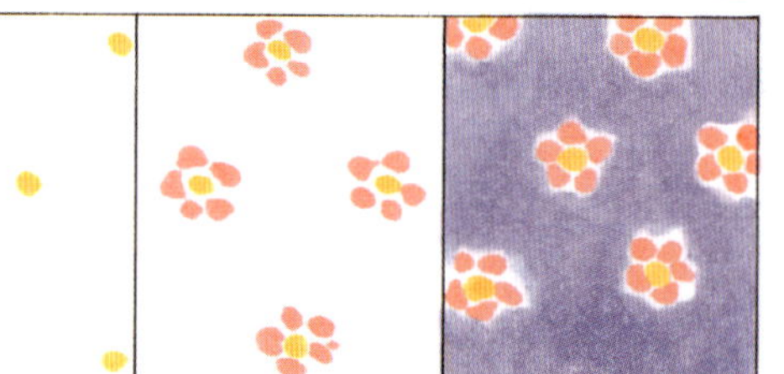

1 Add Y35 in a circle at the top of the △.

2 Use R32 to color the petals. If the fabric is white, this should be all you need.

3 If you want to add a color, just soften the edges around each flower.

Camouflage on the Shoes

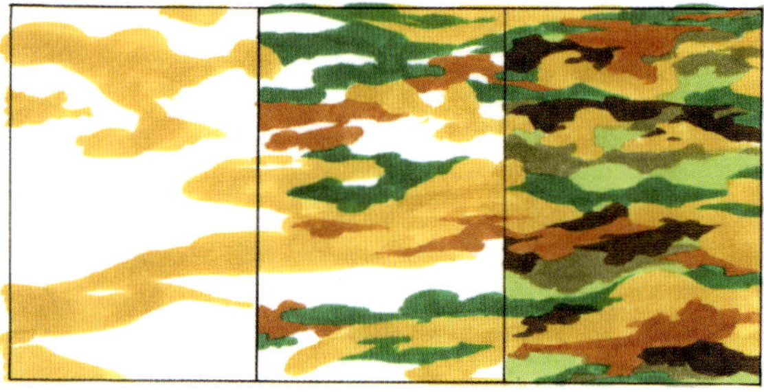

1 Fill some wispy horizontal areas with Y26.

2 Add G19 and E35 in the same manner.

3 Add G85, W7, and Y23 to complete.

Patterns on the Socks

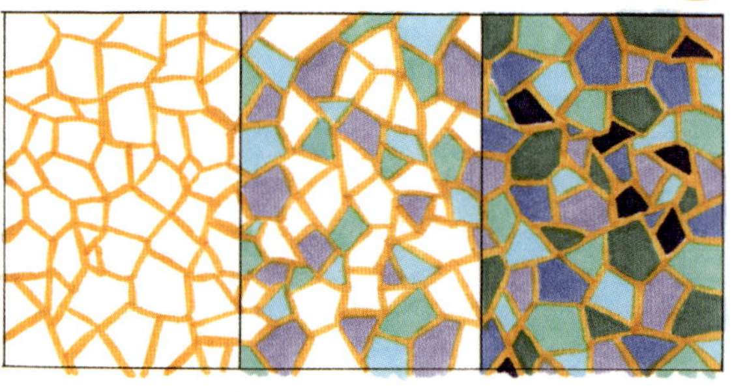

1 Draw the "frames" with YR23.

2 Color with BV02, BG01, and BG13.

3 Apply BG18, B24, and BV08 as far apart as possible.

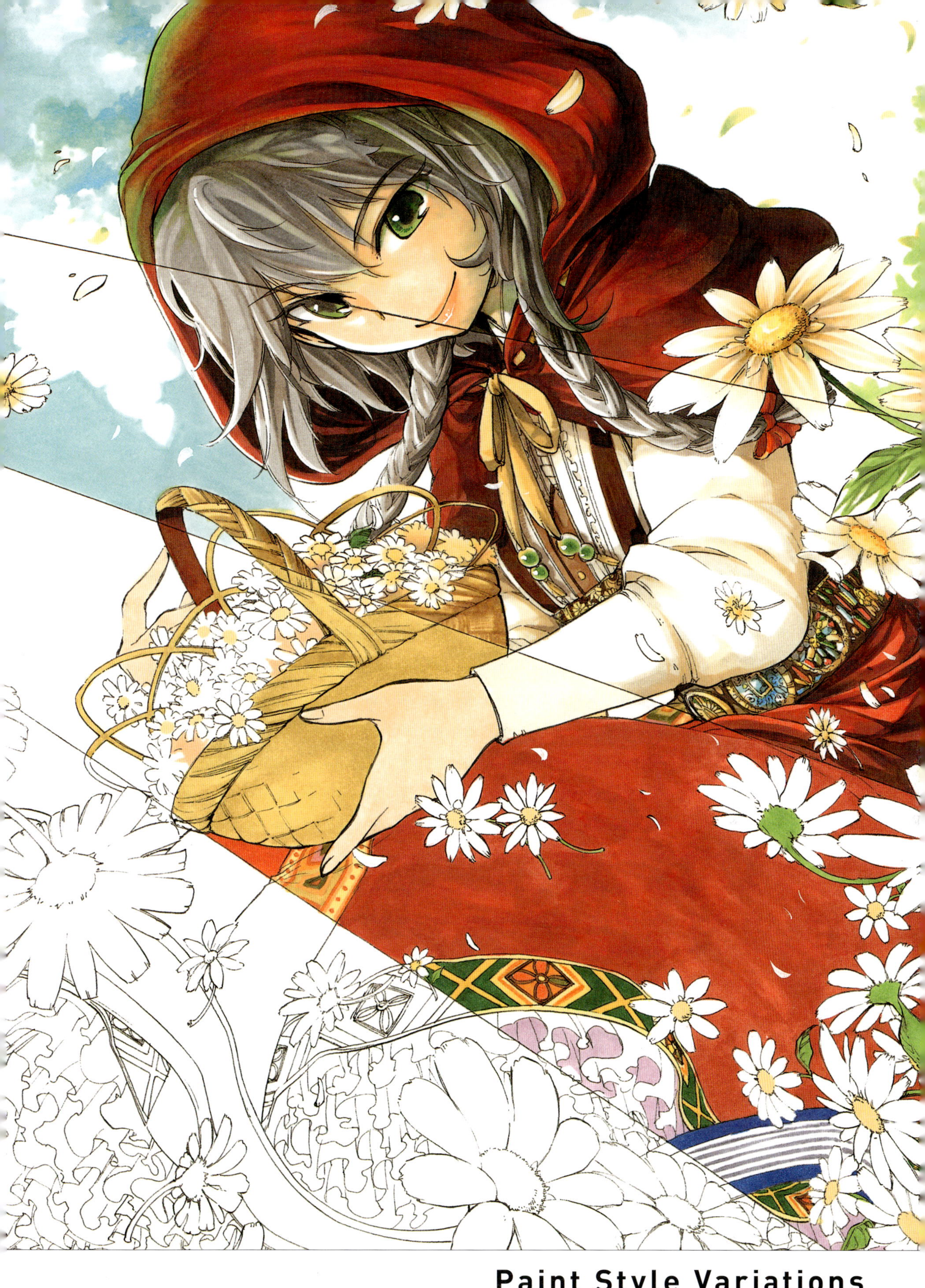

Paint Style Variations

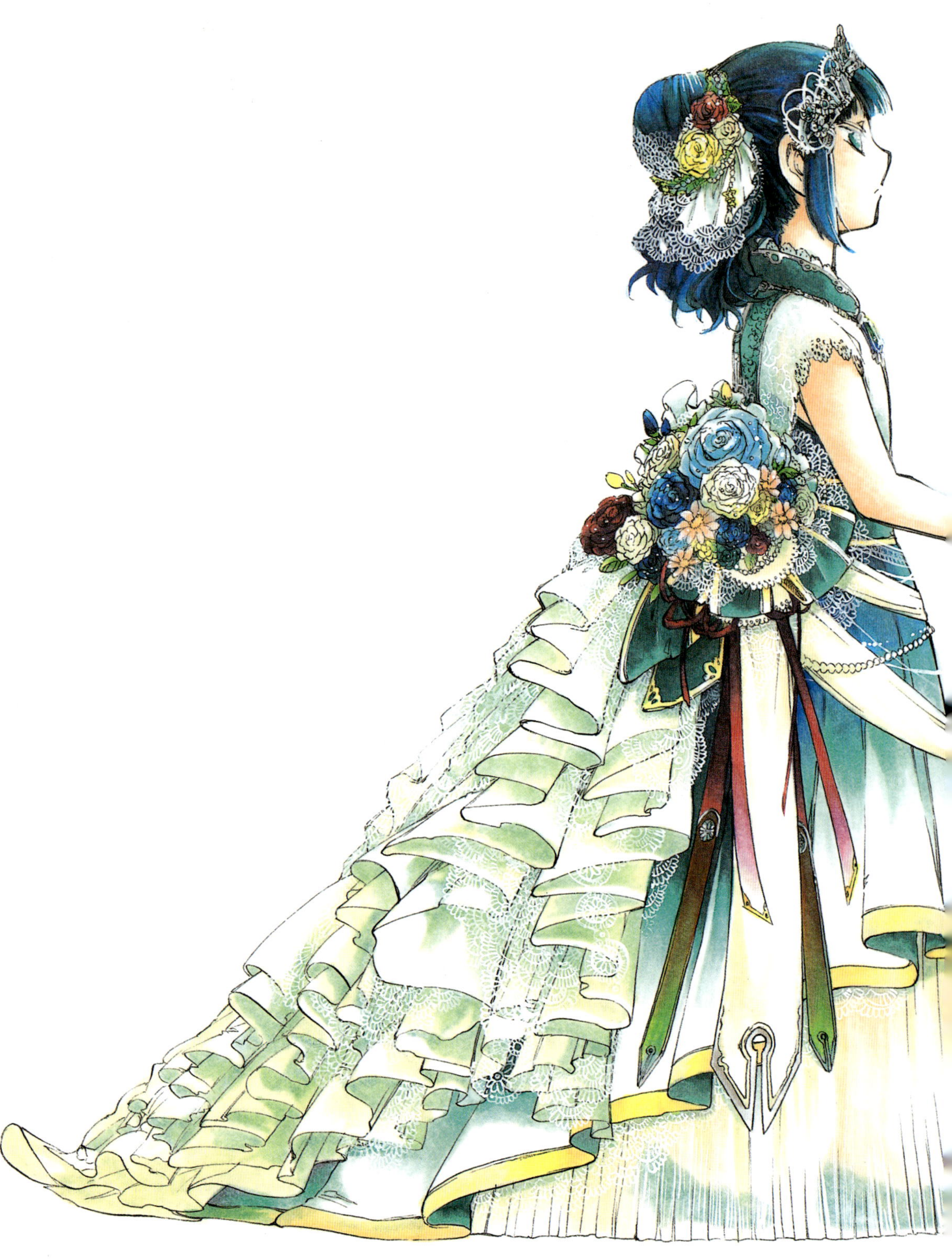

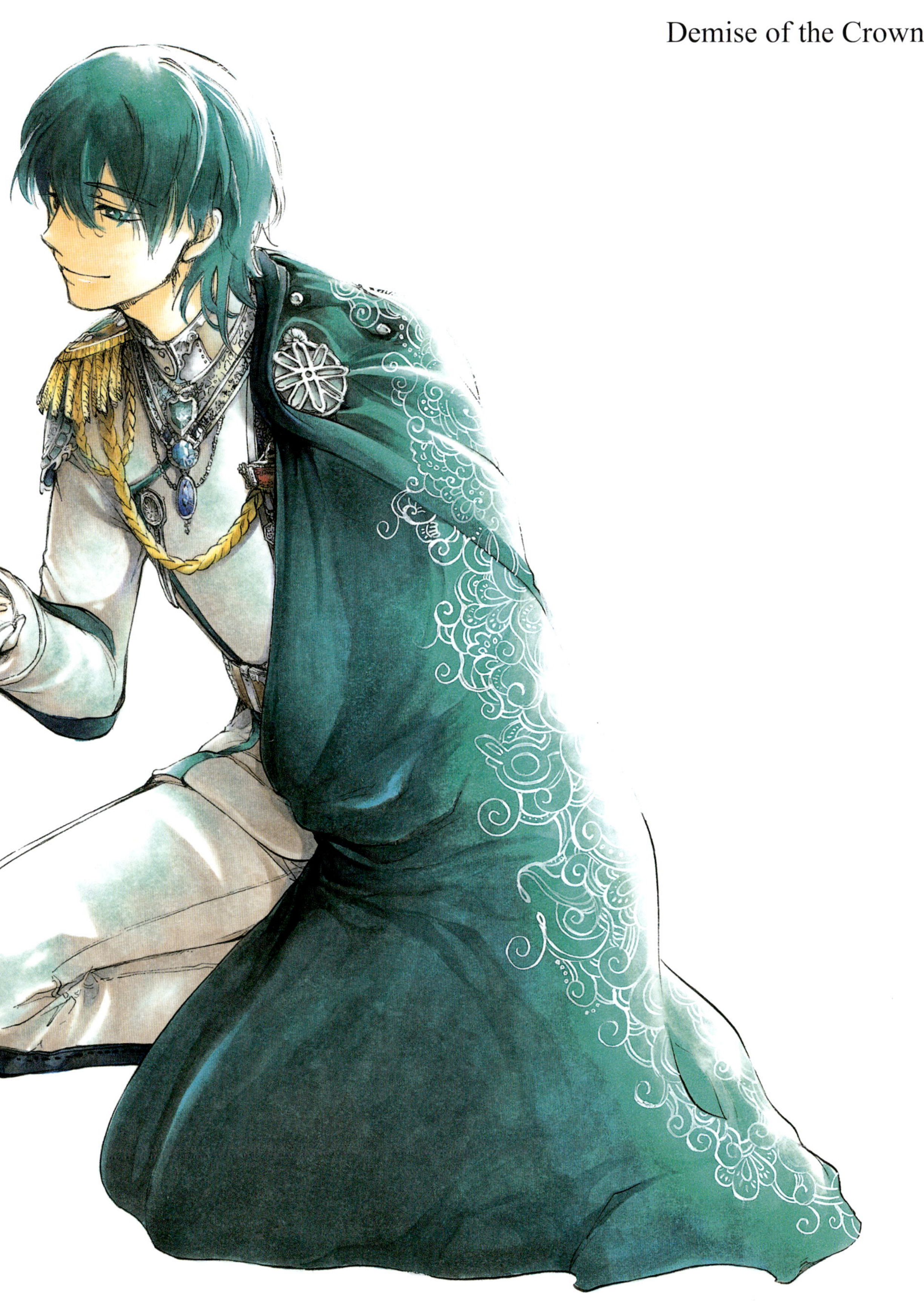

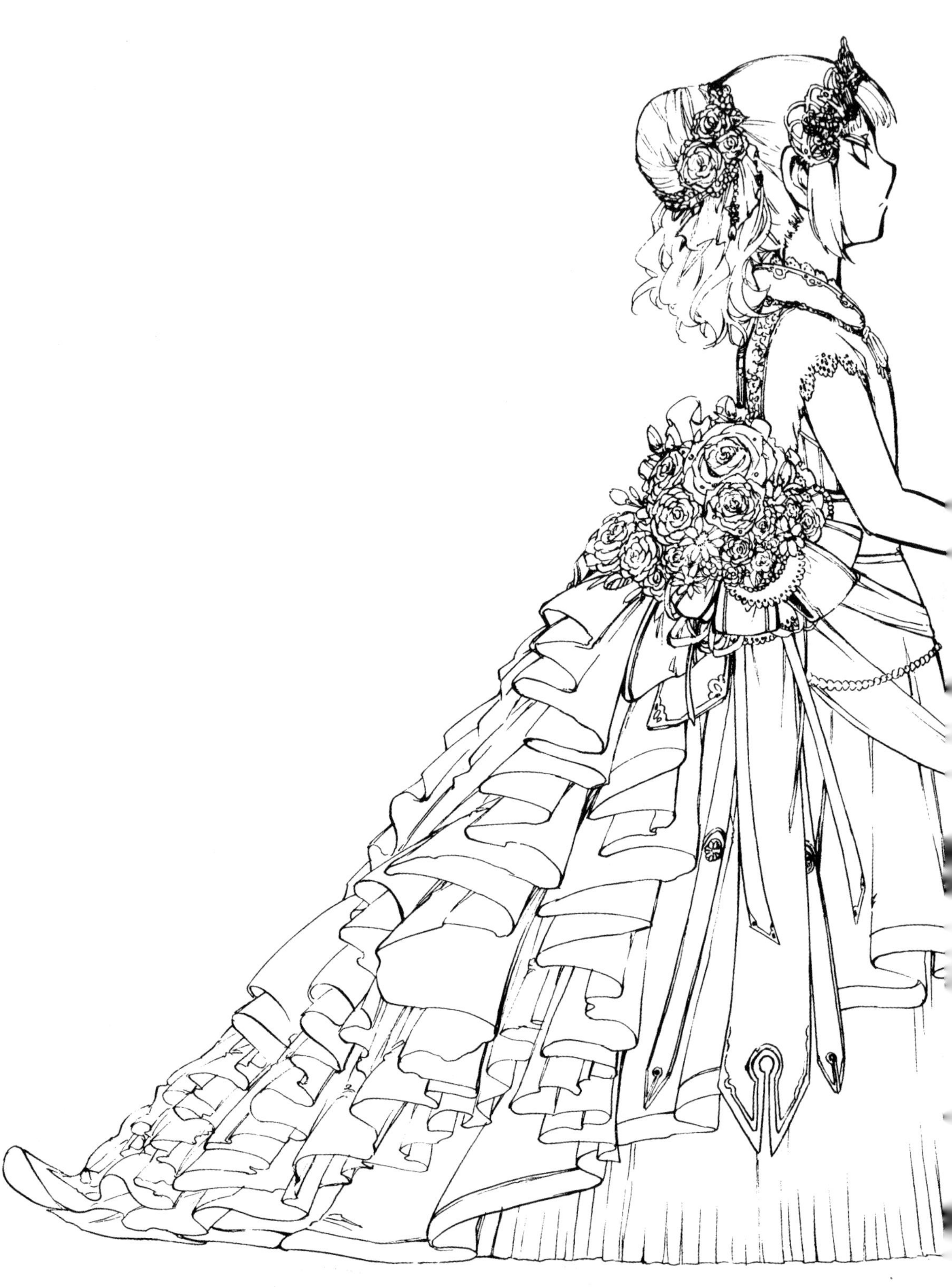

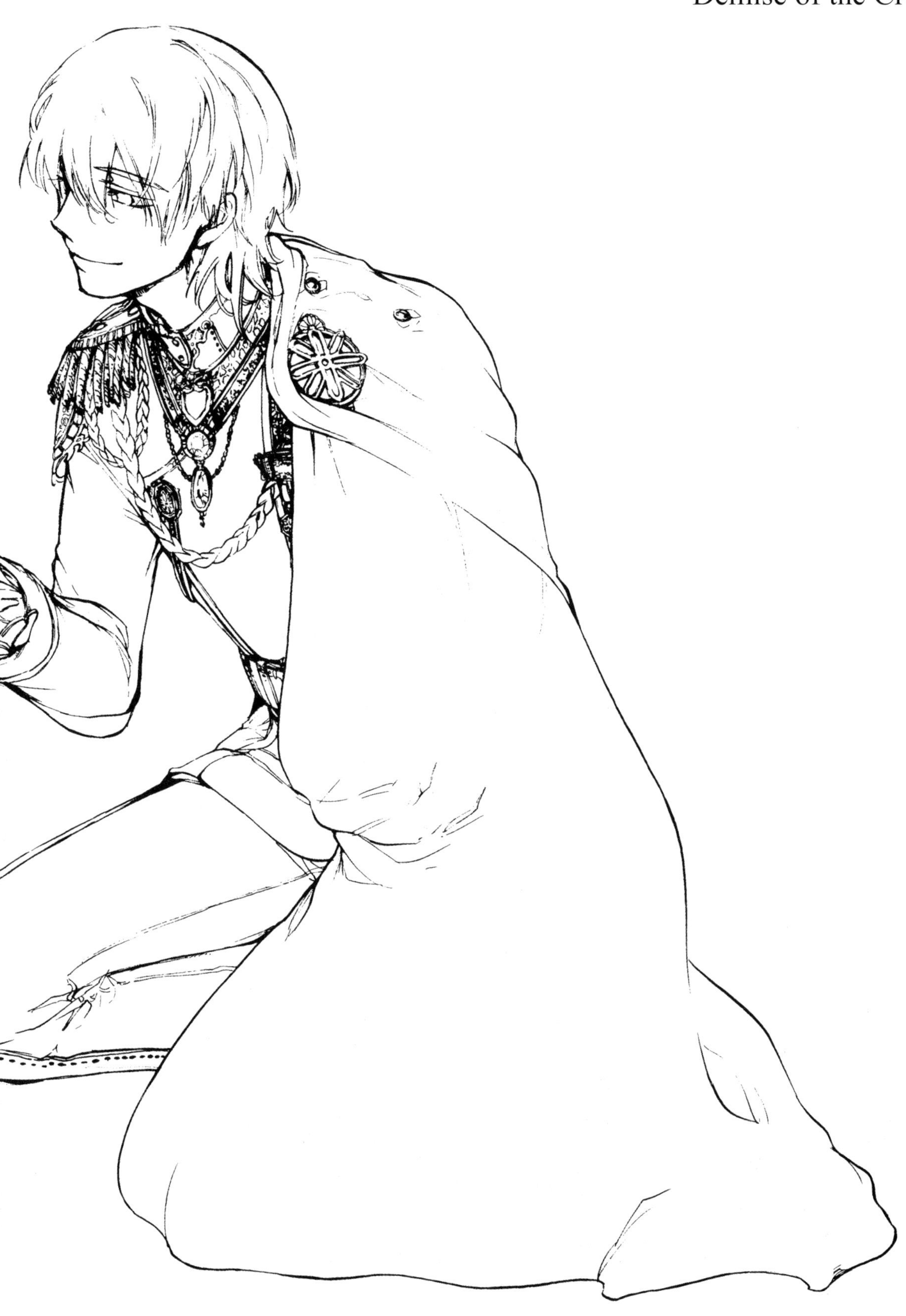

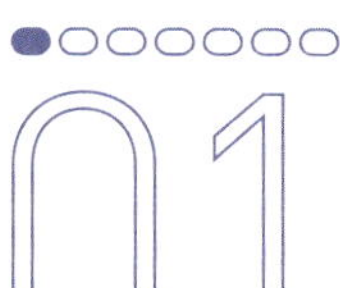

Softening Edges: Using COPIC #0 to Render Light

This technique allows for the use of fewer colors because light is represented by #0 and the native paper color. In addition, softening edges makes it possible to create effective illustrations.

Selected Ink

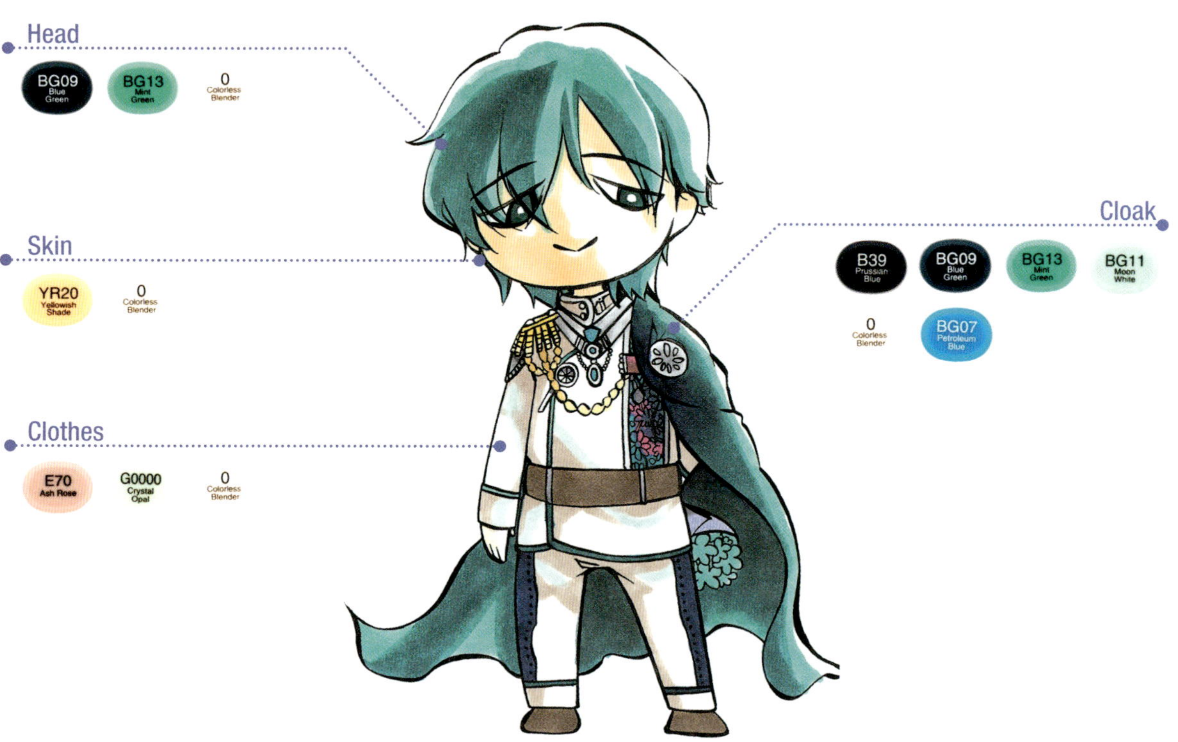

Coloring With a Single Color and #0

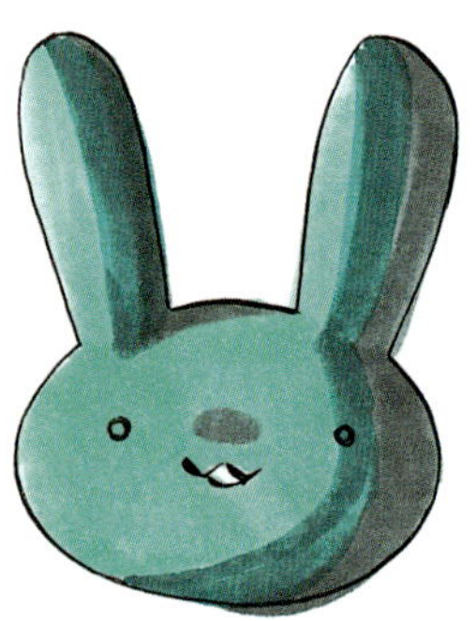

Usually, "light," "neutral colors," and "shadows" are used to create a three-dimensional effect.

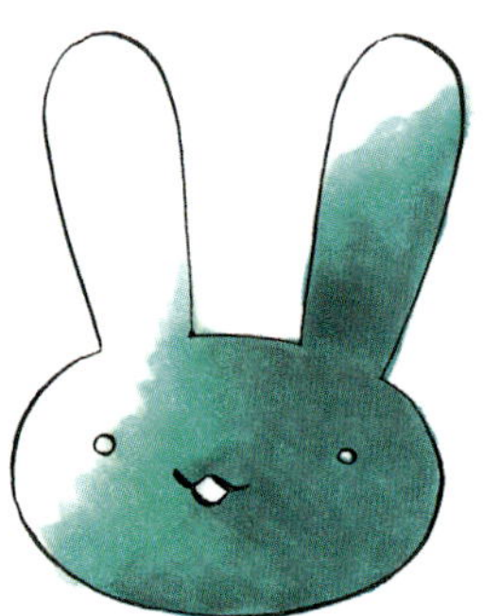

Here, the "light" is represented by blank paper while the "neutral color" is created with a single application. "Shadows" are created by applying more layers of the neutral color. Note that it is almost impossible to do this with dark colors as you would have to use far too much COPIC #0.

Coloring Faces: Effective Use of the Nib

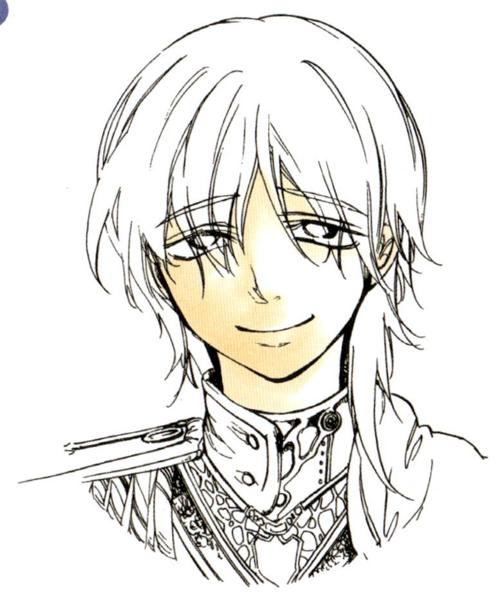

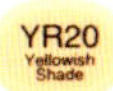

Add shadows with YR20. Use a feathering motion to color in the direction of the light.

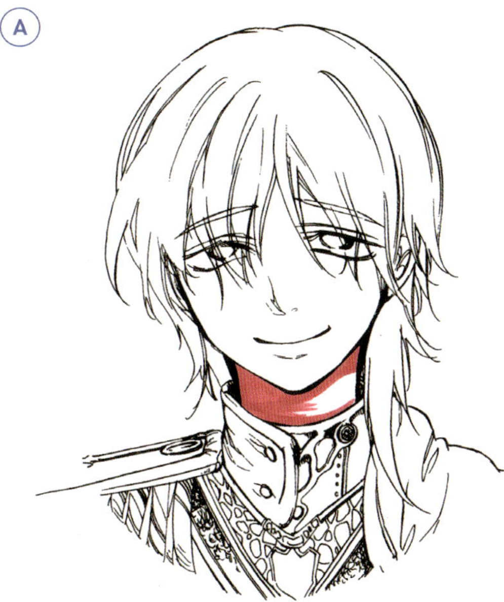

Note, the procedure for softening edges looks like this but we are using a dark color for demonstration purposes. First, color the neck and then soften the edges.

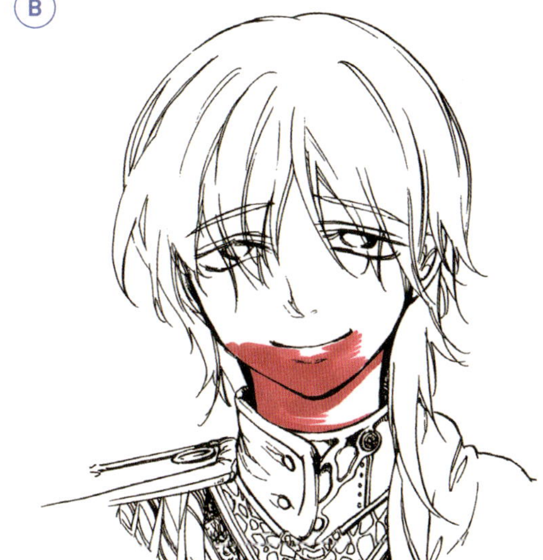

Next, paint under the chin and soften the edges.

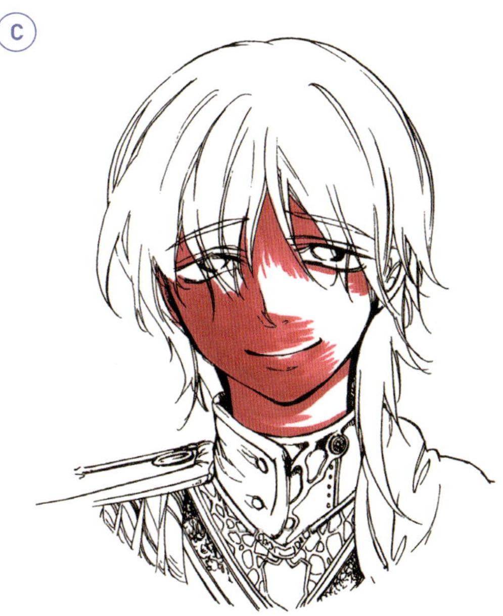

The last step is to go down the nose, forehead, and under the right eye.

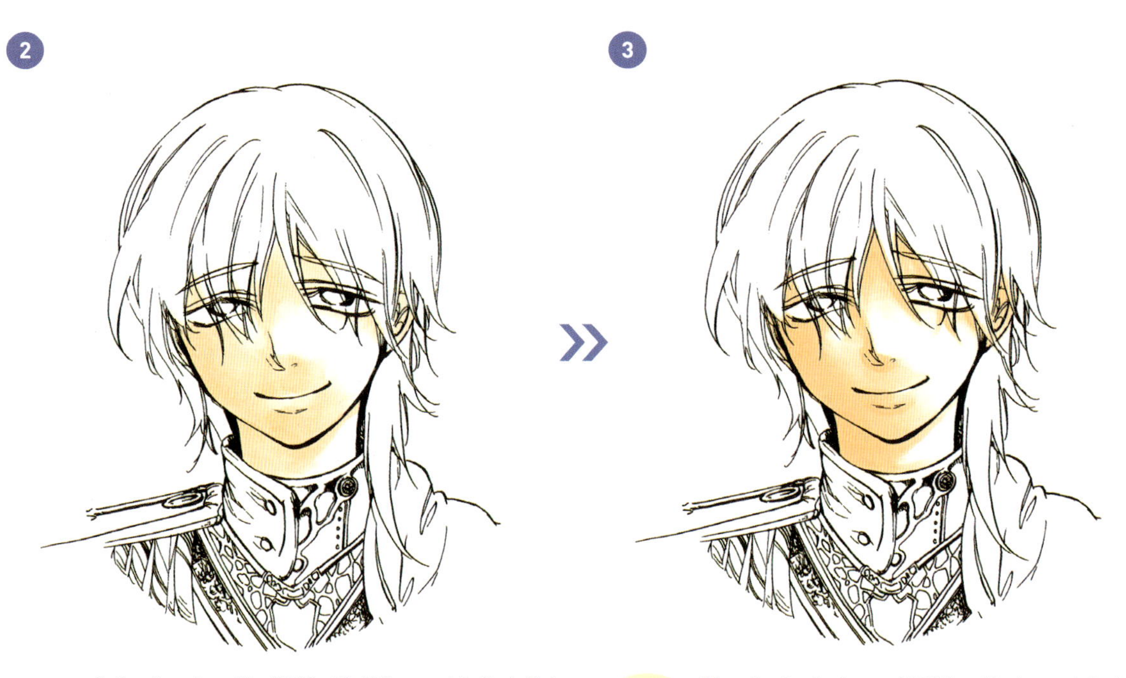

2

Soften the edge of the YR20 with #0 to complete the initial expression of light.

0 Colorless Blender

3

»

After allowing to dry, use YR20 to add a layer of shadows. This will give that wonderful 3D effect. There is no need to gradate again as you are using the same color.

YR20 Yellowish Shade

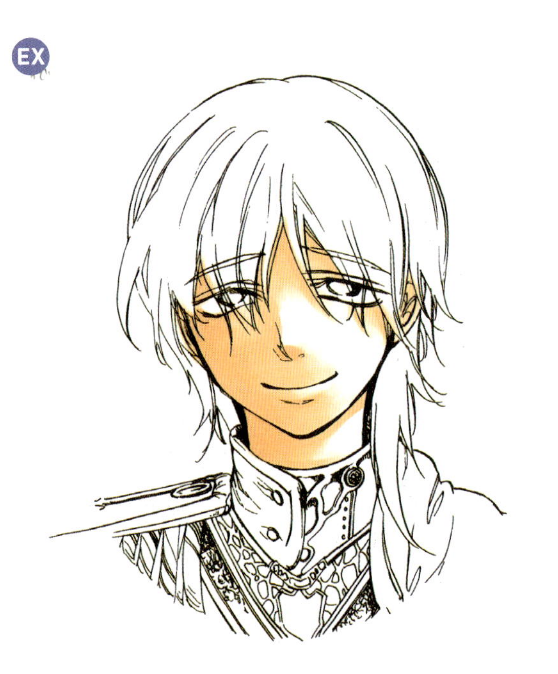

EX

Instead of going over the shadows with the same color, as in step 3, this is what you get when using E21.

E21 Soft Sun

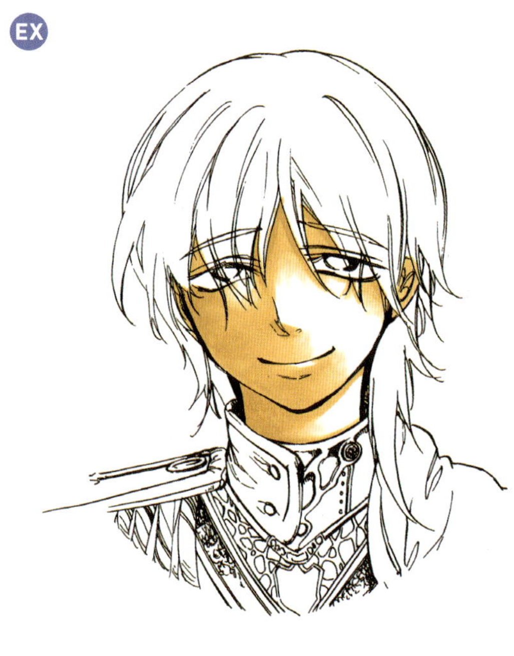

EX

Using YR23 and #0 instead of E21 like at left.

YR23 Yellow Ochre   *0 Colorless Blender*

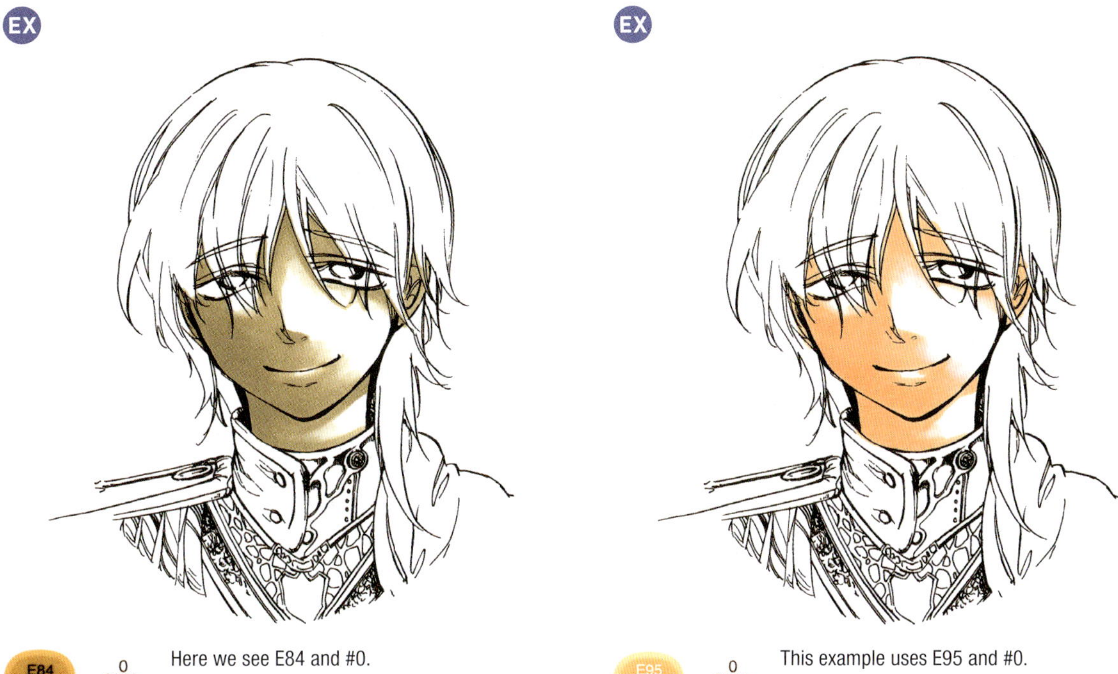

E84
Khaki

0
Colorless
Blender

Here we see E84 and #0.

E95
Tea
Orange

0
Colorless
Blender

This example uses E95 and #0.

Coloring Hair: Pay Attention to Hair Flow

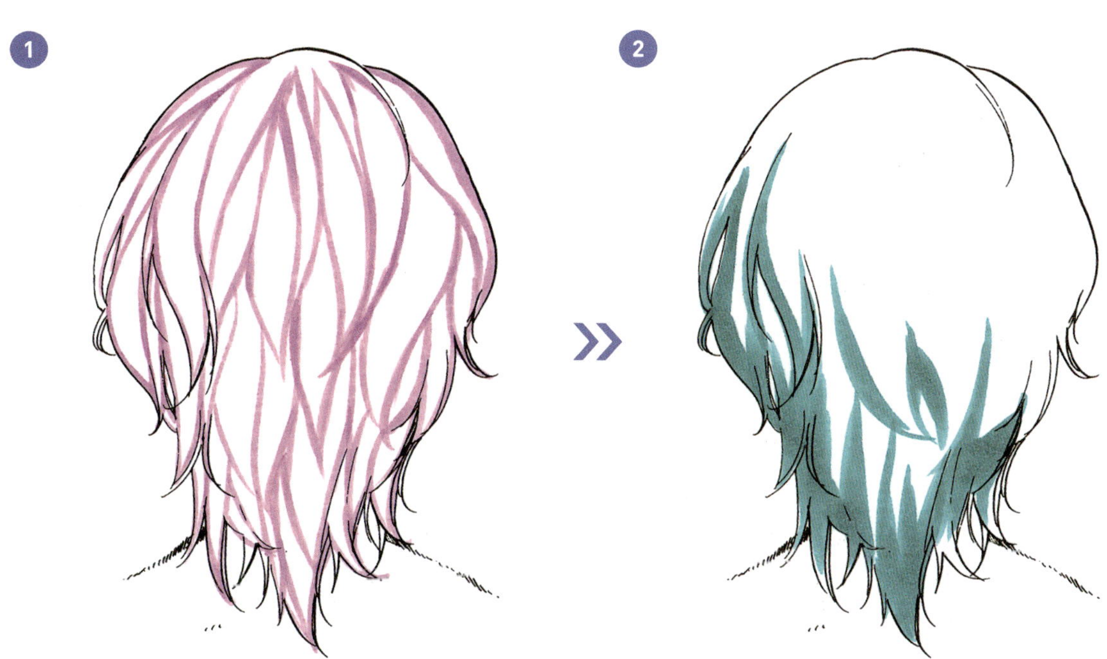

1

First, decide on the flow and any clumping of the hair, as seen here.

2

BG09
Blue
Green

The hair is colored with three colors. Begin with the shadows, adding them quickly with BG09.

3 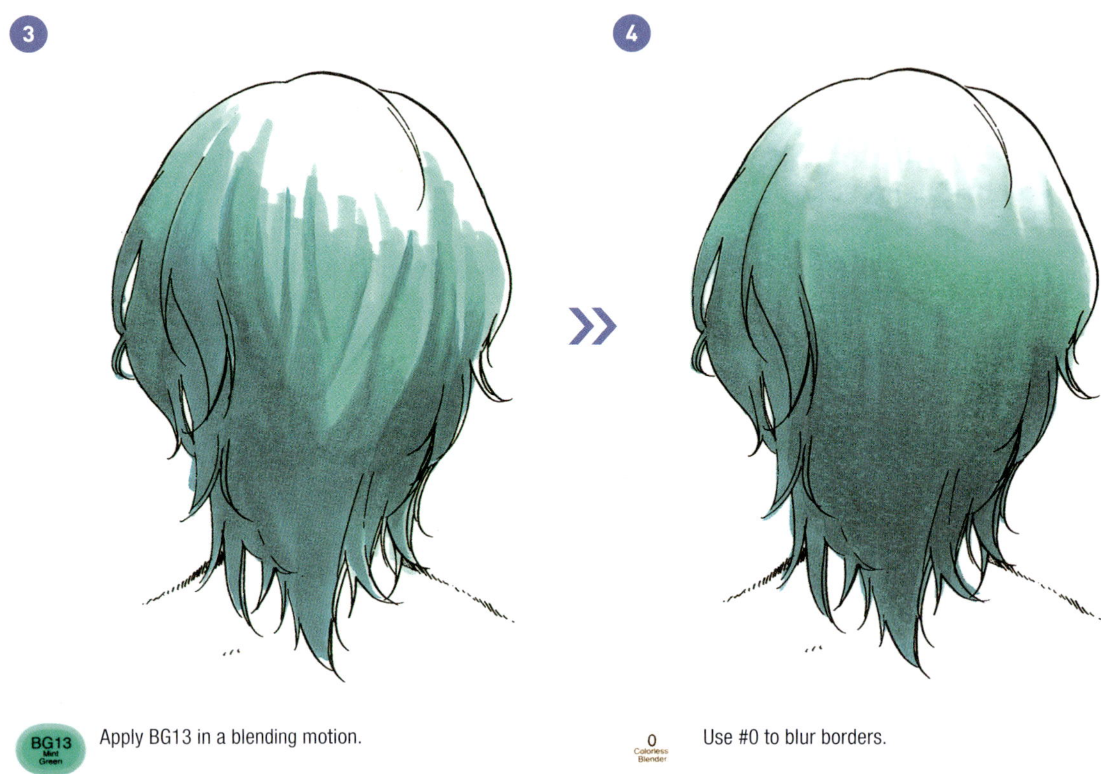

Apply BG13 in a blending motion.

4

Use #0 to blur borders.

5 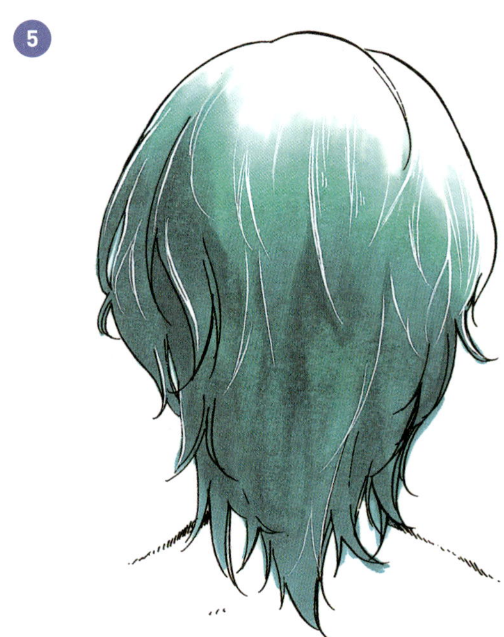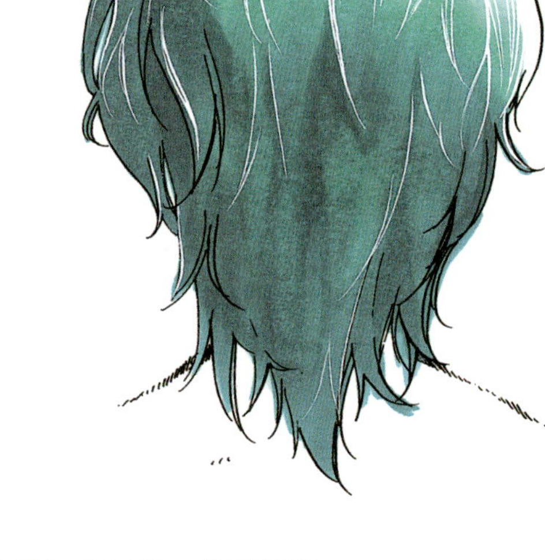

Finish by adding flow with white ink.

EX 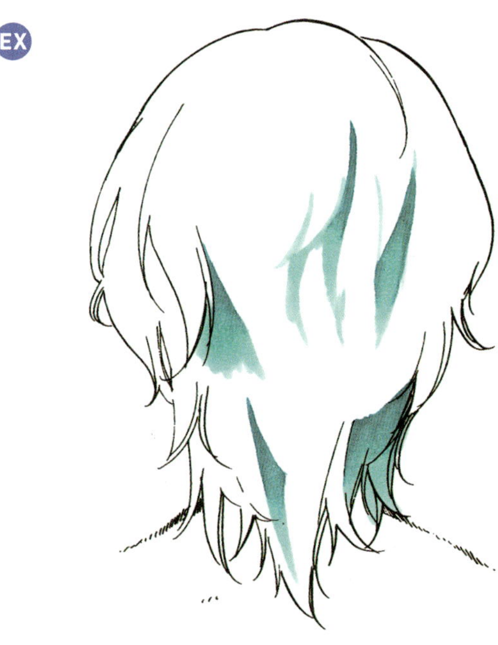

When drawing clumps think about "drawing the shadow of the clump" rather than drawing the clump itself.

Light-Colored Gloves

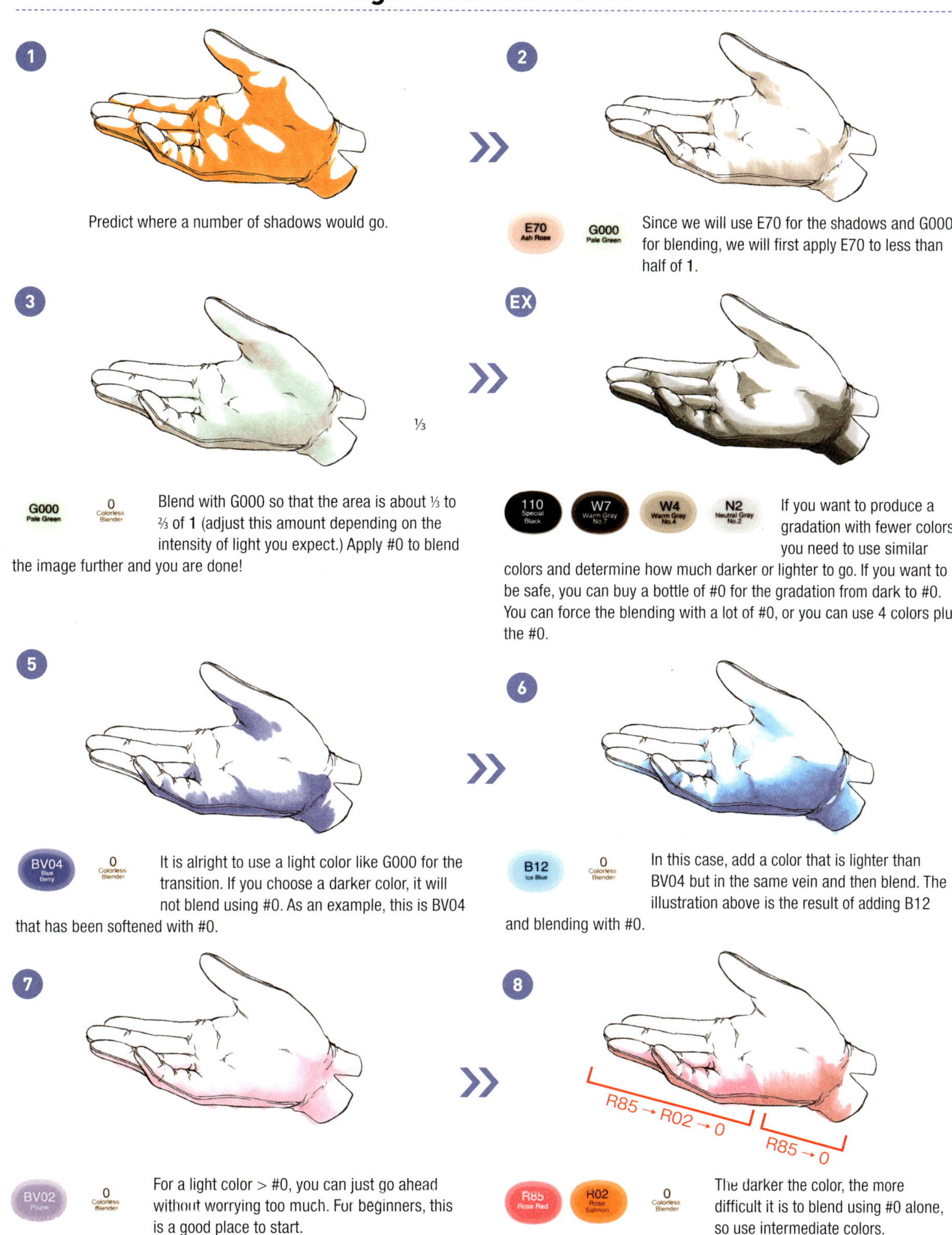

1 Predict where a number of shadows would go.

2 E70 Ash Rose / G000 Pale Green — Since we will use E70 for the shadows and G000 for blending, we will first apply E70 to less than half of **1**.

3 G000 Pale Green / 0 Colorless Blender — Blend with G000 so that the area is about ⅓ to ⅔ of **1** (adjust this amount depending on the intensity of light you expect.) Apply #0 to blend the image further and you are done!

⅓

EX 110 Special Black / W7 Warm Gray No.7 / W4 Warm Gray No.4 / N2 Neutral Gray No.2 — If you want to produce a gradation with fewer colors, you need to use similar colors and determine how much darker or lighter to go. If you want to be safe, you can buy a bottle of #0 for the gradation from dark to #0. You can force the blending with a lot of #0, or you can use 4 colors plus the #0.

5 BV04 Blue Berry / 0 Colorless Blender — It is alright to use a light color like G000 for the transition. If you choose a darker color, it will not blend using #0. As an example, this is BV04 that has been softened with #0.

6 B12 Ice Blue / 0 Colorless Blender — In this case, add a color that is lighter than BV04 but in the same vein and then blend. The illustration above is the result of adding B12 and blending with #0.

7 BV02 Prune / 0 Colorless Blender — For a light color > #0, you can just go ahead without worrying too much. For beginners, this is a good place to start.

8 R85 Rose Red / R02 Rose Salmon / 0 Colorless Blender — The darker the color, the more difficult it is to blend using #0 alone, so use intermediate colors.

#0 is a very powerful blending agent, but it is not compatible with all colors. You may need to go through several colors until you get one that #0 can blend credibly. You can force the blending with a bunch of #0's, by refilling from a bottle, etc., but it is best to decide if you want to use a lot of #0's or you just want to buy a lot of subtly different markers based on your particular style.

Blocking: Wrinkles and Shadows

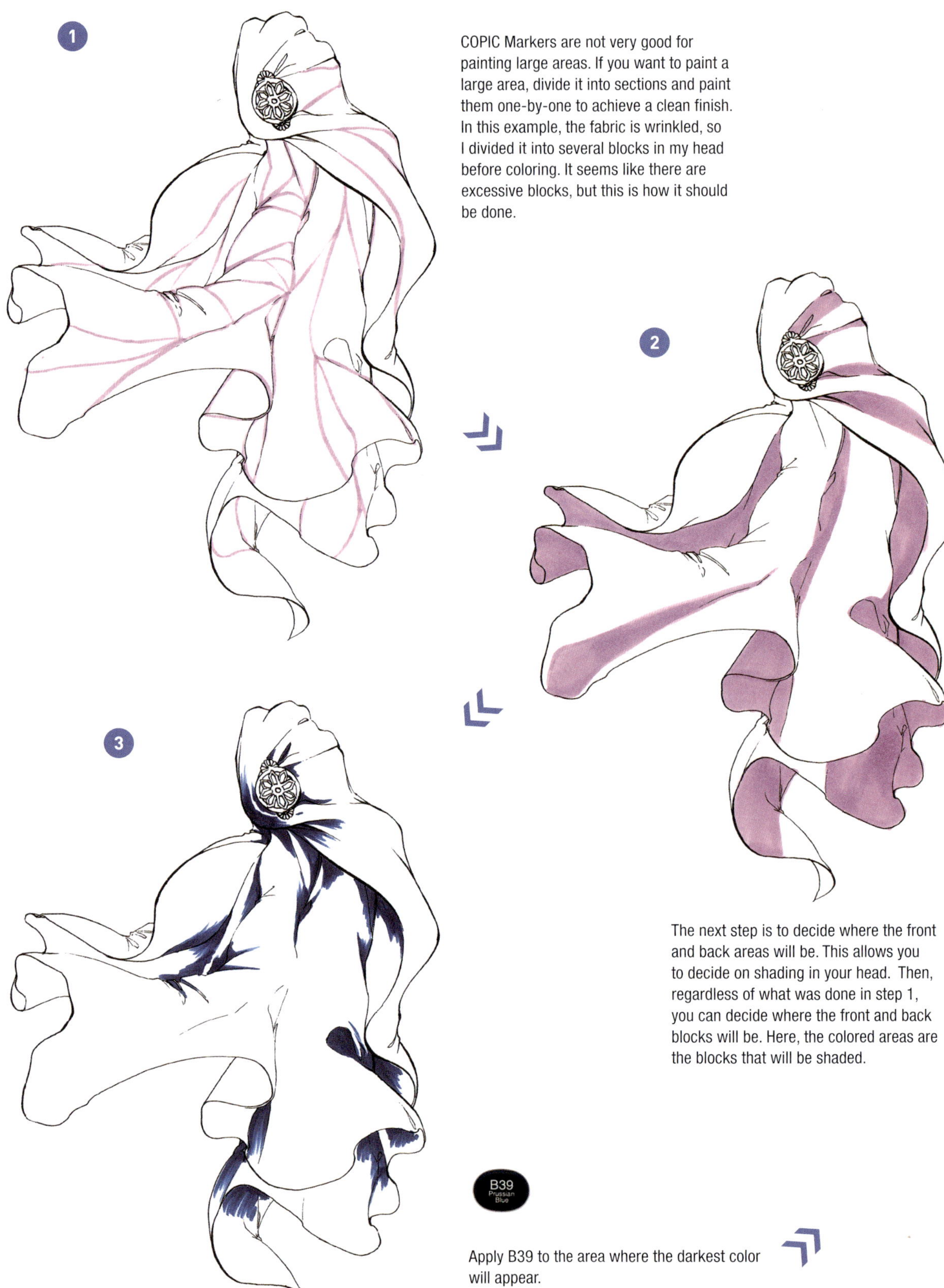

COPIC Markers are not very good for painting large areas. If you want to paint a large area, divide it into sections and paint them one-by-one to achieve a clean finish. In this example, the fabric is wrinkled, so I divided it into several blocks in my head before coloring. It seems like there are excessive blocks, but this is how it should be done.

The next step is to decide where the front and back areas will be. This allows you to decide on shading in your head. Then, regardless of what was done in step 1, you can decide where the front and back blocks will be. Here, the colored areas are the blocks that will be shaded.

B39
Prussian Blue

Apply B39 to the area where the darkest color will appear.

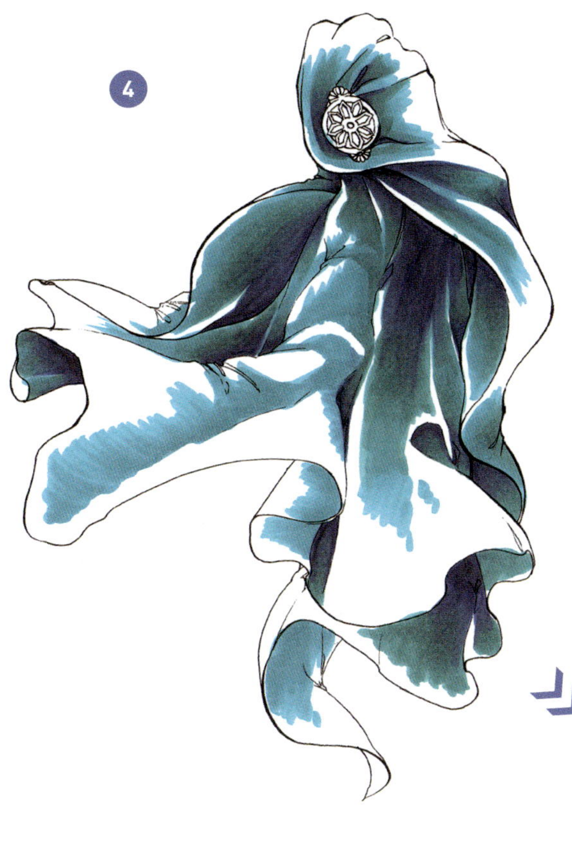

4

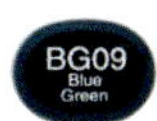
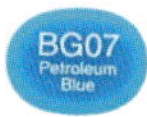

Apply BG09 and then BG07 over the B39. Blend. There are three more color steps, so take that into account and leave some blank space.

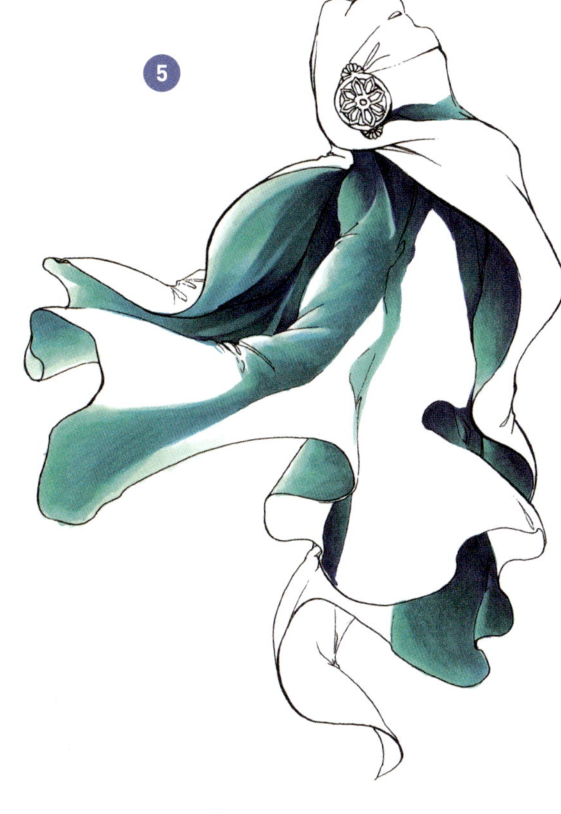

5

Apply BG13, then BG11 and overlay #0 to blend the colors in. The actual painting process is divided into sections like this. Each section is colored separately.

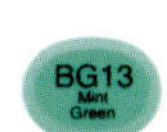
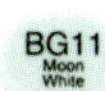

6

Finally, add white ink to finish.

Overlaying Dark Colors on Light Colors

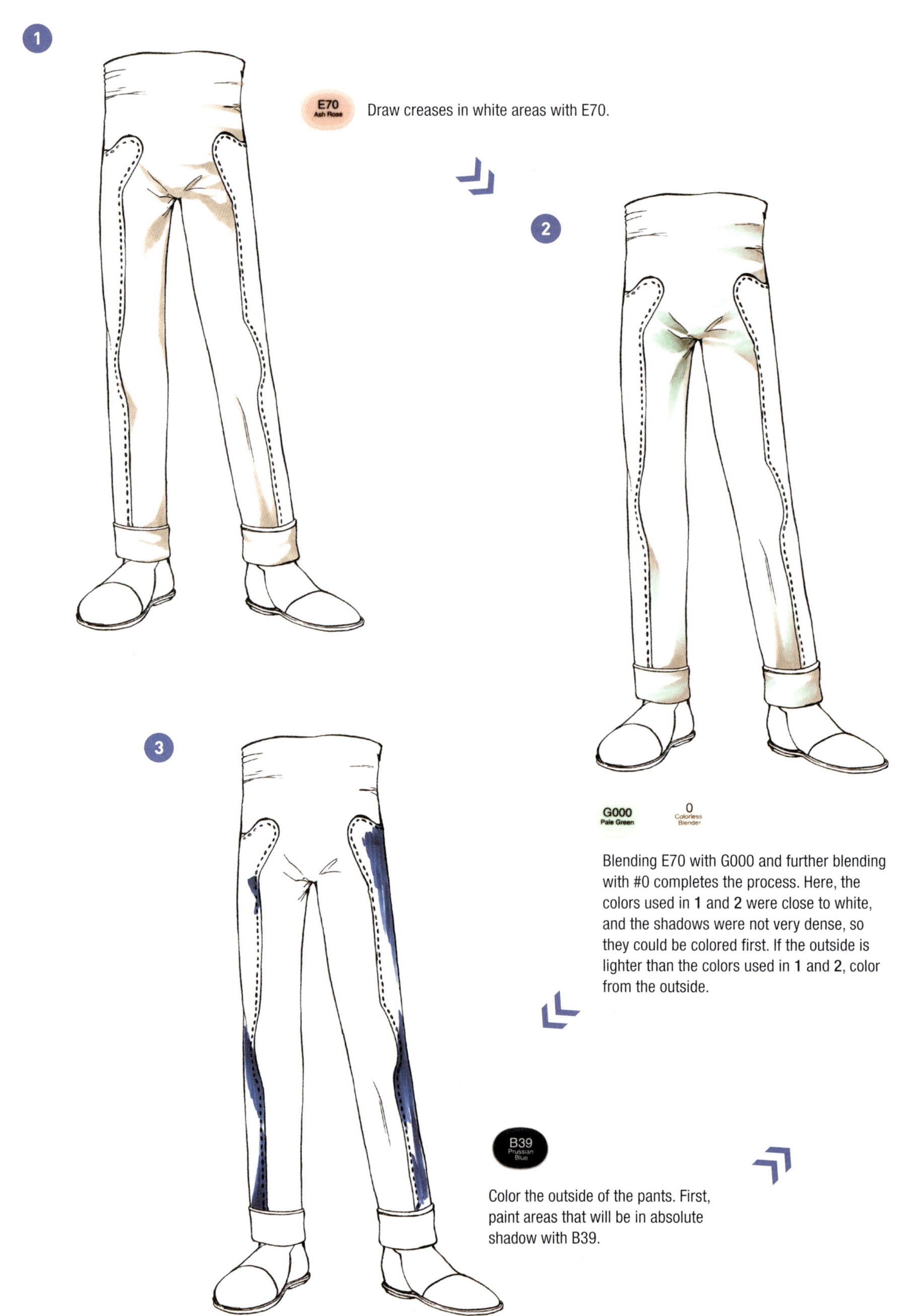

Draw creases in white areas with E70.

Blending E70 with G000 and further blending with #0 completes the process. Here, the colors used in 1 and 2 were close to white, and the shadows were not very dense, so they could be colored first. If the outside is lighter than the colors used in 1 and 2, color from the outside.

Color the outside of the pants. First, paint areas that will be in absolute shadow with B39.

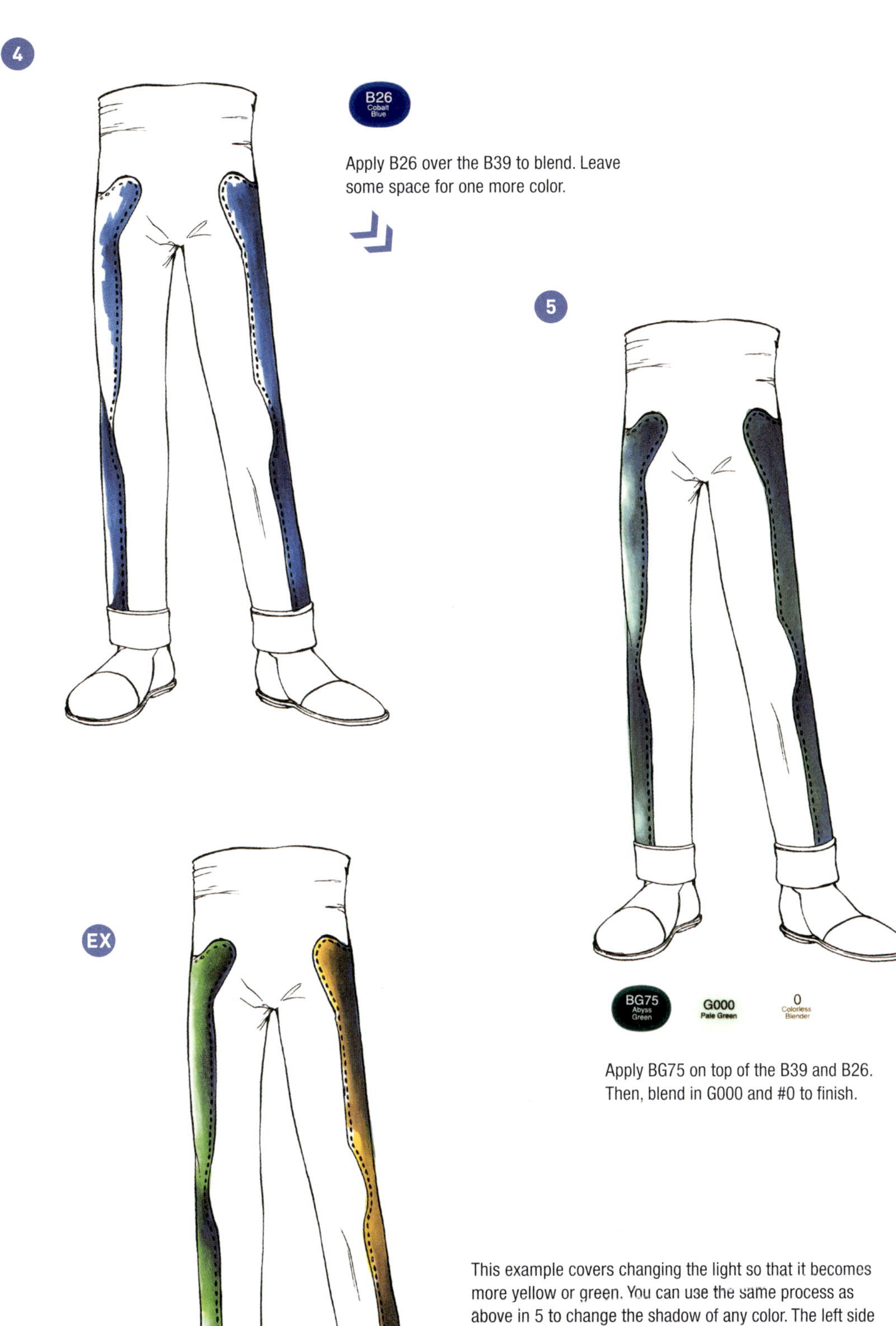

Apply B26 over the B39 to blend. Leave some space for one more color.

Apply BG75 on top of the B39 and B26. Then, blend in G000 and #0 to finish.

This example covers changing the light so that it becomes more yellow or green. You can use the same process as above in 5 to change the shadow of any color. The left side goes from B39 > B26 > YG17 > G21 to #0 while the right goes from B39 > B26 > E25 > YR23 > Y08 to #0. Note that if you are using a color that is far from blue, such as red, you will need to change the transition color significantly.

Tran

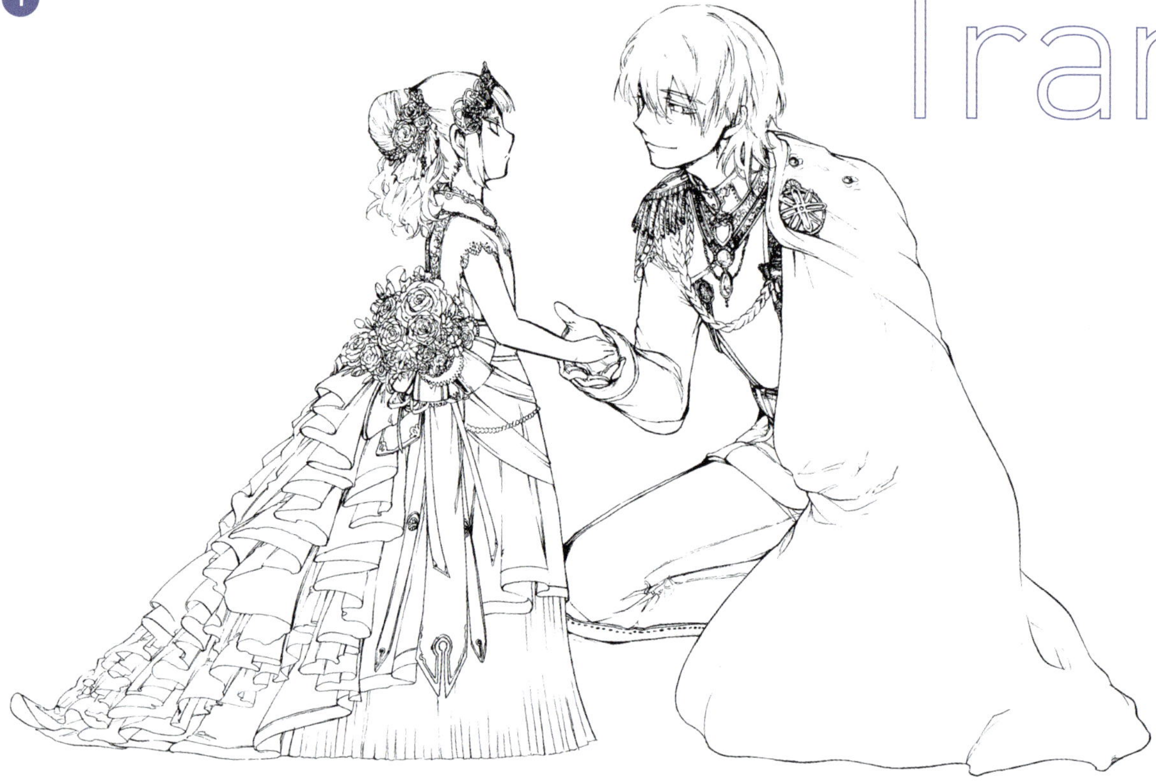

2

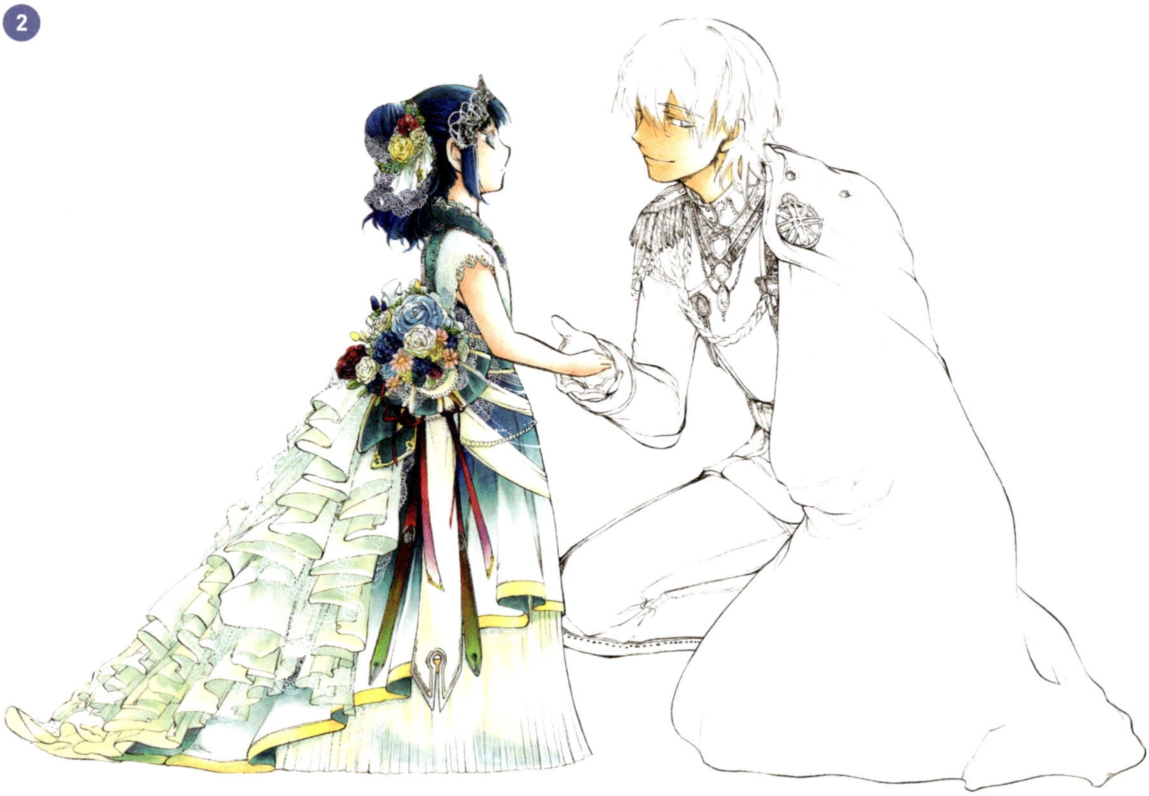

3

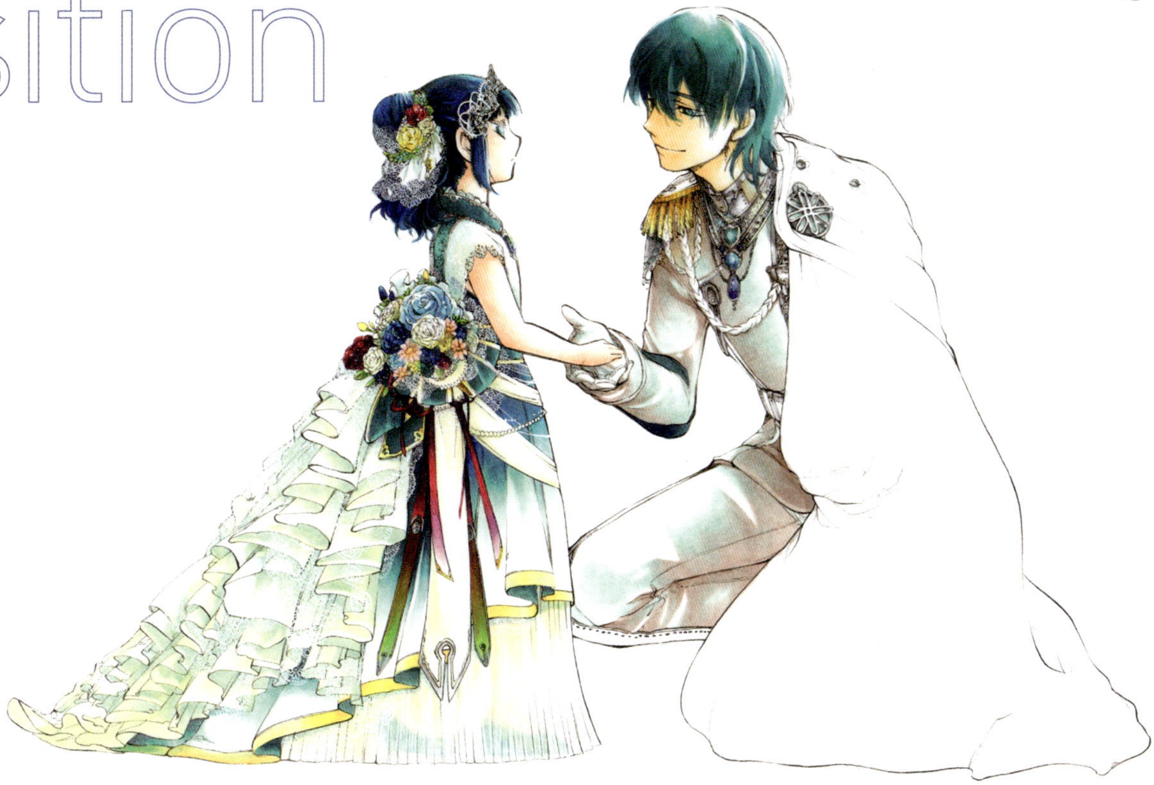

4

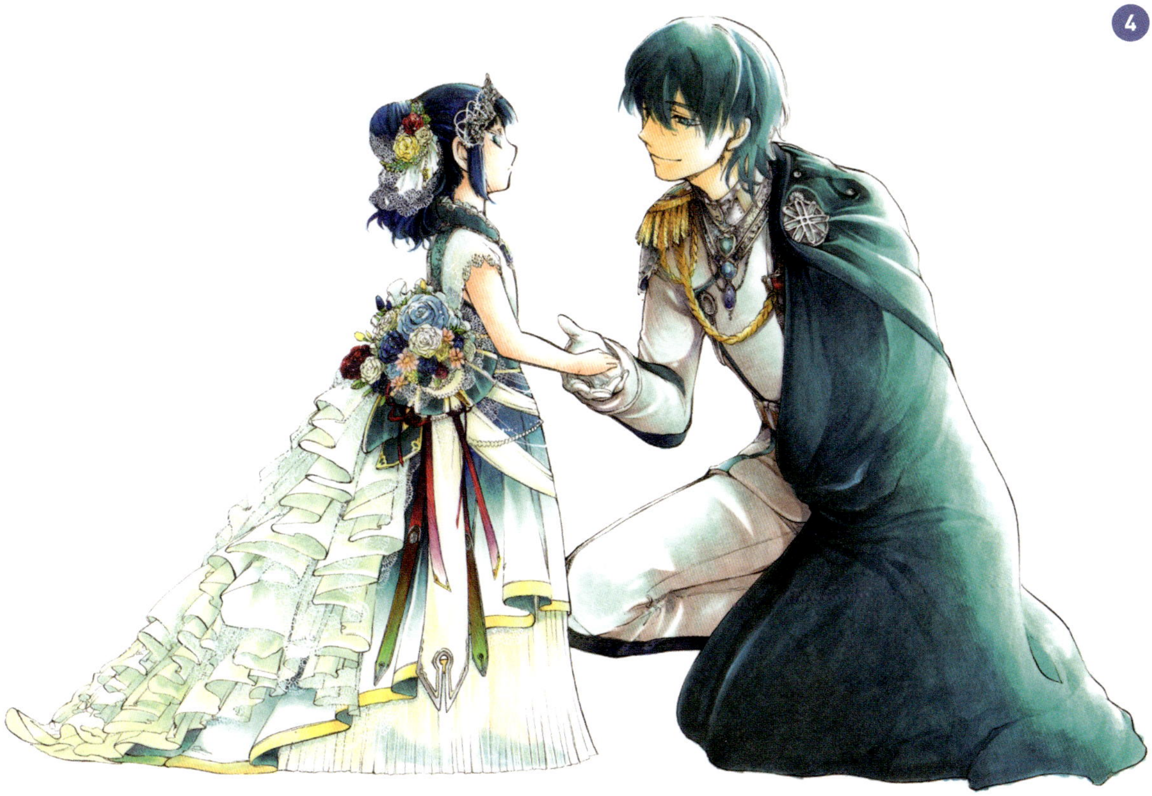

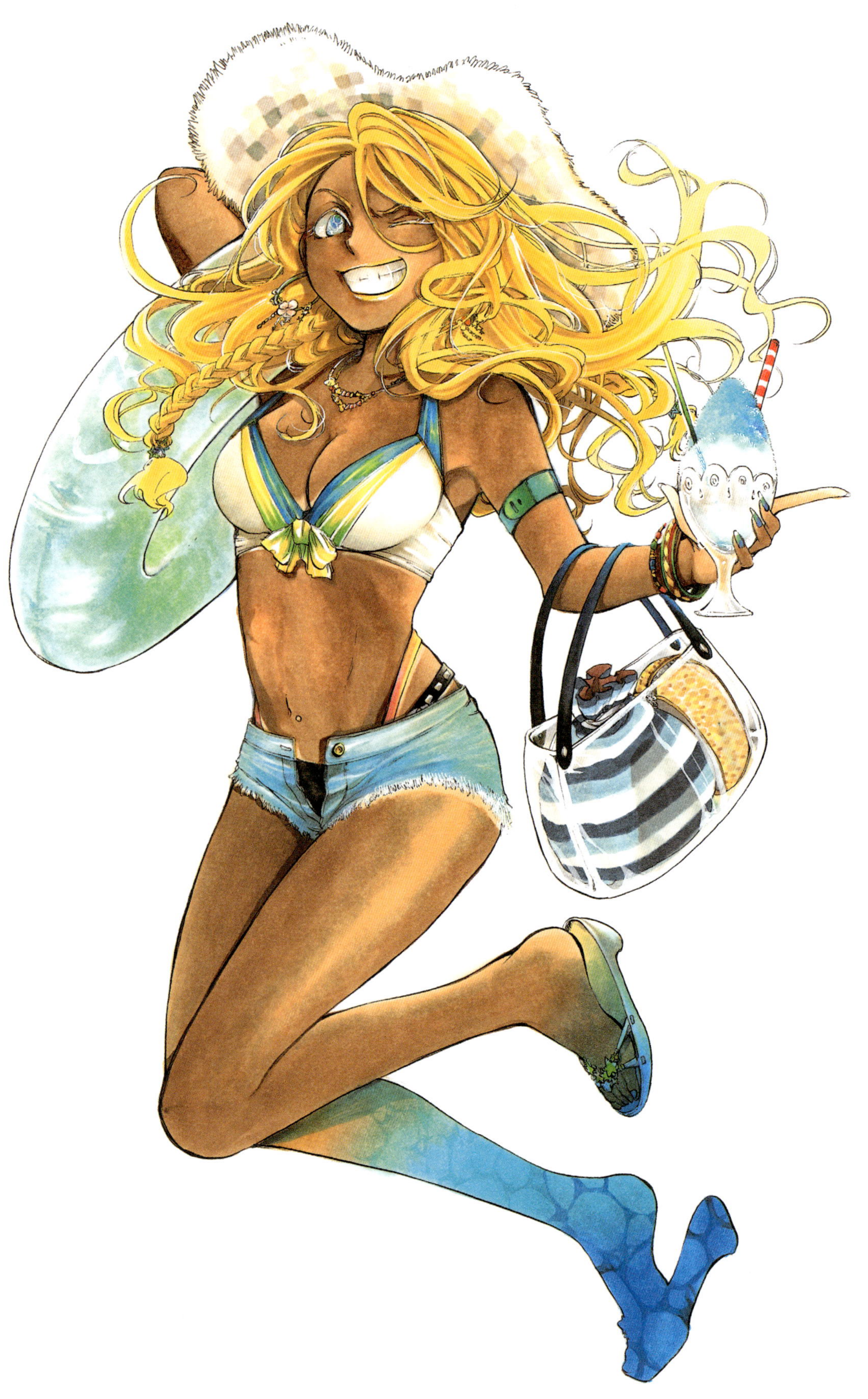

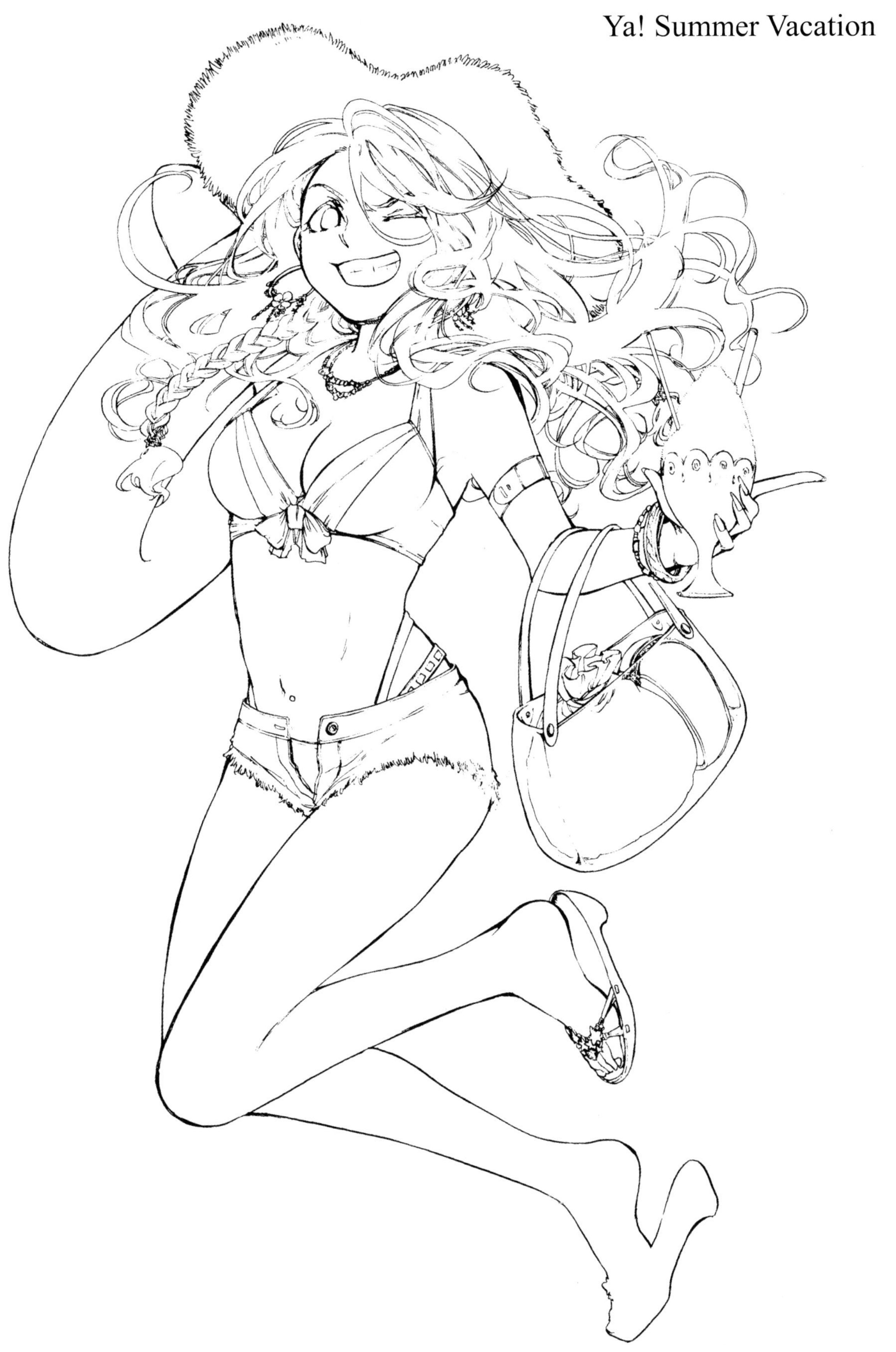

Gradating without Blending Shadows

This is a technique that uses basic blending, but also colors the shadows succinctly. The result is a slightly cartoonish coloring job. This is recommended for people who are not good at gradation.

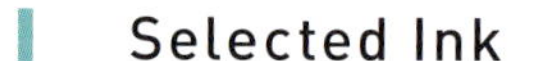

Selected Ink

Hair

- YR23 Yellow Ochre
- Y08 Acid Yellow
- Y11 Pale Yellow

Skin

- E35 Chamois
- E21 Soft Sun
- E47 Dark Brown

Floaty

- B0000 Pale Celestine
- G20 Wax White
- YG11 Mignonette
- BG02 New Blue

Bikini Bottom/Cutoffs

- BG93 Green Gray
- BG02 New Blue
- B95 Light Grayish Cobalt
- G20 Wax White
- B01 Mint Blue

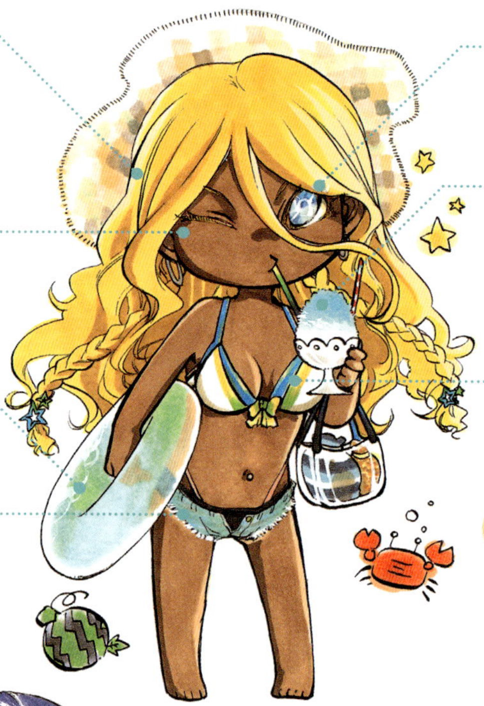

Eyes

- B01 Mint Blue
- B23 Phthalo Blue
- FBG2 Fluorescent Dull B.G.

Syrup

- B01 Mint Blue
- B23 Phthalo Blue
- FBG2 Fluorescent Dull B.G.

Bikini (Top)

- B05 Process Blue
- FBG2 Fluorescent Dull B.G.
- Y11 Pale Yellow

+

- YG91 Putty
- E43 Dull Ivory
- BG90 Gray Sky
- 0 Colorless Blender

+

- YG25 Celadon Green
- Y08 Acid Yellow
- Y04 Acacia

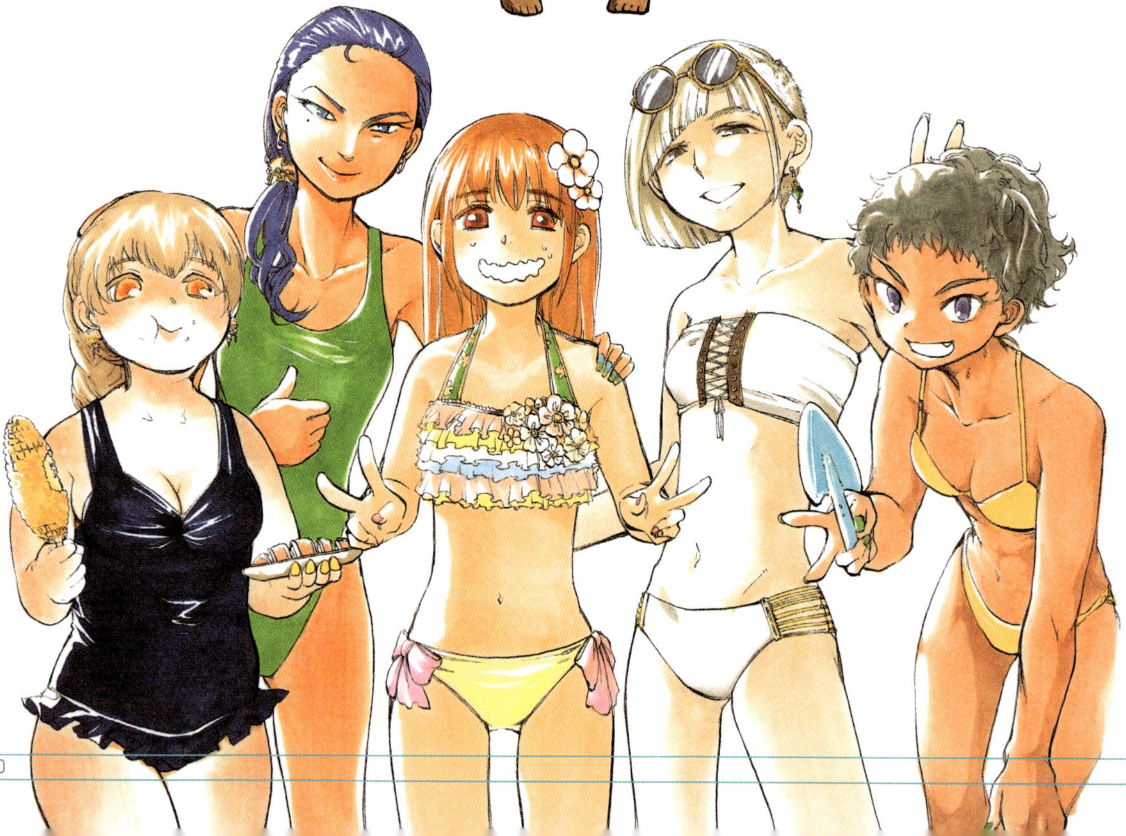

Glassy Eyes

1

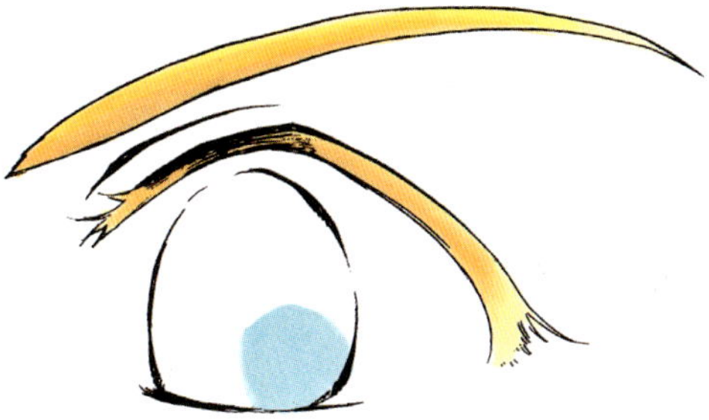

Color a "contact lens" that is slightly off-sized using B01.

B01 Mint Blue

2

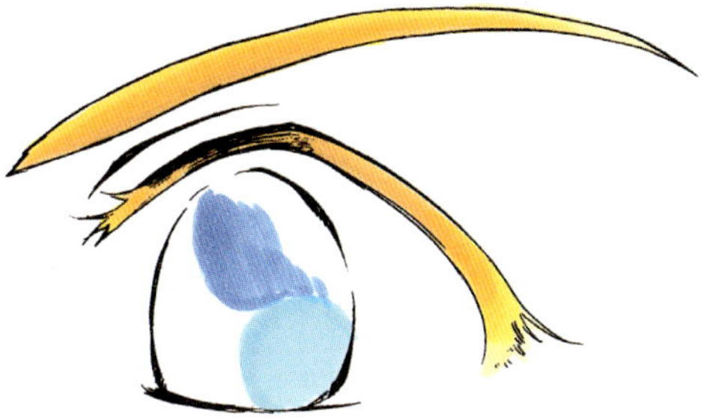

Add B23 above the contact lens. Draw it out from the edge of the eye.

B23 Phthalo Blue

3

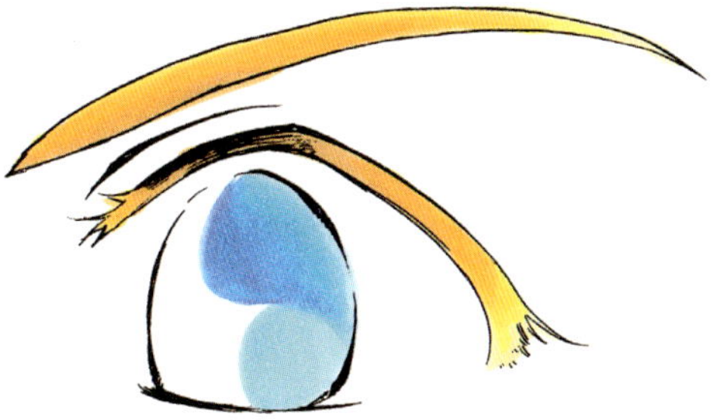

Lay FBG2 and B52 over **2** to blend. Adding FBG2 will make the eye glitter.

FBG2 Fluorescent Dull B.G. **B52** Soft Greenish Blue

4

Color the lower left corner with the same colors. Use a lower percentage of B23 on the lower part.

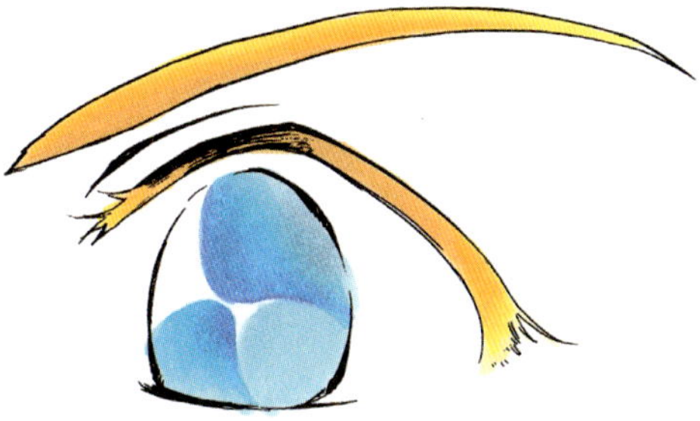

B23 Phthalo Blue **B52** Soft Greenish Blue **FBG2** Fluorescent Dull B.G.

5

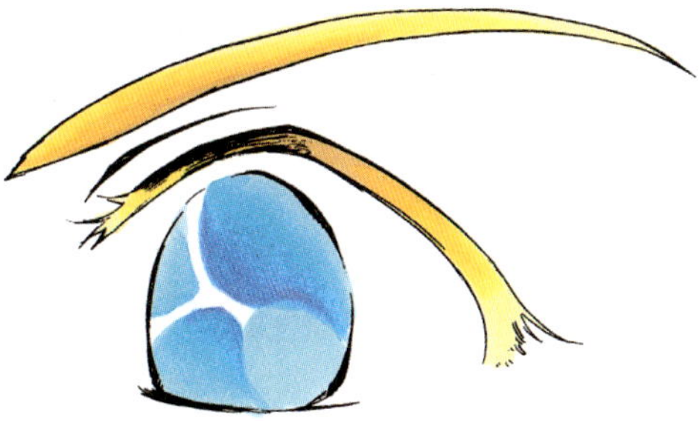

Apply color to the upper left. Do not use B23 here. The key is to leave white space as shown.

B52 Soft Greenish Blue **FBG2** Fluorescent Dull B.G.

6

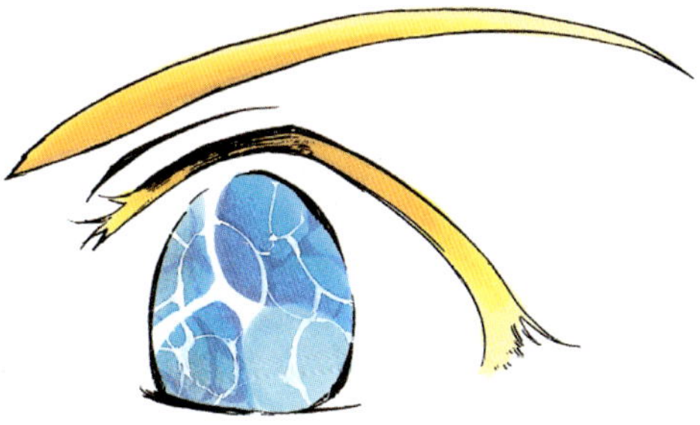

Draw water-like patterns with B23. Then do the same over the entire eye with white ink.

B23 Phthalo Blue

Tanned Face

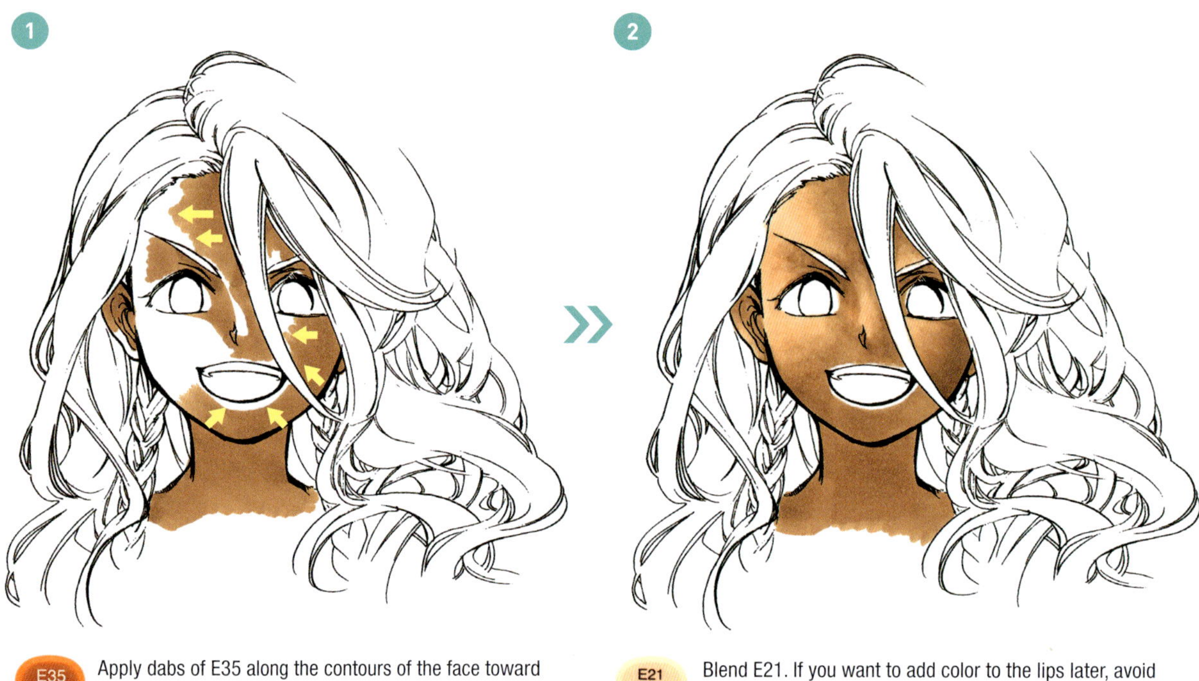

1 Apply dabs of E35 along the contours of the face toward the nose. Apply horizontally on the forehead.

(E35 Chamois)

2 Blend E21. If you want to add color to the lips later, avoid applying color to them now.

(E21 Soft Sun)

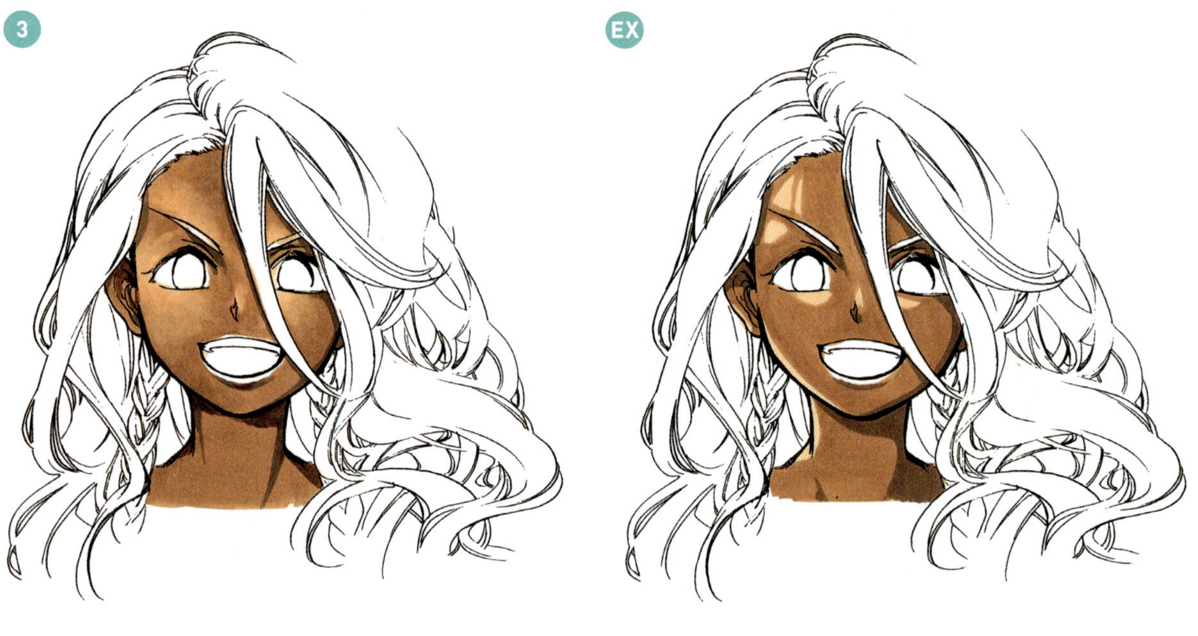

3 Add shadows with E47. Feel free to apply strongly and then you're done.

(E47 Dark Brown)

EX This example is done in an anime style.

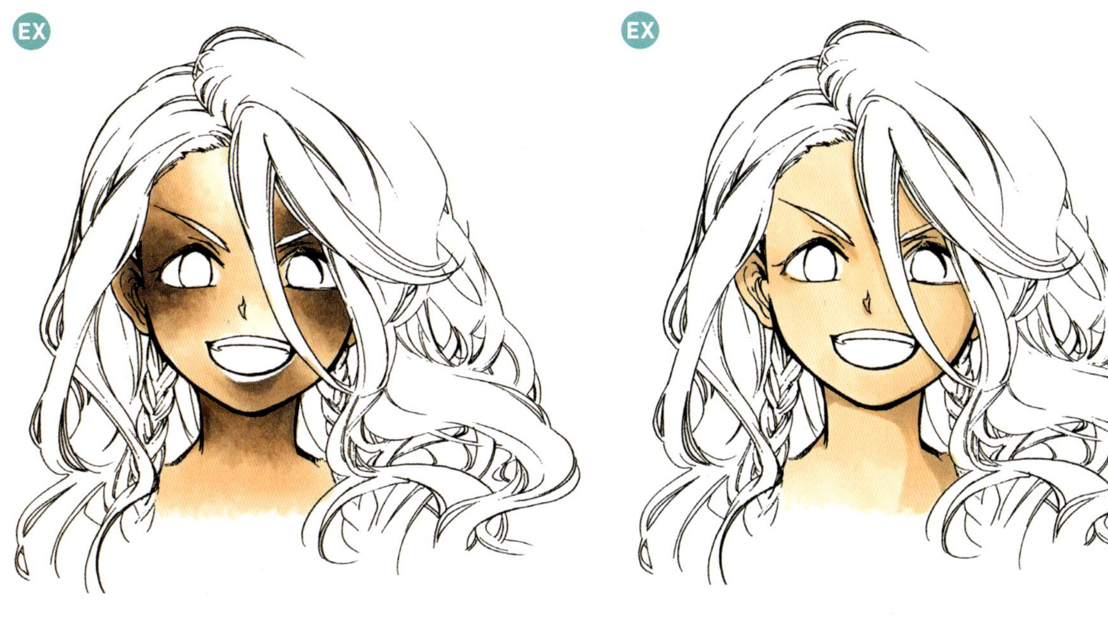

This is what it looks like when blurred.

E55 Light Camel   **YR20** Yellowish Shade   **E21** Soft Sun

If E55, YR20, and E21 are used you will obtain a lighter skin color.

Wavy Blond Hair

1

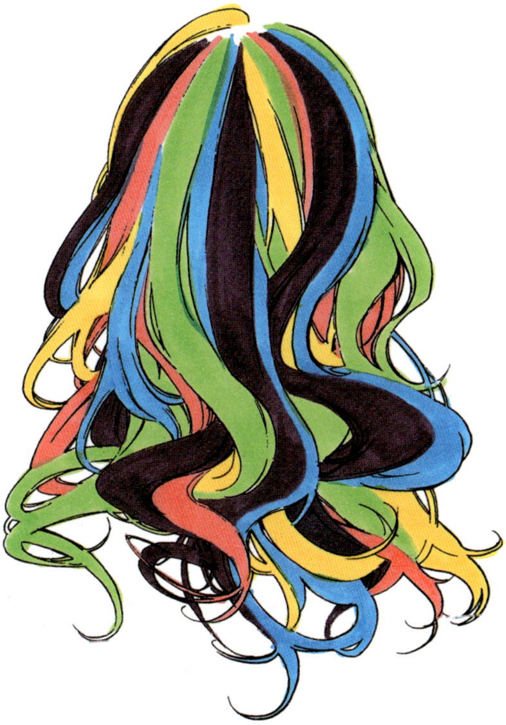

First, get a rough idea of the waves in the hair. Here is a rough idea of the blocking. The more of these blocks you have, the sleeker the hair will look.

2

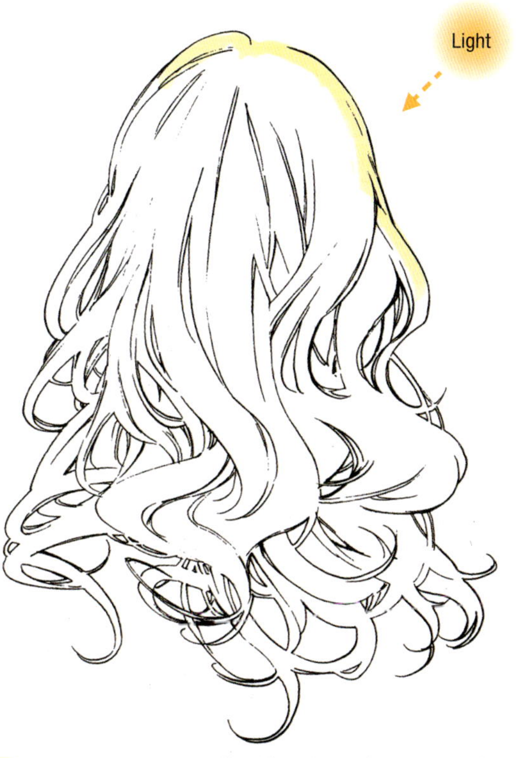

Y11 Pale Yellow

Fill the light side with Y11. First, draw a frame around the area you don't want to jut out.

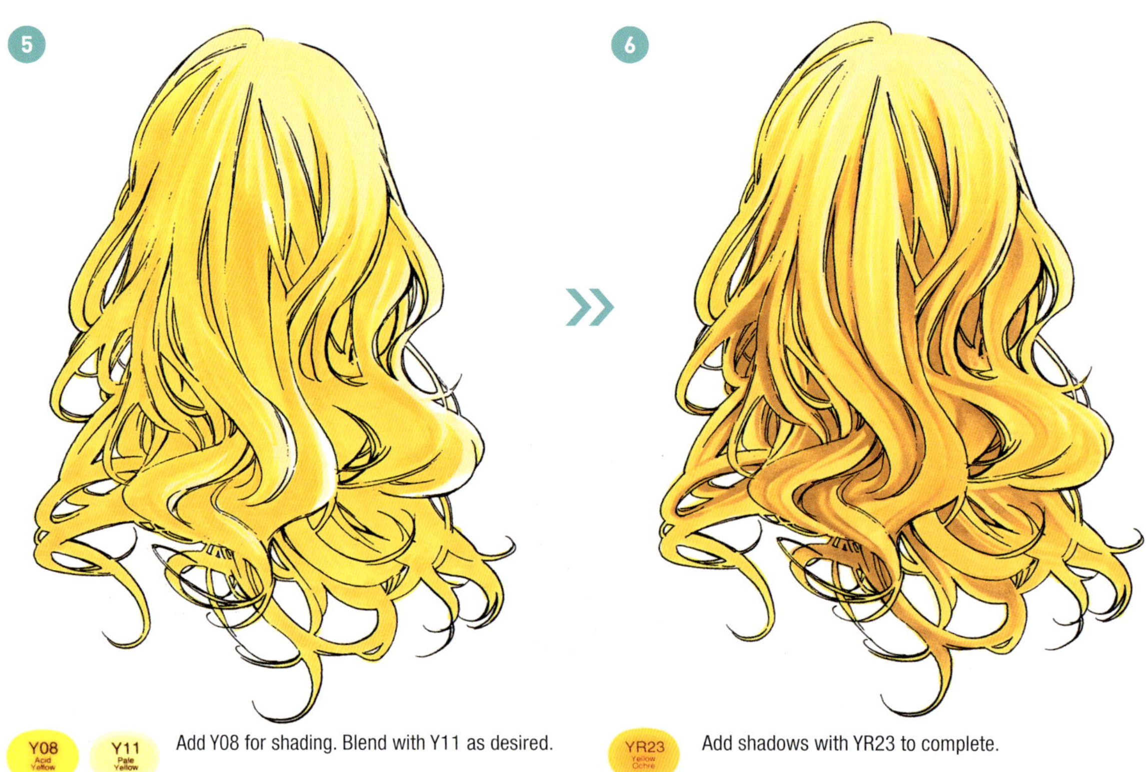

3

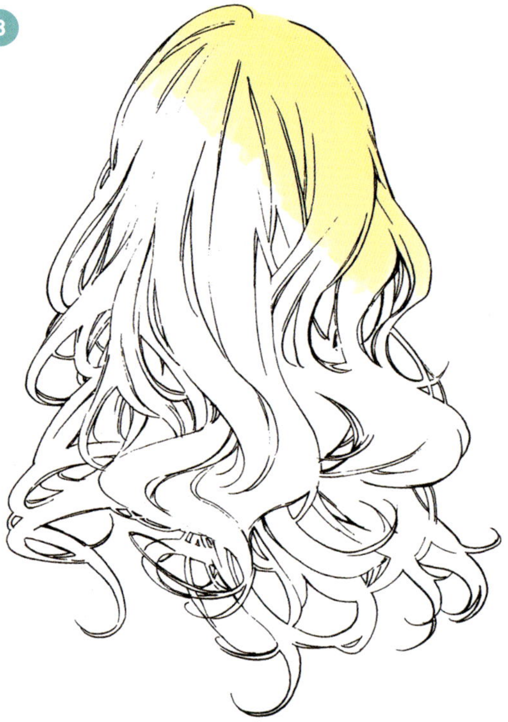

Y11 Pale Yellow — If you add Y11 from the frame towards the center, there's less risk of color bleeding outside the hair outline.

4

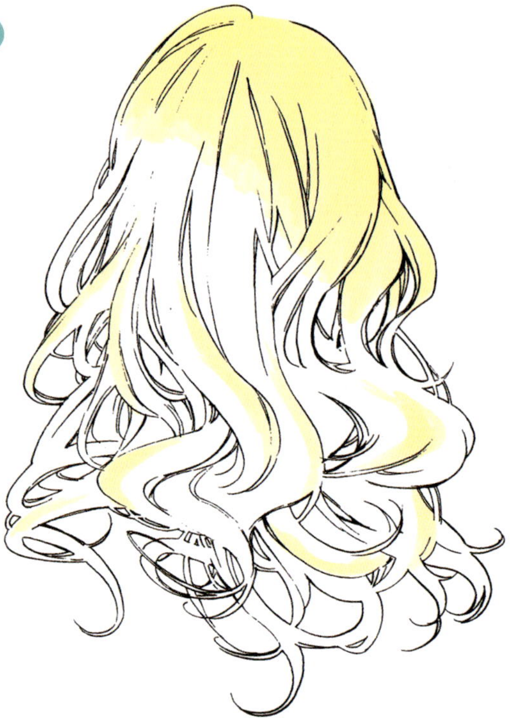

Y11 Pale Yellow — Add Y11 to the "middle and bottom" of the hair where the light hits.

5

Y08 Acid Yellow / Y11 Pale Yellow — Add Y08 for shading. Blend with Y11 as desired.

6

YR23 Yellow Ochre — Add shadows with YR23 to complete.

Braided Hair

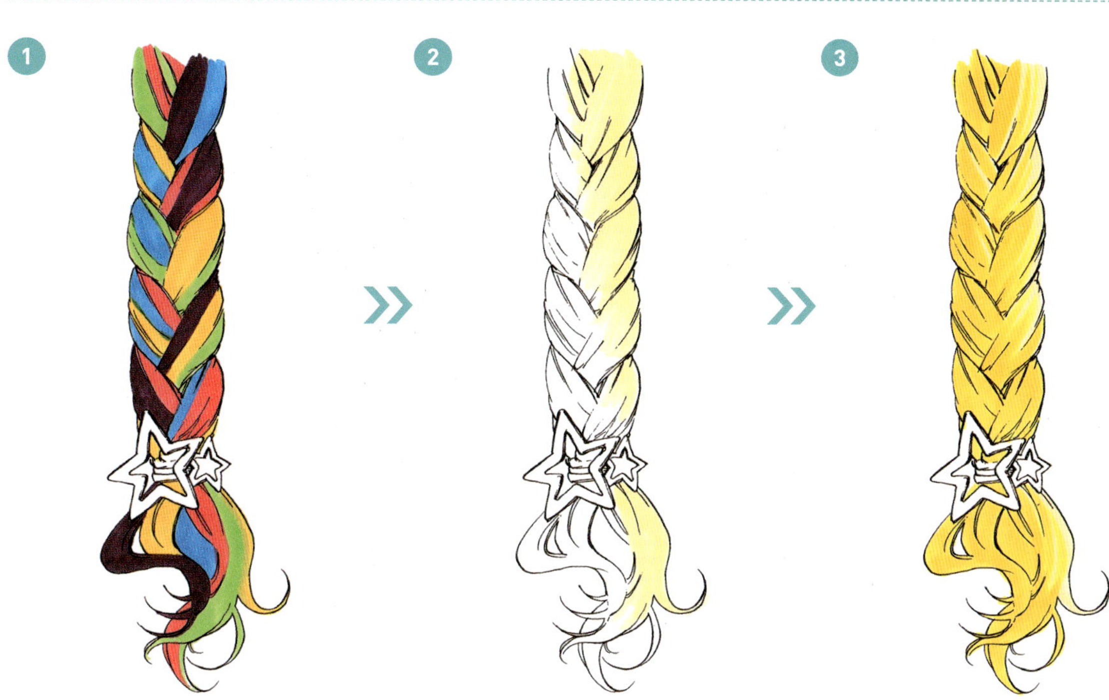

1 Roughly determine the blocking as you did in the previous section, Wavy Blond Hair.

2 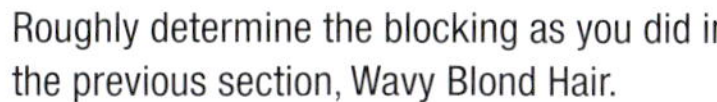 Quickly color with Y11.

3 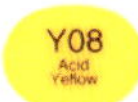 Apply Y08 to produce a better color transition.

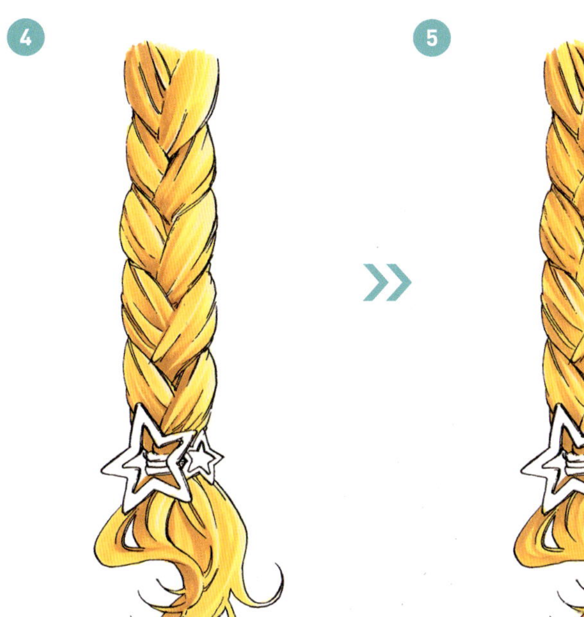

4 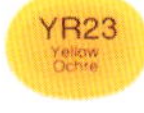 Add shadows with YR23 to finish.

5 You can add white ink as desired.

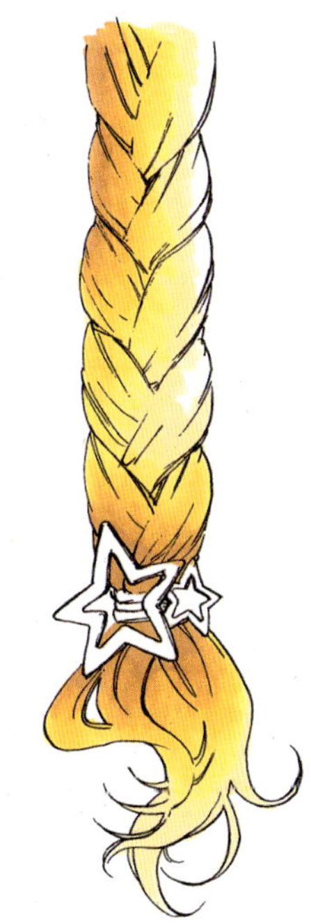

EX This is what it looks like when the colors are blended.

Tanned Skin and the Expression of Shadows

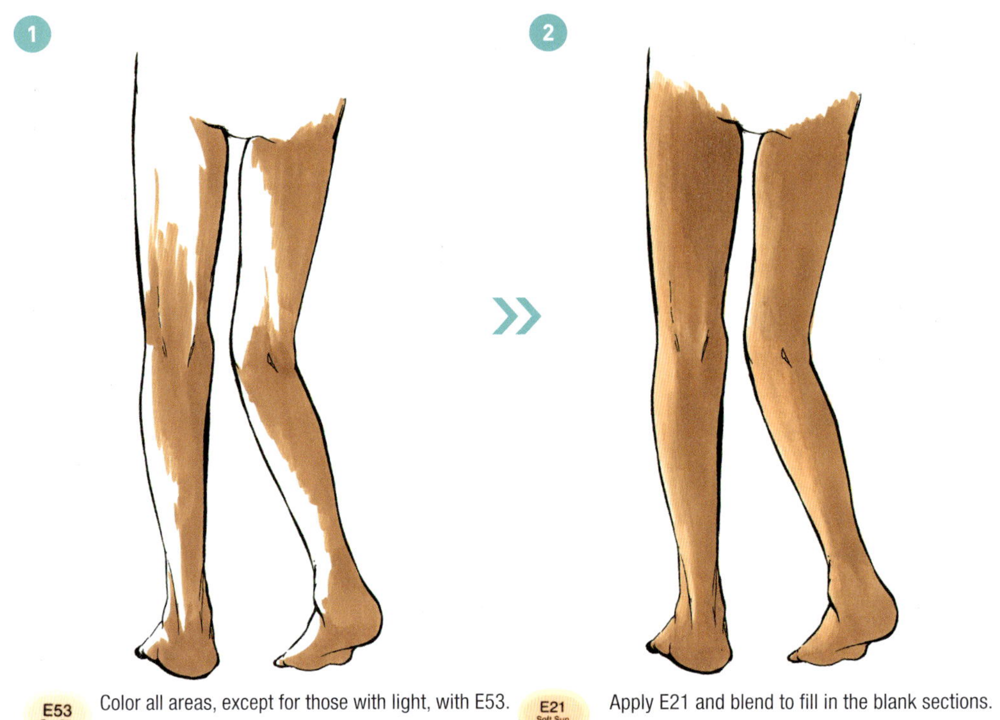

1 Color all areas, except for those with light, with E53.

E53 Raw Silk

2 Apply E21 and blend to fill in the blank sections.

E21 Soft Sun

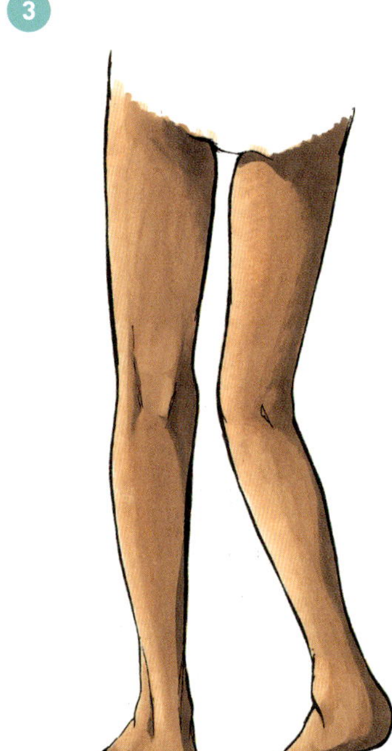

3

E47 Dark Brown

Add E47 to create a 3D feel on the legs using the shadows to complete.

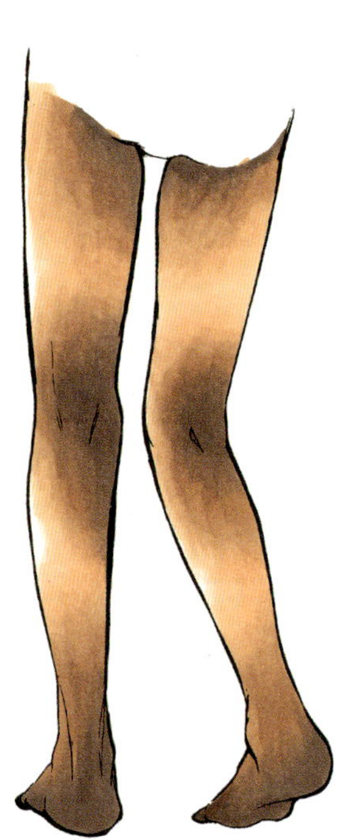

EX

This is what it looks like when the colors are blended.

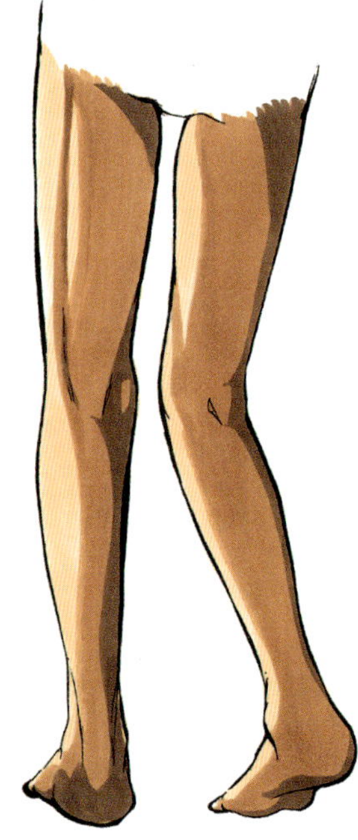

EX

This is an anime-style example.

Textures for Swimsuits and Cutoffs

 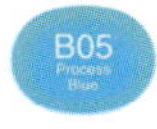 After coloring with B05, add in some FBG02 to produce thick line-like light. Create several lines of light (white areas) and connect some of them delicately.

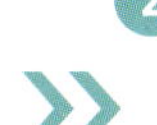 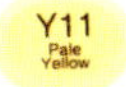 Fill the "light" area created in **1** with Y11 and try not to touch the blue as much as possible to prevent mixing colors and turning the blue part green.

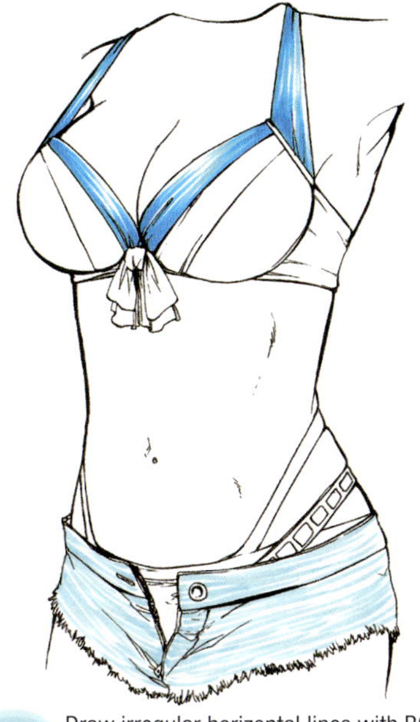

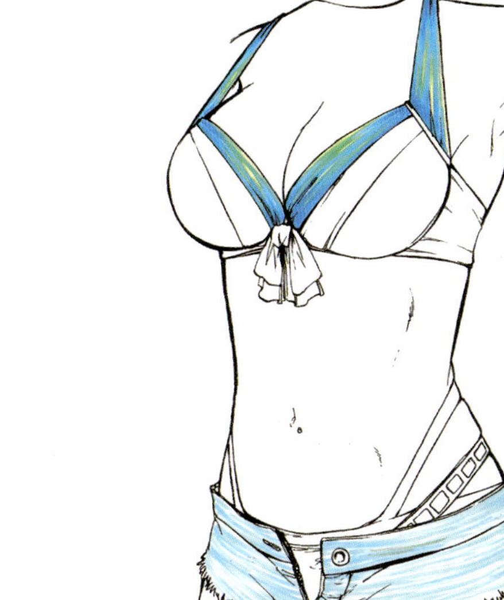

Draw irregular horizontal lines with BG02.

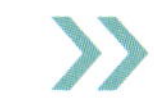 Draw horizontal lines that are thinner than **1** with B95.

 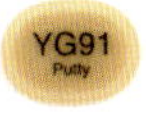 Apply YG91 slightly larger than the shadow. Blend it with BG90.

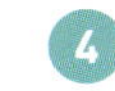  Soften the edges of BG90 using #0 to produce roundness and add accents with E42.

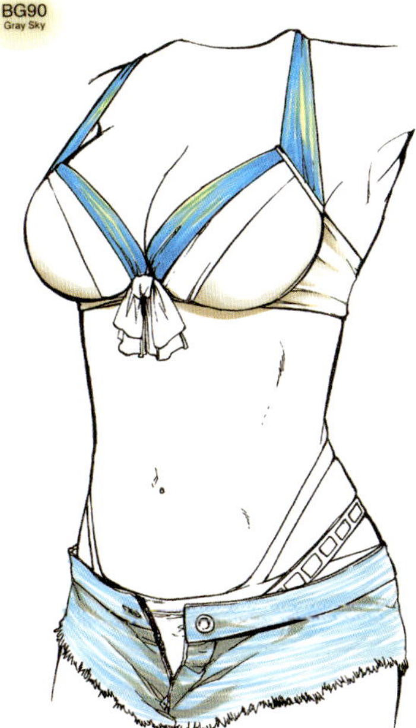

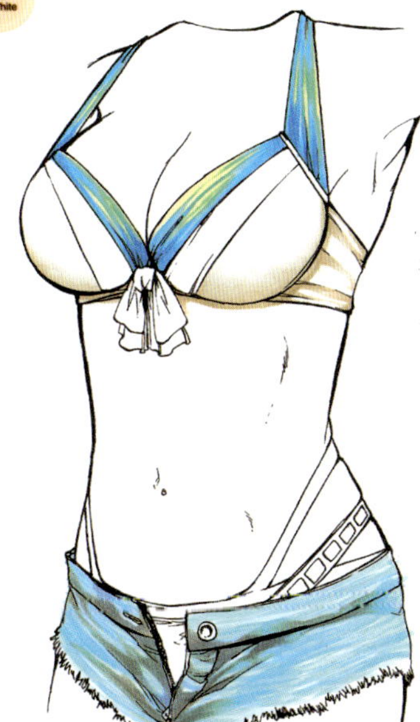

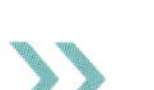 Add creases with BG93.

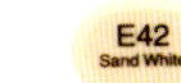 Apply B95 at the base of the creases and horizontal lines all over with B01.

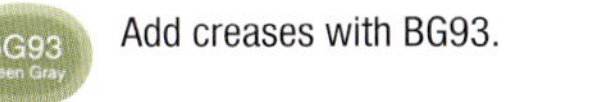 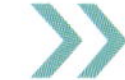 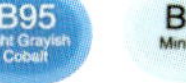

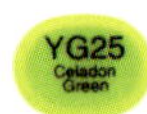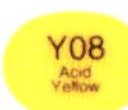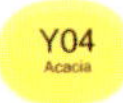

In a similar manner to when we first added blue, color the middle of the bikini top with YG25 > Y08 > Y04.

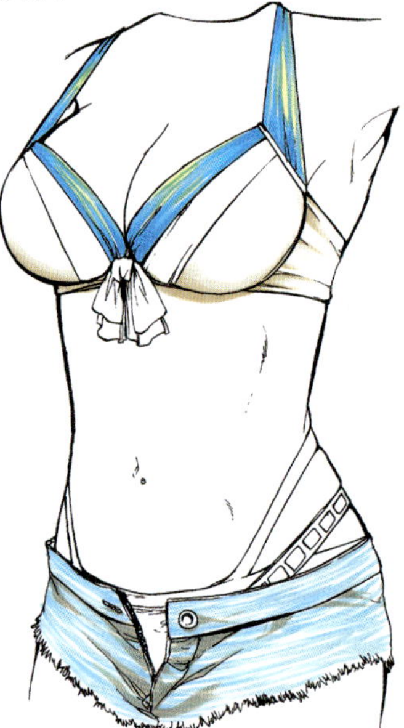

G20 Wax White — Add a thin layer of G20.

6 Finish by adding "shine" with white ink on the bikini top.

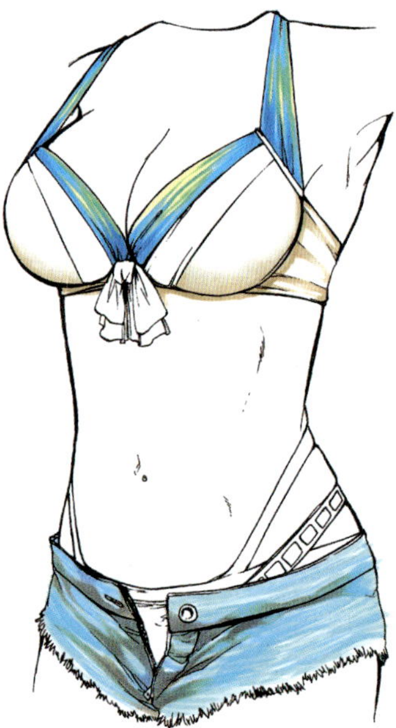

Add white ink to finish.

1

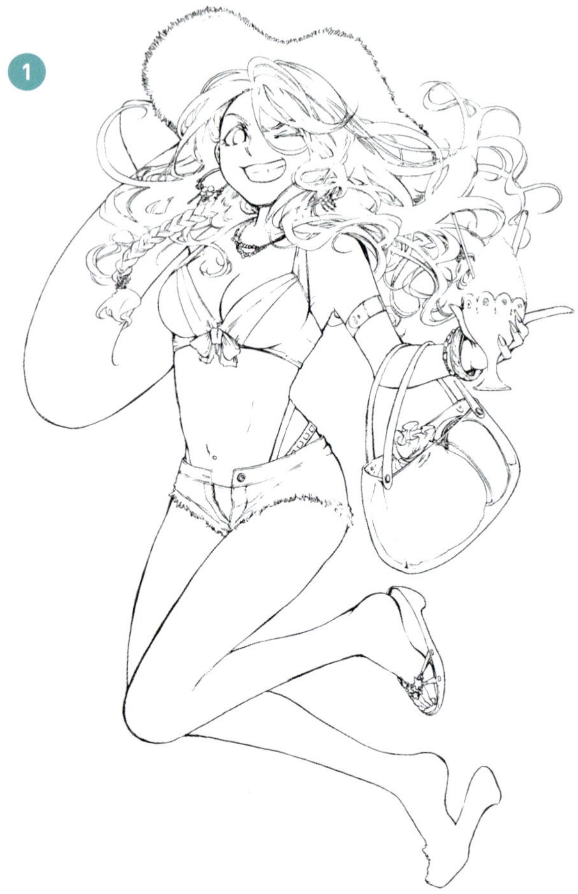

Progress >>

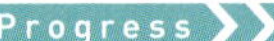

2

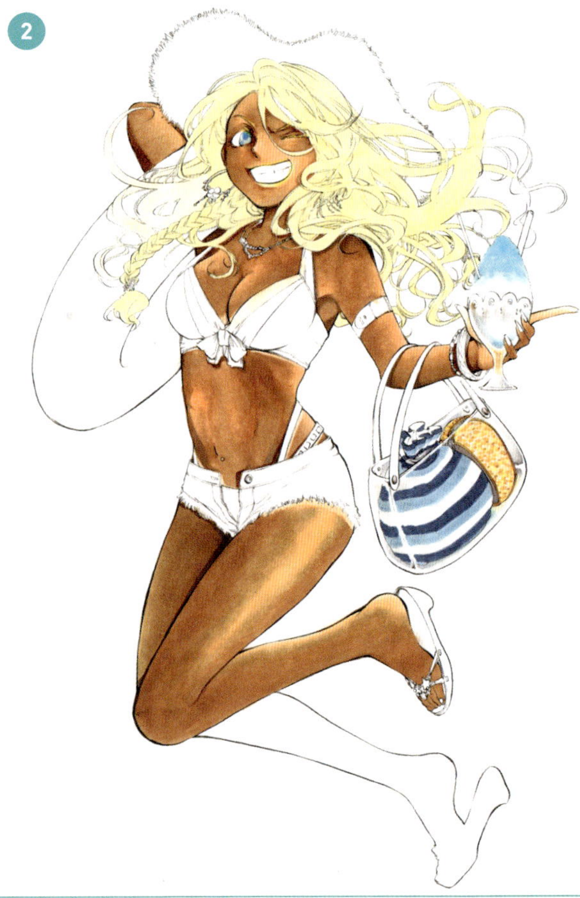

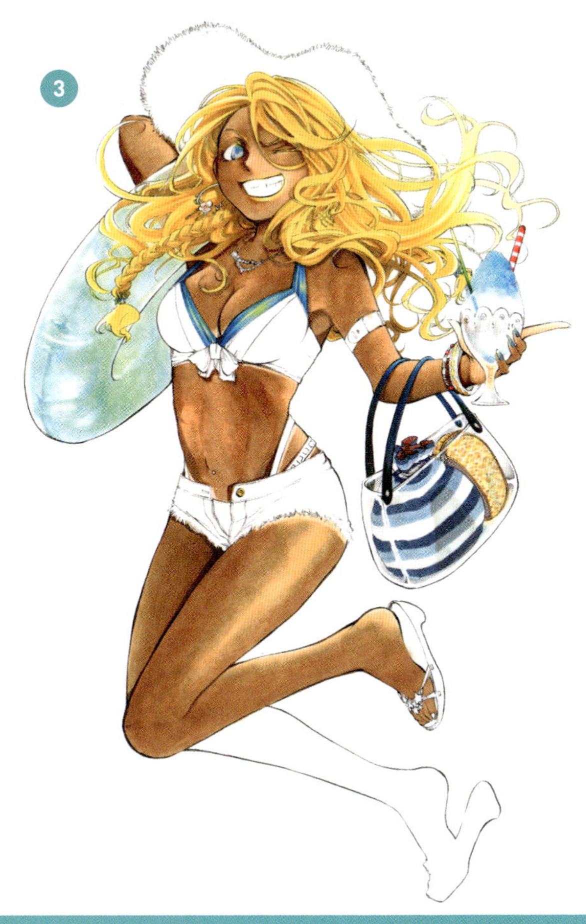

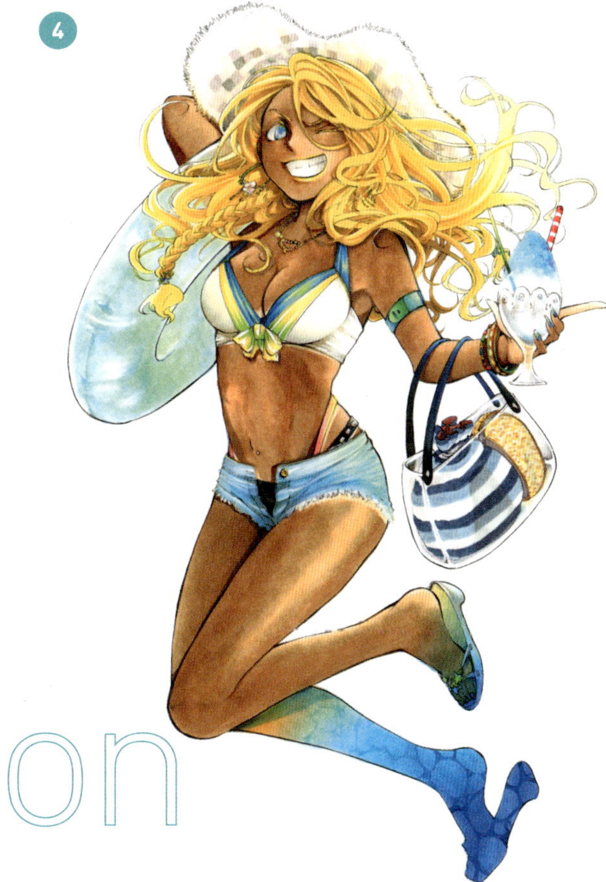

Transition

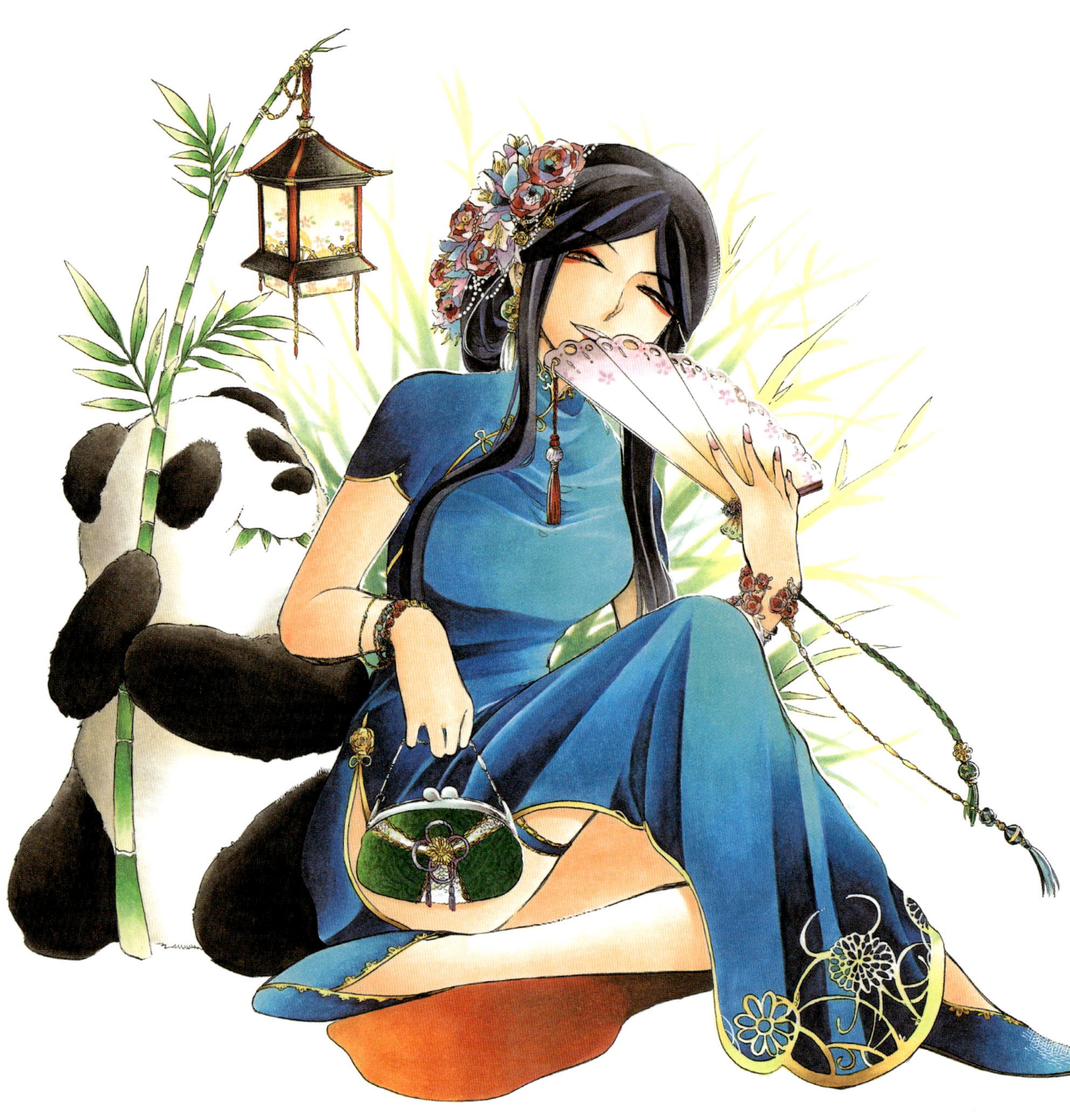

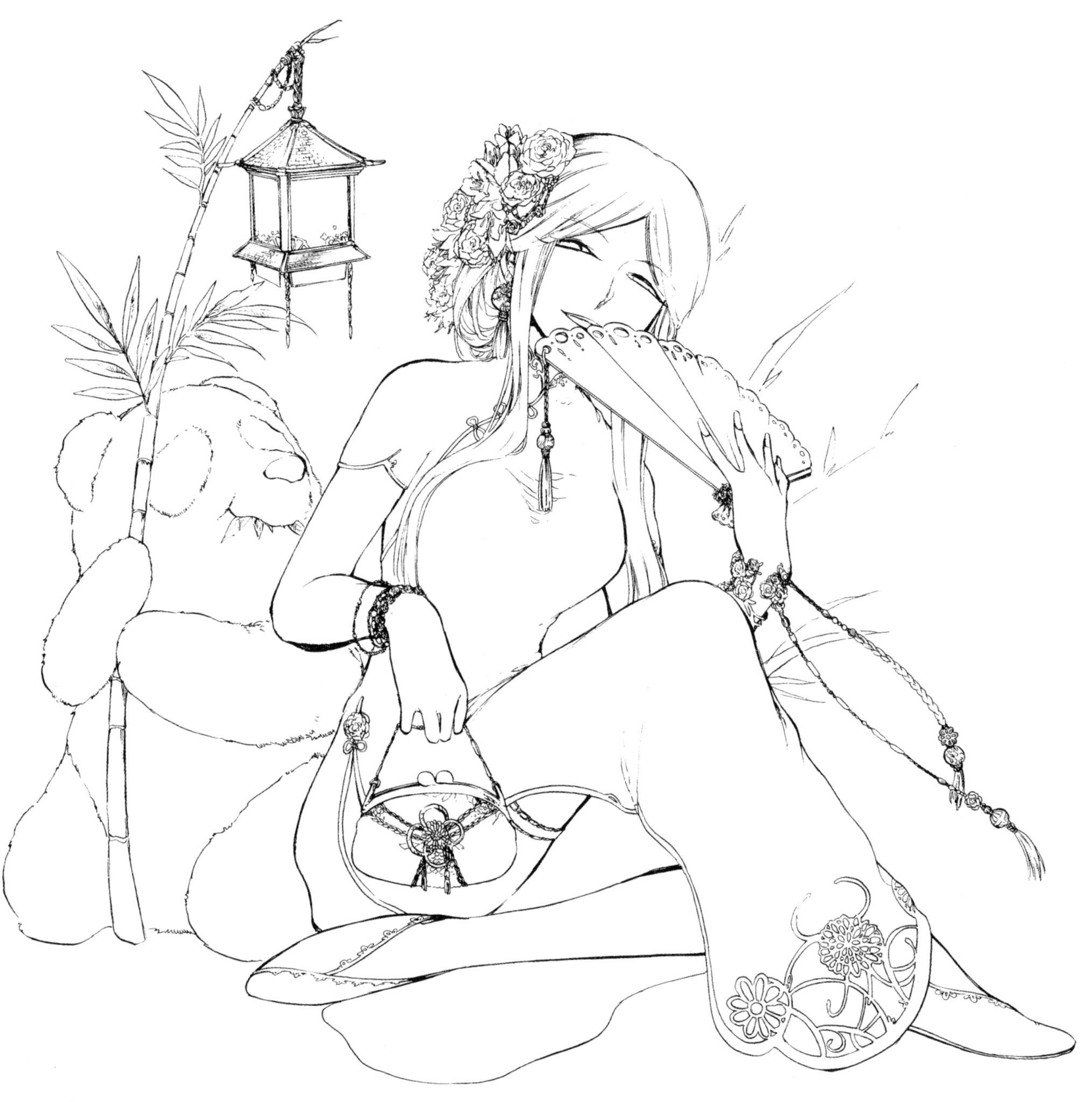

Coloring with Gradation and Almost No Shadows

This technique makes the image look like a shadow by changing the gradation colors, but without actually adding any shadow colors. It gives the impression of a design drawing and reduces the number of colors.

Selected Ink

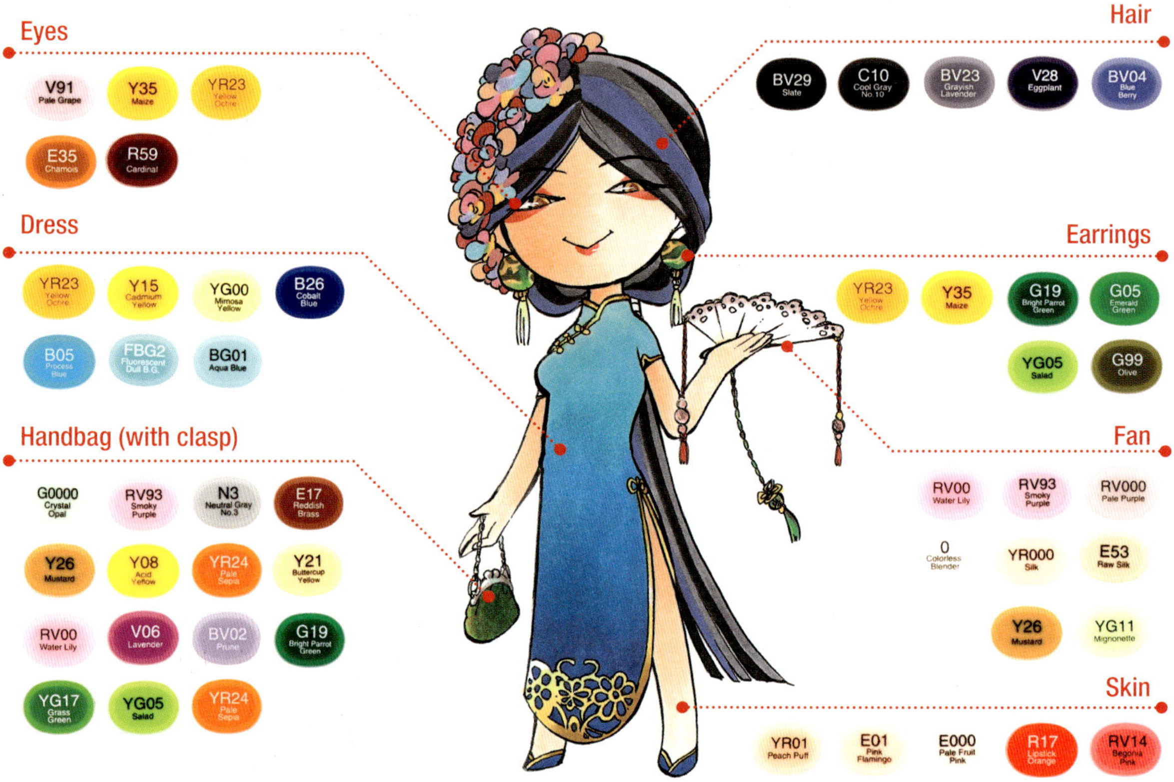

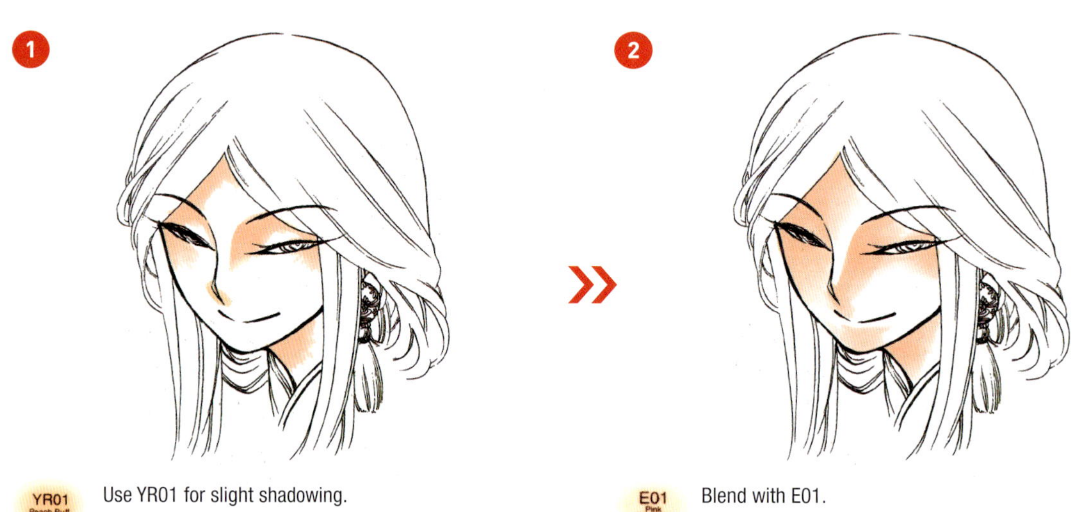

Eyes

| V91 Pale Grape | Y35 Maize | YR23 Yellow Ochre |
| E35 Chamois | R59 Cardinal | |

Dress

| YR23 Yellow Ochre | Y15 Cadmium Yellow | YG00 Mimosa Yellow | B26 Cobalt Blue |
| B05 Process Blue | FBG2 Fluorescent Dull B.G. | BG01 Aqua Blue | |

Handbag (with clasp)

G0000 Crystal Opal	RV93 Smoky Purple	N3 Neutral Gray No.3	E17 Reddish Brass
Y26 Mustard	Y08 Acid Yellow	YR24 Pale Sepia	Y21 Buttercup Yellow
RV00 Water Lily	V06 Lavender	BV02 Prune	G19 Bright Parrot Green
YG17 Grass Green	YG05 Salad	YR24 Pale Sepia	

Hair

| BV29 Slate | C10 Cool Gray No.10 | BV23 Grayish Lavender | V28 Eggplant | BV04 Blue Berry |

Earrings

| YR23 Yellow Ochre | Y35 Maize | G19 Bright Parrot Green | G05 Emerald Green |
| YG05 Salad | G99 Olive | | |

Fan

RV00 Water Lily	RV93 Smoky Purple	RV000 Pale Purple
0 Colorless Blender	YR000 Silk	E53 Raw Silk
Y26 Mustard	YG11 Mignonette	

Skin

| YR01 Peach Puff | E01 Pink Flamingo | E000 Pale Fruit Pink | R17 Lipstick Orange | RV14 Begonia Pink |

Use Shading to Create a Three-Dimensional Effect

1 »» **2**

YR01 Peach Puff — Use YR01 for slight shadowing.

E01 Pink Flamingo — Blend with E01.

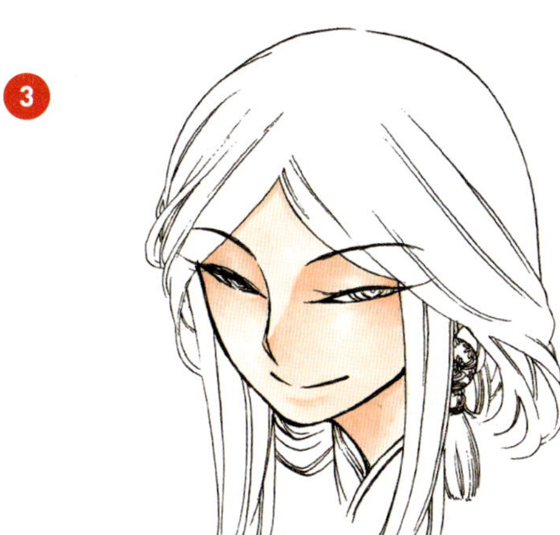

3

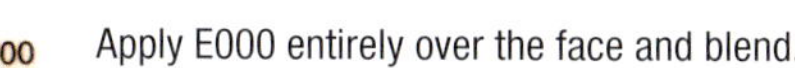
E000
Pale Fruit
Pink

Apply E000 entirely over the face and blend.

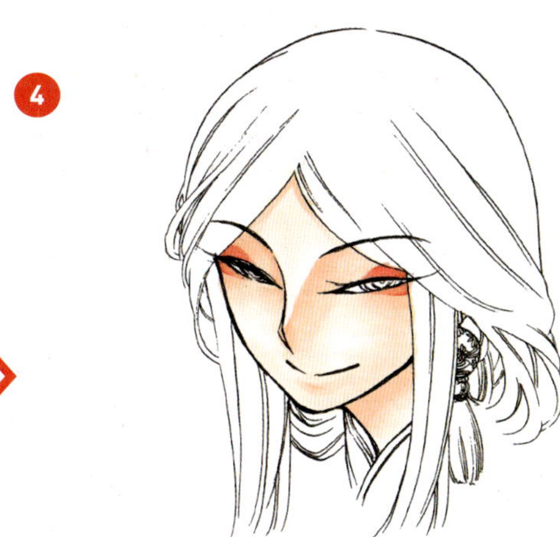

4

R17
Lipstick
Orange

RV14
Begonia
Pink

R32
Peach

To complete the look, use R17 to outline outer edges of the eyes, and then use RV14 and R32 to gradate.

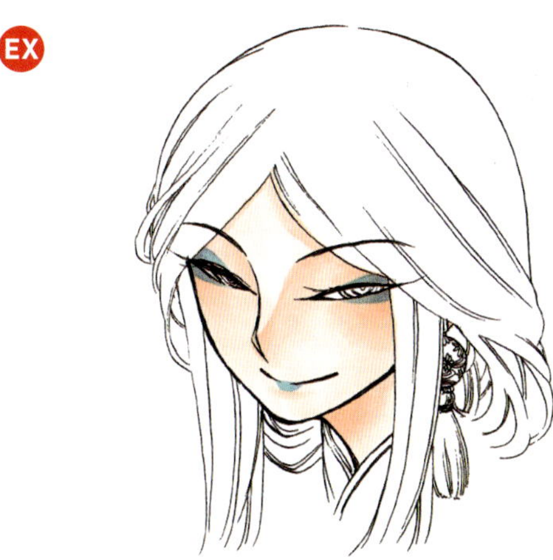

EX

B95
Light Grayish
Cobalt

BG53
Ice Mint

Example 1: Uses different colors. Outline with B95 and apply BG53.

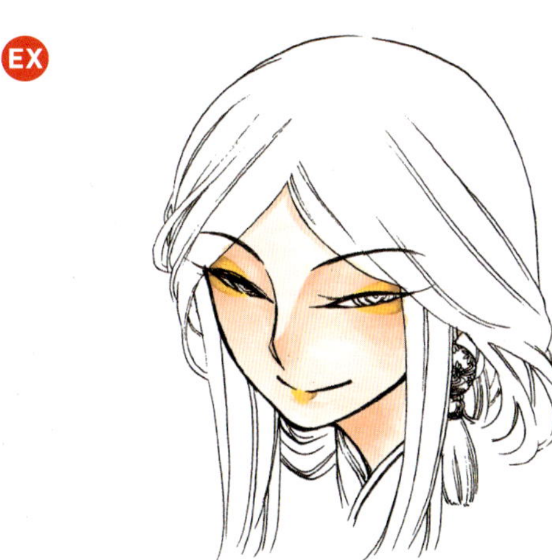

EX

E35
Chamois

Y08
Acid
Yellow

Example 2: Yet another set of colors. Outline with E35 and apply Y08.

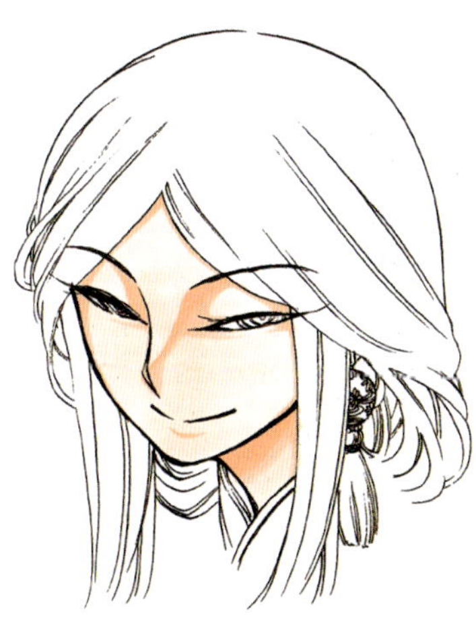

EX

This is an anime-style example.

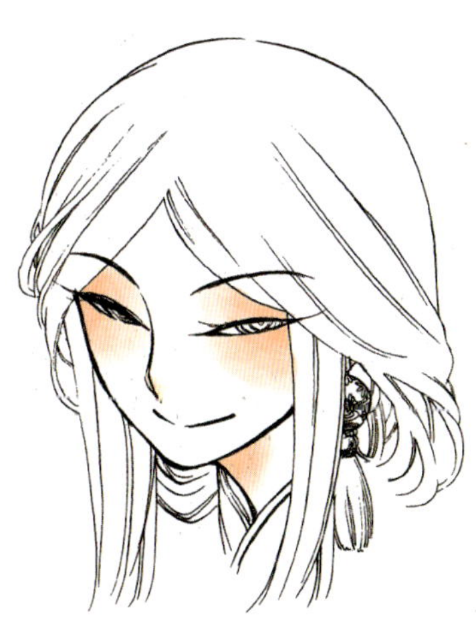

EX

Here's how a light-colored, blended version would look.

Expressive Narrow Eyes

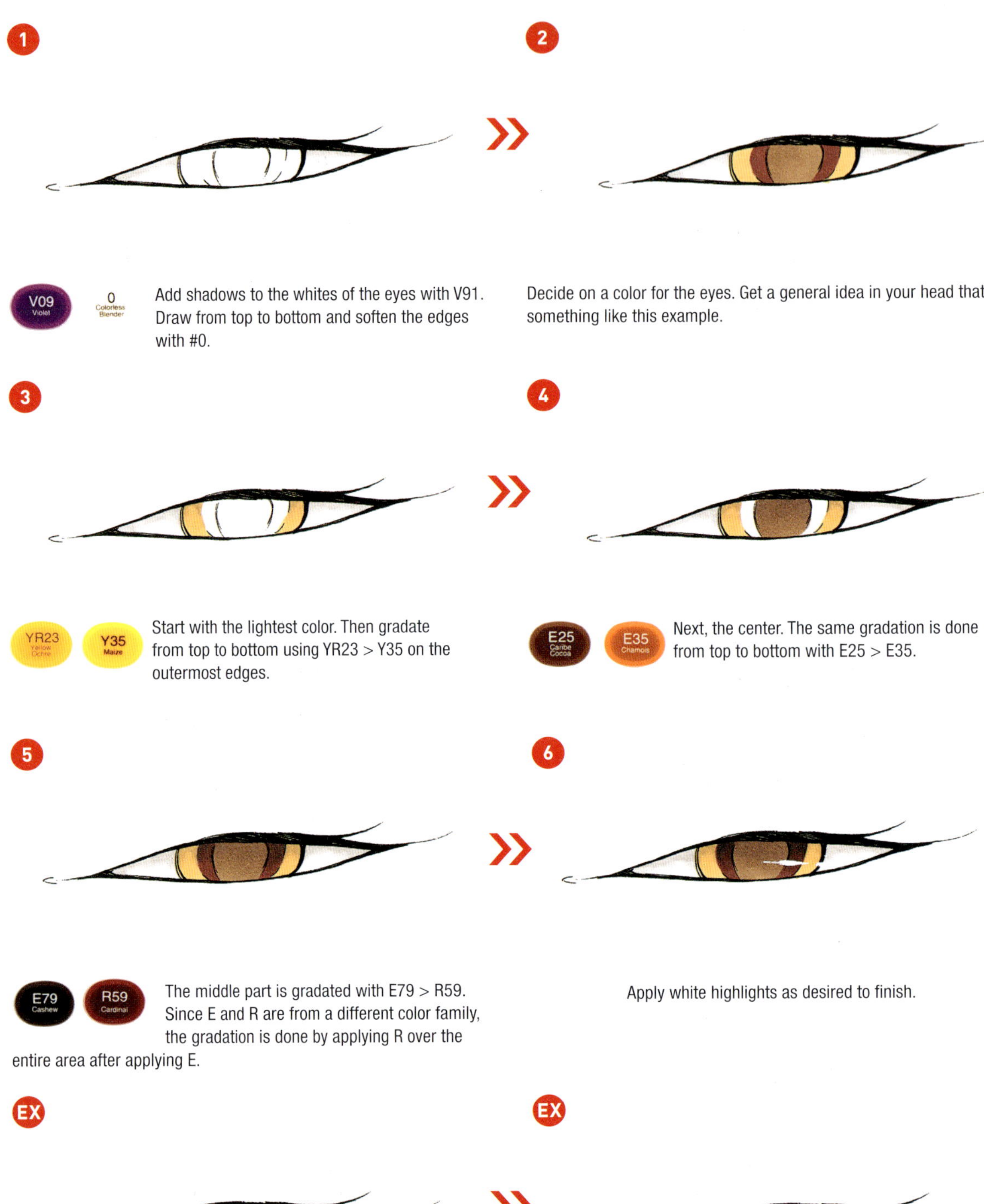

1 Add shadows to the whites of the eyes with V91. Draw from top to bottom and soften the edges with #0.

(V09 Violet, 0 Colorless Blender)

2 Decide on a color for the eyes. Get a general idea in your head that is something like this example.

3 Start with the lightest color. Then gradate from top to bottom using YR23 > Y35 on the outermost edges.

(YR23 Yellow Ochre, Y35 Maize)

4 Next, the center. The same gradation is done from top to bottom with E25 > E35.

(E25 Caribe Cocoa, E35 Chamois)

5 The middle part is gradated with E79 > R59. Since E and R are from a different color family, the gradation is done by applying R over the entire area after applying E.

(E79 Cashew, R59 Cardinal)

6 Apply white highlights as desired to finish.

EX Example 1: Using different colors. This one is from the blue family.

EX Example 2: Using different colors. This one is from the green family.

Slightly Reddened Lips

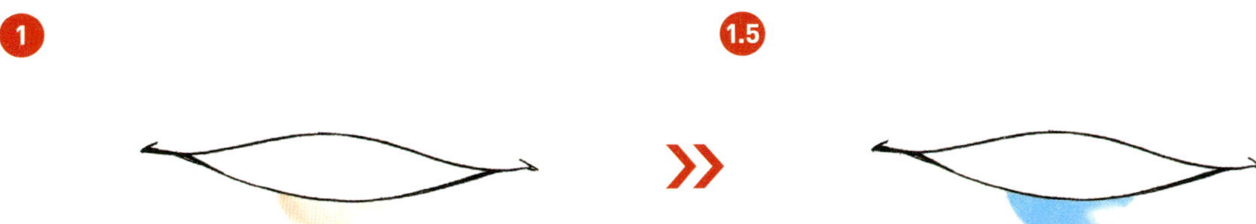

1

1.5

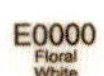 E0000 Floral White  0 Colorless Blender

Use E0000 to establish the shape and #0 to add light.

1 It is difficult to see clearly so this example uses a different color.

2

3

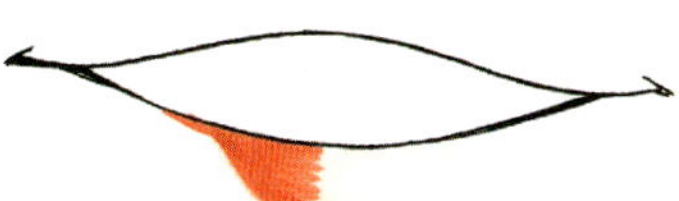

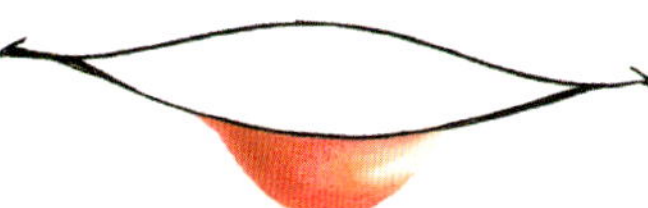

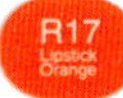 R17 Lipstick Orange

Add R17 from the direction of the shadow.

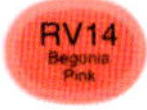 RV14 Begonia Pink  E0000 Floral White

Blend RV14 over R17. Then, apply E0000 to blend these two colors further and link the area where #0 was applied in **1**.

4

EX

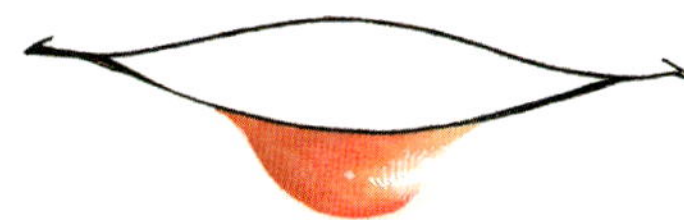

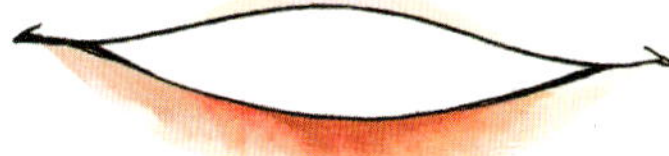

Add white highlights to complete.

This example has the color spreading out from the center like a stain.

EX

EX

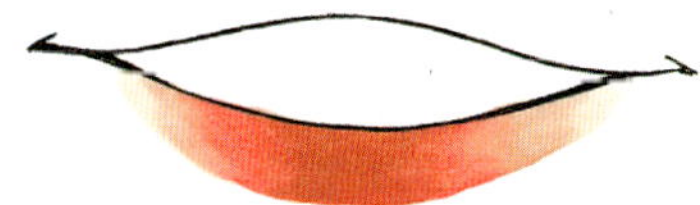

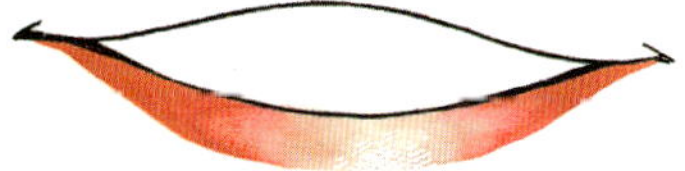

This example has the color spreading from the center to the left and right.

This example softens the edges from the outside toward the center.

Loose Black Hair

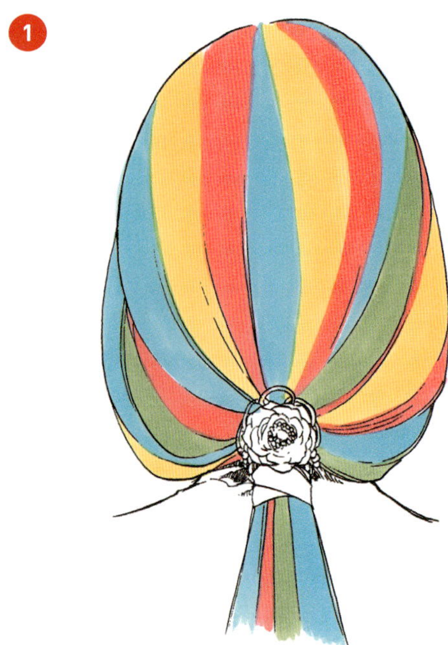

1

First, let's prepare. Divide the hair into blocks in your mind like this. Think of it more like a bunch of bands, not bundles or clumps this time.

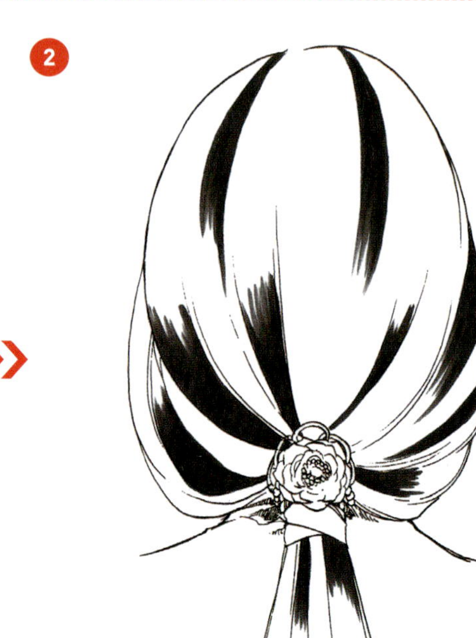

2

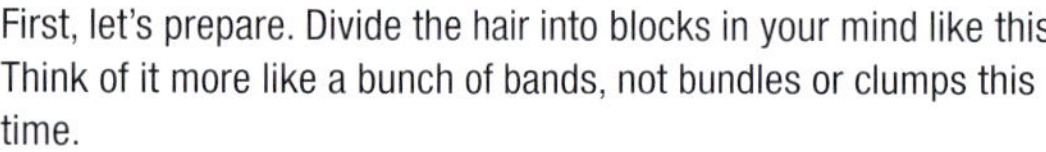

Apply C10 to the blocks you have just envisioned, but make sure they aren't side-by-side and don't join together.

C10
Cool Gray
No.10

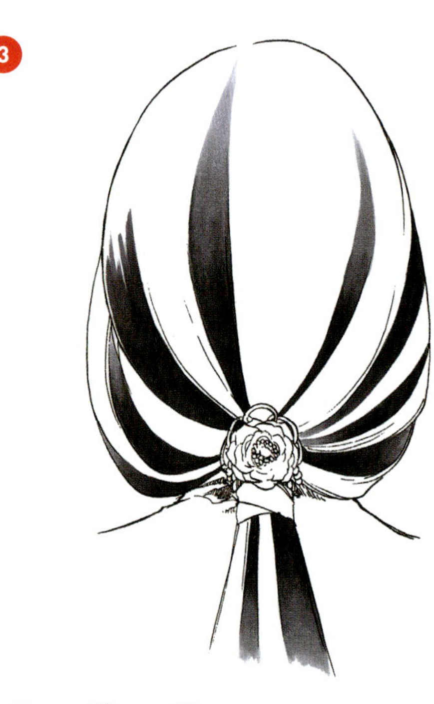

3

BV29 Slate · V28 Eggplant · BV23 Grayish Lavender

Apply BV29 > V28 > BV23 on the C10 blocks to produce gradation.

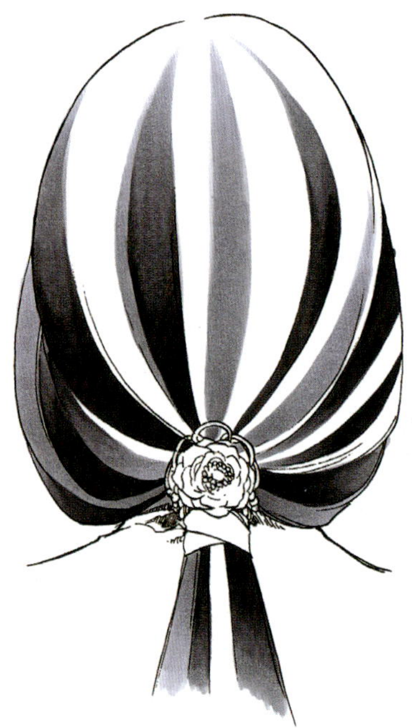

4

V28 Eggplant · BV23 Grayish Lavender

Next, gradate the empty spaces with V28 > BV23.

 **5**

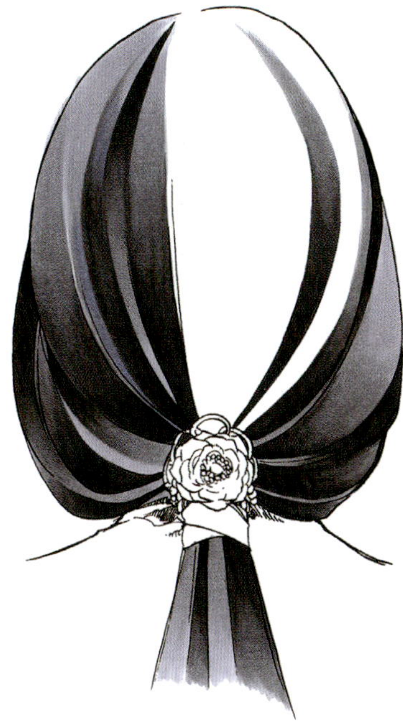

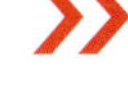

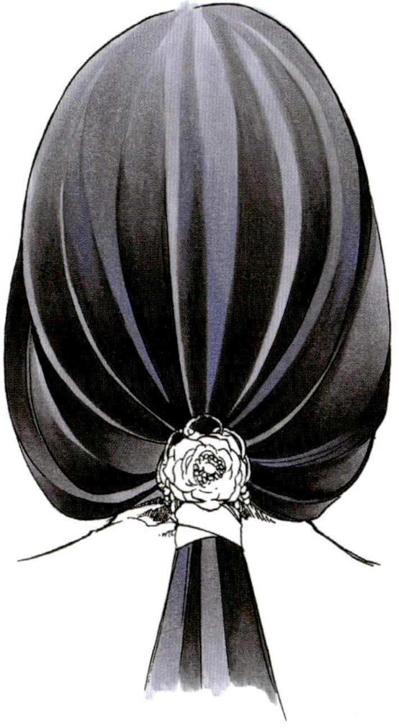 **6**

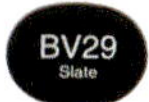 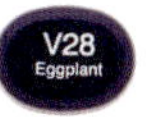 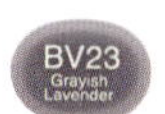

BV29 Slate **V28** Eggplant **BV23** Grayish Lavender

Apply gradations, in the opposite direction, next to the areas colored in 3.

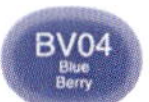 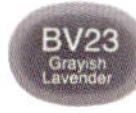

BV04 Blue Berry **BV23** Grayish Lavender

For accents, add BV04 to the V28 gradient and blend with BV23.

 **7**

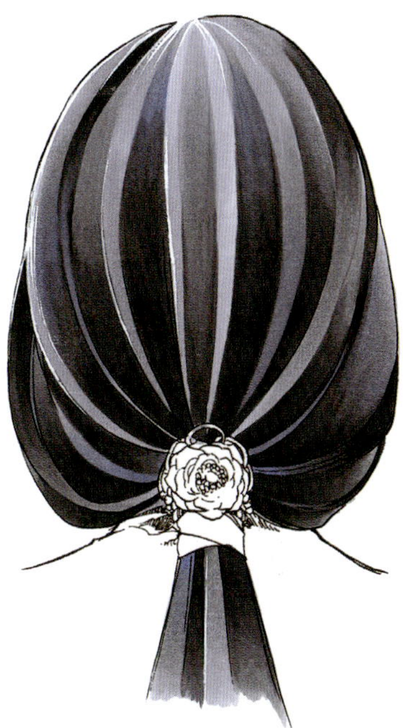

Follow the flow of the hair. Add in some white if you like, and you're done!

 **EX**

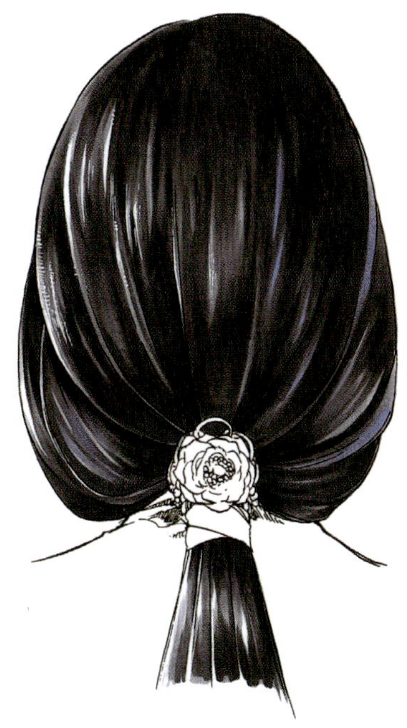

This example has a glossy finish, but uses the same color.

1

2

3

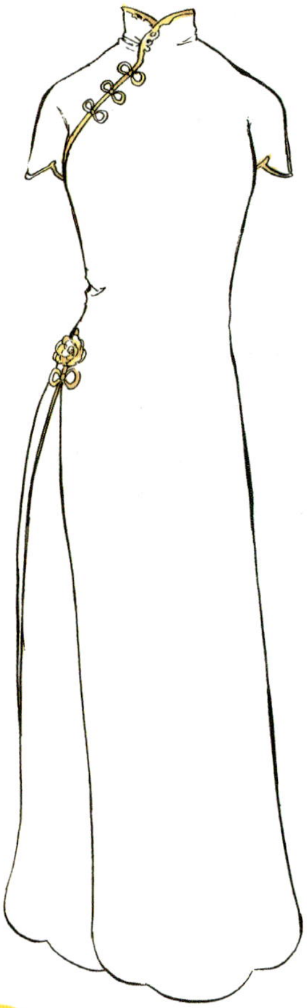

YR23
Yellow
Ochre

Y15
Cadmium
Yellow

Start with the gold on the outer edge. Use YR23 > Y15.

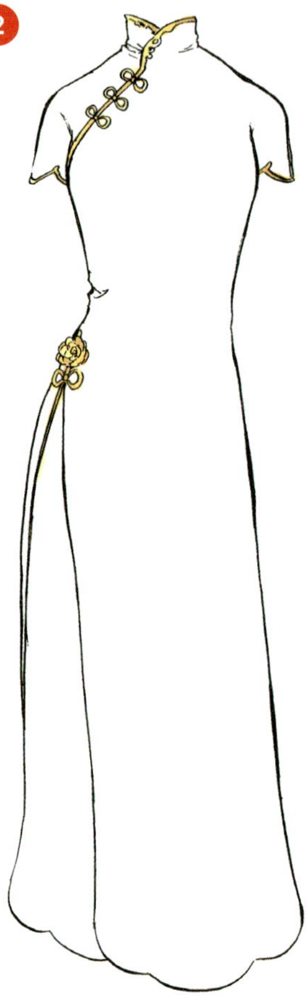

YG00
Mimosa
Yellow

Color the entire edge with YG00 and you're done!

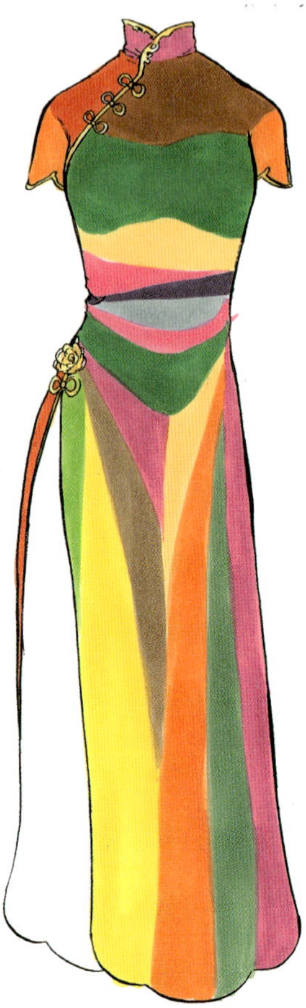

For the clothing part, first divide into blocks in your mind like this.

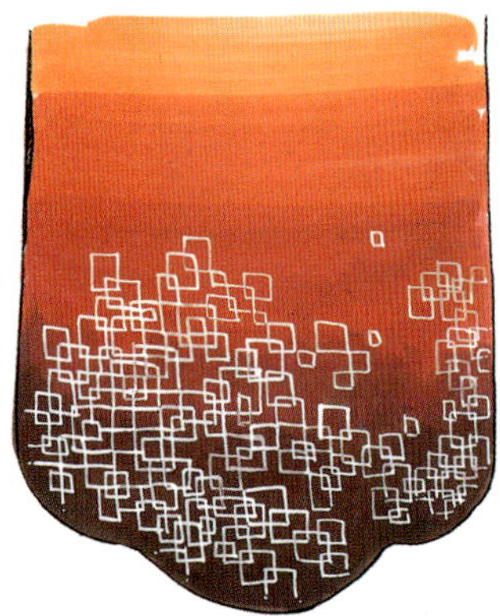

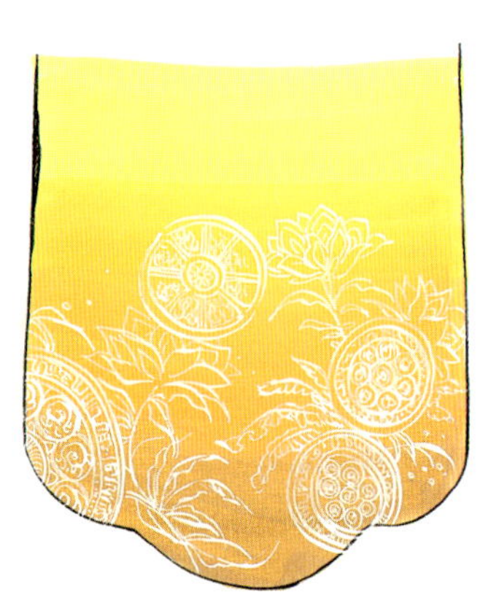

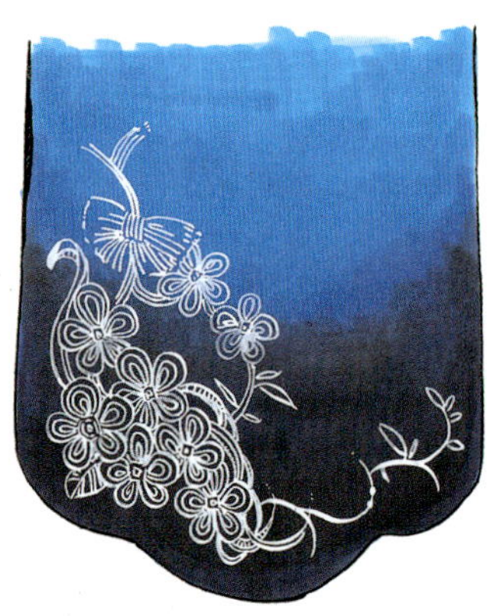

Samples of White Patterning on Chinese-Style Dresses

4

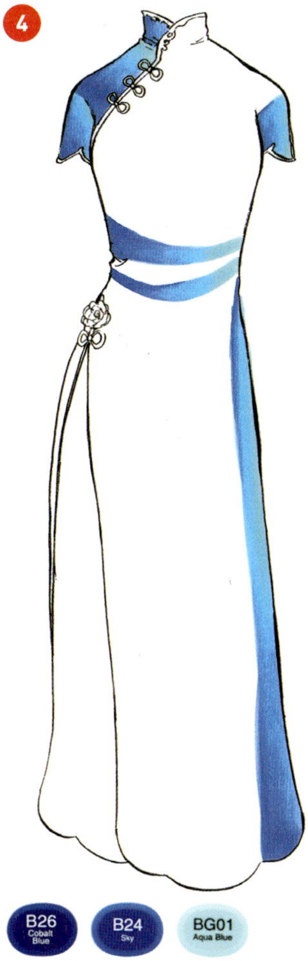

B26 Cobalt Blue B24 Sky BG01 Aqua Blue

Gradations by block: B26 > B24 > BG01.

5

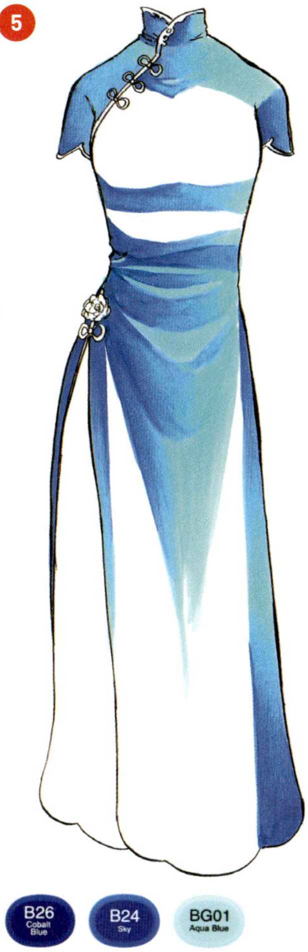

B26 Cobalt Blue B24 Sky BG01 Aqua Blue

Begin with easy to color areas and work your way along.

6

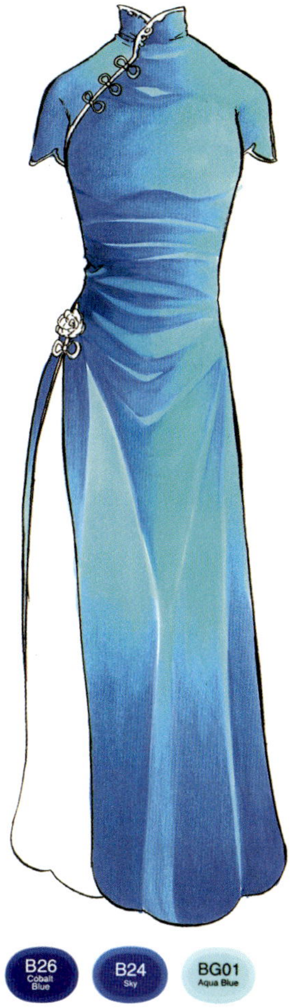

B26 Cobalt Blue B24 Sky BG01 Aqua Blue

Once you have colored them all, you're done!

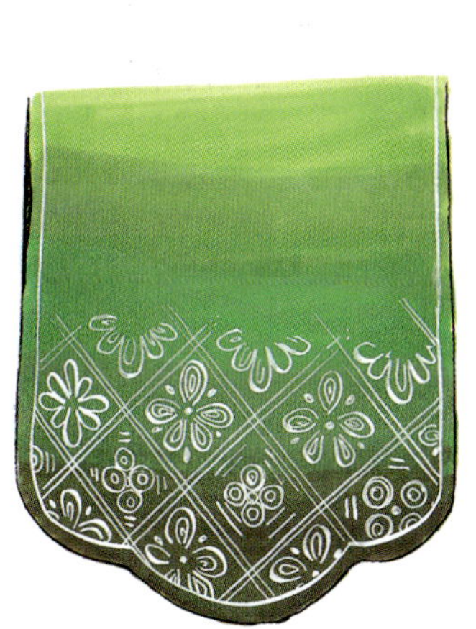

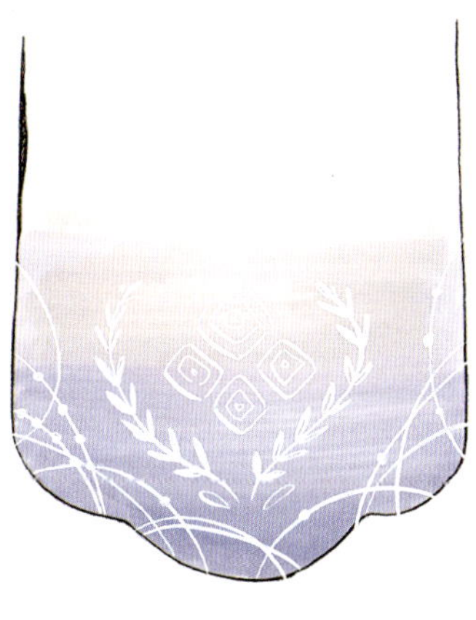

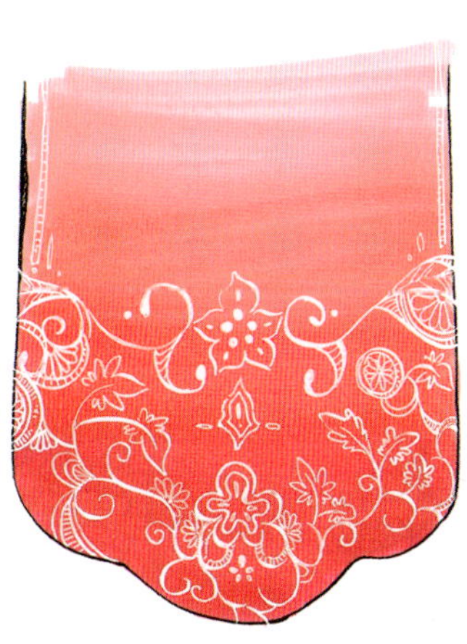

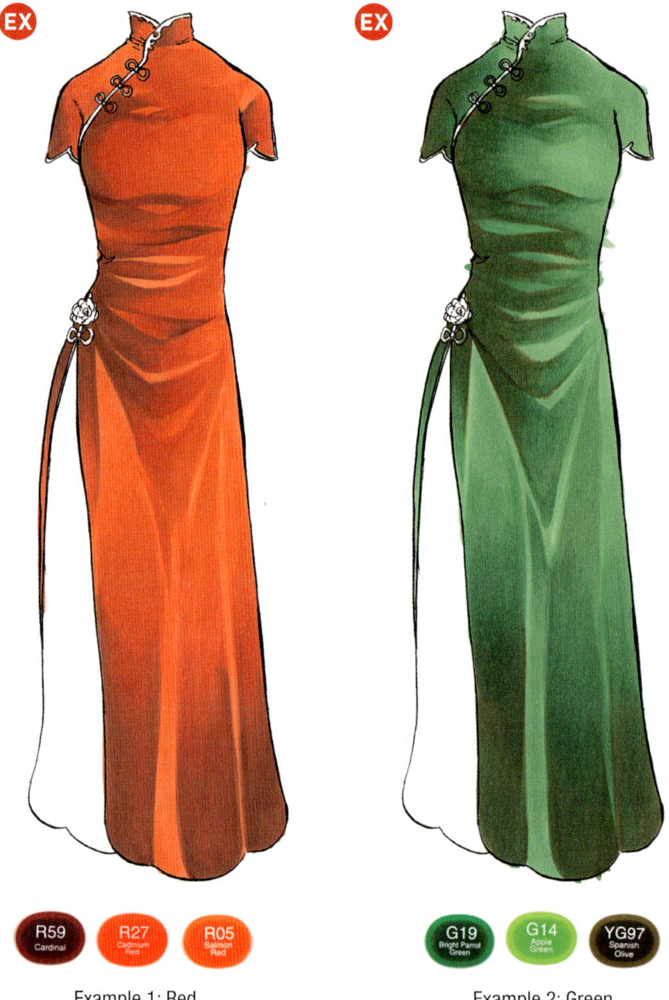

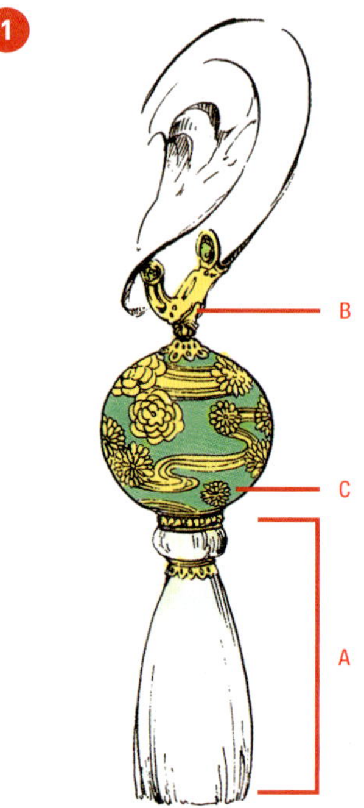

Decide on the general color in your mind. Since we'll be painting light colors first, the order will be A, B, and then C.

Example 1: Red

Example 2: Green

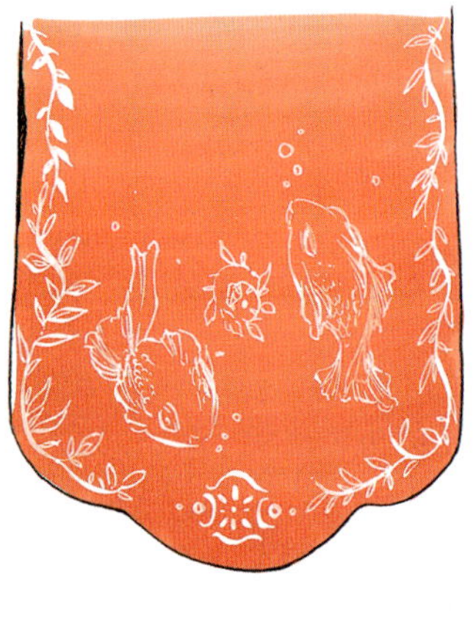

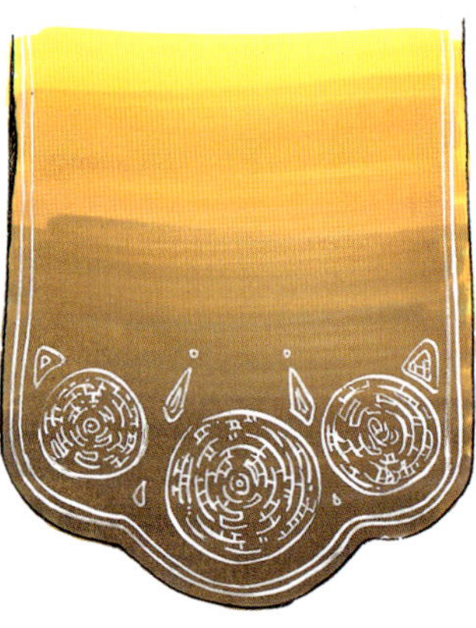

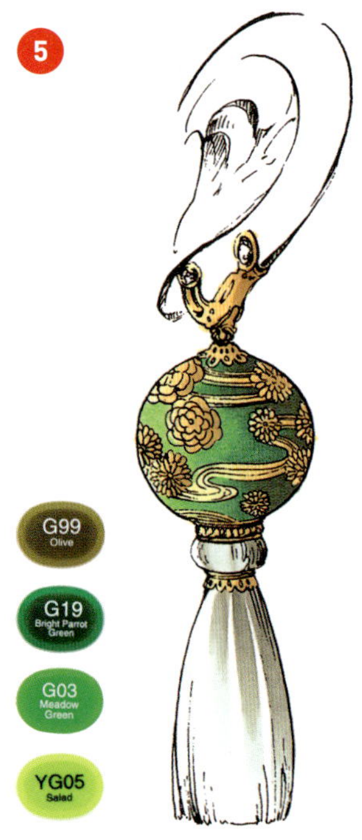

Section C. Color from shade to light with G99 > G19 > G03 > YG05.

Earring

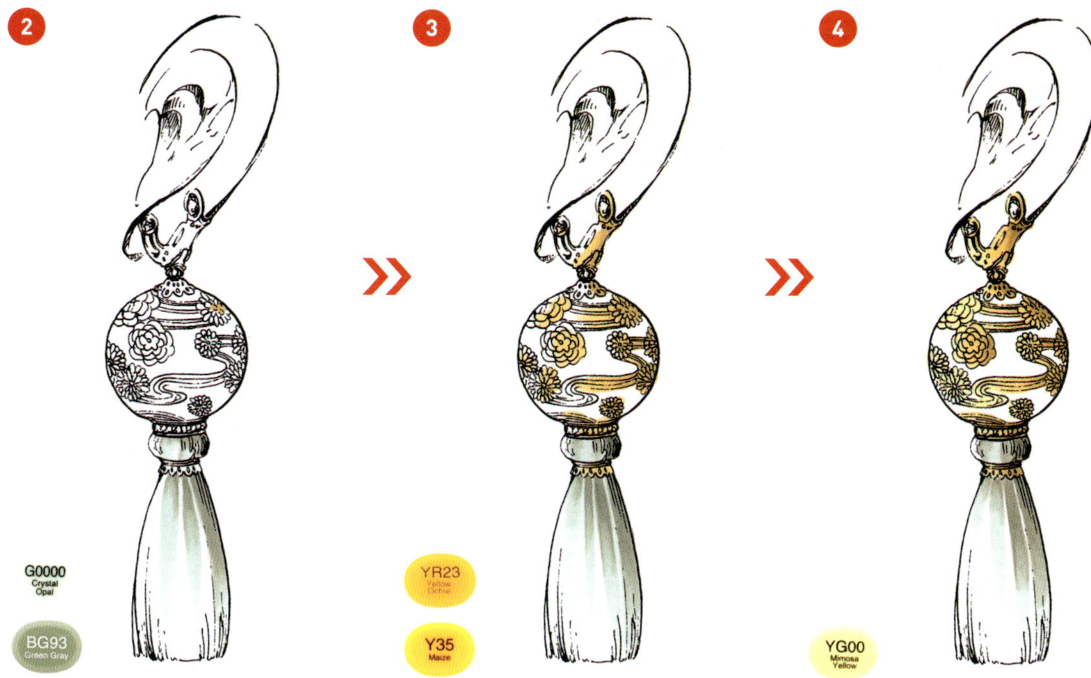

2

G0000
Crystal Opal

BG93
Green Gray

Starting from A, color the base color of the tassel with G0000 and apply BG93 to gradate. Divide the block from the opposite side of the light, and reduce the ratio of BG93.

3

YR23
Yellow Ochre

Y35
Maize

Add shadows to B using YR23 > Y35. Separate them according to the pattern.

4

YG00
Mimosa Yellow

B is completed with YG00 colored light.

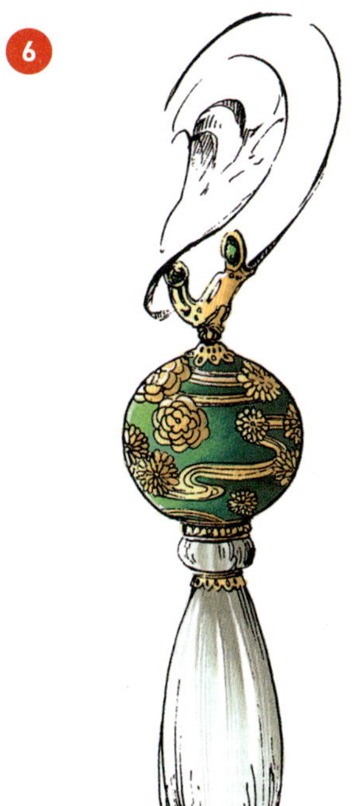

6

For part B, add white to match the pattern. For part C, add white to match the sphere. That's it, you're done!

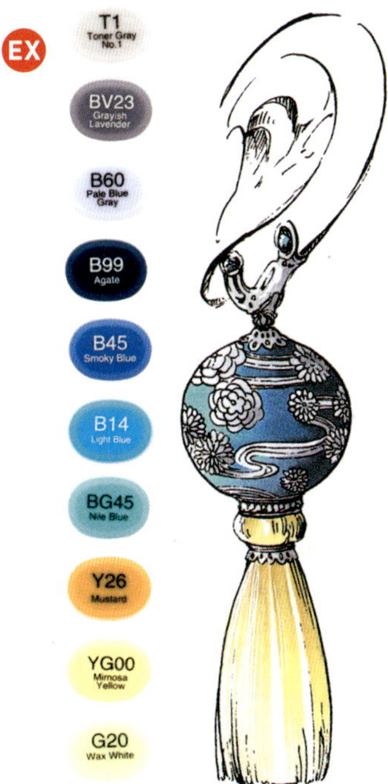

EX

T1
Toner Gray No.1

BV23
Grayish Lavender

B60
Pale Blue Gray

B99
Agate

B45
Smoky Blue

B14
Light Blue

BG45
Nile Blue

Y26
Mustard

YG00
Mimosa Yellow

G20
Wax White

Example 1: Using different colors: BV23, B60, T1 for the base, B99, B45, B14, BG45 for the sphere, and Y26, YG00, G20 for the tassels.

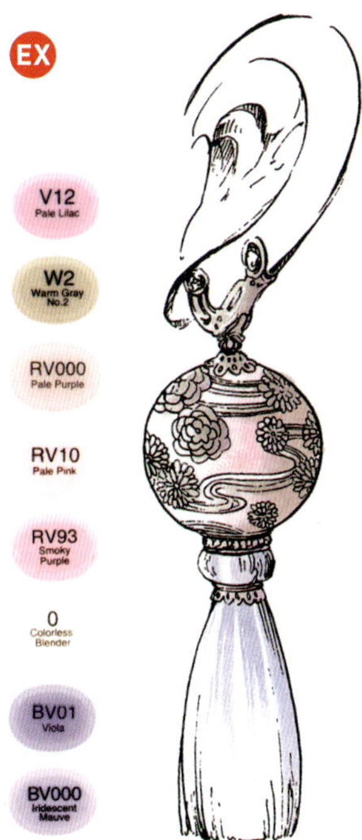

EX

V12
Pale Lilac

W2
Warm Gray No.2

RV000
Pale Purple

RV10
Pale Pink

RV93
Smoky Purple

0
Colorless Blender

BV01
Viola

BV000
Iridescent Mauve

Example 2: With different colors: V12, W2, RV000 for the base, RV10, RV93, #0 for the sphere, and BV01, BV000, #0 for the tassel.

Light-Colored Fans

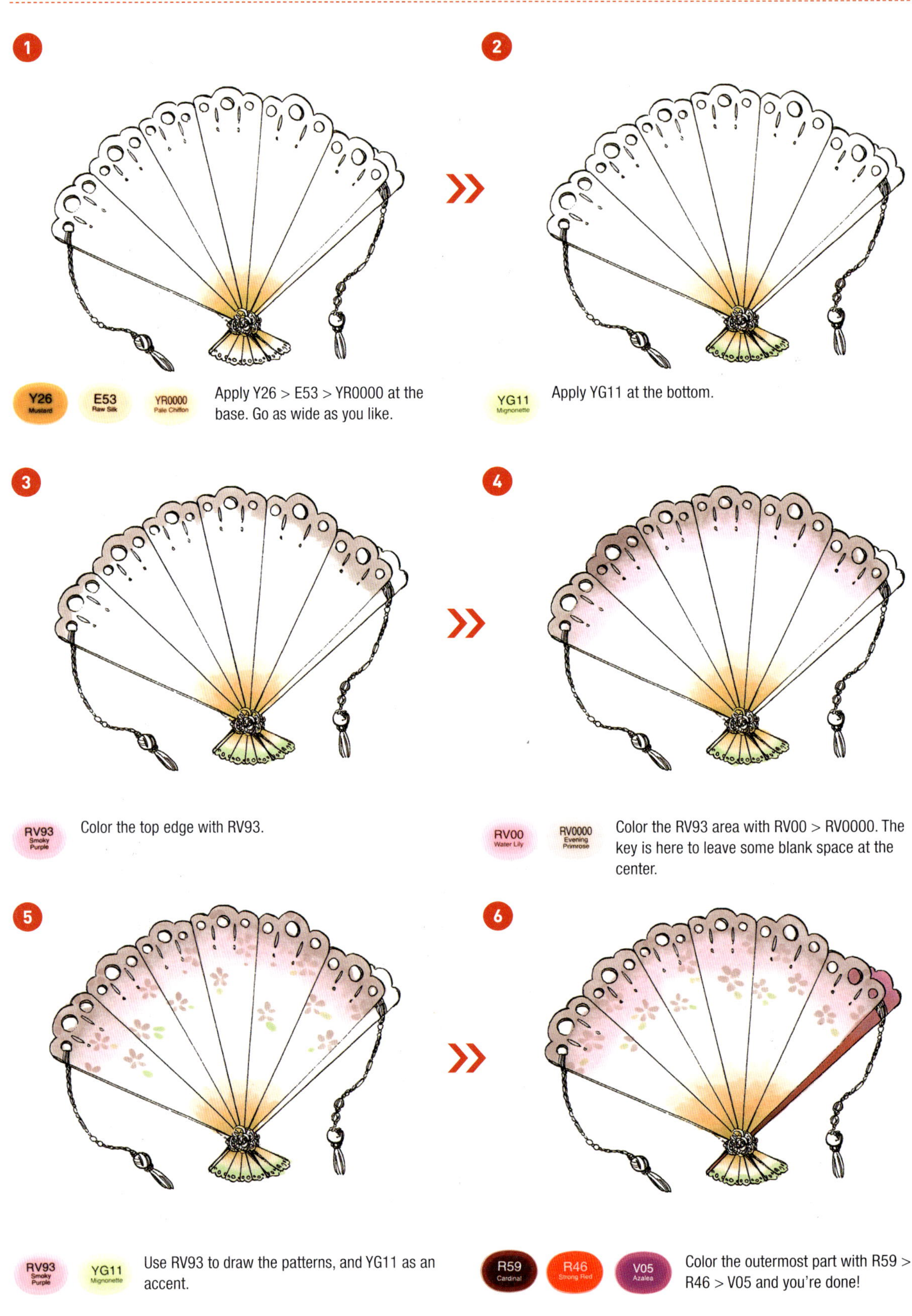

1

Y26 Mustard **E53** Raw Silk **YR0000** Pale Chiffon

Apply Y26 > E53 > YR0000 at the base. Go as wide as you like.

2

YG11 Mignonette

Apply YG11 at the bottom.

3

RV93 Smoky Purple

Color the top edge with RV93.

4

RV00 Water Lily **RV0000** Evening Primrose

Color the RV93 area with RV00 > RV0000. The key is here to leave some blank space at the center.

5

RV93 Smoky Purple **YG11** Mignonette

Use RV93 to draw the patterns, and YG11 as an accent.

6

R59 Cardinal **R46** Strong Red **V05** Azalea

Color the outermost part with R59 > R46 > V05 and you're done!

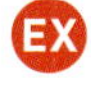 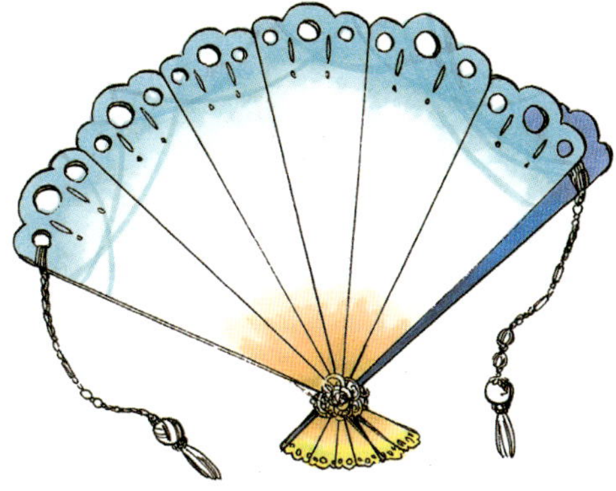

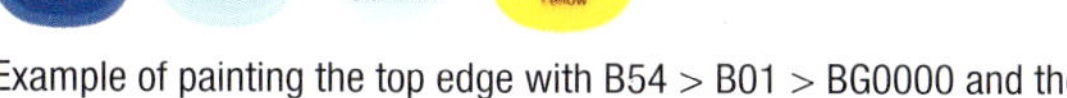

Example of painting the top edge with B54 > B01 > BG0000 and the base with Y08.

 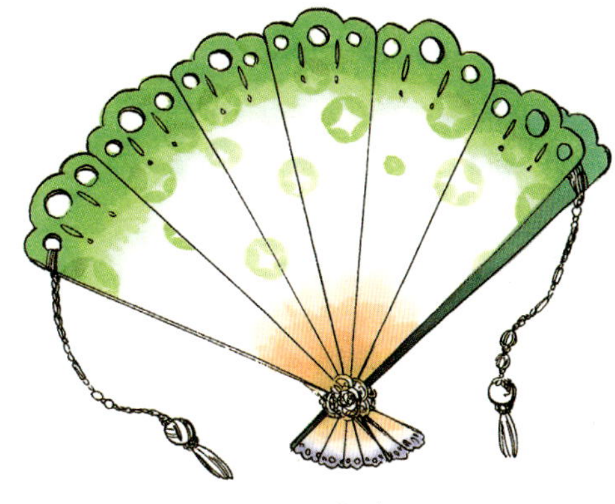

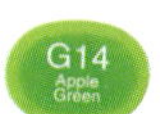 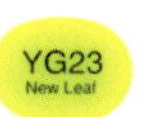 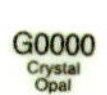 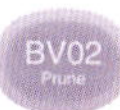

Example with the top edge using G14 > YG23 > G0000 and the base using BV02.

Handbag with Clasp

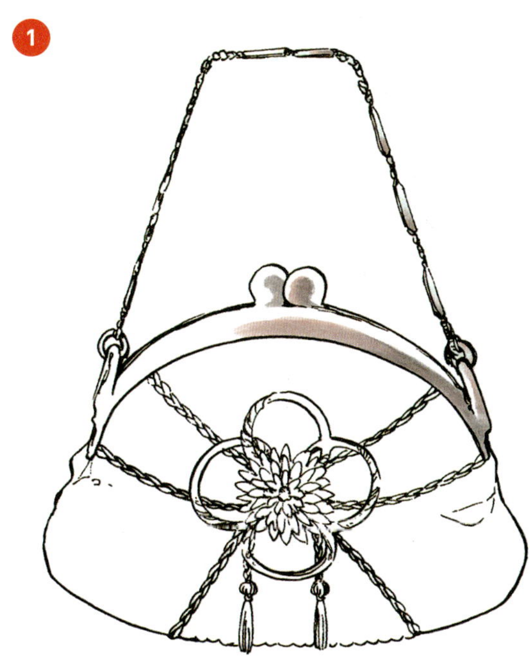

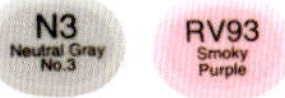

First color the clasp: Use N3 > RV93 for the shadows.

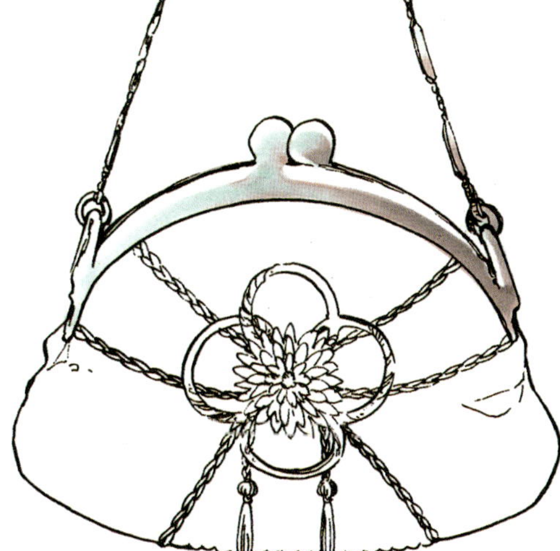

Use G000 to blend in the direction of the light, while still leaving some white areas.

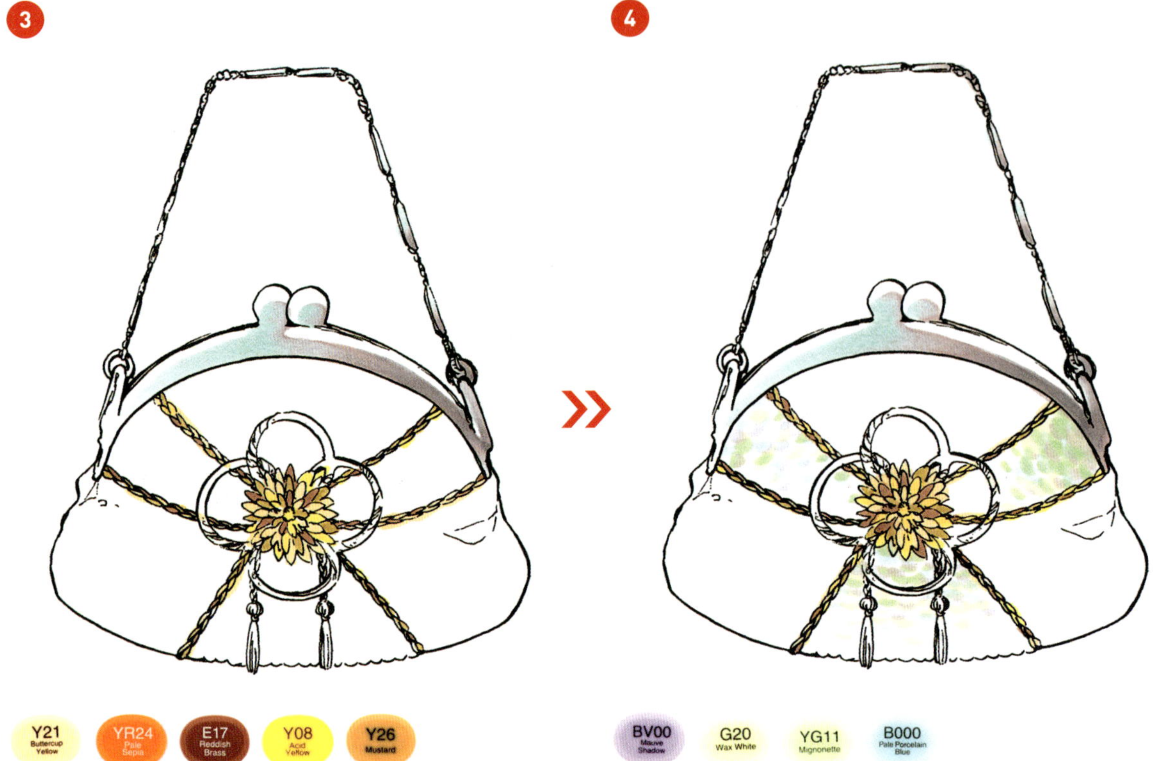

3

Y21 Buttercup Yellow · YR24 Pale Sepia · E17 Reddish Brass · Y08 Acid Yellow · Y26 Mustard

Paint the flower and string with Y21, YR24, E17, Y08, Y26, being sure to separate the colors.

4

BV00 Mauve Shadow · G20 Wax White · YG11 Mignonette · B000 Pale Porcelain Blue

Paint the body with BV00, G20, YG11, and B000, making sure to separate the colors. If you paint in a semicircle, it will look like scales.

5

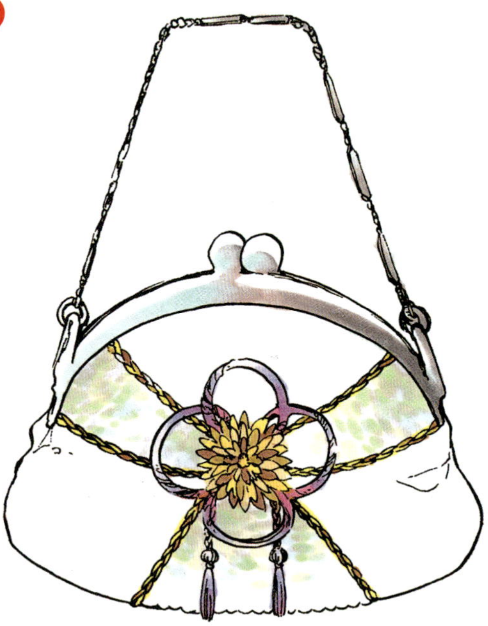

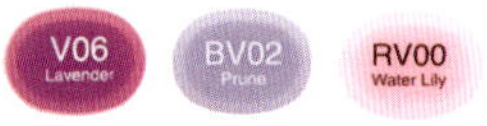

V06 Lavender · BV02 Prune · RV00 Water Lily

Paint the center string with V6 > BV02 > RV00. At this point, paint from the center outward. This is the best way to paint the accessories.

6

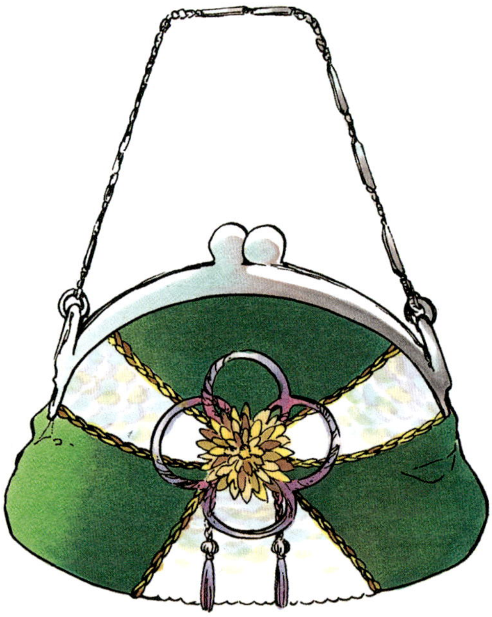

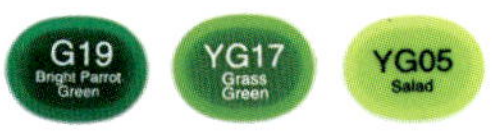

G19 Bright Parrot Green · YG17 Grass Green · YG05 Salad

Apply the base coat using G19 > YG17 > YG05.

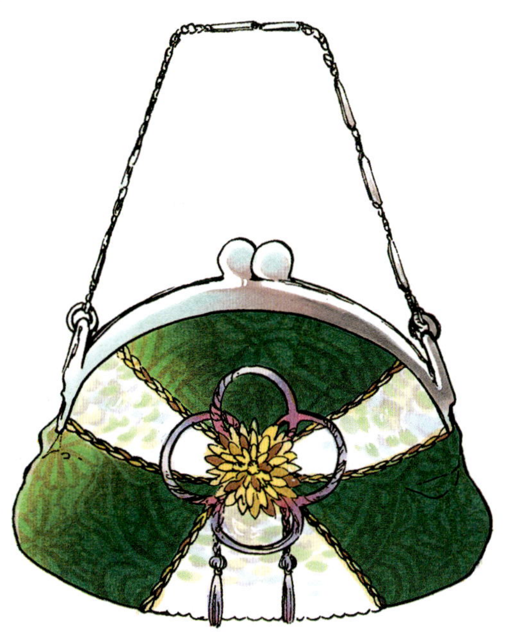

7

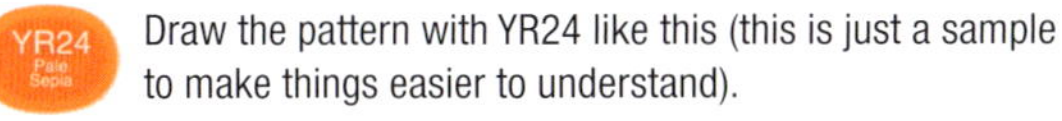

YR24 Pale Sepia — Draw the pattern with YR24 like this (this is just a sample to make things easier to understand).

8

Add white highlights and it is complete!

1

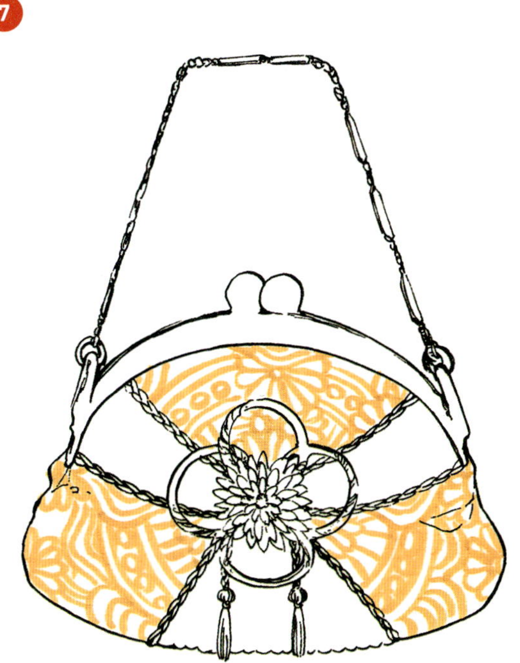

Transition

Transition

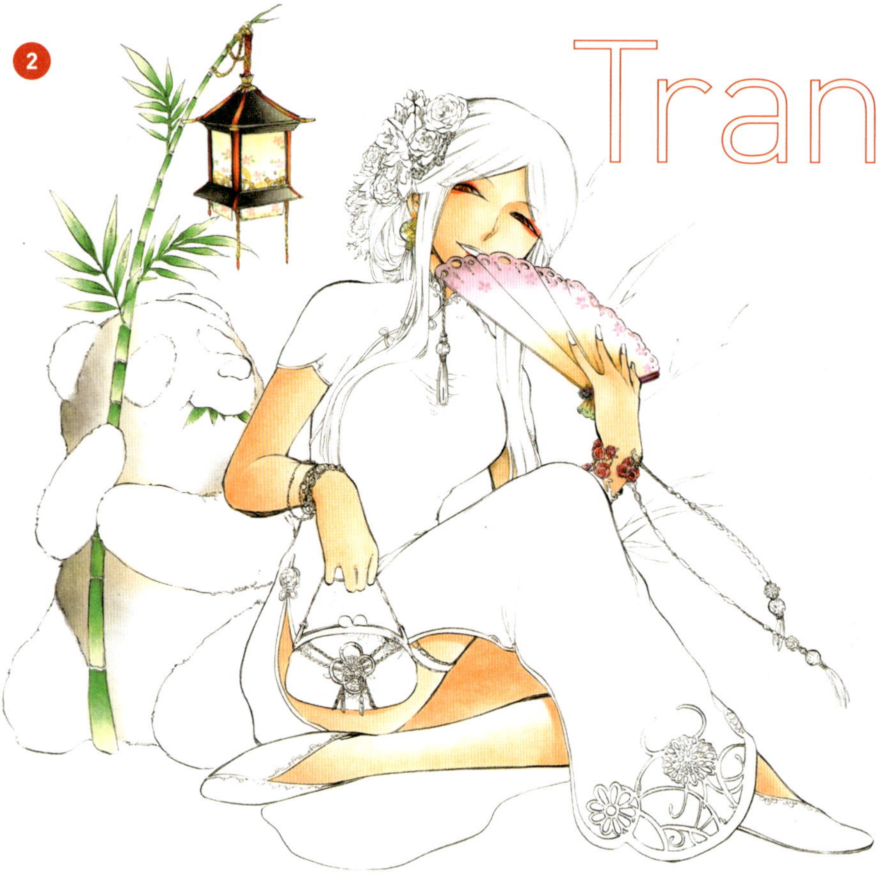

Progress >>

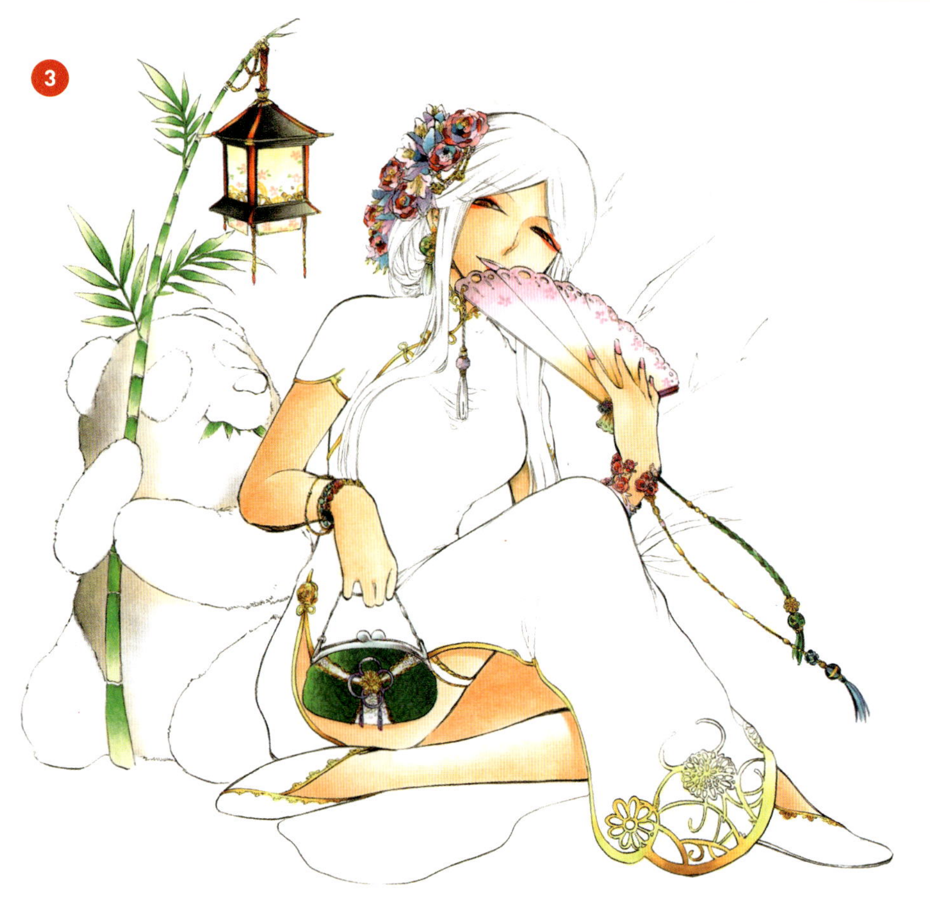

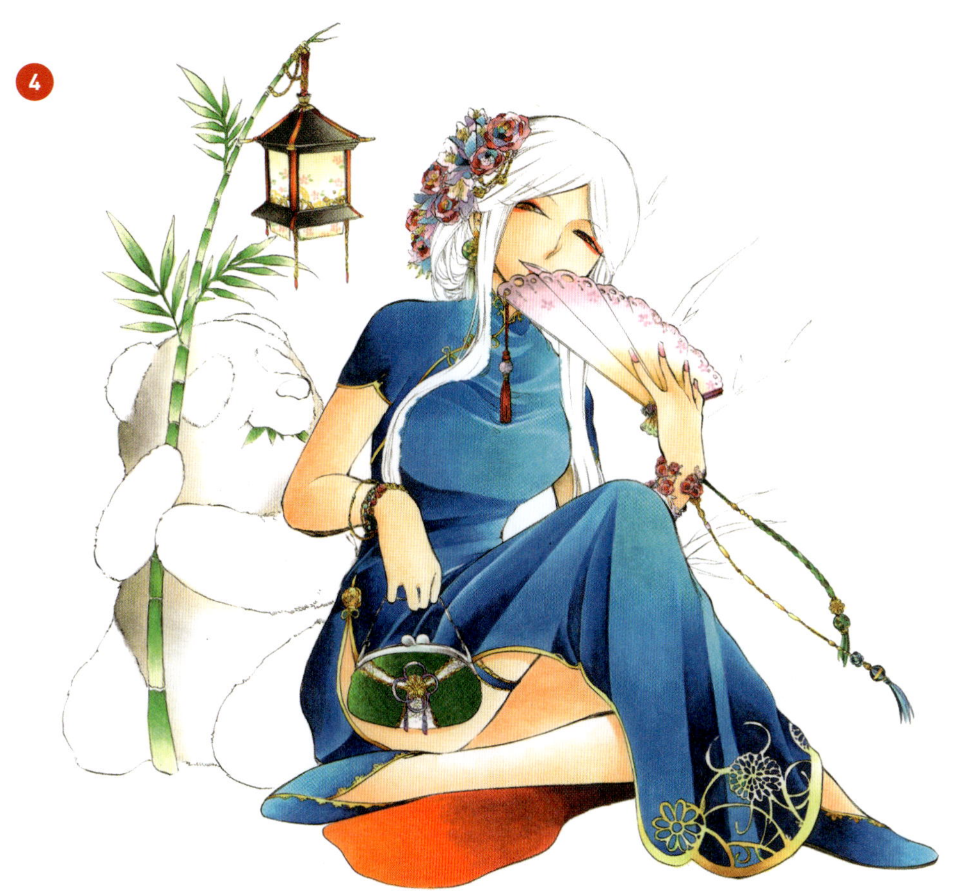

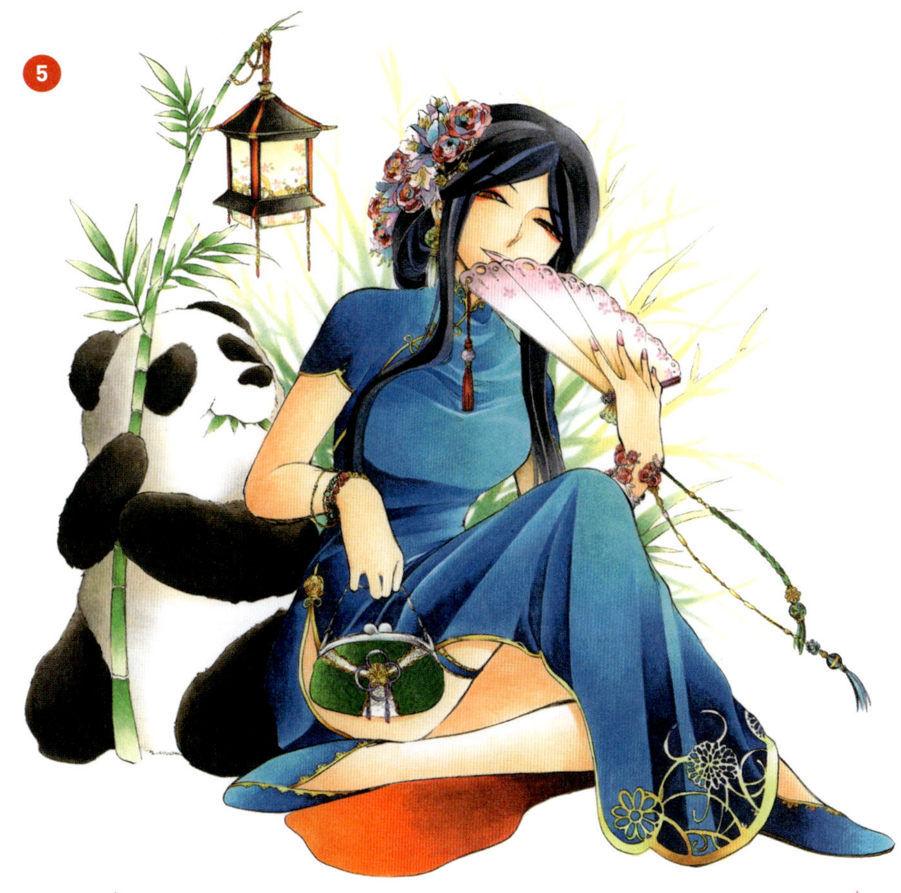

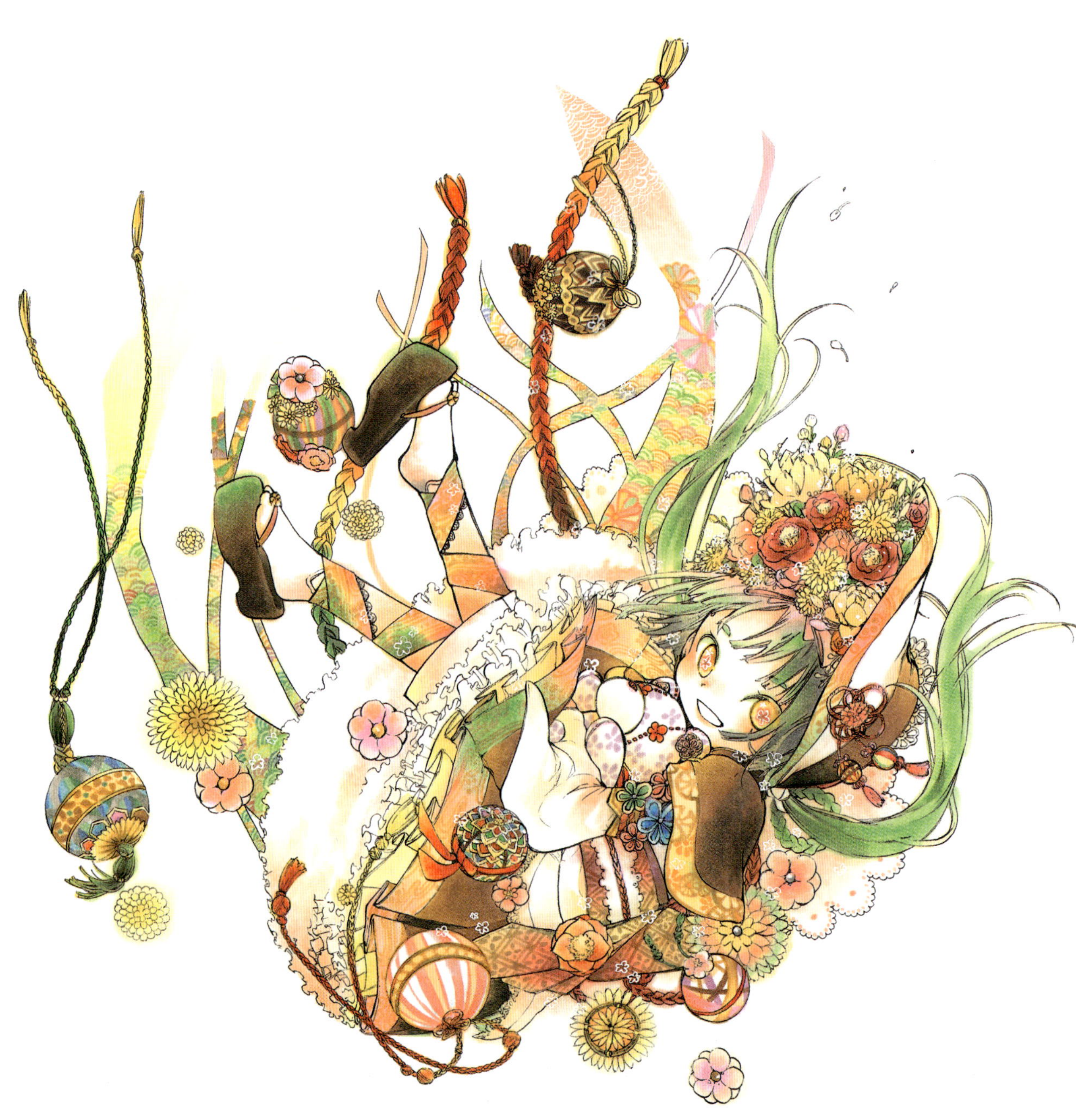

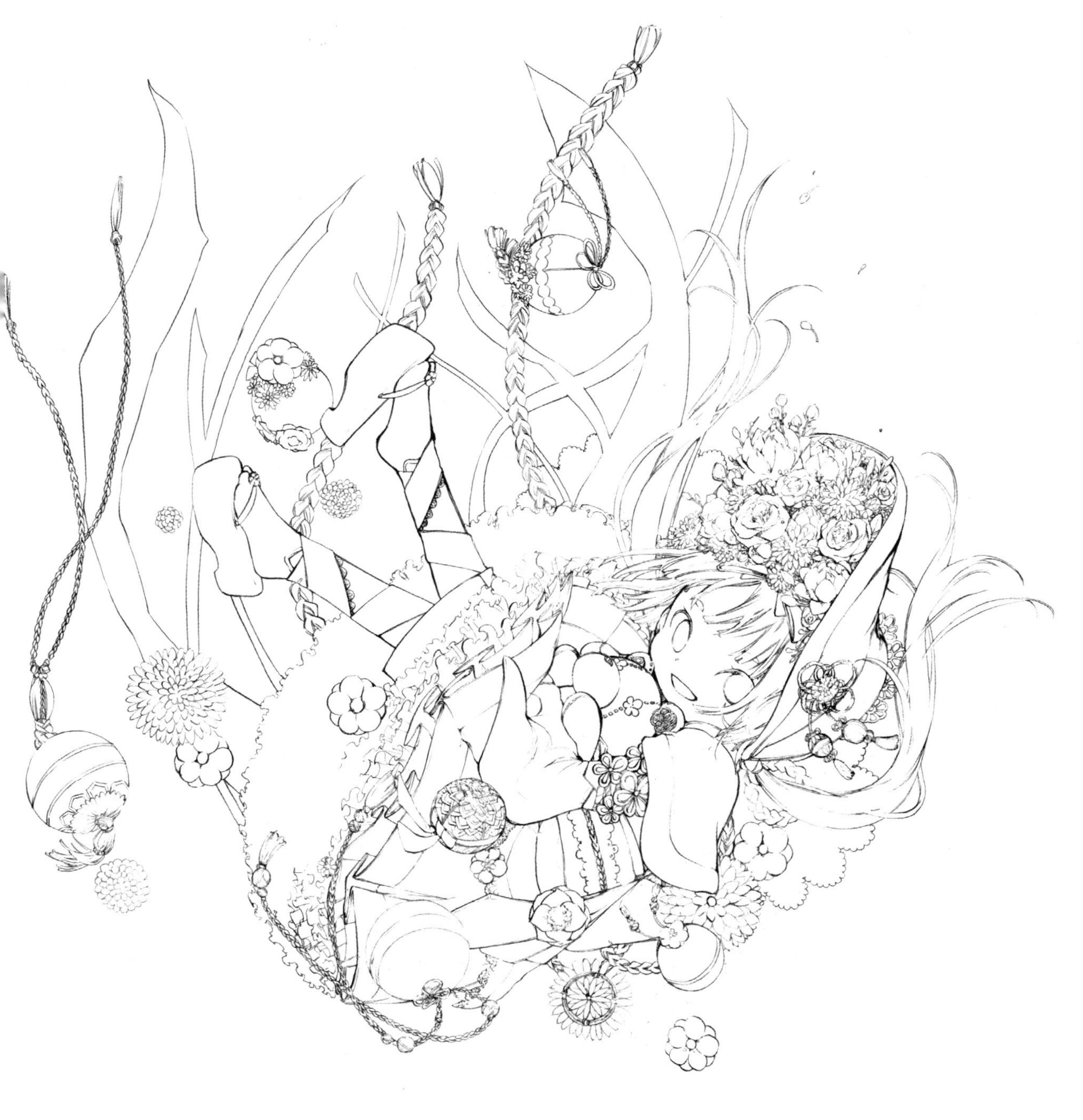

Blending with Multiple Light Colors

This is a technique that uses a large number of colors and blends them to create a soft and gentle atmosphere. It is worry-free coloring since light colors are blended overflowing to a neighboring area.

Selected Ink

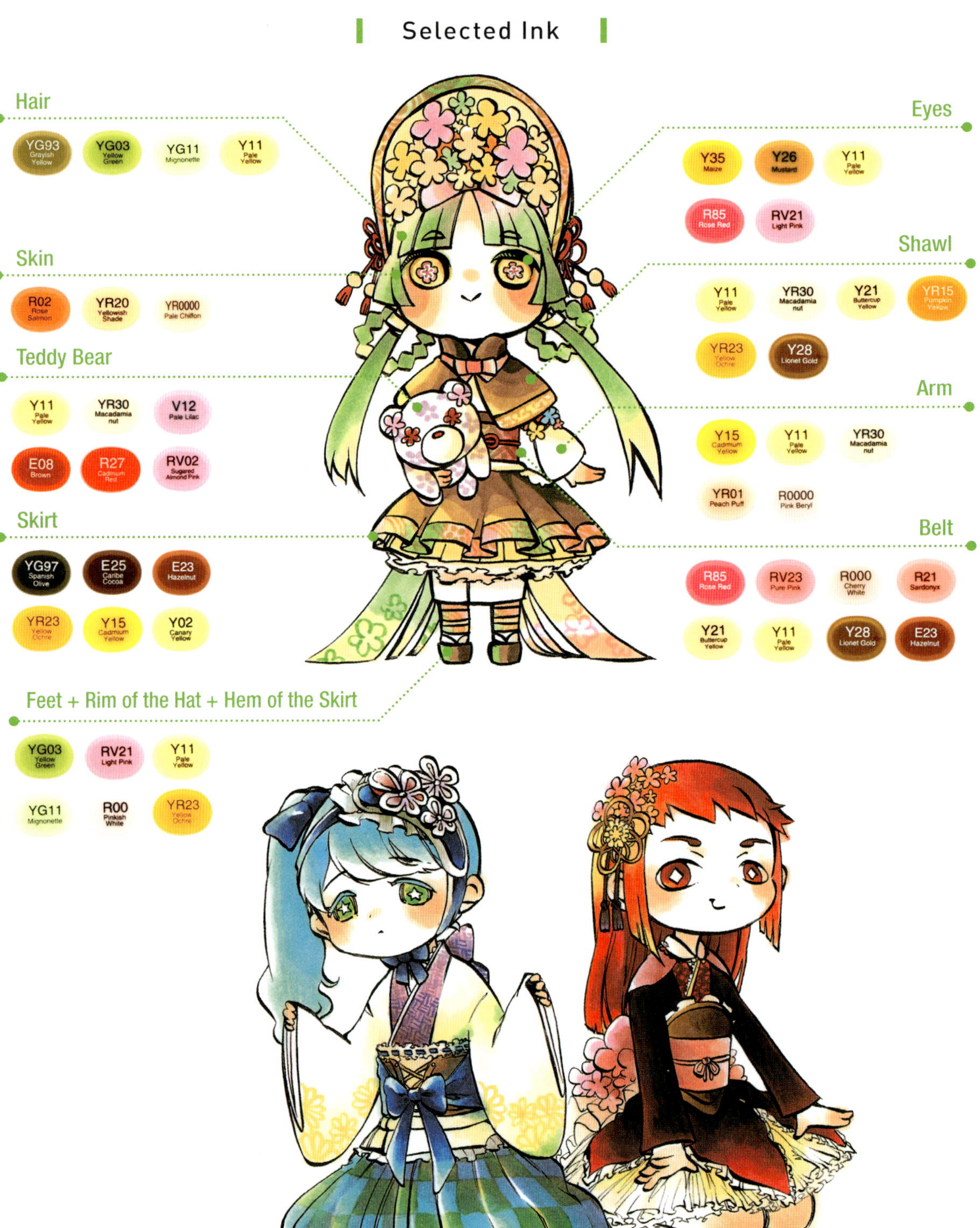

Hair

- YG93 Grayish Yellow
- YG03 Yellow Green
- YG11 Mignonette
- Y11 Pale Yellow

Skin

- R02 Rose Salmon
- YR20 Yellowish Shade
- YR0000 Pale Chiffon

Teddy Bear

- Y11 Pale Yellow
- YR30 Macadamia nut
- V12 Pale Lilac
- E08 Brown
- R27 Cadmium Red
- RV02 Sugared Almond Pink

Skirt

- YG97 Spanish Olive
- E25 Caribe Cocoa
- E23 Hazelnut
- YR23 Yellow Ochre
- Y15 Cadmium Yellow
- Y02 Canary Yellow

Feet + Rim of the Hat + Hem of the Skirt

- YG03 Yellow Green
- RV21 Light Pink
- Y11 Pale Yellow
- YG11 Mignonette
- R00 Pinkish White
- YR23 Yellow Ochre

Eyes

- Y35 Maize
- Y26 Mustard
- Y11 Pale Yellow
- R85 Rose Red
- RV21 Light Pink

Shawl

- Y11 Pale Yellow
- YR30 Macadamia nut
- Y21 Buttercup Yellow
- YR15 Pumpkin Yellow
- YR23 Yellow Ochre
- Y28 Lionet Gold

Arm

- Y15 Cadmium Yellow
- Y11 Pale Yellow
- YR30 Macadamia nut
- YR01 Peach Puff
- R0000 Pink Beryl

Belt

- R85 Rose Red
- RV23 Pure Pink
- R000 Cherry White
- R21 Sardonyx
- Y21 Buttercup Yellow
- Y11 Pale Yellow
- Y28 Lionet Gold
- E23 Hazelnut

Flower-Shaped Pupil

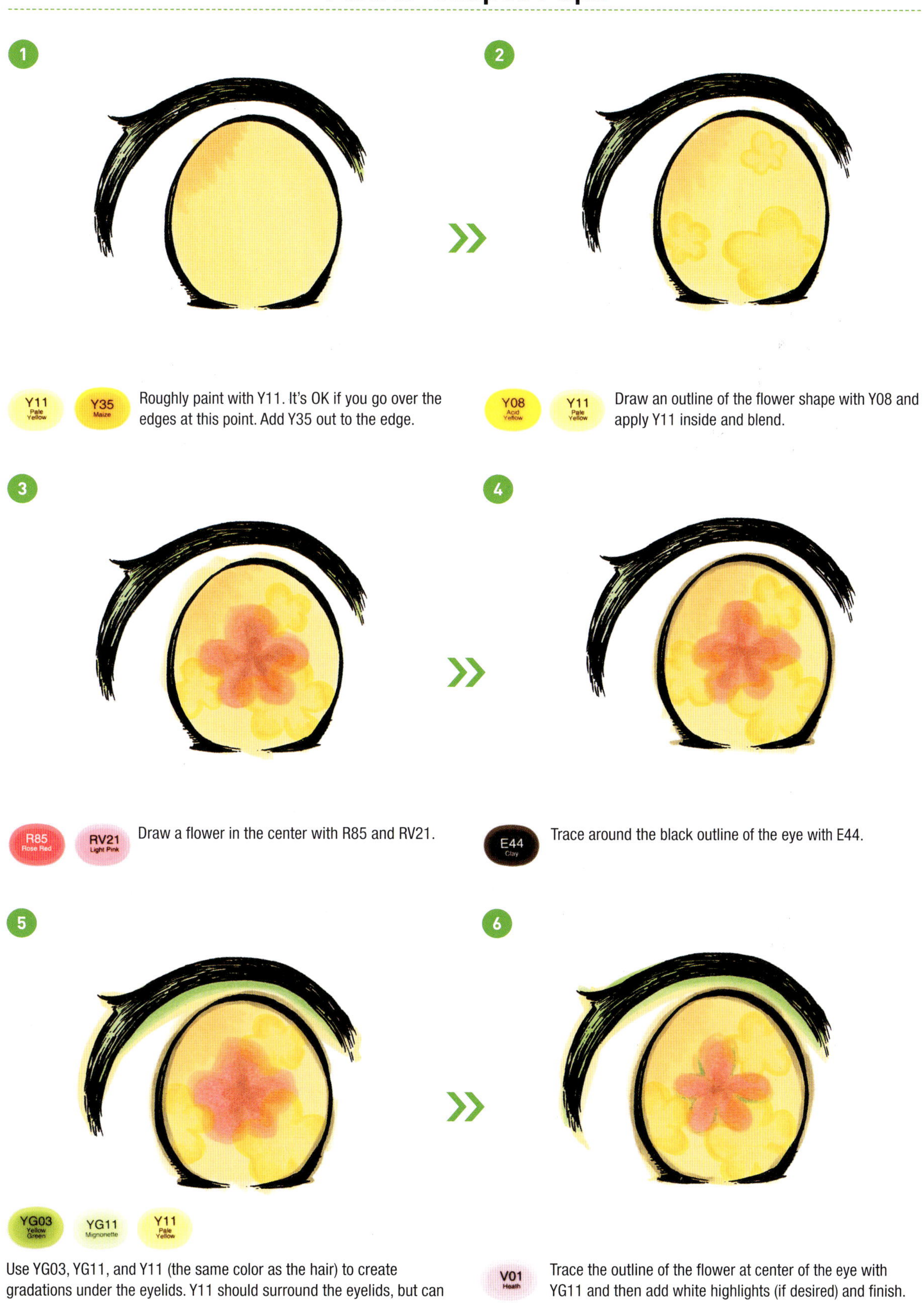

1

Y11 Pale Yellow   **Y35** Maize — Roughly paint with Y11. It's OK if you go over the edges at this point. Add Y35 out to the edge.

2

Y08 Acid Yellow   **Y11** Pale Yellow — Draw an outline of the flower shape with Y08 and apply Y11 inside and blend.

3

R85 Rose Red   **RV21** Light Pink — Draw a flower in the center with R85 and RV21.

4

E44 Clay — Trace around the black outline of the eye with E44.

5

YG03 Yellow Green   **YG11** Mignonette   **Y11** Pale Yellow — Use YG03, YG11, and Y11 (the same color as the hair) to create gradations under the eyelids. Y11 should surround the eyelids, but can extend over.

6

V01 Heath — Trace the outline of the flower at center of the eye with YG11 and then add white highlights (if desired) and finish.

Facial Expressions with Blending

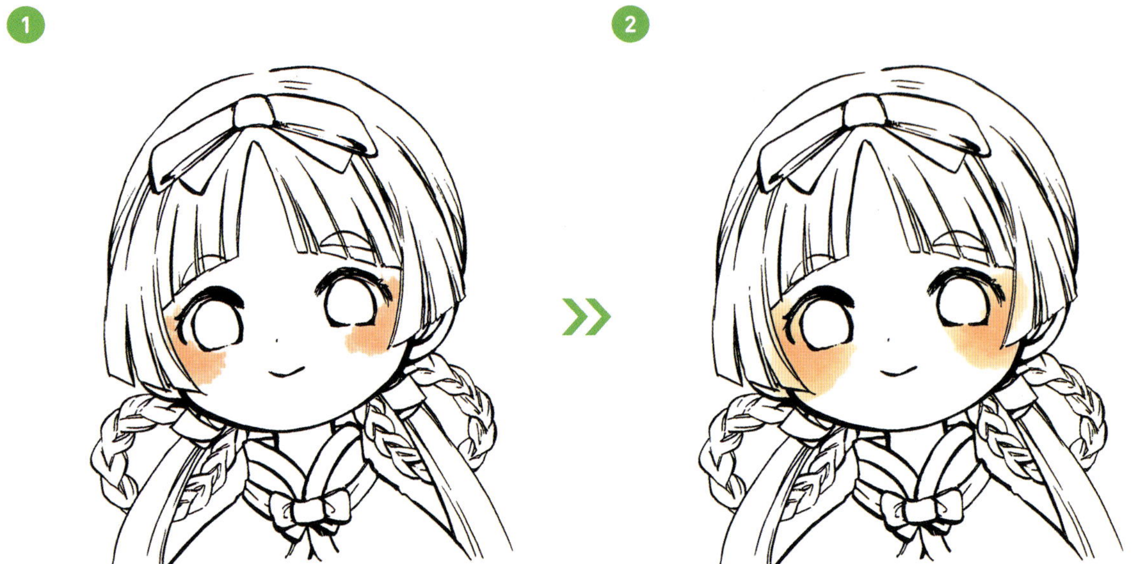

1 Apply R02 in a large circle at the outer corner of the eyes. Apply from the center outward since it will blend with other colors.

R02 — Rose Salmon

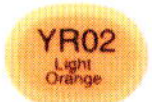

2 Apply YR02 over R02 and soften the edges. Purposefully spread ink outward a little. Layer the colors as you trace the edges to produce a nice smooth look.

YR02 — Light Orange

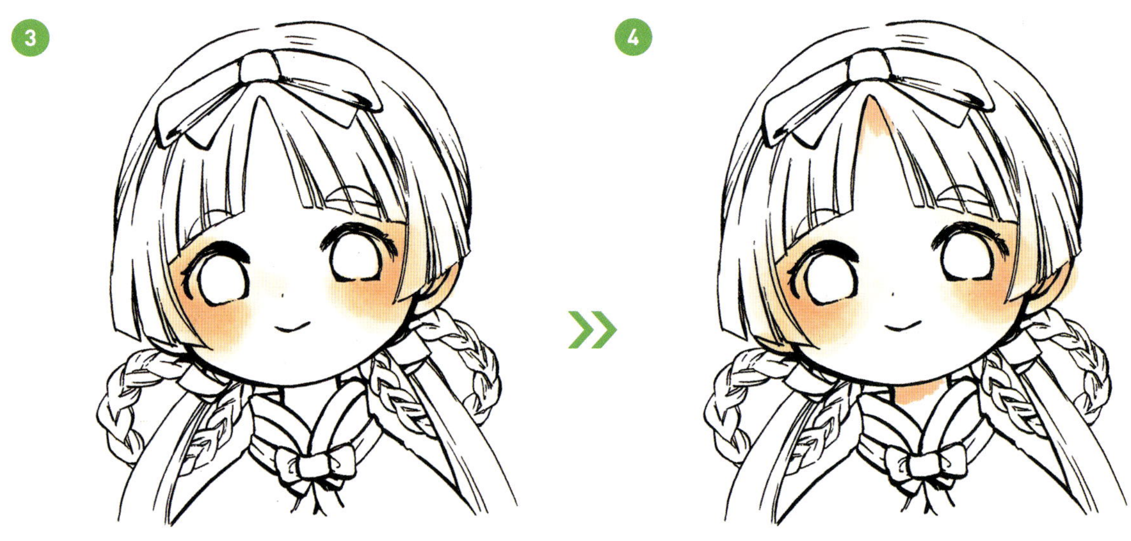

3 Apply YR0000 to the entire area and blend. Let it spread as much as you like. Even if you let it spread a bit too much, it will just become part of the design!

YR0000 — Pale Chiffon

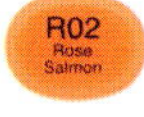

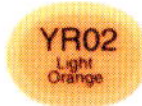

4 Similar to 3, start by applying R02 on the ears and neck and then add YR20 and YR0000 and blend. As far as overflow goes, use a little for R02, a larger amount for YR20, and an even larger amount for YR0000.

R02 — Rose Salmon · YR02 — Light Orange · YR0000 — Pale Chiffon

⑤ 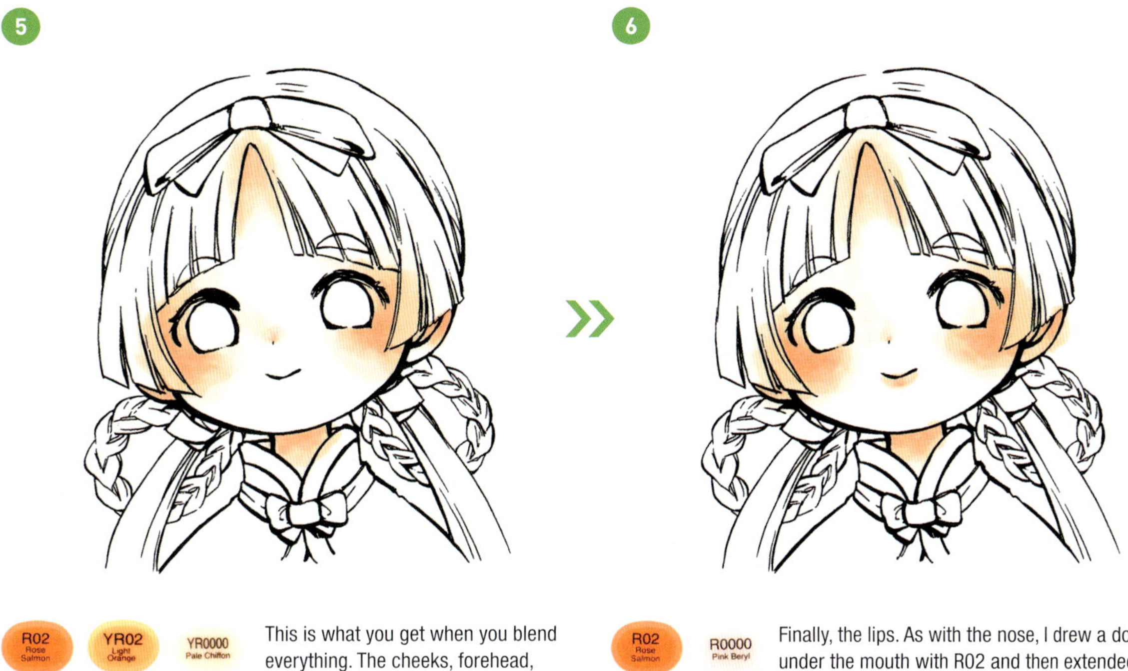

R02 Rose Salmon · YR02 Light Orange · YR0000 Pale Chiffon — This is what you get when you blend everything. The cheeks, forehead, ears, neck, and nose received a "dot" of R02 which was then blended with YR0000.

⑥

R02 Rose Salmon · R0000 Pink Beryl — Finally, the lips. As with the nose, I drew a dot under the mouth with R02 and then extended it to both sides with R0000.

Green Hair Being Hit by Light

① 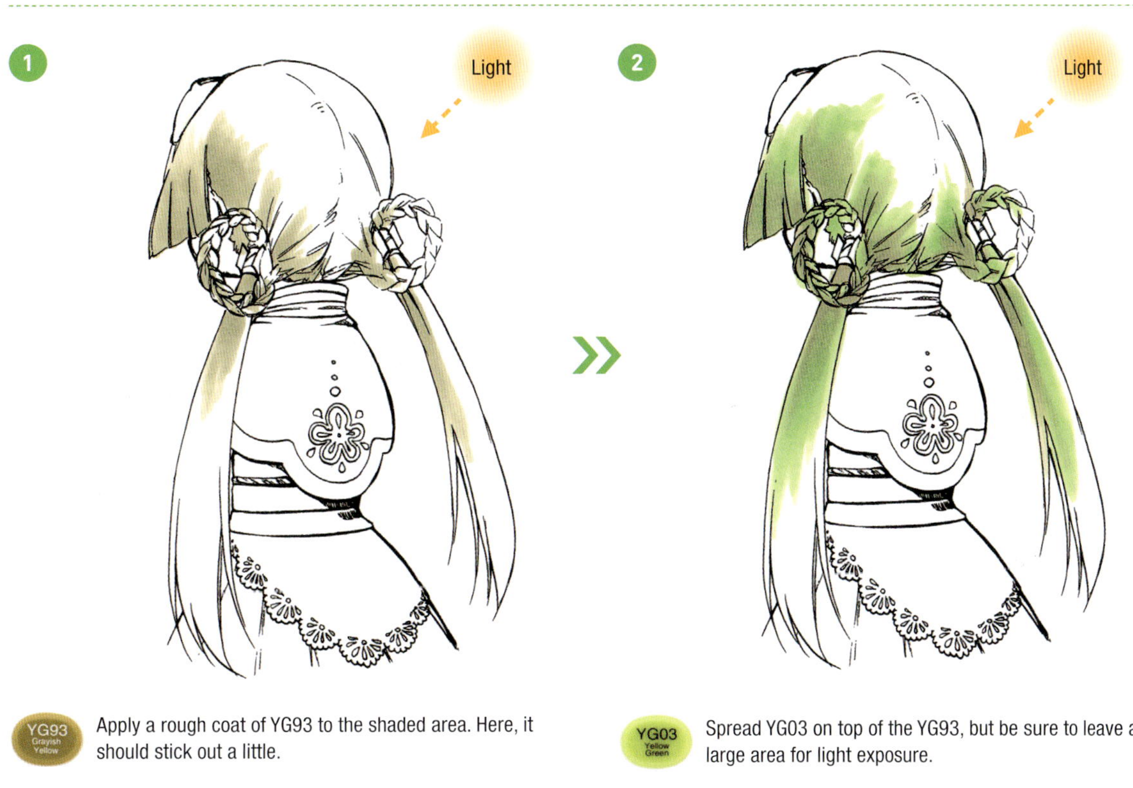

YG93 Grayish Yellow — Apply a rough coat of YG93 to the shaded area. Here, it should stick out a little.

②

YG03 Yellow Green — Spread YG03 on top of the YG93, but be sure to leave a large area for light exposure.

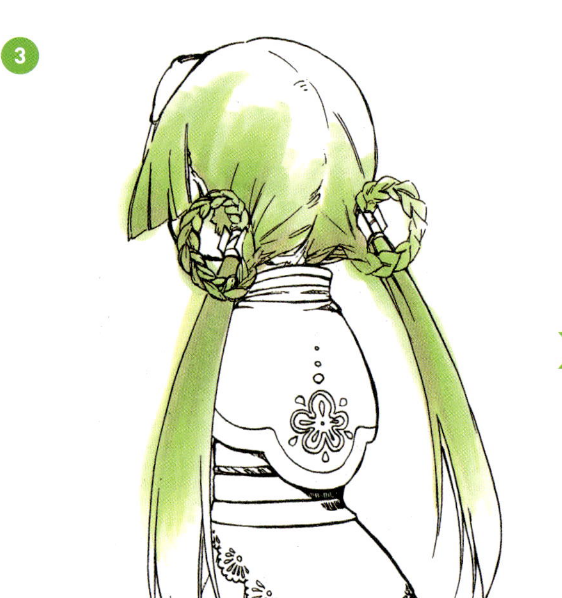

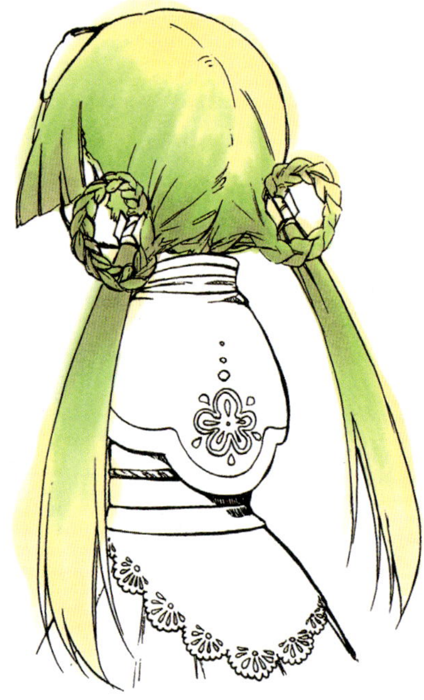

YG11
Mignonette

Apply another coat of YG11 on top of 2. Spread it all over the top of 2, but be careful not to spread it on the skin.

YG11
Mignonette

Apply YG11 over everything and blend the colors applied from 1 to 3. Spread the colors out boldly. The side that is exposed to light should be fuller.

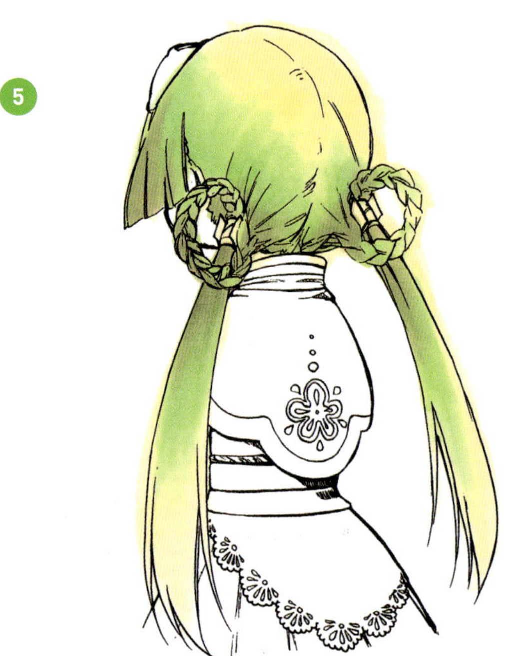

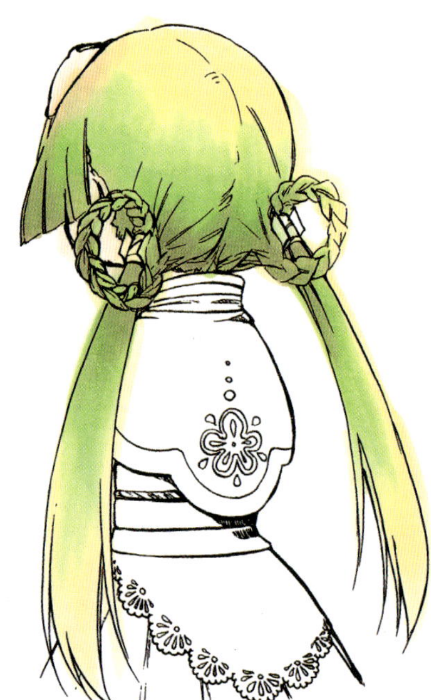

YG93
Grayish Yellow **YG11**
Mignonette

Use YG93 and YG11 to draw in the thin areas, and also color over the shadows to make them darker.

YG93
Grayish Yellow **YG11**
Mignonette **YG03**
Yellow Green

Depending on the color of the skin or ribbon, you may need to worry about color bleeding. In such cases, paint the overhang of the skin or ribbon at the end. This will allow for a clean, complete project.

Japanese-Style Clothing Texture (*Obi*)

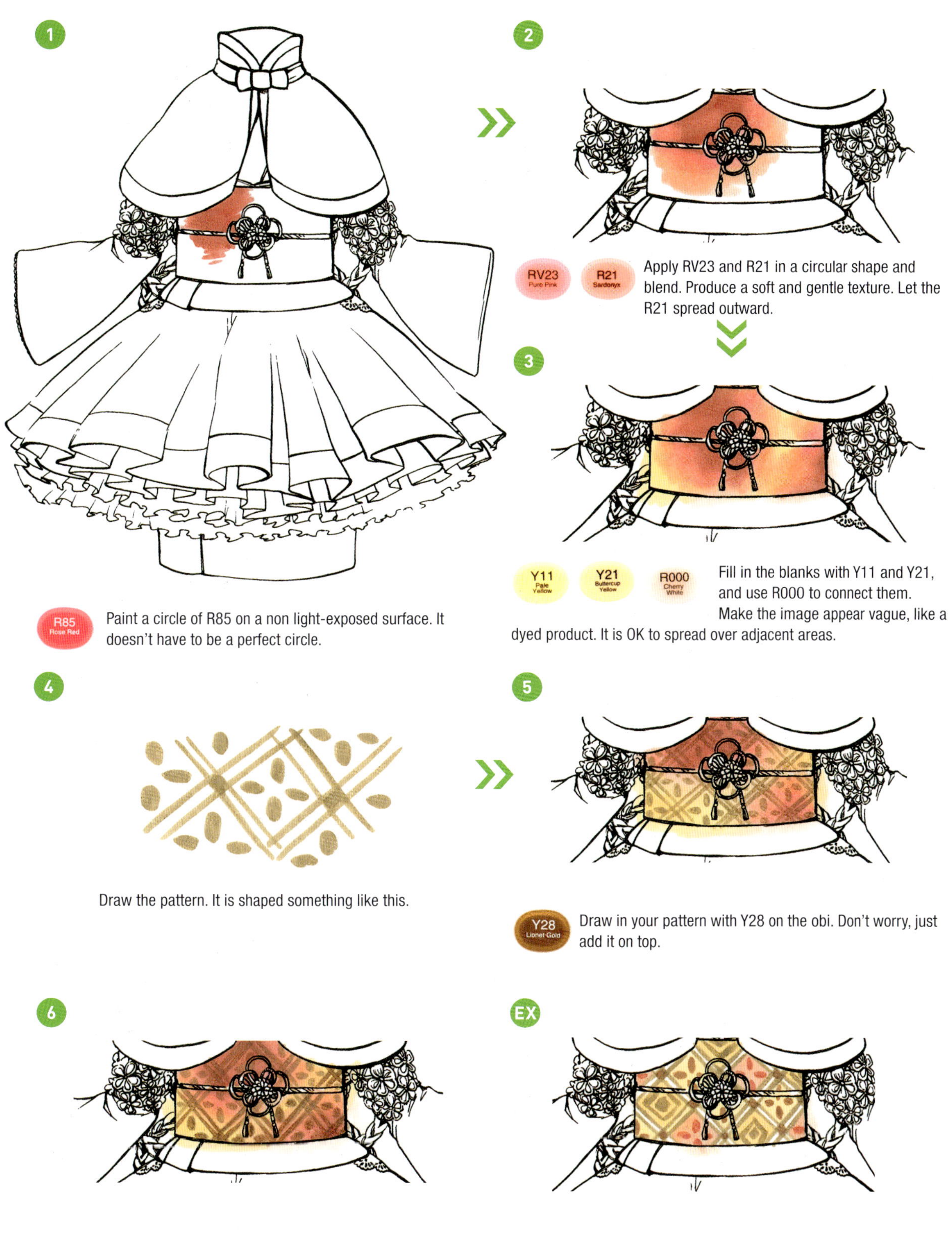

1 — **R85** Rose Red
Paint a circle of R85 on a non light-exposed surface. It doesn't have to be a perfect circle.

2 — **RV23** Pure Pink · **R21** Sardonyx
Apply RV23 and R21 in a circular shape and blend. Produce a soft and gentle texture. Let the R21 spread outward.

3 — **Y11** Pale Yellow · **Y21** Buttercup Yellow · **R000** Cherry White
Fill in the blanks with Y11 and Y21, and use R000 to connect them. Make the image appear vague, like a dyed product. It is OK to spread over adjacent areas.

4 — Draw the pattern. It is shaped something like this.

5 — **Y28** Lionet Gold
Draw in your pattern with Y28 on the obi. Don't worry, just add it on top.

6 — **E23** Hazelnut
Trace the bottom of Y28 with E23 to create a 3D effect.

EX — It also works to use the colors from 1 to 6 as a pattern itself. Don't forget to deliberately spread color over 3.

Skirt and Mantle

1 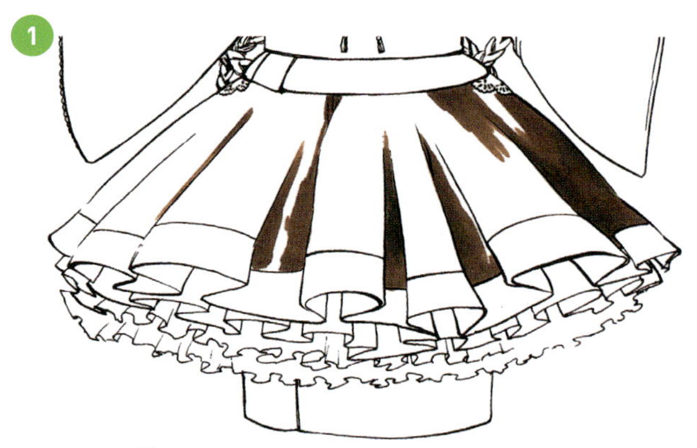

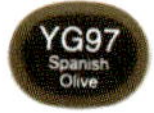 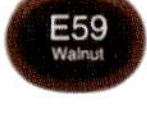

While blending YG97 with E59, draw the part that will become the shadow. It can be colored any way you wish, but be careful not to overflow the edges.

2 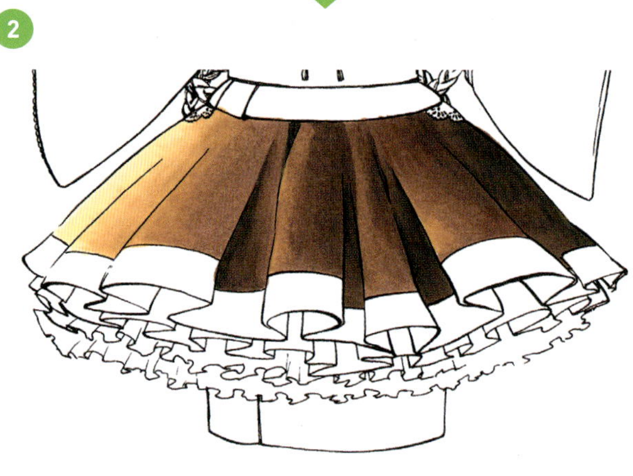

Apply gradation using YR23 > Y11 > YR30.

3 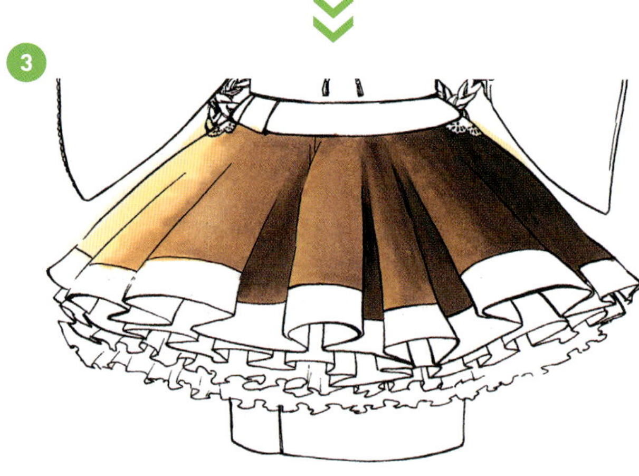

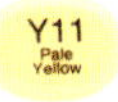

Finally, apply Y11 over everything and soften the light areas. It's OK to if color spreads beyond the edge.

1 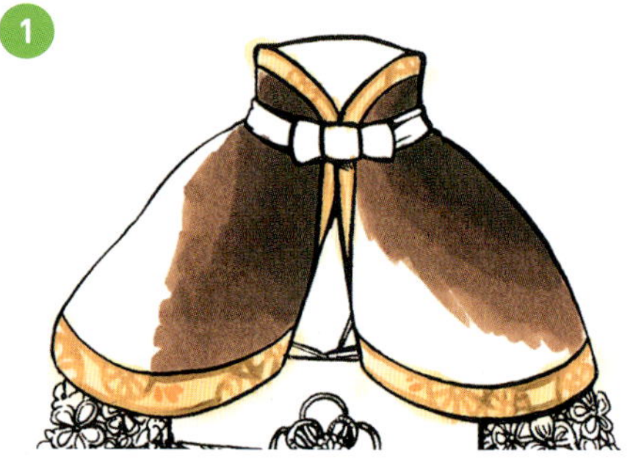

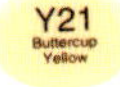 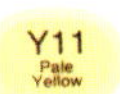 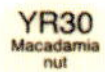

Apply Y21 to a portion of the mantle and blend with Y11 and YR30. Y11 and YR30 can be spread over to neighboring areas.

2 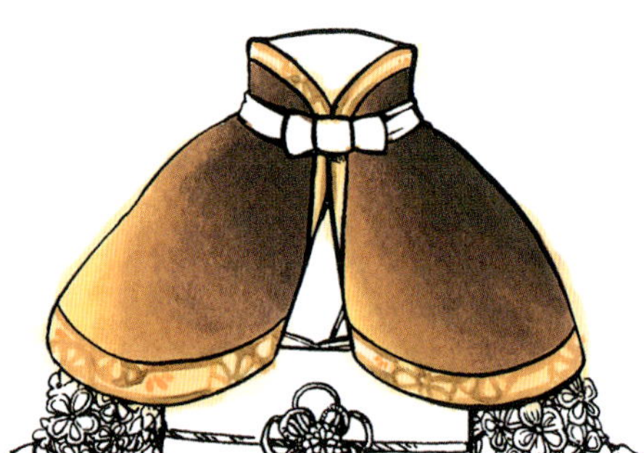

 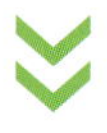

The blending tends to bleed, so let it sit for about 20 minutes after 1. Then, draw the pattern with YR33.

3 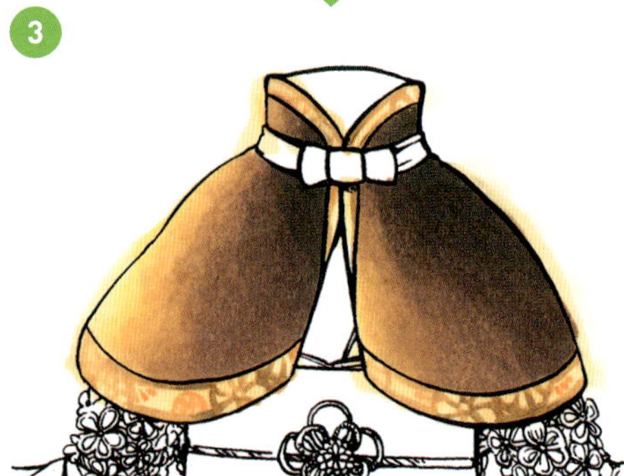

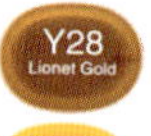 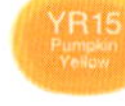

Partially overlay Y28 to YR23. Do not entirely cover YR23 with Y28. Add a little more to the pattern with YR15 and the edge is done!

Inside the Skirt and the Hem of the Mantle

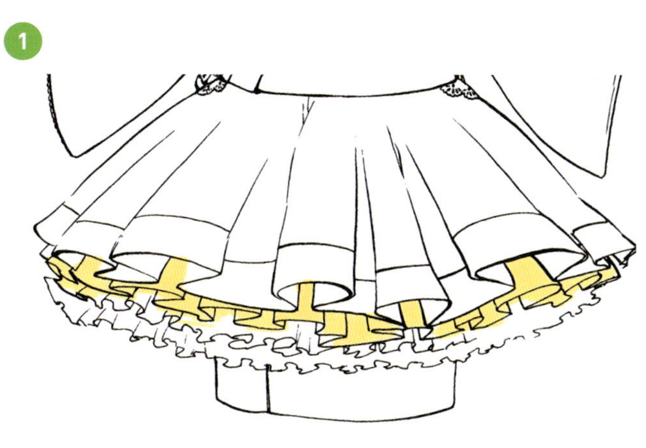

1 Y15 Cadmium Yellow — Color the second ruffle from the top with Y15. It doesn't have to be precise.

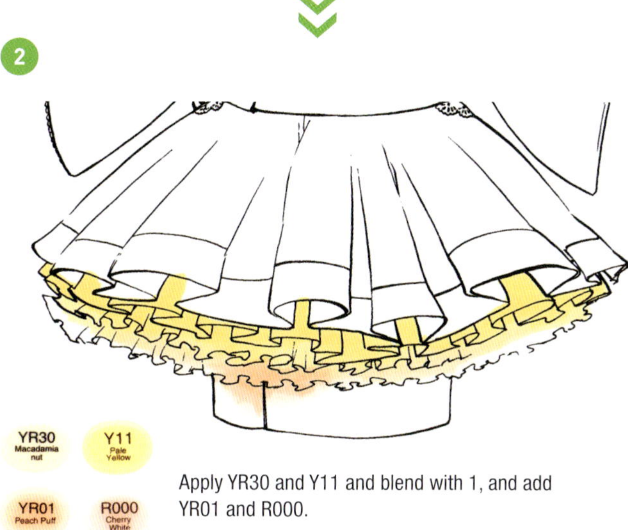

2 YR30 Macadamia nut / Y11 Pale Yellow / YR01 Peach Puff / R000 Cherry White — Apply YR30 and Y11 and blend with 1, and add YR01 and R000.

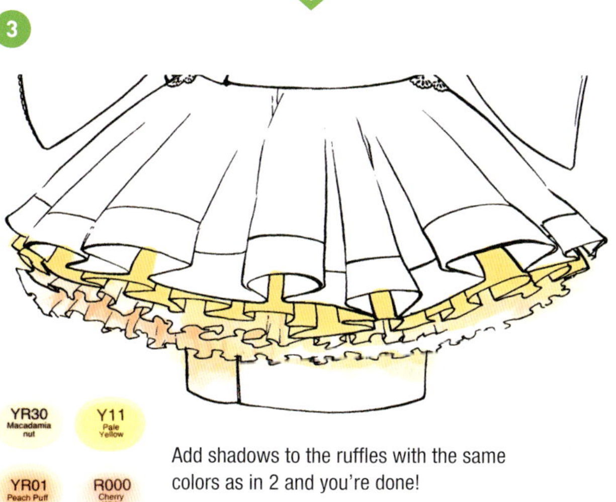

3 YR30 Macadamia nut / Y11 Pale Yellow / YR01 Peach Puff / R000 Cherry White — Add shadows to the ruffles with the same colors as in 2 and you're done!

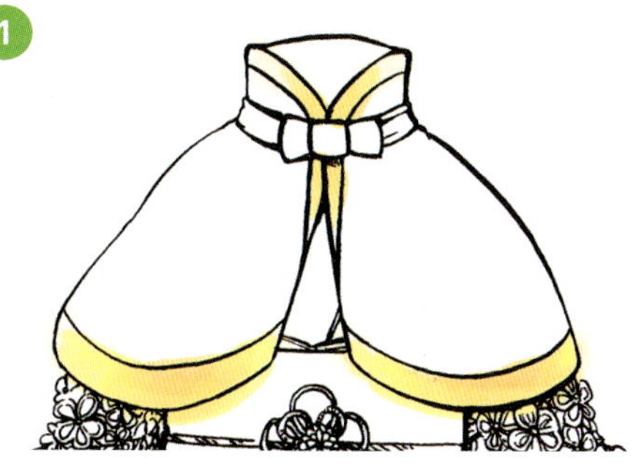

1 YG97 Spanish Olive / E59 Walnut / E25 Caribe Cocoa — 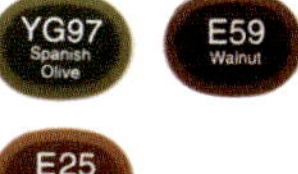 Color shadows in the following order: YG97 > E59 > E25. Keep spreading color to neighboring areas as minimum as possible.

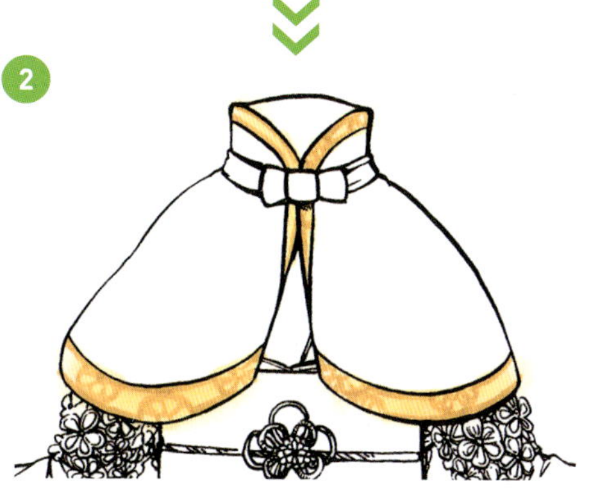

2 YR23 Yellow Ochre / Y15 Cadmium Yellow / Y11 Pale Yellow — 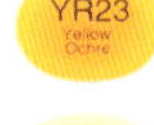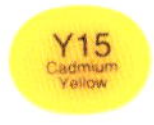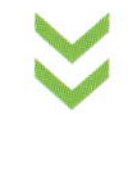 Then blend with YR23 > Y15 > Y11. It's OK if these three colors spread over to neighboring areas.

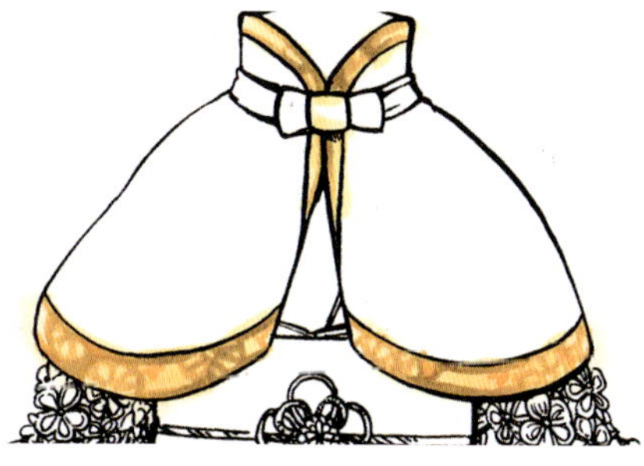

3 Y11 Pale Yellow — 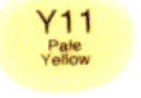 Apply Y11, in the direction of the light, in a circular motion. Blend to finish. It's OK to overflow here too.

Coloring Feet and Shoes

 **YG00** Mimosa Yellow

1 Apply YG0. Be careful not to overflow.

 **YG11** Mignonette

2 Blend with YG11 and Y11. For a cute look be sure to apply in a circular motion. It is OK to overflow here.

 **RV21** Light Pink

3 Apply RV21 to the opposite margins, making sure that it doesn't spill into the already painted sections. Be careful not to overflow.

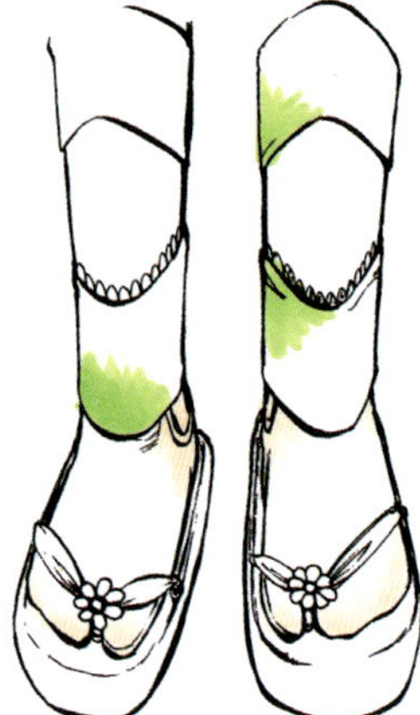

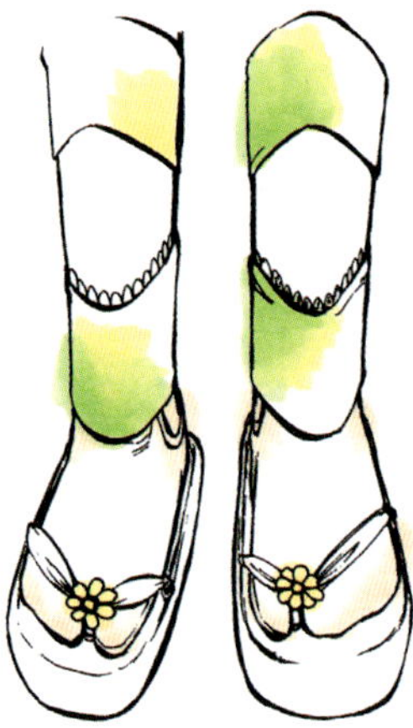

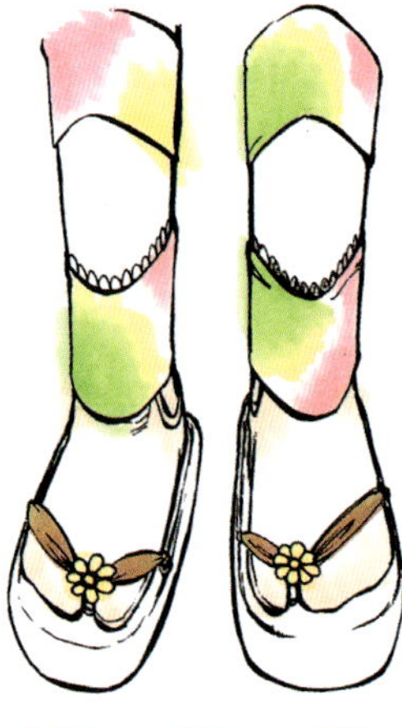

R00 Pinkish White

Color heels and toes with R00.

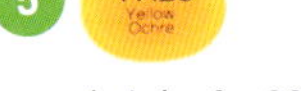 **Y21** Buttercup Yellow   **Y11** Pale Yellow

Put Y21 in the center of the flower. Go around the flower and apply Y11 that protrudes slightly.

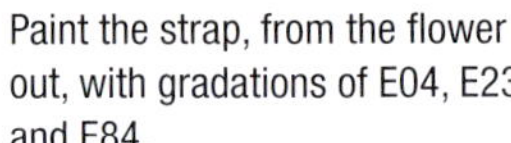 **E04** Lipstick Natural   **E23** Hazelnut   **E84** Khaki

Paint the strap, from the flower out, with gradations of E04, E23, and E84.

4  **R00** Pinkish White   **Y11** Pale Yellow

Blend the RV21 with R00 and Y11. Connect with the parts colored in 2. It's OK, if it spread out to adjacent areas.

5 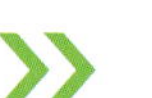 **YR23** Yellow Ochre

Let dry for 20 to 30 minutes, then add in patterns with YR23.

6 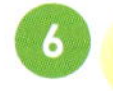 **YG00** Mimosa Yellow   **YG11** Mignonette   **Y11** Pale Yellow   **RV21** Light Pink

R00 Pinkish White   **Y11** Pale Yellow

Fill in the gaps between the patterns with the colors used in 1 to 4 as you desire to complete.

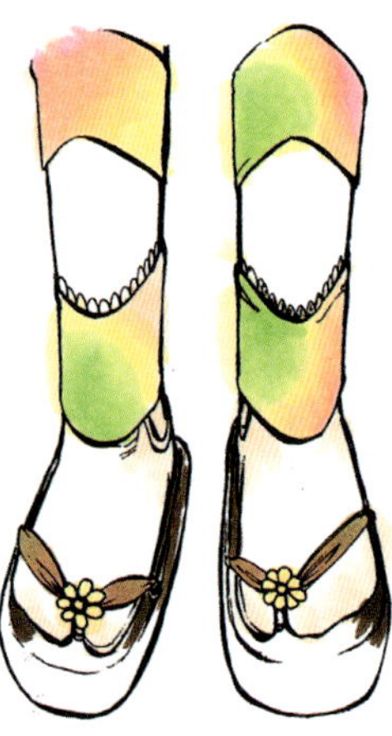

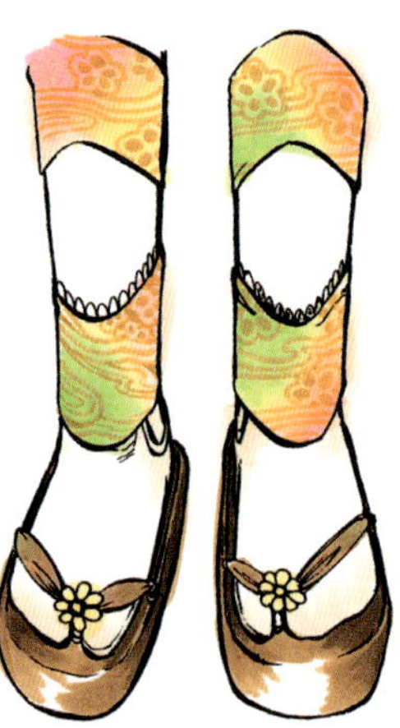

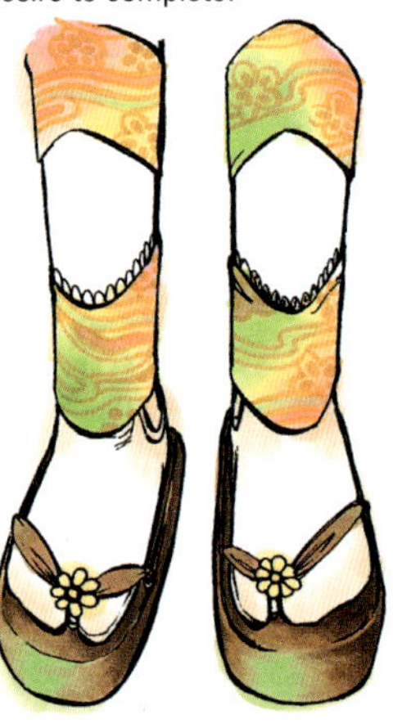

E89 Pecan

Apply E89 to the area where the darkest shadows form.

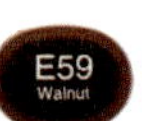 **E59** Walnut   **E23** Hazelnut

Soften the edges of E89 with E59 and E23. The E23 can spread over outside of the edge but leave out where the light hits.

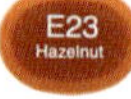 **Y11** Pale Yellow

Add your favorite color to the leftover light area. In this case, Y11 was added. It's OK to overflow here too.

Decorative Flowers

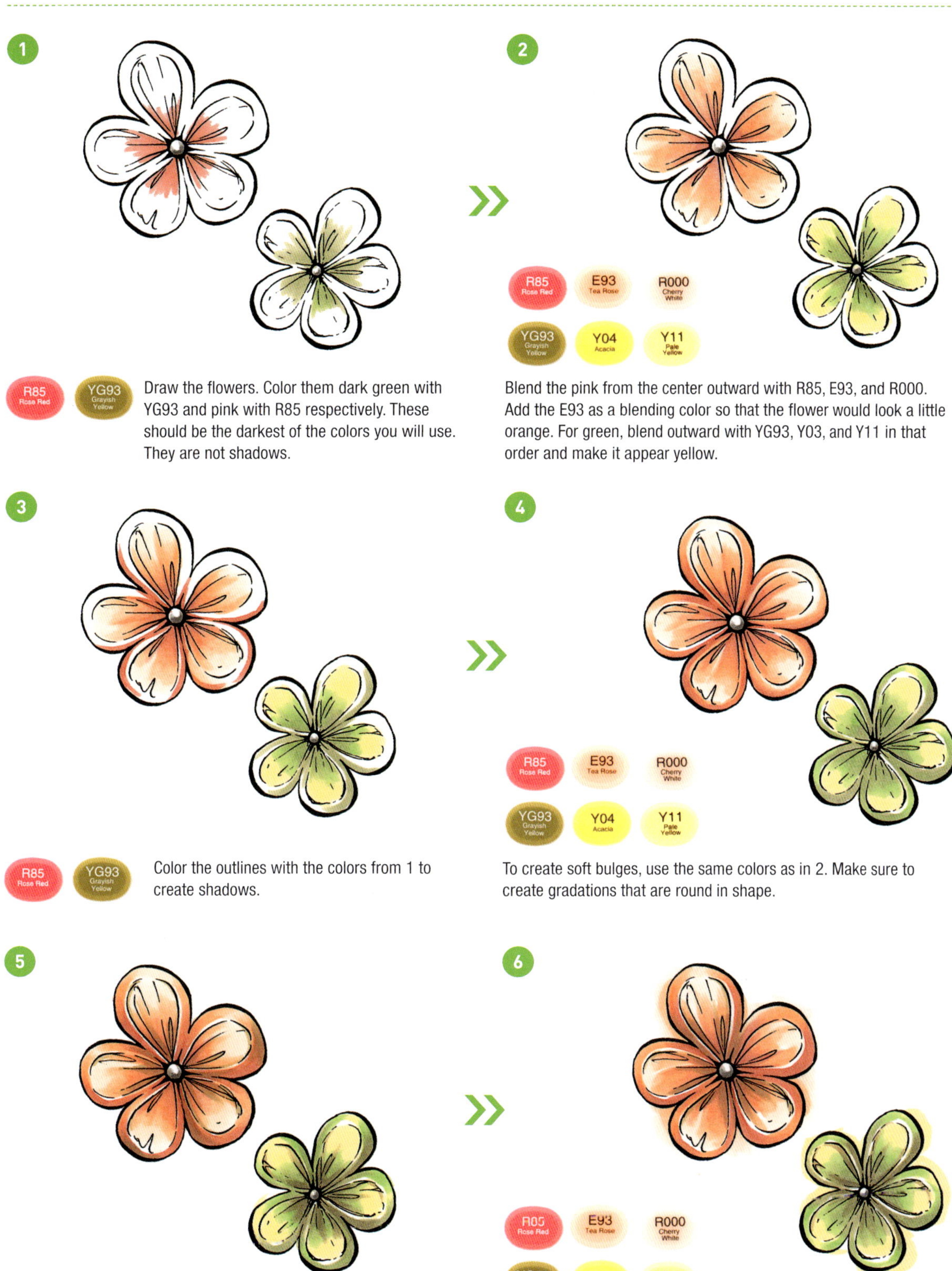

1 — R85 (Rose Red), YG93 (Grayish Yellow)

Draw the flowers. Color them dark green with YG93 and pink with R85 respectively. These should be the darkest of the colors you will use. They are not shadows.

2 — R85 (Rose Red), E93 (Tea Rose), R000 (Cherry White), YG93 (Grayish Yellow), Y04 (Acacia), Y11 (Pale Yellow)

Blend the pink from the center outward with R85, E93, and R000. Add the E93 as a blending color so that the flower would look a little orange. For green, blend outward with YG93, Y03, and Y11 in that order and make it appear yellow.

3 — R85 (Rose Red), YG93 (Grayish Yellow)

Color the outlines with the colors from 1 to create shadows.

4 — R85 (Rose Red), E93 (Tea Rose), R000 (Cherry White), YG93 (Grayish Yellow), Y04 (Acacia), Y11 (Pale Yellow)

To create soft bulges, use the same colors as in 2. Make sure to create gradations that are round in shape.

5 — E84 (Khaki)

Lightly shade with E84.

6 — R85 (Rose Red), E93 (Tea Rose), R000 (Cherry White), YG93 (Grayish Yellow), Y04 (Acacia), Y11 (Pale Yellow)

If the colors don't overflow properly, just go back and let the color spread. Then, you're done!

Transiti

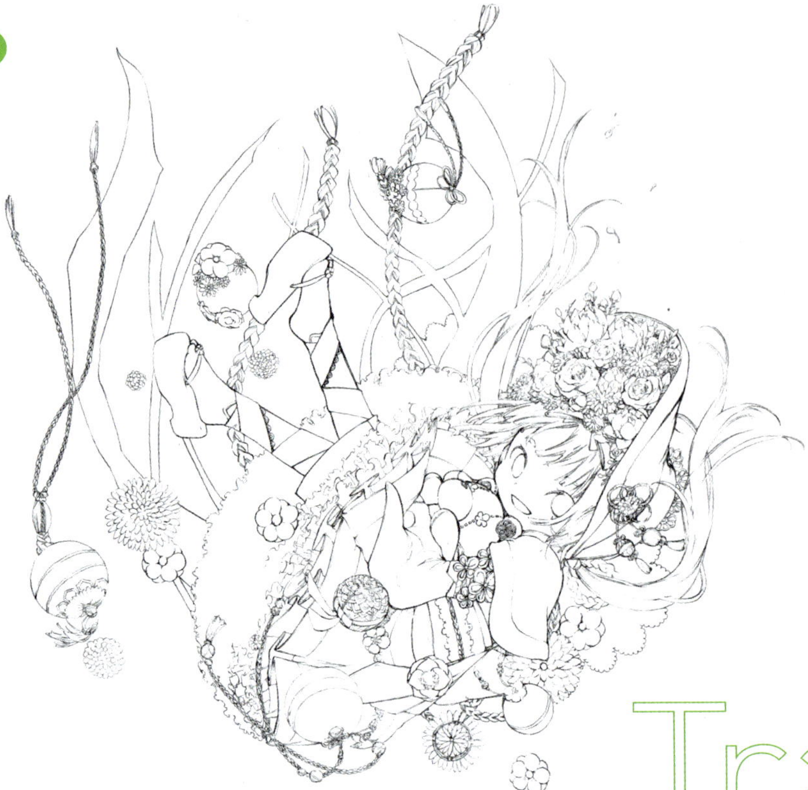

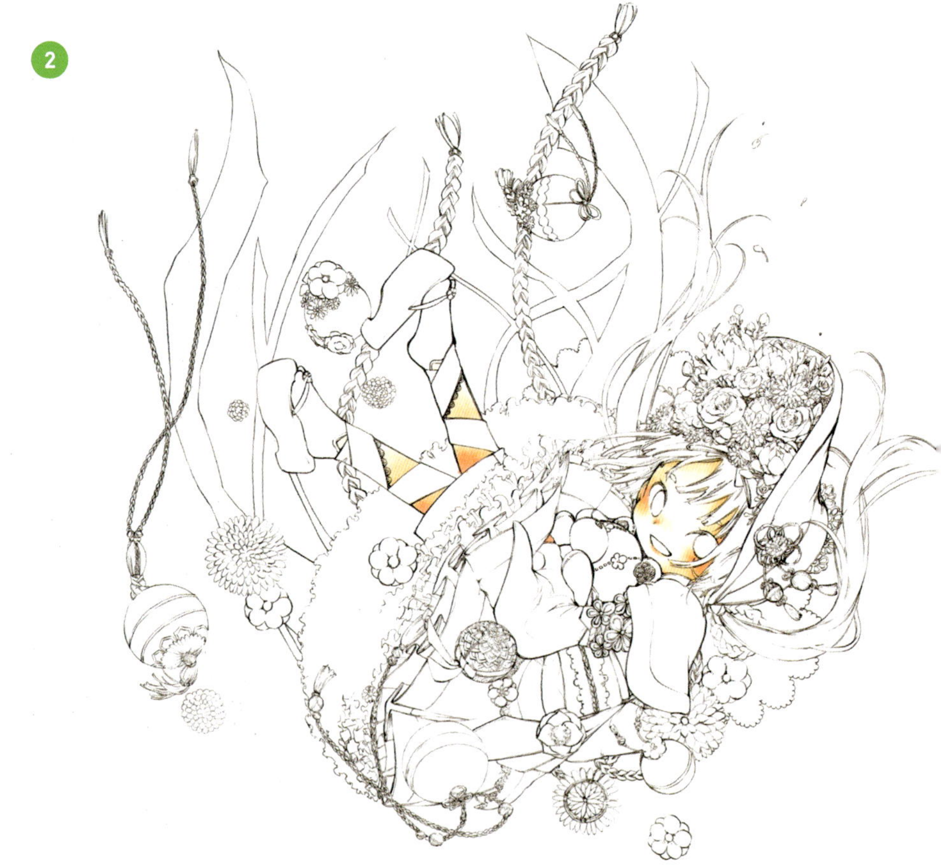

3

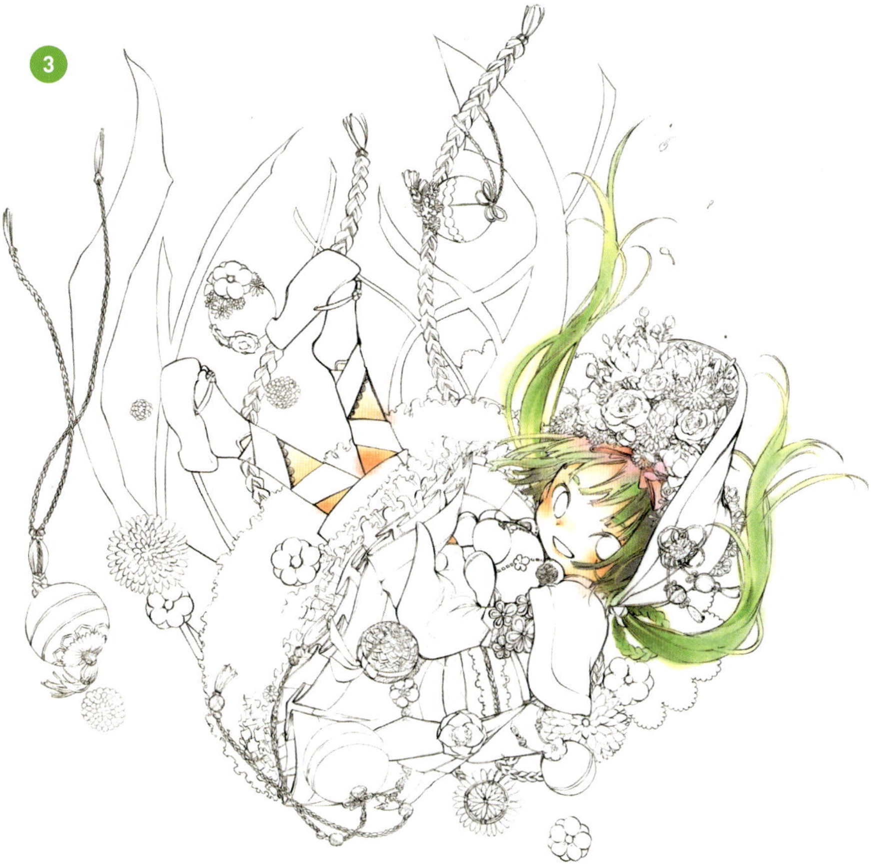

on

Next >>

4

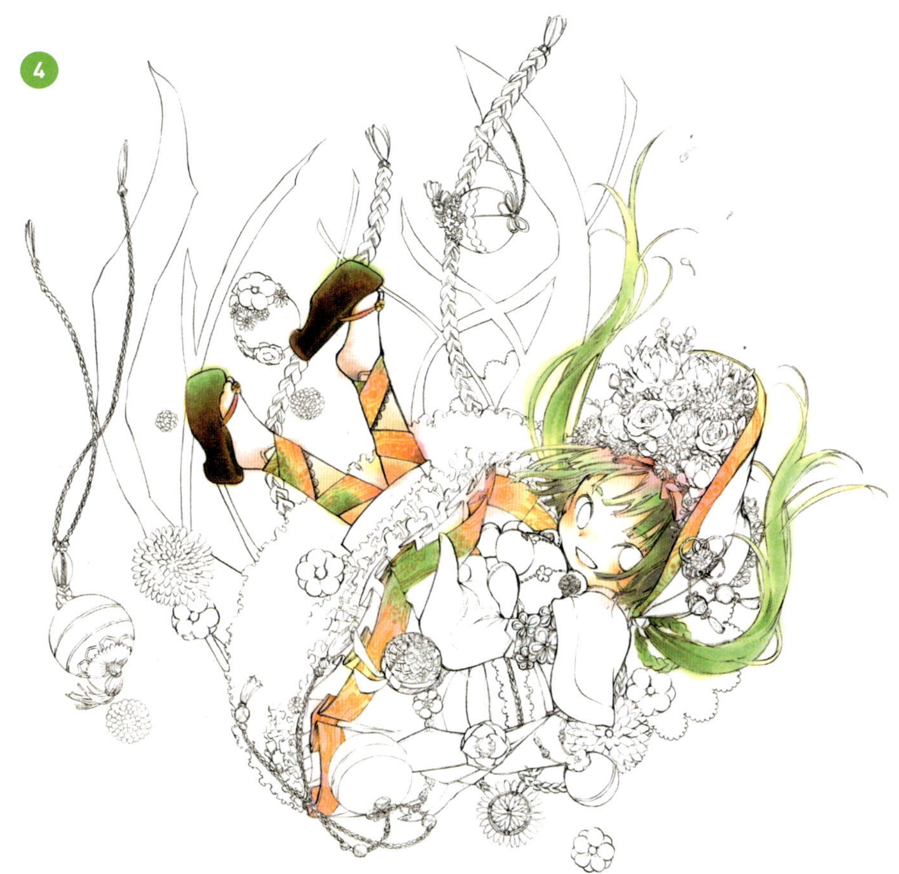

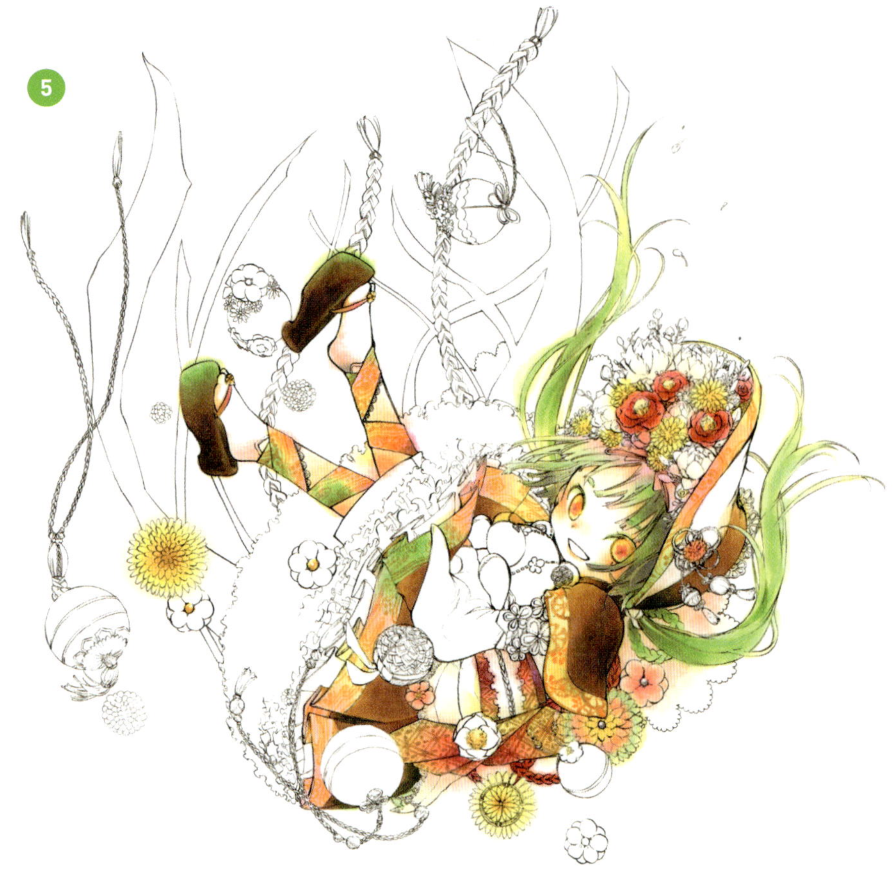

6

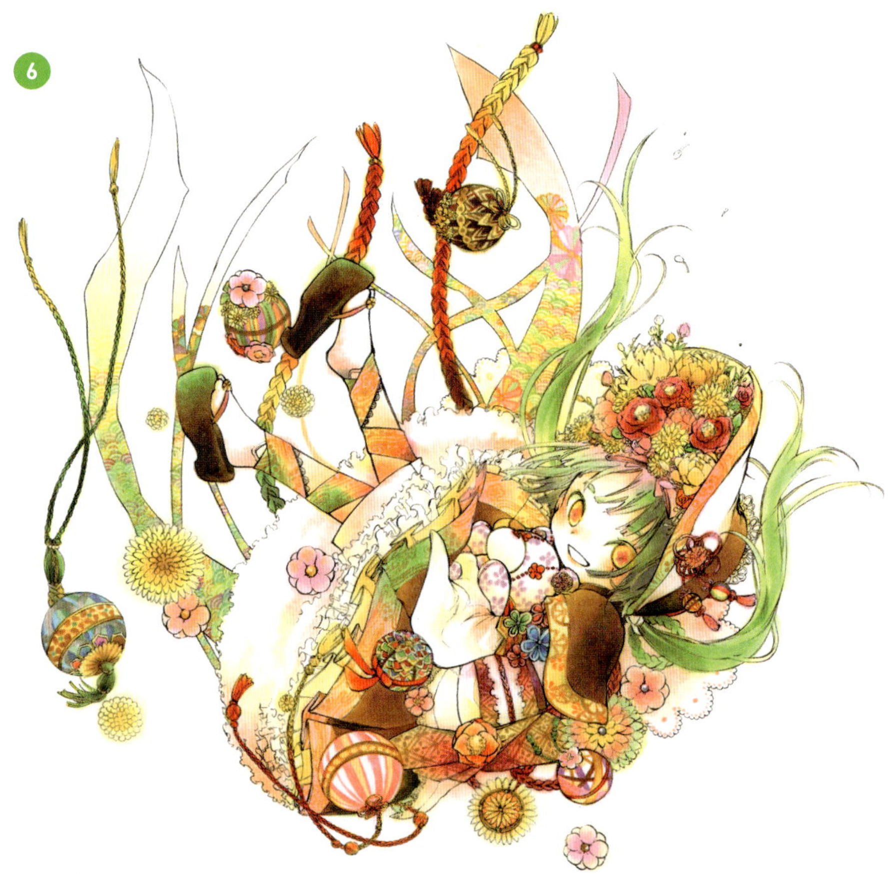

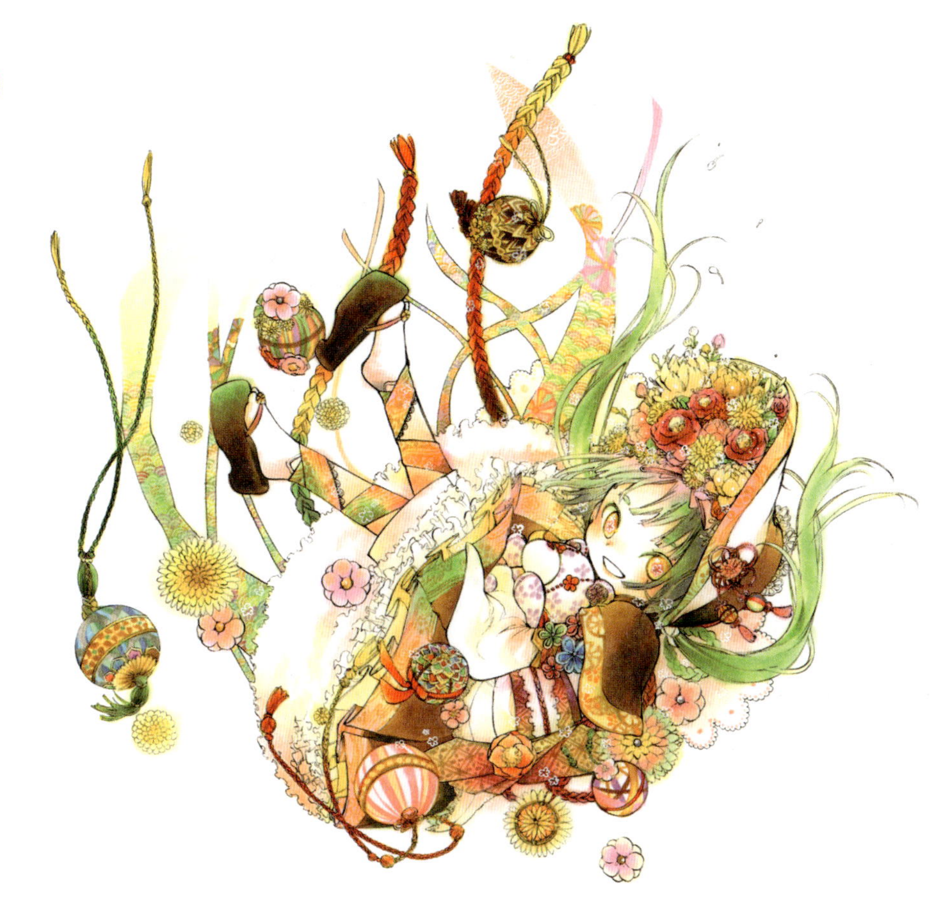

Transition

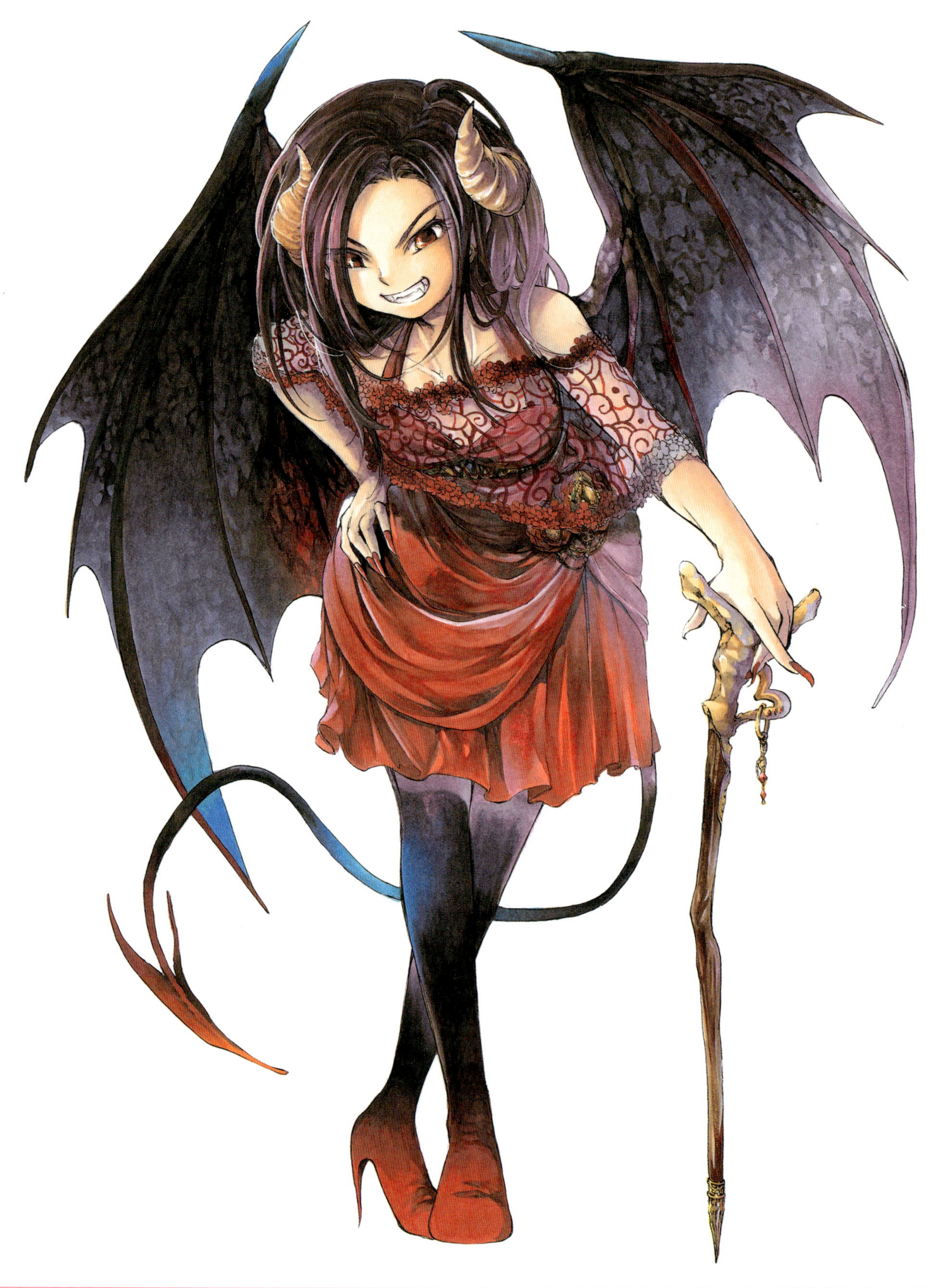

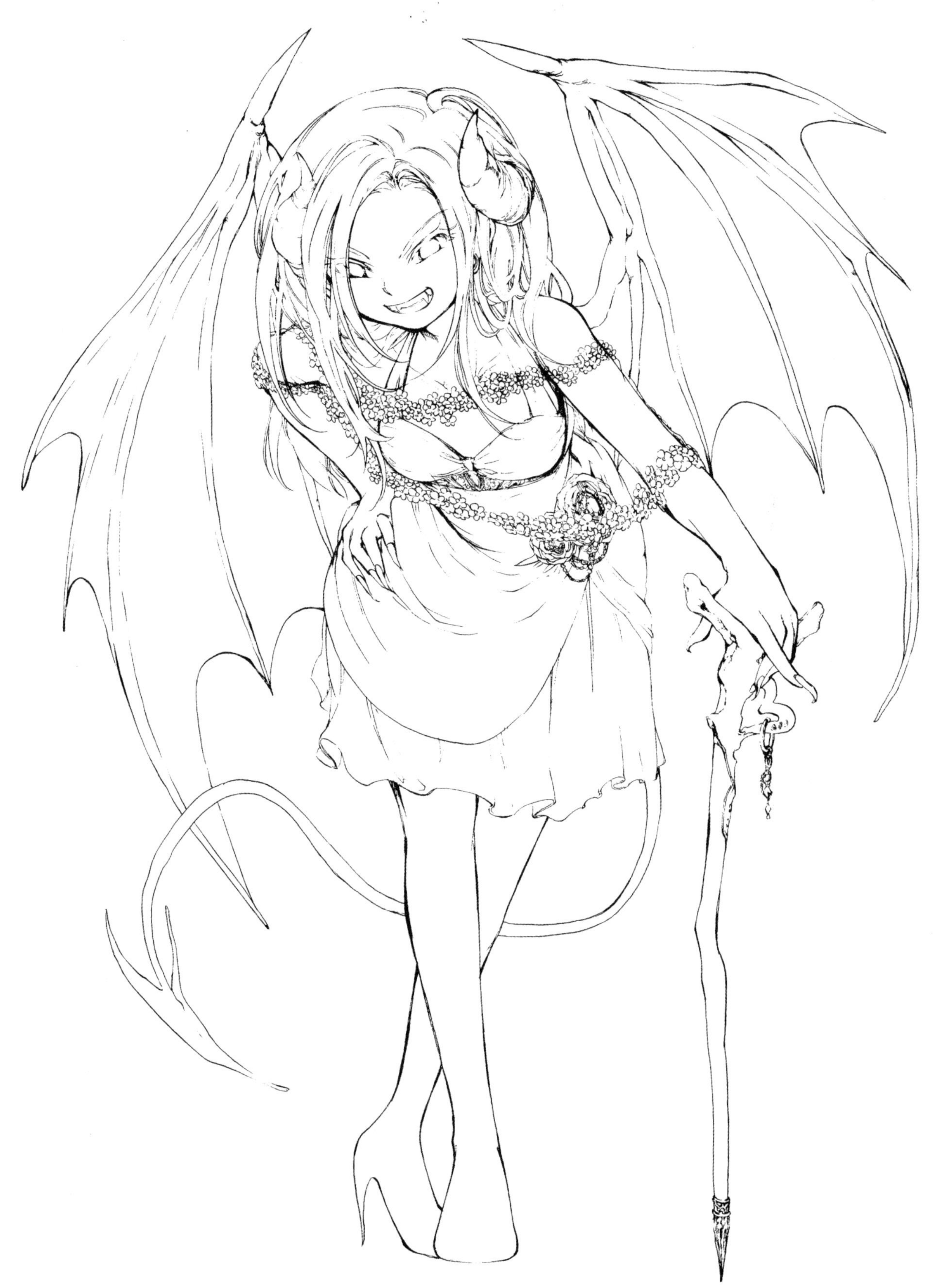

Fill Shadows with Special Colors

This is a technique that uses colored shadows to create expressions that match the location and atmosphere of the character. You have to think first about the colors and then unify them, but this allows you to achieve unique results.

Selected Ink

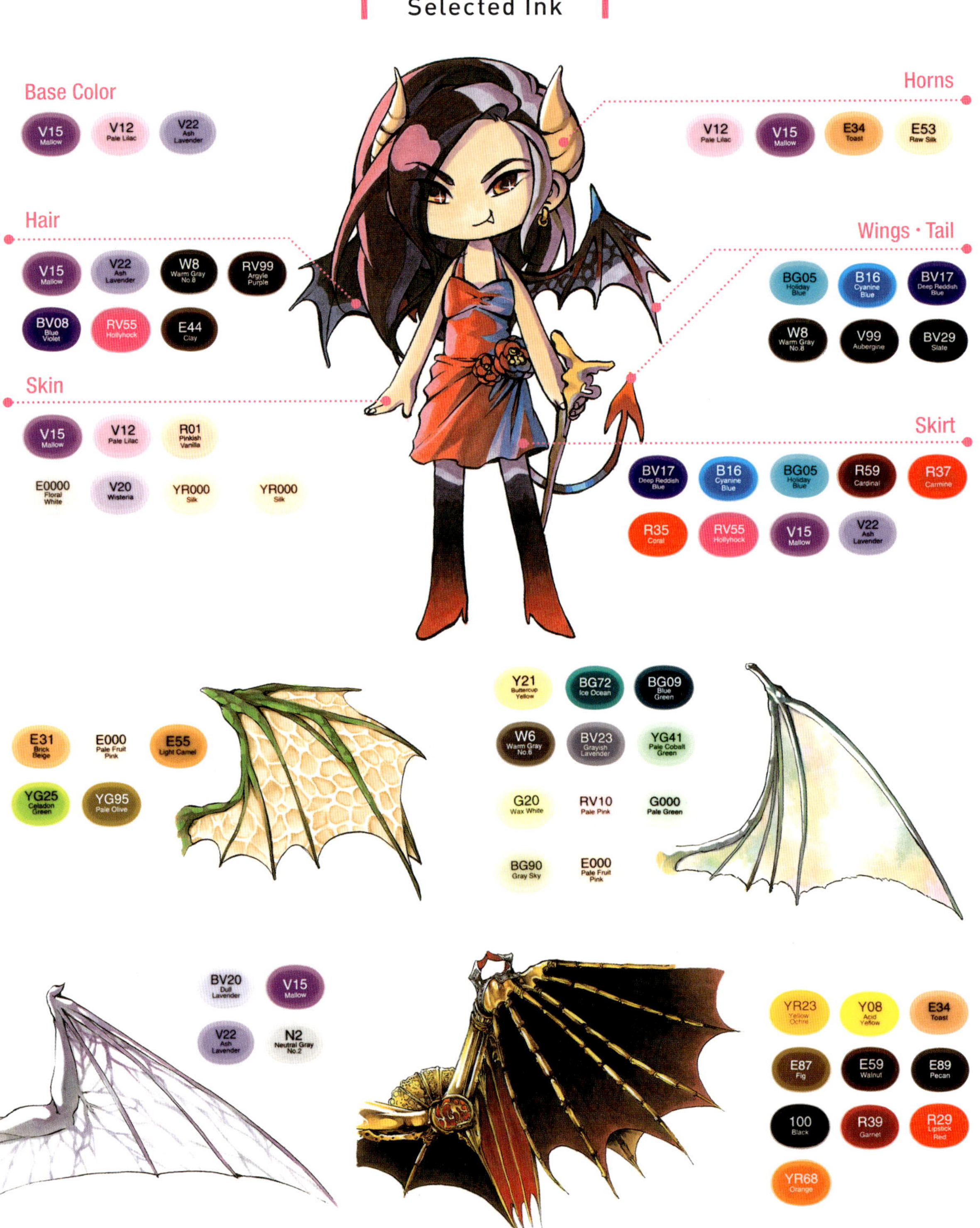

Red Eyes

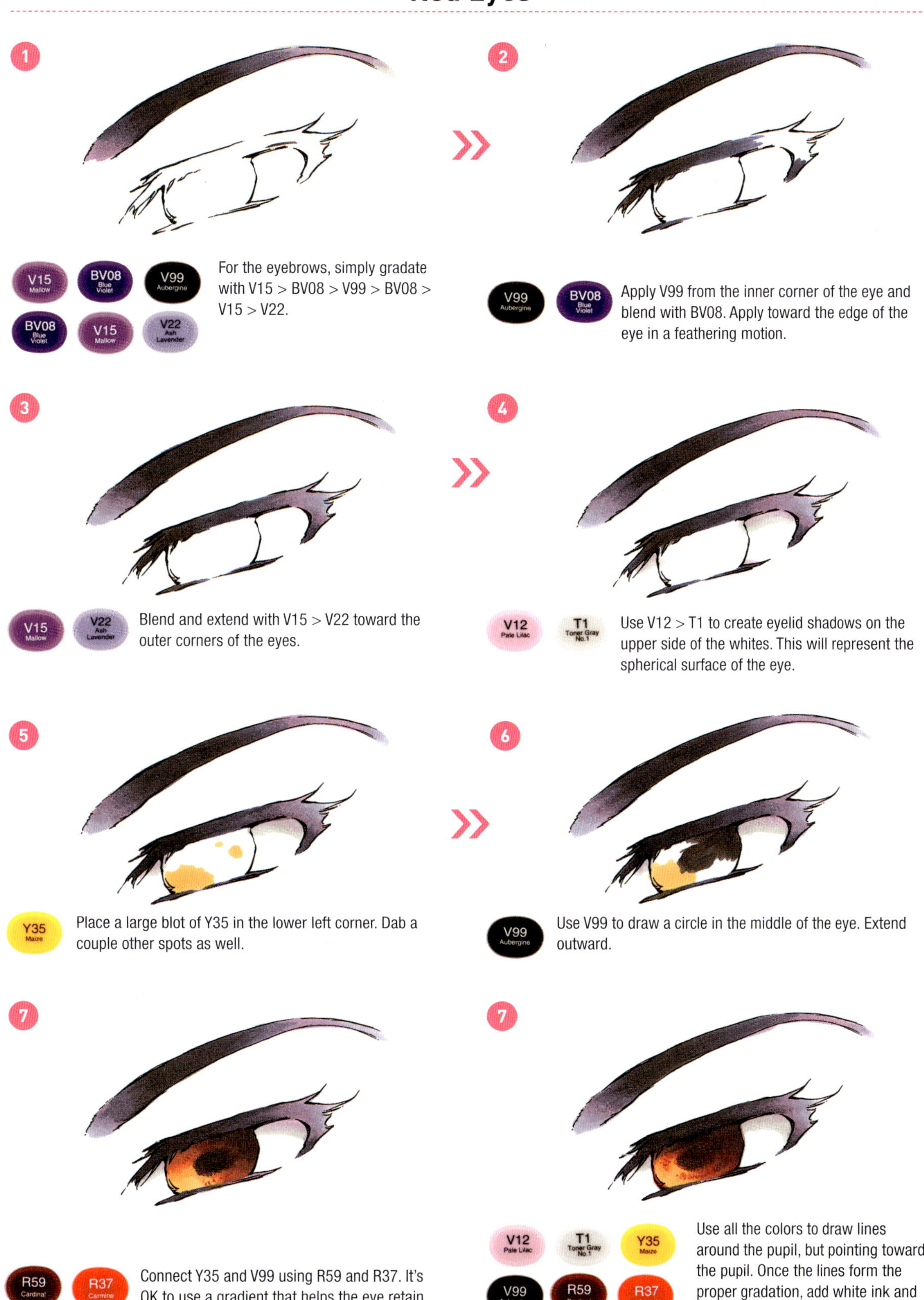

1 For the eyebrows, simply gradate with V15 > BV08 > V99 > BV08 > V15 > V22.

V15 Mallow · BV08 Blue Violet · V99 Aubergine · BV08 Blue Violet · V15 Mallow · V22 Ash Lavender

2 Apply V99 from the inner corner of the eye and blend with BV08. Apply toward the edge of the eye in a feathering motion.

V99 Aubergine · BV08 Blue Violet

3 Blend and extend with V15 > V22 toward the outer corners of the eyes.

V15 Mallow · V22 Ash Lavender

4 Use V12 > T1 to create eyelid shadows on the upper side of the whites. This will represent the spherical surface of the eye.

V12 Pale Lilac · T1 Toner Gray No.1

5 Place a large blot of Y35 in the lower left corner. Dab a couple other spots as well.

Y35 Maize

6 Use V99 to draw a circle in the middle of the eye. Extend outward.

V99 Aubergine

7 Connect Y35 and V99 using R59 and R37. It's OK to use a gradient that helps the eye retain its shape.

R59 Cardinal · R37 Carmine

7 Use all the colors to draw lines around the pupil, but pointing toward the pupil. Once the lines form the proper gradation, add white ink and you're done!

V12 Pale Lilac · T1 Toner Gray No.1 · Y35 Maize · V99 Aubergine · R59 Cardinal · R37 Carmine

Purple Shadows and Skin

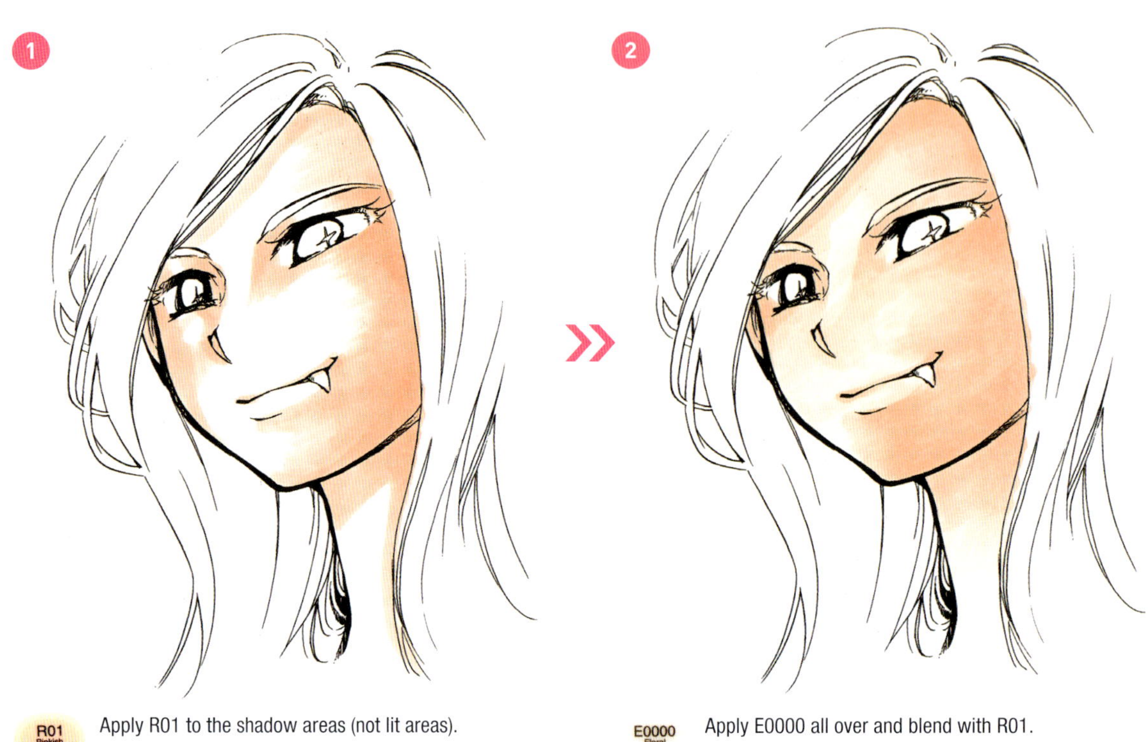

1 Apply R01 to the shadow areas (not lit areas).

R01 Pinkish Vanilla

2 Apply E0000 all over and blend with R01.

E0000 Floral White

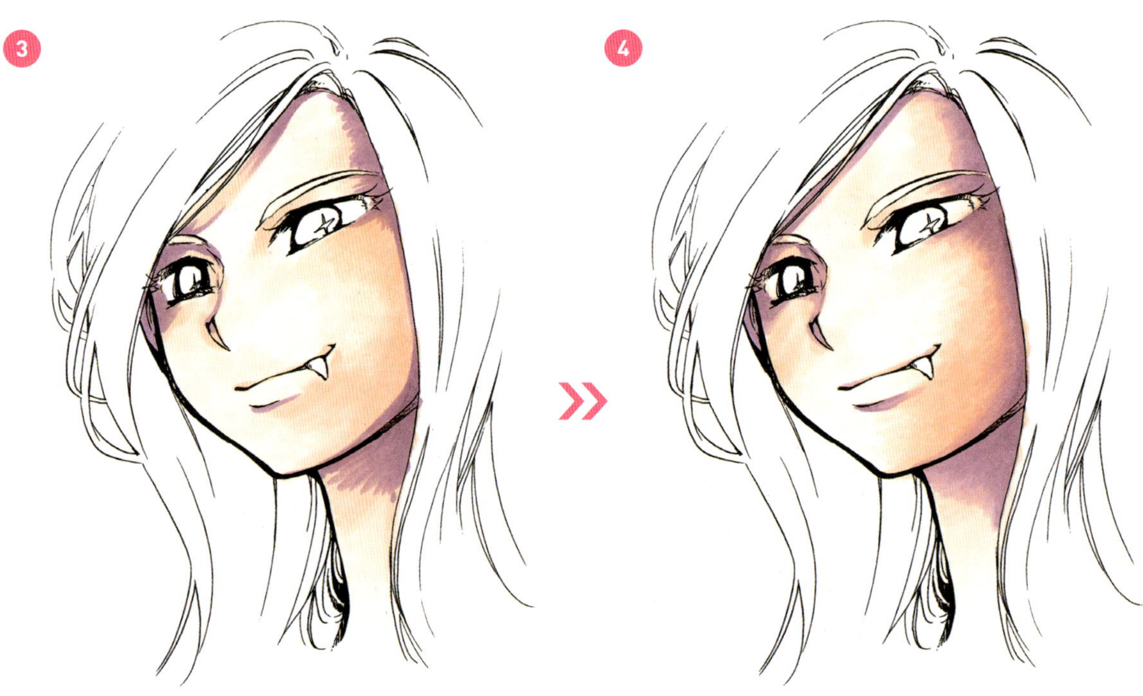

3 Place V15 on the darkest shadows. It's easiest to later blend the shadows by adding the color in a feathering motion.

V15 Mallow

4 Use V12 to blend the V15. In this case, it is OK to make the color a little intense. In this picture, the hair is darker than the skin, so it can overflow. However, if the hair color is lighter, be careful not to overflow.

V12 Pale Lilac

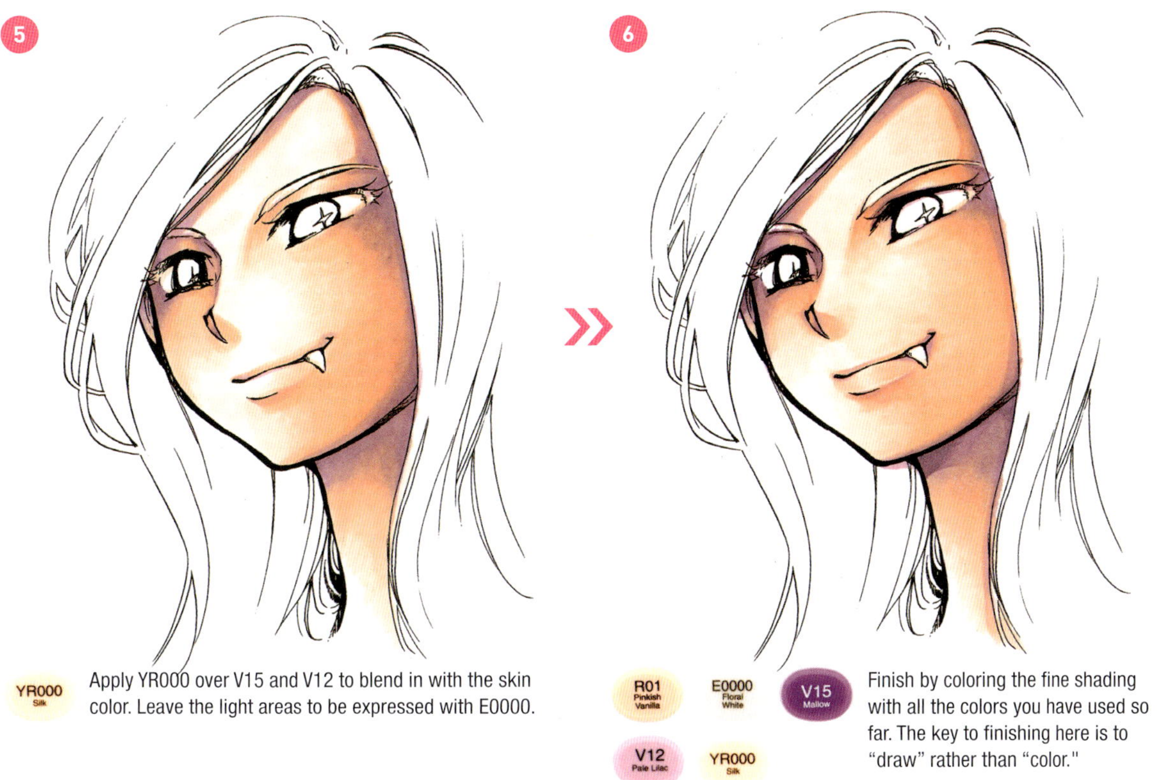

5

YR000 Silk

Apply YR000 over V15 and V12 to blend in with the skin color. Leave the light areas to be expressed with E0000.

6

R01 Pinkish Vanilla	E0000 Floral White	V15 Mallow
V12 Pale Lilac	YR000 Silk	

Finish by coloring the fine shading with all the colors you have used so far. The key to finishing here is to "draw" rather than "color."

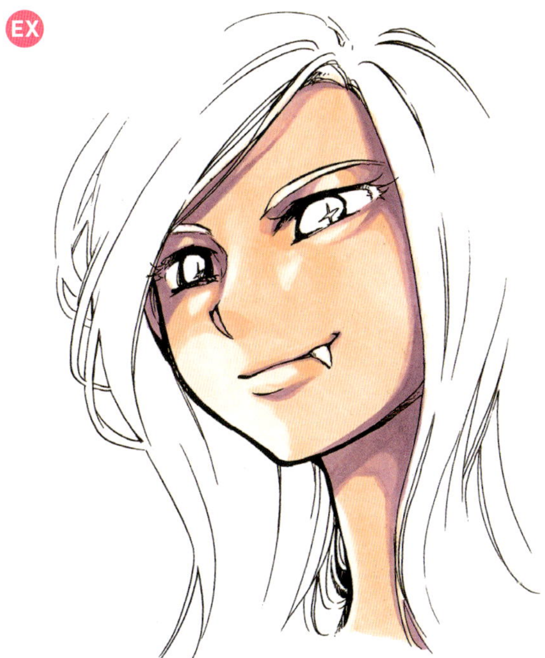

EX

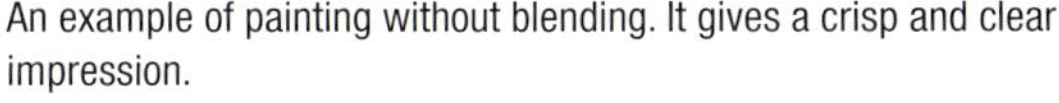

An example of painting without blending. It gives a crisp and clear impression.

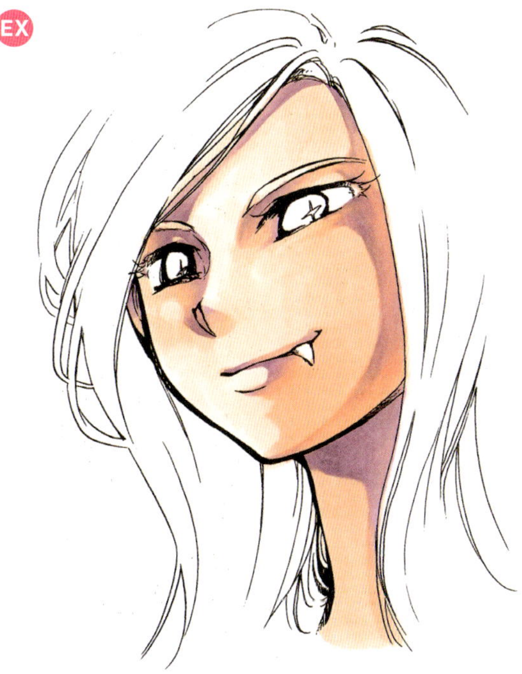

EX

The darkest shadows are placed at the boundary between light and shadow, and blend so that they fade toward the back. If you don't know where to put the shadows, you won't be able to apply them well. It is also difficult to correct if you weren't able to achieve the desired outcome, but it has the advantage of making the skin look brighter.

Hair Flow and Shine

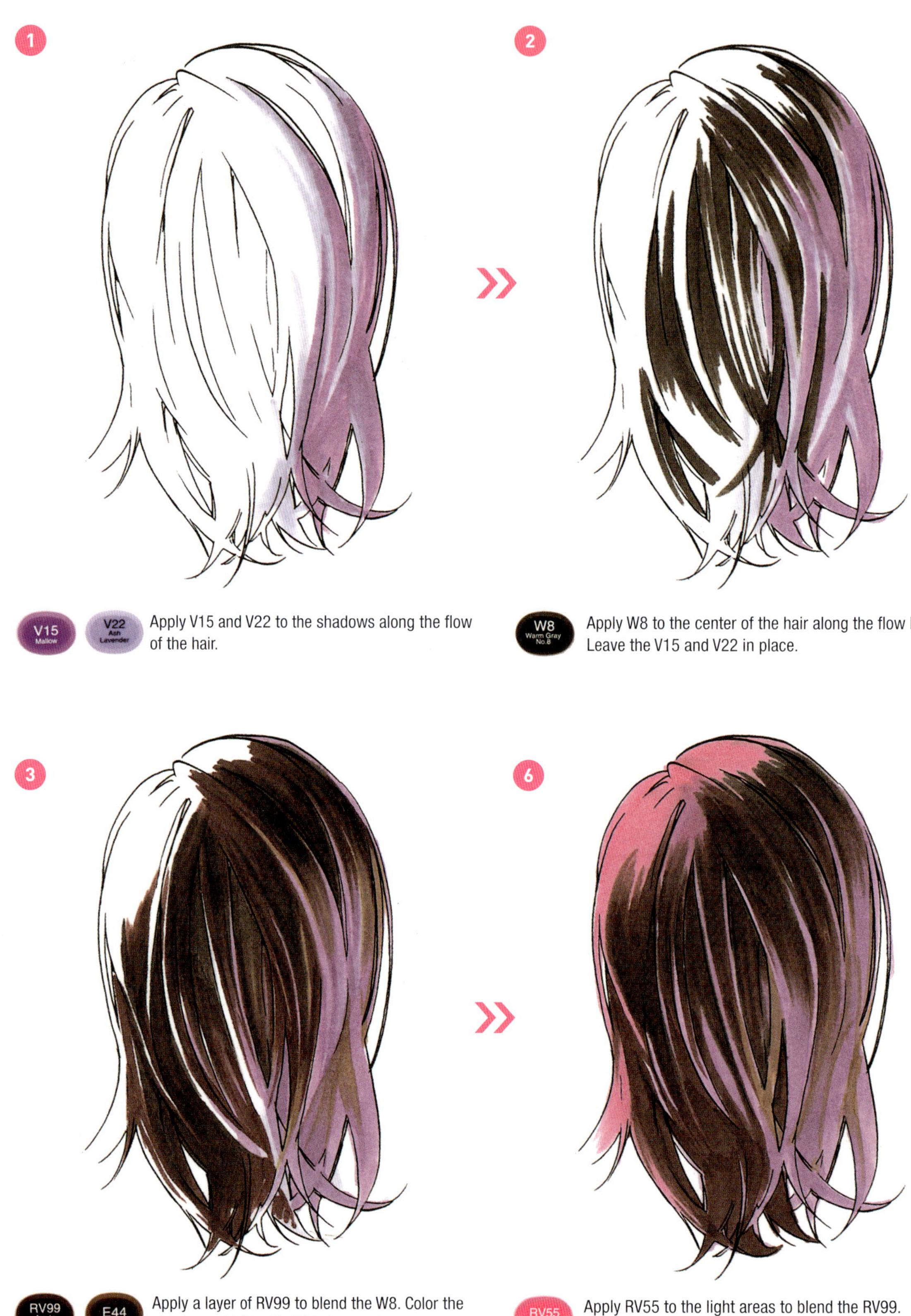

1 Apply V15 and V22 to the shadows along the flow of the hair.

V15 Mallow · V22 Ash Lavender

2 Apply W8 to the center of the hair along the flow line. Leave the V15 and V22 in place.

W8 Warm Gray No.8

3 Apply a layer of RV99 to blend the W8. Color the shadows of V15 with E44. Be sure to leave out any light areas.

RV99 Argyle Purple · E44 Clay

6 Apply RV55 to the light areas to blend the RV99.

RV55 Hollyhock

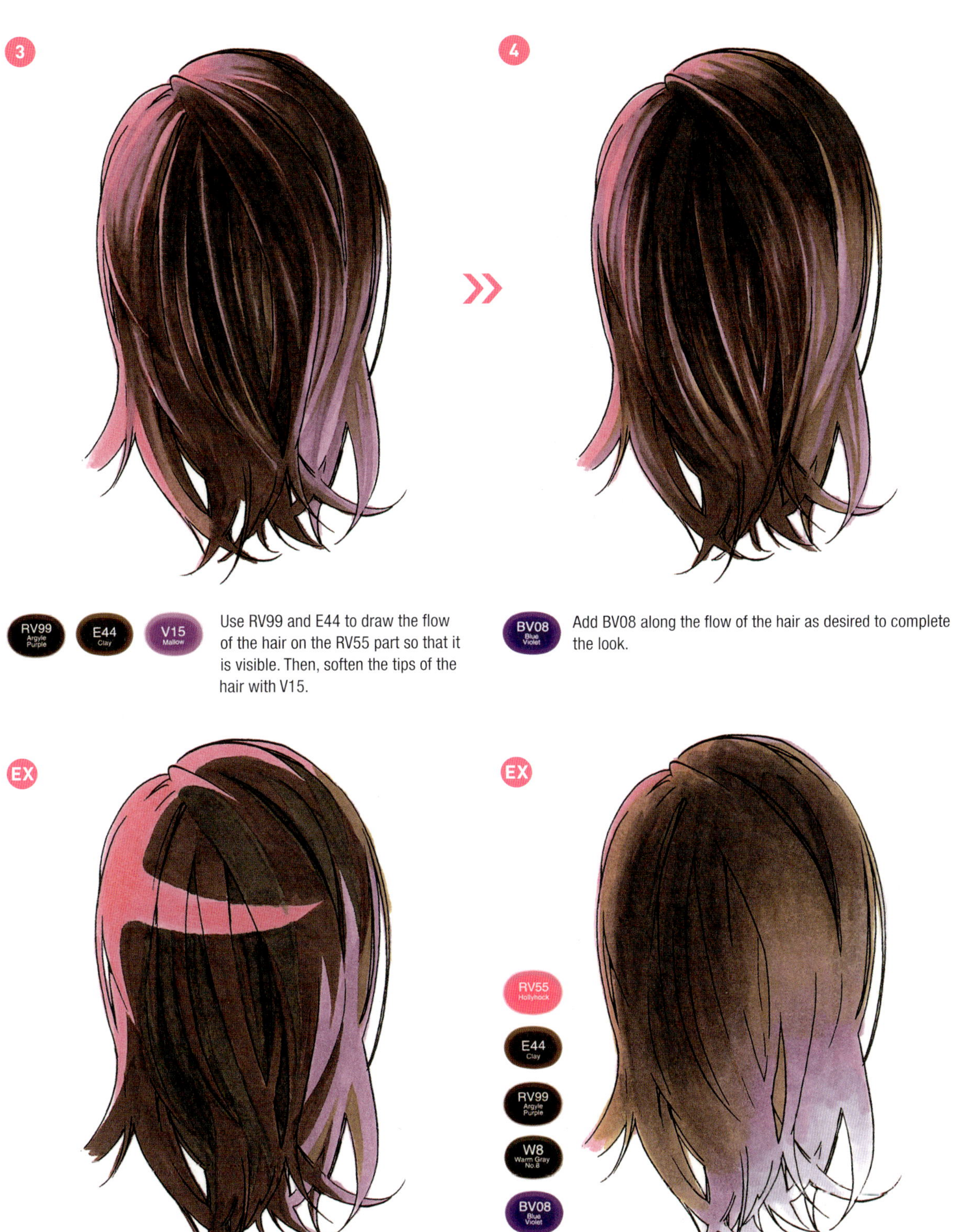

3

Use RV99 and E44 to draw the flow of the hair on the RV55 part so that it is visible. Then, soften the tips of the hair with V15.

RV99 Argyle Purple · E44 Clay · V15 Mallow

4

Add BV08 along the flow of the hair as desired to complete the look.

BV08 Blue Violet

EX

This is what it looks like when it's painted crisply.

EX

RV55 Hollyhock · E44 Clay · RV99 Argyle Purple · W8 Warm Gray No.8 · BV08 Blue Violet · V15 Mallow · V22 Ash Lavender

Here's the whole thing gradated.

Various Shadow Examples

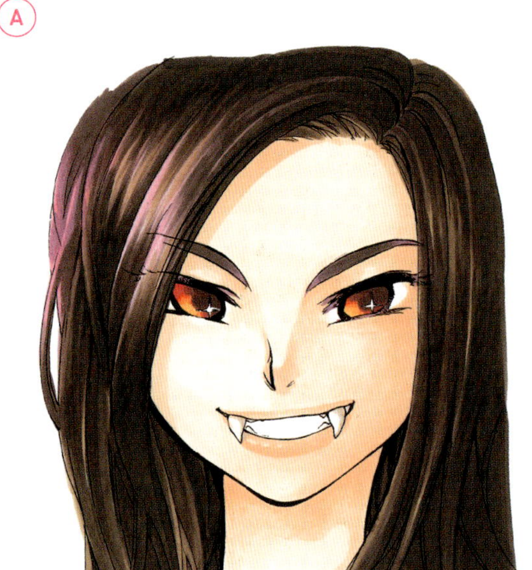

(A)

We have added color to the shadows in the other samples, but this is what it would look like without any shadow coloring.

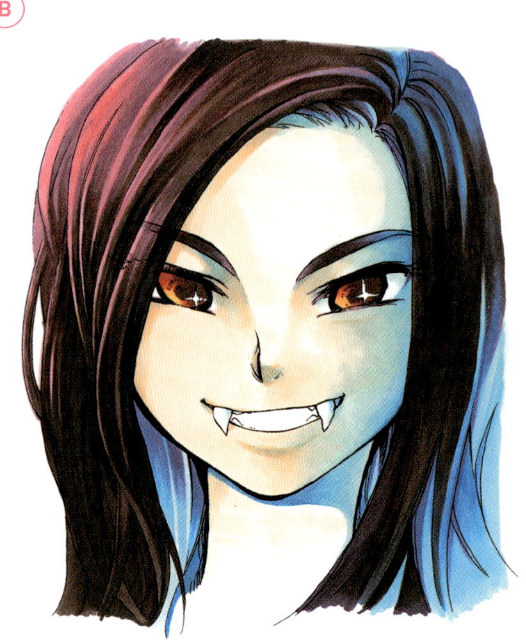

(B)

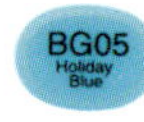 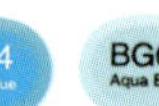 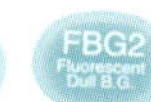

Example 1: This is what it looks like with added blue shadows.

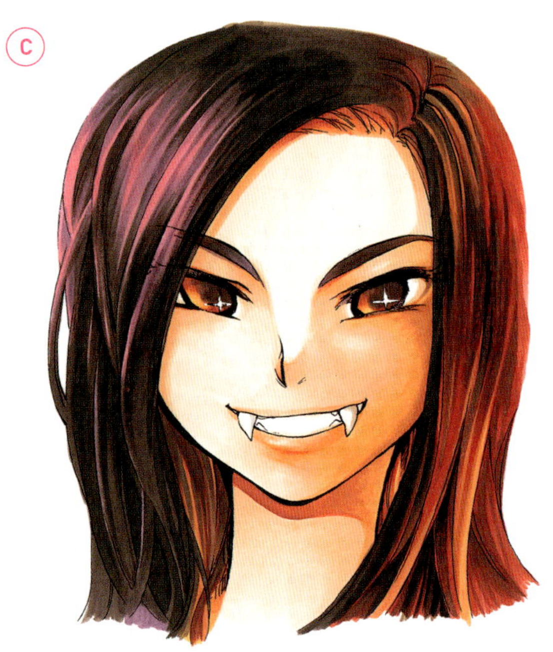

(C)

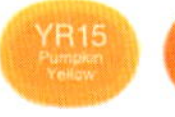 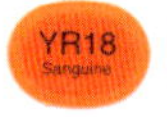 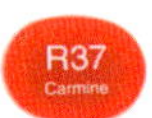 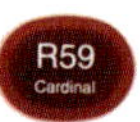

Example 2: Yellow shading leads to this look.

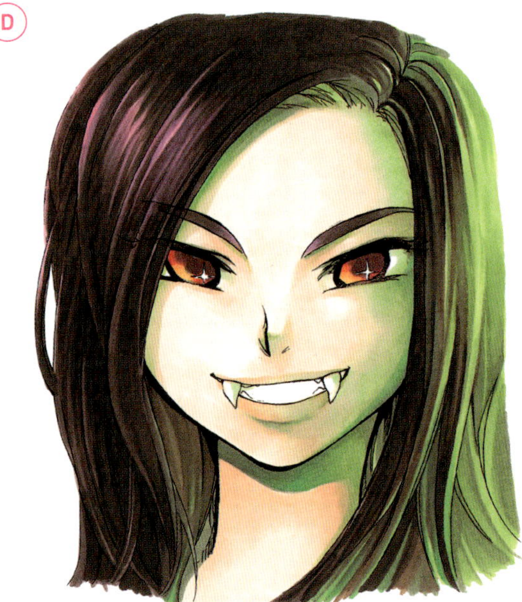

(D)

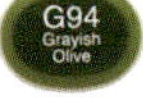 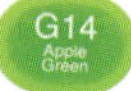 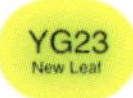 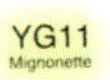

Example 3: Here we added green shadows.

Dress Shadows and Creases

 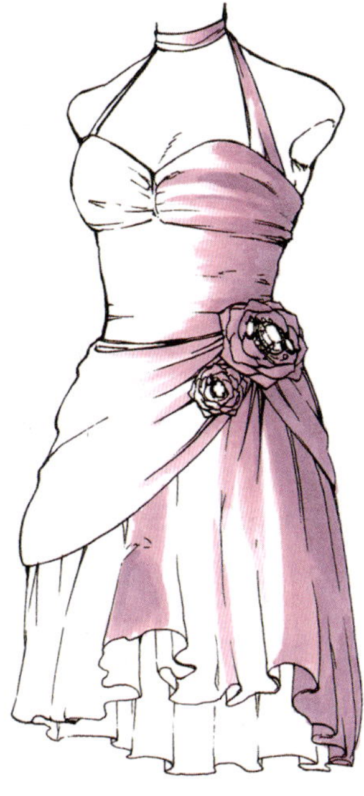

 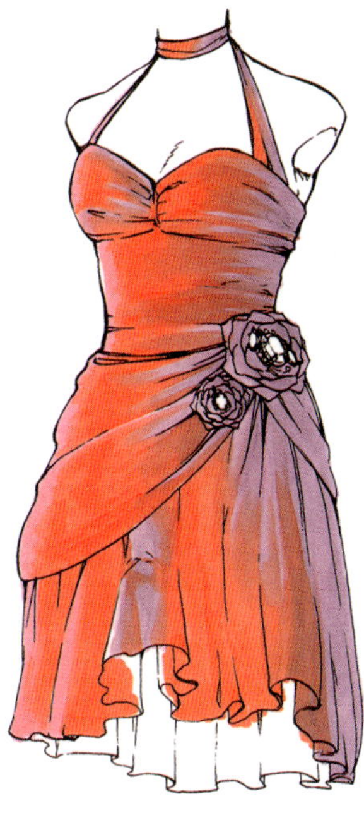

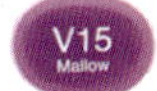 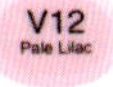 Color the shadows with V15 and then blend with V12. You don't need to be precise, just go with the flow.

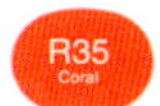 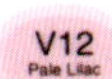 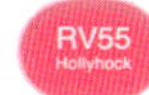 Leave the shadows and lit areas of V15 and V12 alone, but color the remaining areas with R35. Blend the R35 with V12 and then go on to blend the light side with RV55.

 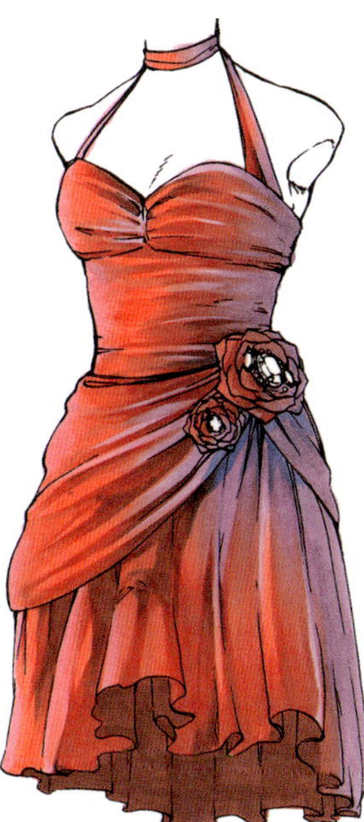

 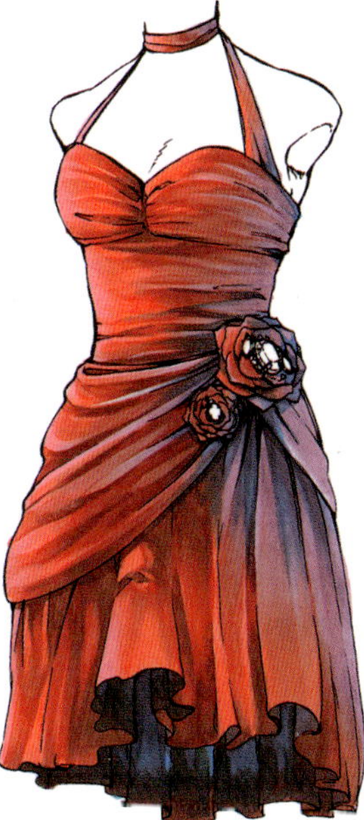

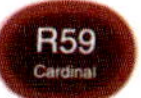 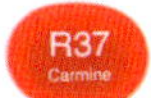 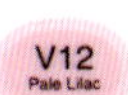 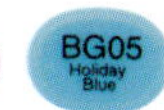 Darken the shadows with R59 and R37. Here, it is best to blend the shadows in the middle. Use V12 to blend the areas where V12 intersects with other colors. If you add shadows to the V12, the other colors will look better. In this case, BG05 is used.

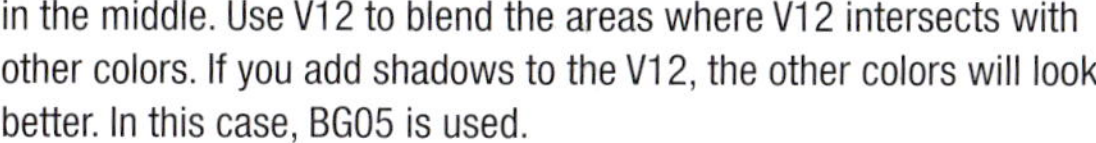

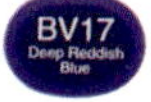 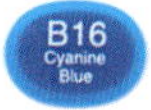 Use BV17 and B16 to add in creases and shadows. Make sure you use fine lines for this finishing touch!

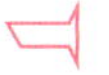

Rendering Feet with Special Colors

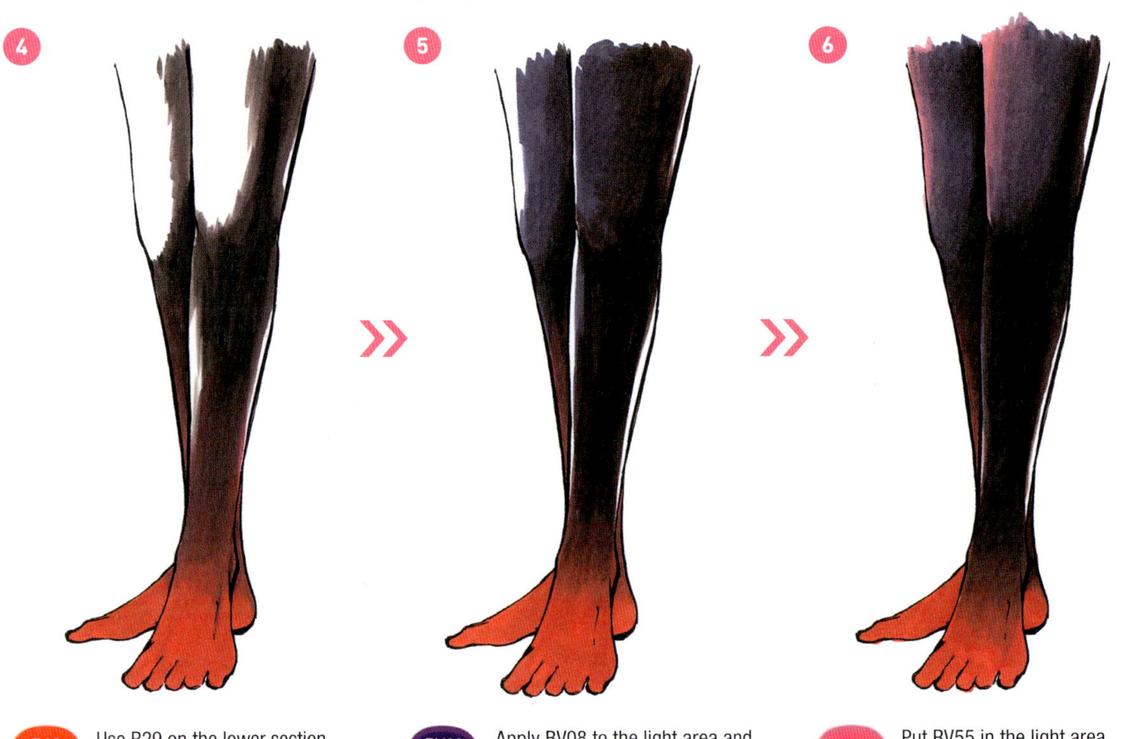

1 — W10 (Warm Gray No.10): Place W10 in the shadow of the knee and along the muscle of the thigh.

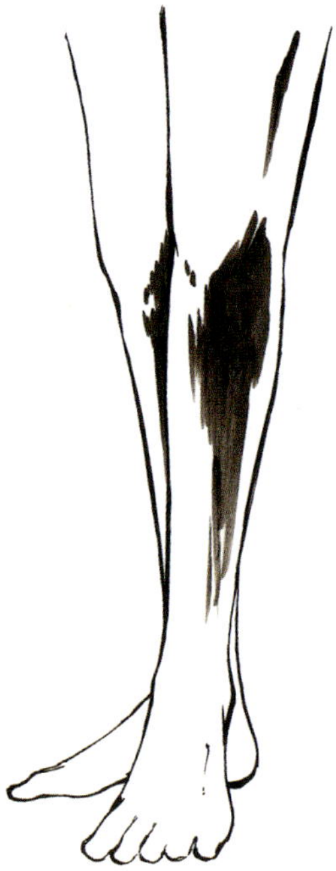

2 — V99 (Aubergine): Dissolve the W10 with V99 and spread it out a bit. However, make sure to leave both sides alone as the light and shadows will be lighter than this.

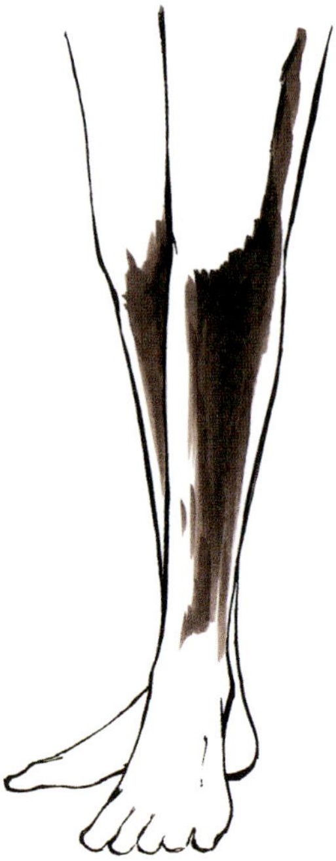

3 — RV69 (Peony): Spread the V99 further with RV69.

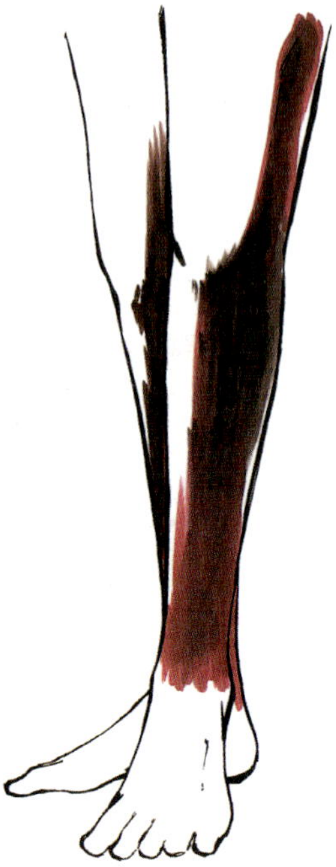

4 — R29 (Lipstick Red): Use R29 on the lower section.

5 — BV08 (Blue Violet): Apply BV08 to the light area and blend it. Leave a little space to add another layer of light.

6 — RV55 (Hollyhock): Put RV55 in the light area.

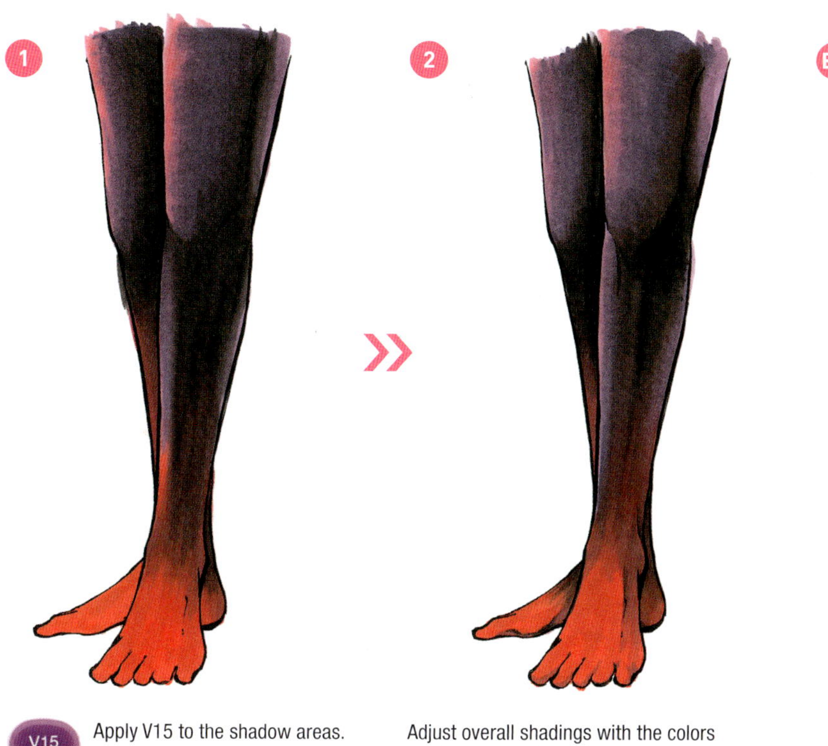

1

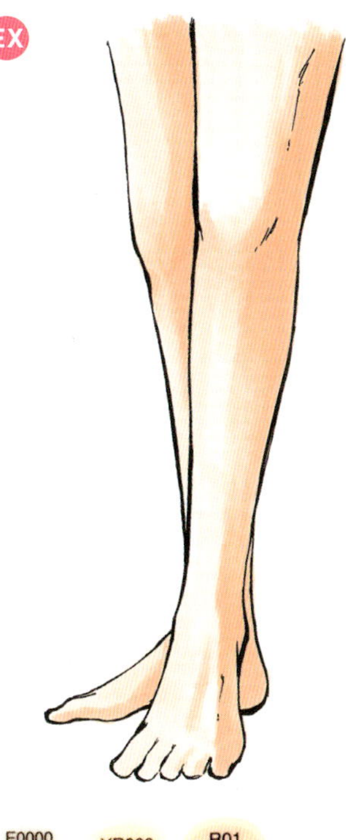

2

EX

V15 Mallow — Apply V15 to the shadow areas.

Adjust overall shadings with the colors you've used so far to finish.

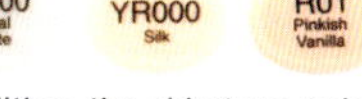

E0000 Floral White   YR000 Silk   R01 Pinkish Vanilla

In addition, the skin tone using E0000, YR000, and R01 looks like this.

Spiral Horns

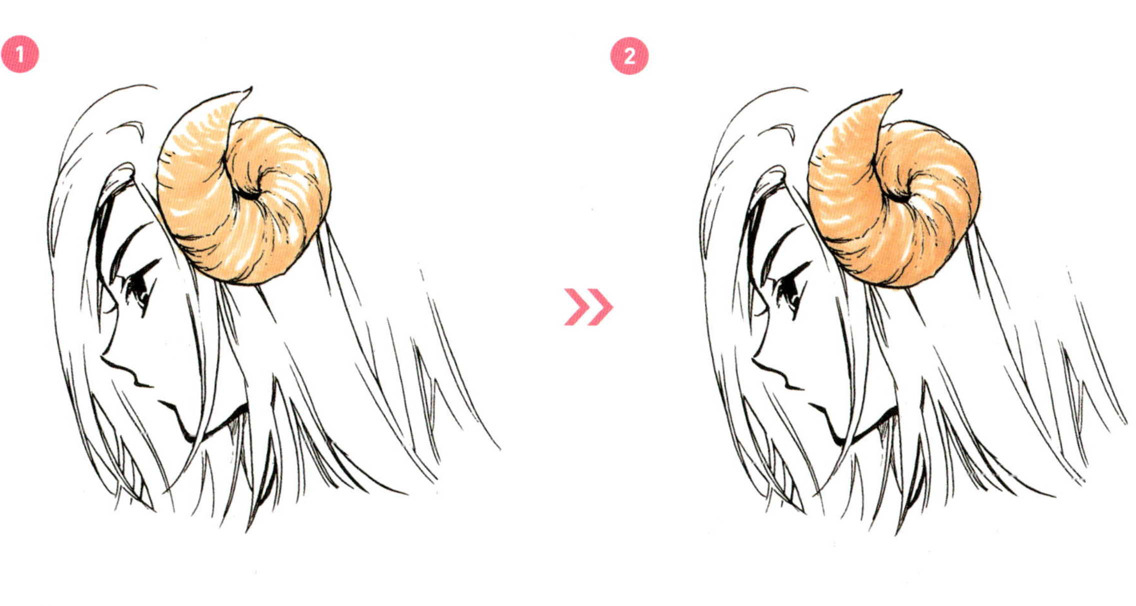

1

2

E53 Raw Silk — Lightly trace the corner grooves with E53.

E53 Raw Silk — Allow to dry and then use E53 to add grooves again. Do this two or three times. Be sure to leave the areas that will be light.

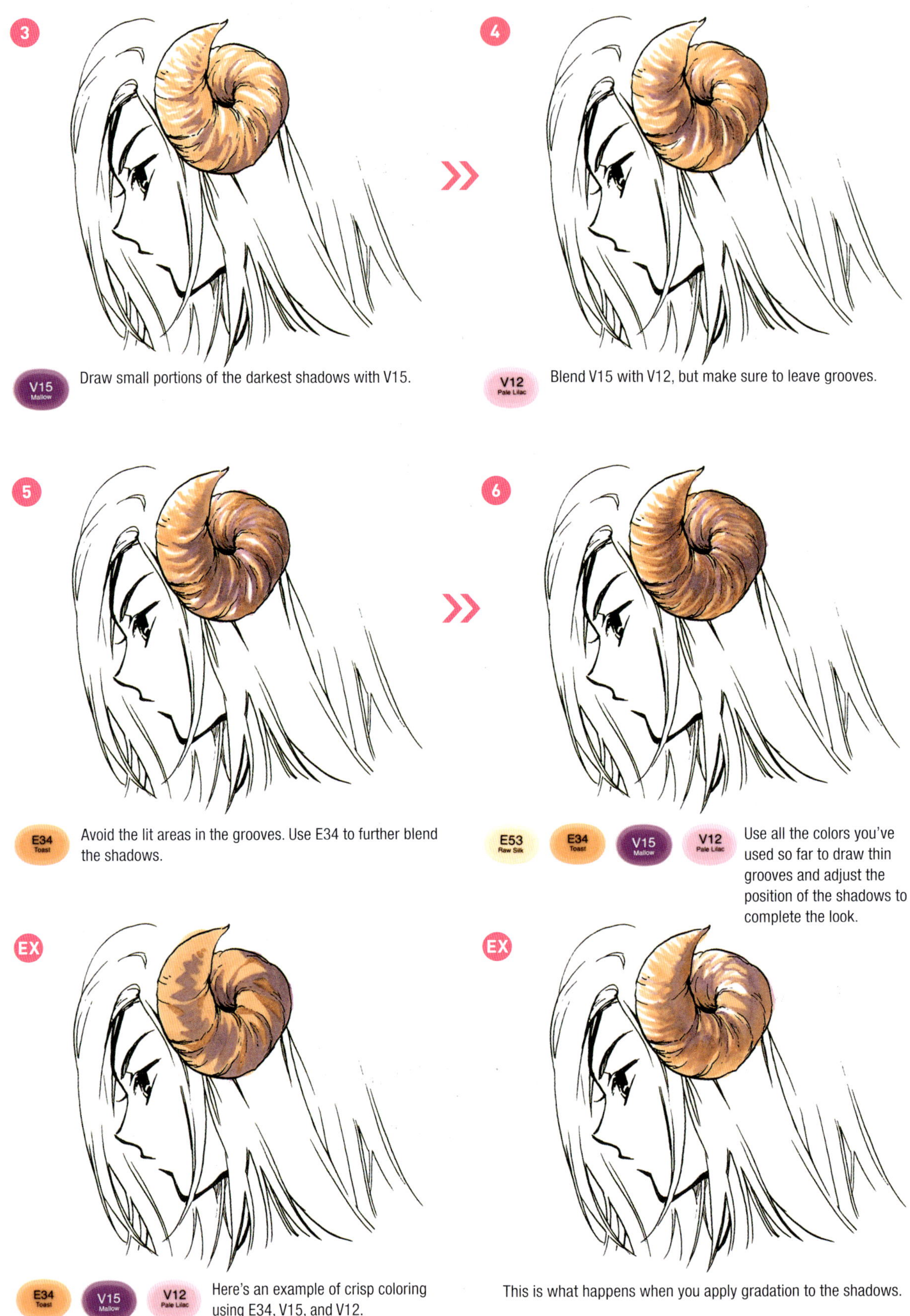

3 Draw small portions of the darkest shadows with V15.

V15 Mallow

4 Blend V15 with V12, but make sure to leave grooves.

V12 Pale Lilac

5 Avoid the lit areas in the grooves. Use E34 to further blend the shadows.

E34 Toast

6 Use all the colors you've used so far to draw thin grooves and adjust the position of the shadows to complete the look.

E53 Raw Silk   E34 Toast   V15 Mallow   V12 Pale Lilac

EX Here's an example of crisp coloring using E34, V15, and V12.

E34 Toast   V15 Mallow   V12 Pale Lilac

EX This is what happens when you apply gradation to the shadows.

Lips that Match the Color of Skin

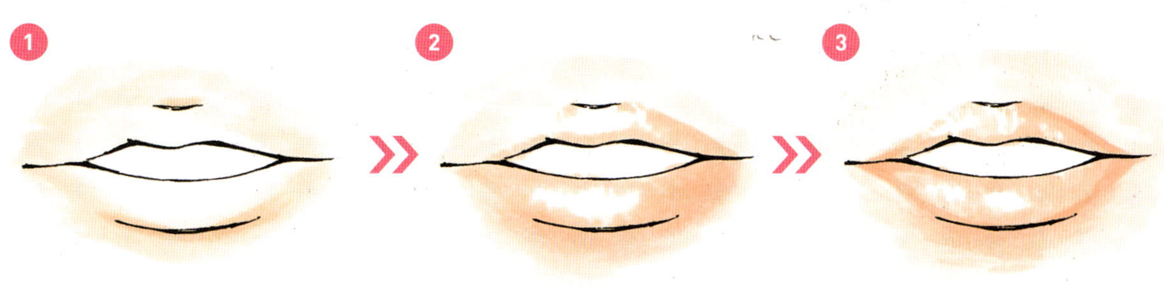

1

0 Colorless Blender

Paint the skin while leaving the lip area white.

2

YR000 Silk

Think about the fullness of the lips and draw vertical curves with YR000. This will be the base color. At this point, leave the areas where the light will shine.

3

R01 Pinkish Vanilla

Use R01 to draw the lip outline. The direction of the light should be just hinted at.

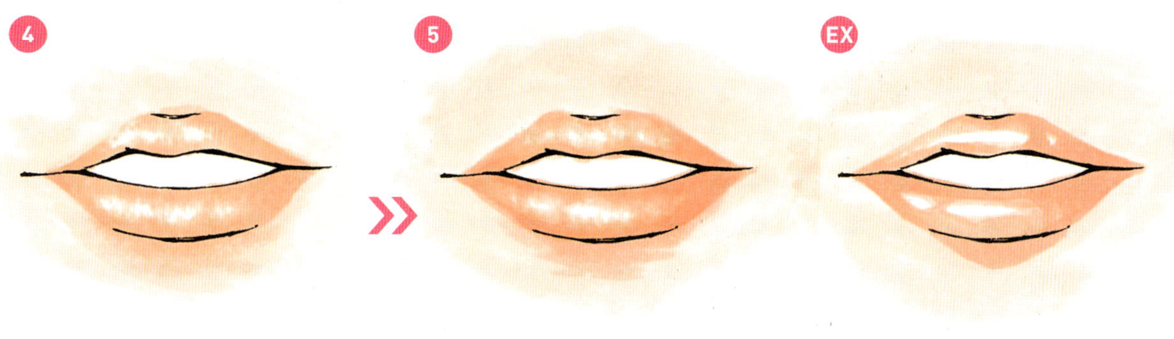

4

R01 Pinkish Vanilla

To keep the curve from **2** intact, go over it vertically with R01.

5

YR000 Silk

R01 Pinkish Vanilla

Apply a few more layers and you're done. Keep in mind that the light should be in a line.

EX

This is a crisply colored example.

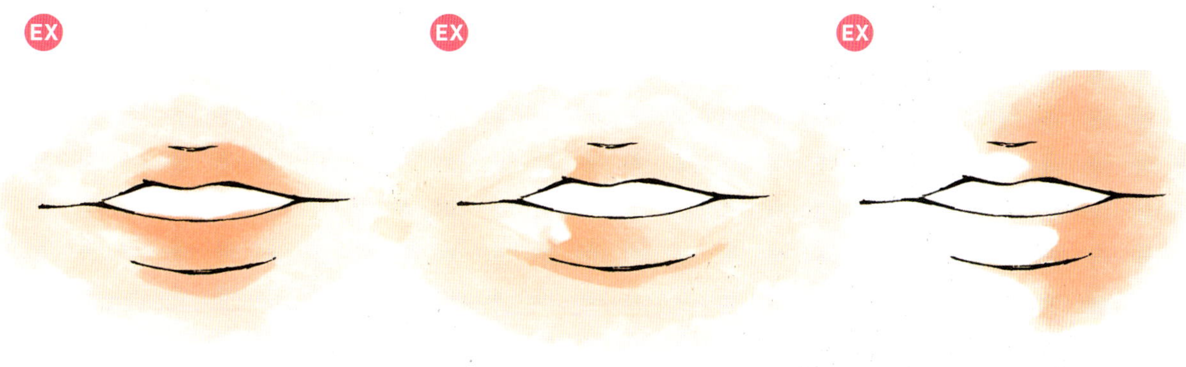

EX

An example of a simple gradation from the center outward.

EX

Create lit areas and then gradate from there.

EX

An example that uses #0 for the light and has skin tone only on the shadows.

Bat-Like Wings

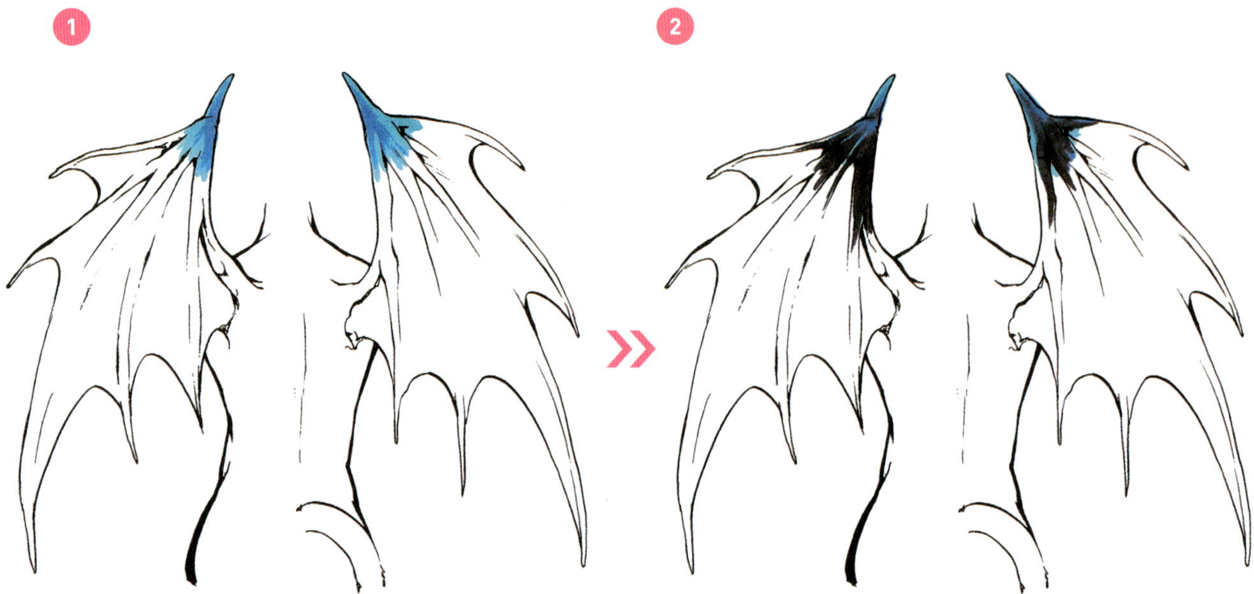

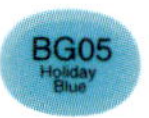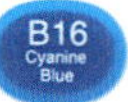 Apply BG05 to the tips. Then, use B16 to add a hint of shadow.

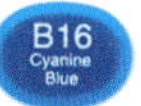 Spread the B16 with BV29, then apply another coat of B16 to the border to create a gradient (be careful not to go beyond the bone areas).

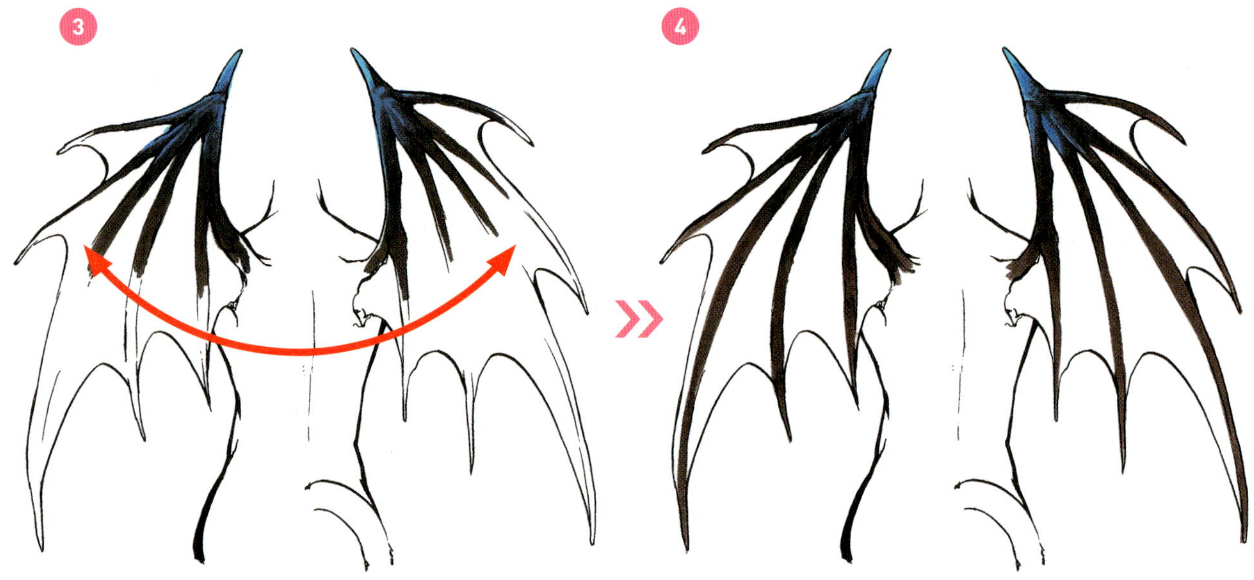

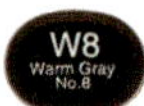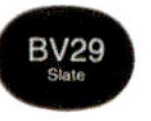 Apply W8 while aligning the lengths to produce the appearance of arched wings. Then blend with BV29.

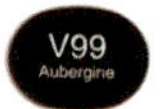 Use V99 to extend the color of the bone area to the tips of the wings. If you want to change the color, pick one that can transition from V99 easily.

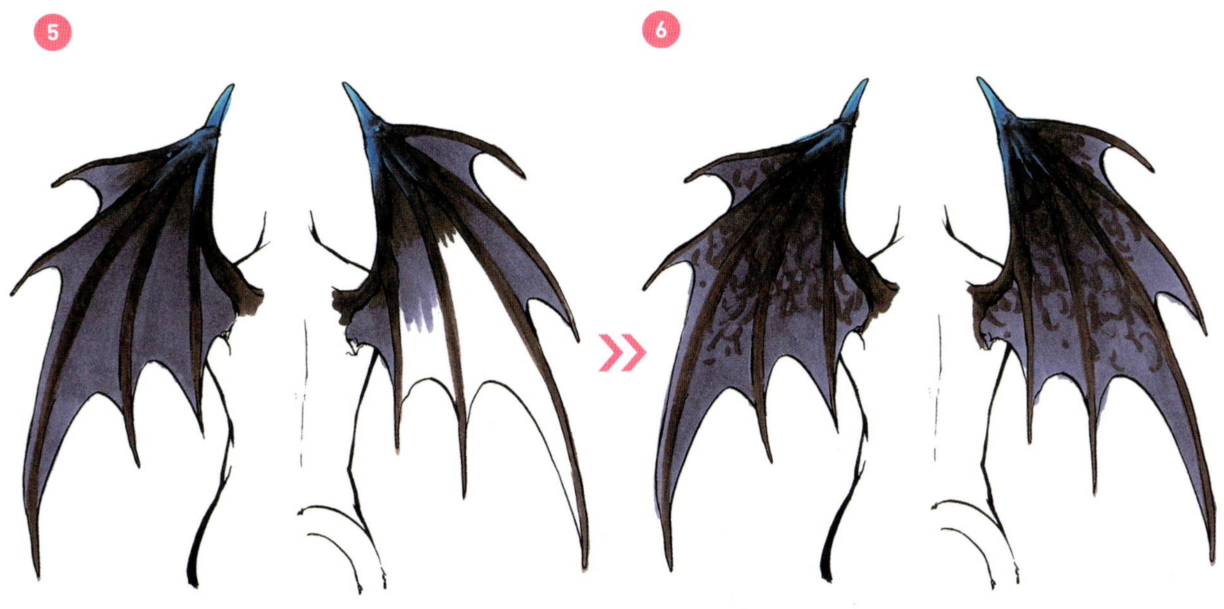

5

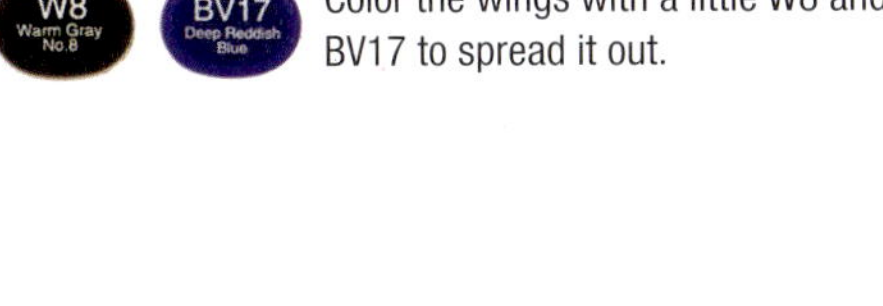

W8 Warm Gray No.8 **BV17** Deep Reddish Blue — Color the wings with a little W8 and then use BV17 to spread it out.

6

V99 Aubergine **BV17** Deep Reddish Blue — Use V99 to roughly draw shapes like wood shavings. Make sure the density decreases from the top of the wing to the bottom. Blend V17 in the spaces to create a stitched look.

7

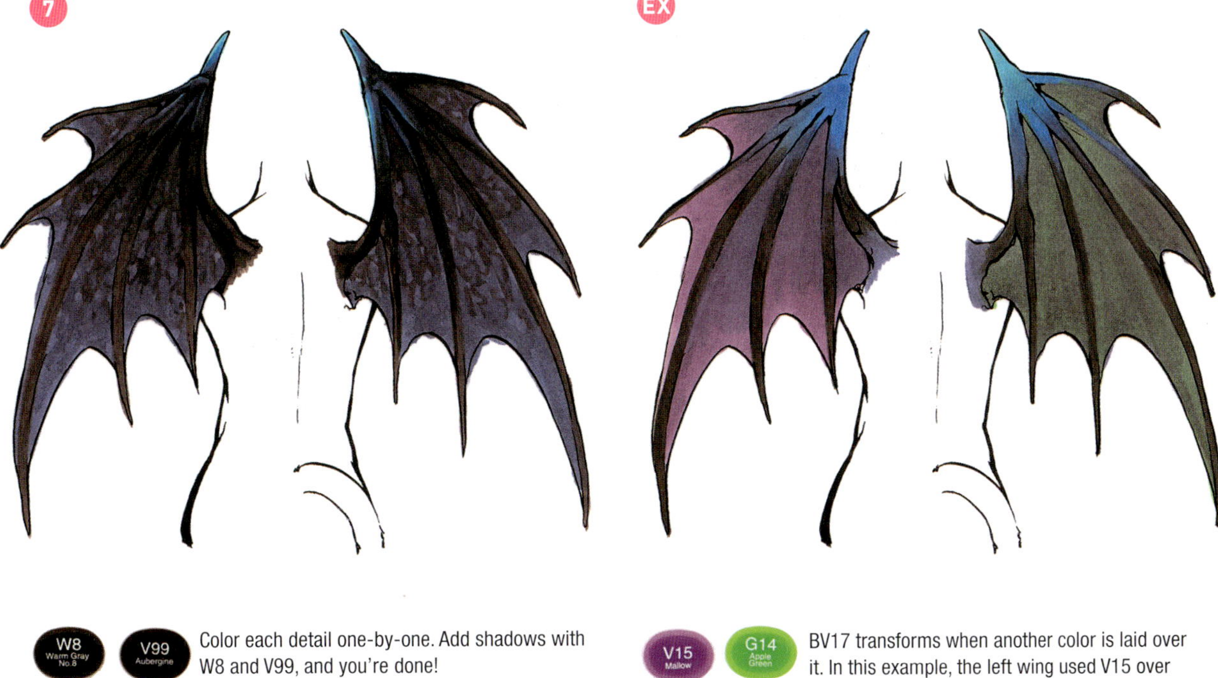

W8 Warm Gray No.8 **V99** Aubergine — Color each detail one-by-one. Add shadows with W8 and V99, and you're done!

EX

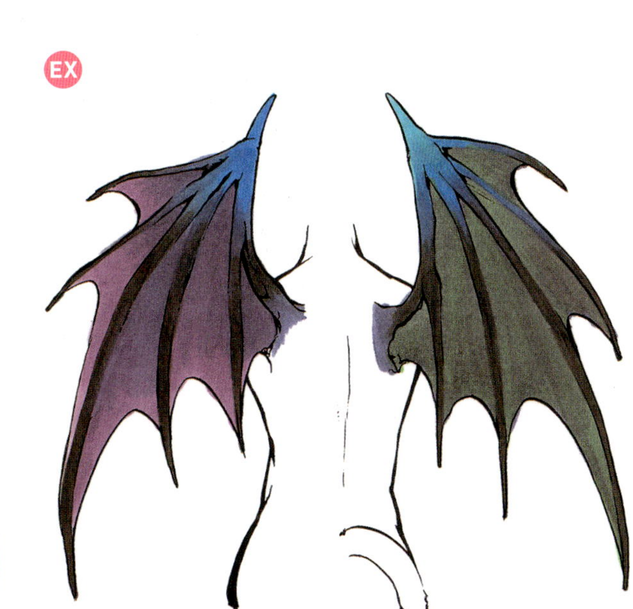

V15 Mallow **G14** Apple Green — BV17 transforms when another color is laid over it. In this example, the left wing used V15 over BV17, and the right wing used G14 over BV17. Have fun trying out different patterns!

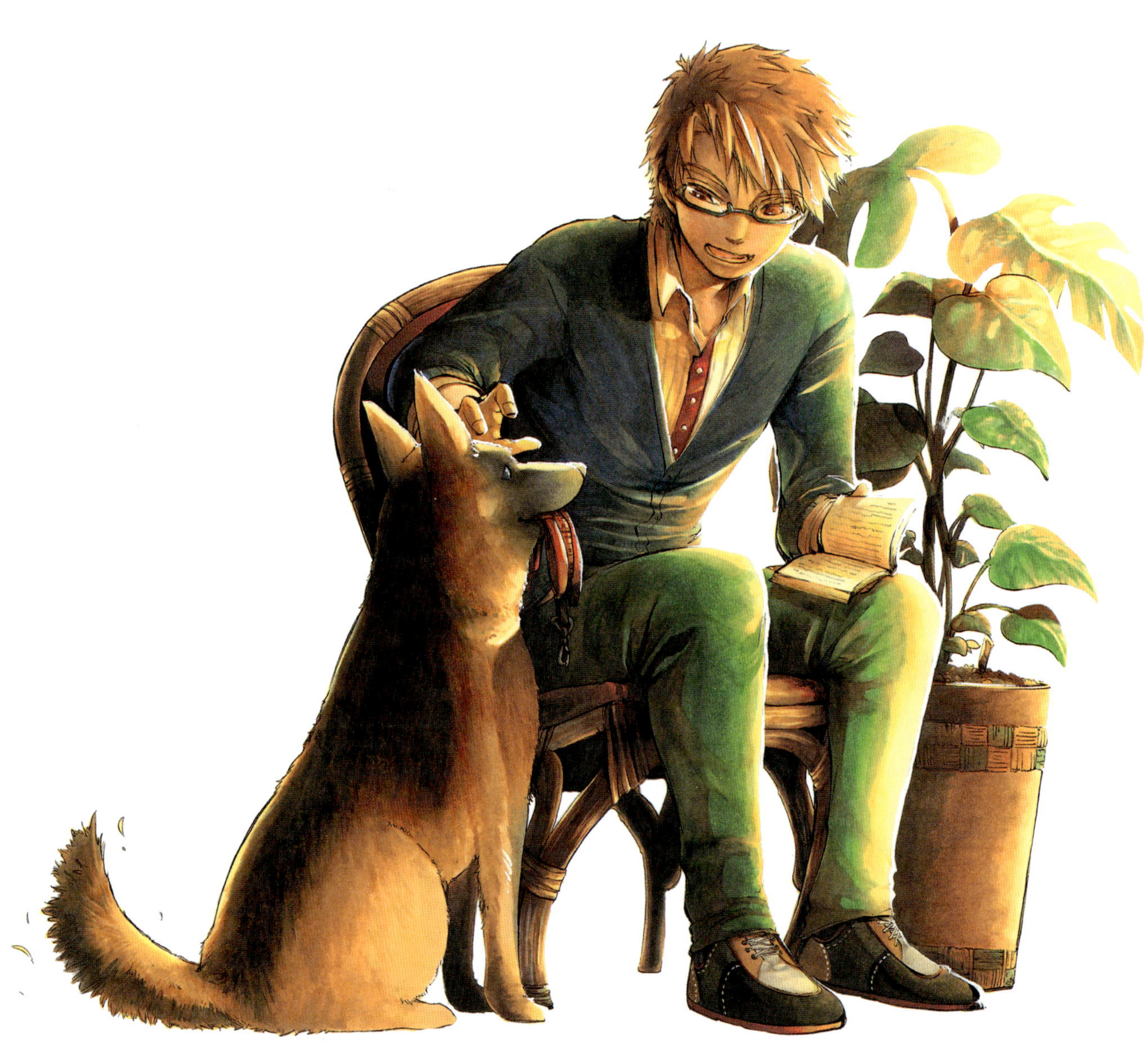

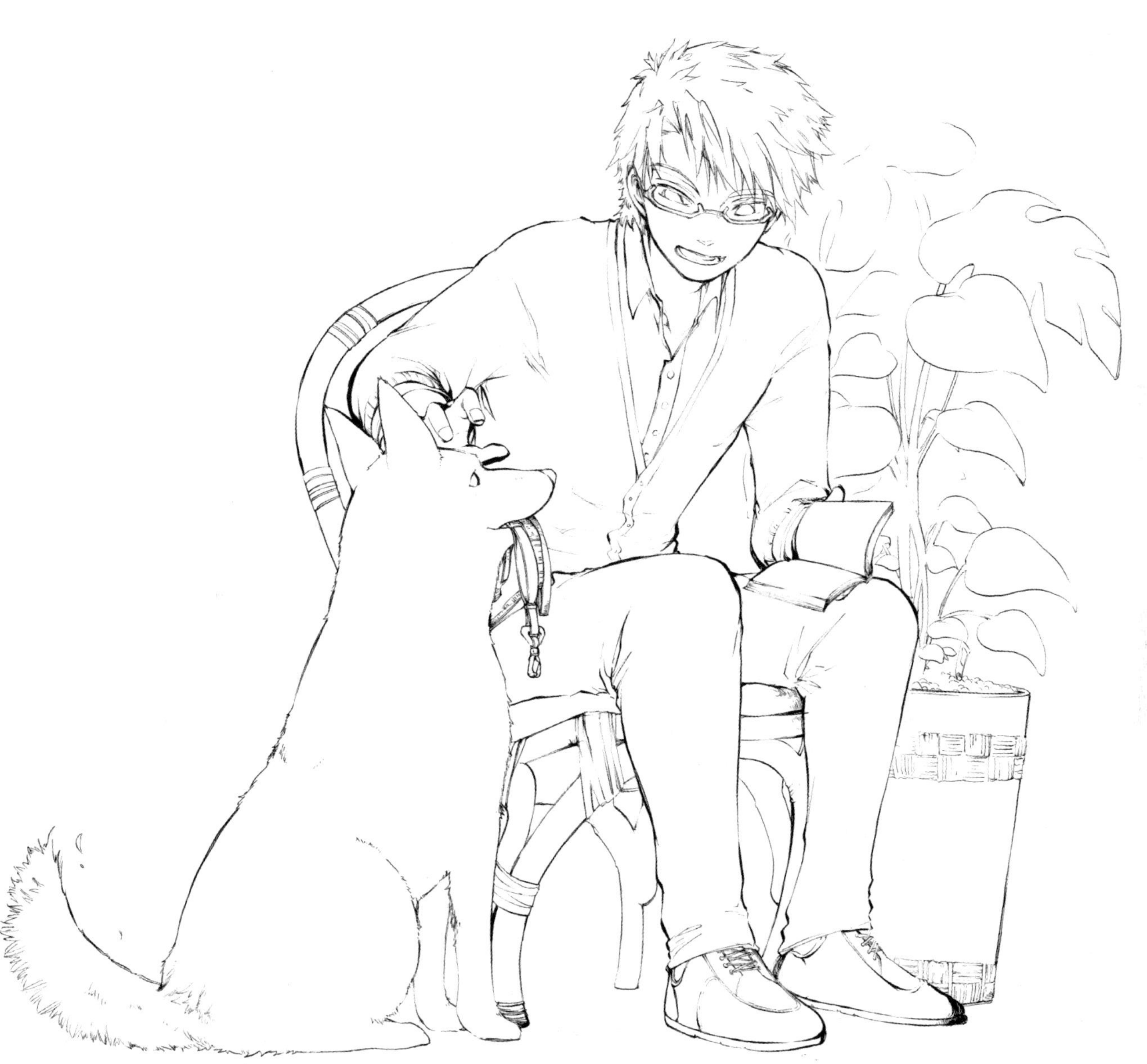

06 Color Selection by Backlighting

This is a technique for making colored light. This example shows how to create a backlit situation with strong yellow light.

Selected Ink

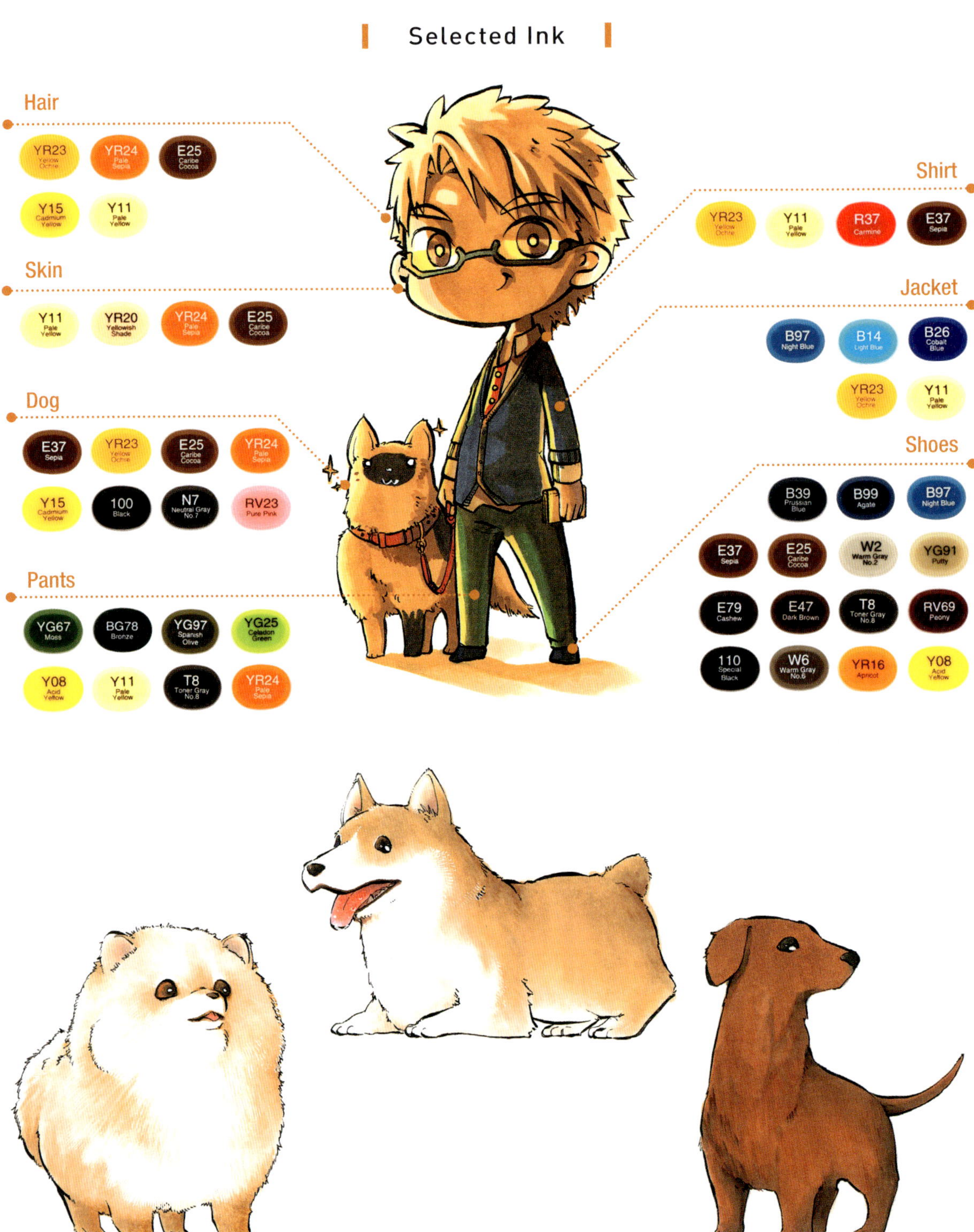

Glasses and Eyes

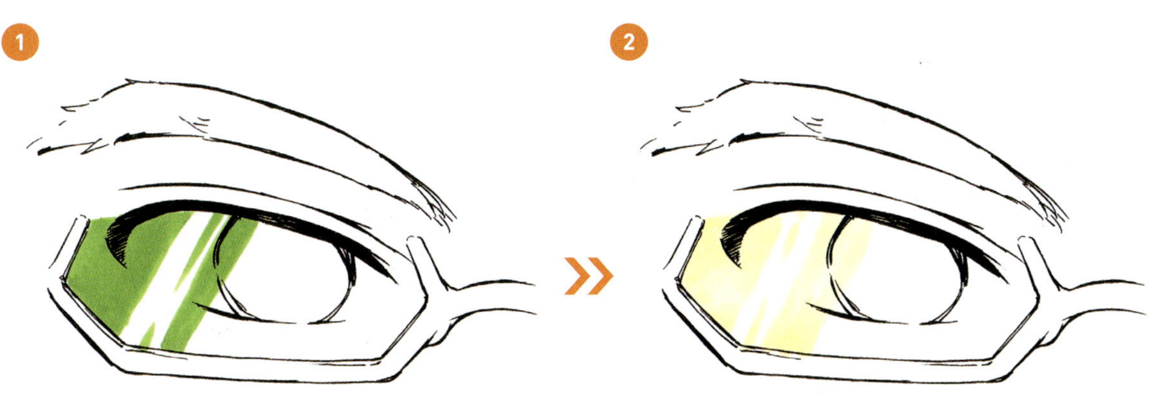

1 Determine the light part of the glasses. This example used YG25 just to clearly show how this is done.

2

Y11 — Pale Yellow

If you want the light to be pure white, you can just leave it uncolored. Or, color it normally and then add a layer of white ink. In this case, use yellow for the light and highlight with a lighter color. Use Y11 as in **1**.

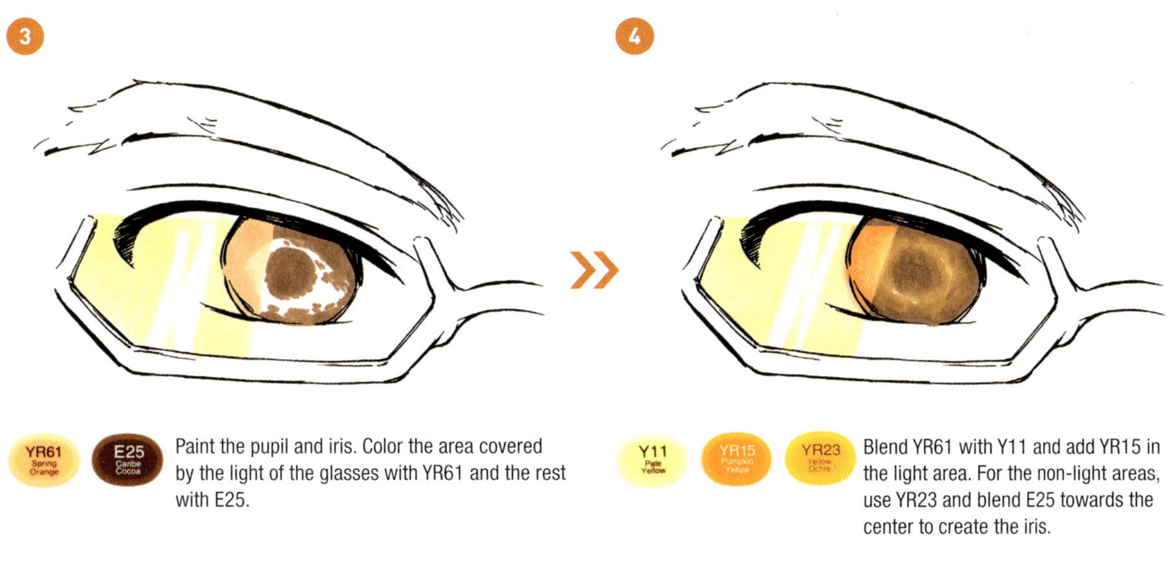

3

YR61 — Spring Orange · E25 — Caribe Cocoa

Paint the pupil and iris. Color the area covered by the light of the glasses with YR61 and the rest with E25.

4

Y11 — Pale Yellow · YR15 — Pumpkin Yellow · YR23 — Yellow Ochre

Blend YR61 with Y11 and add YR15 in the light area. For the non-light areas, use YR23 and blend E25 towards the center to create the iris.

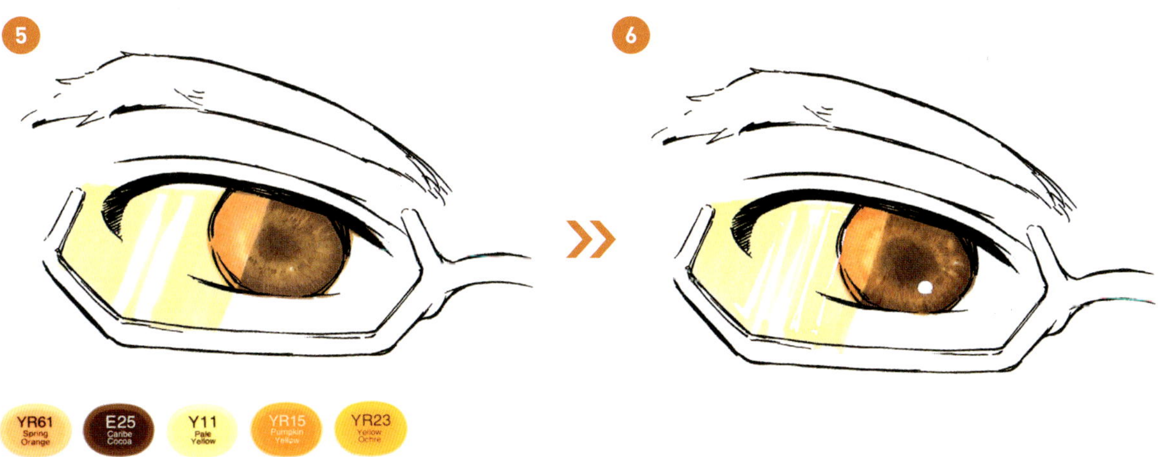

5

YR61 — Spring Orange · E25 — Caribe Cocoa · Y11 — Pale Yellow · YR15 — Pumpkin Yellow · YR23 — Yellow Ochre

Use the colors from **2** to **4** and adjust as desired.

6 Use white ink to express specular light spots to complete.

Backlit Skin

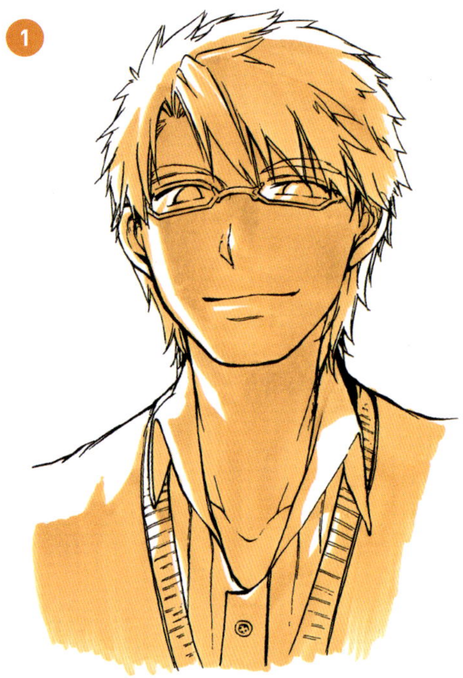

1

The skin is expressed through backlighting. Here's an image of the shaded area.

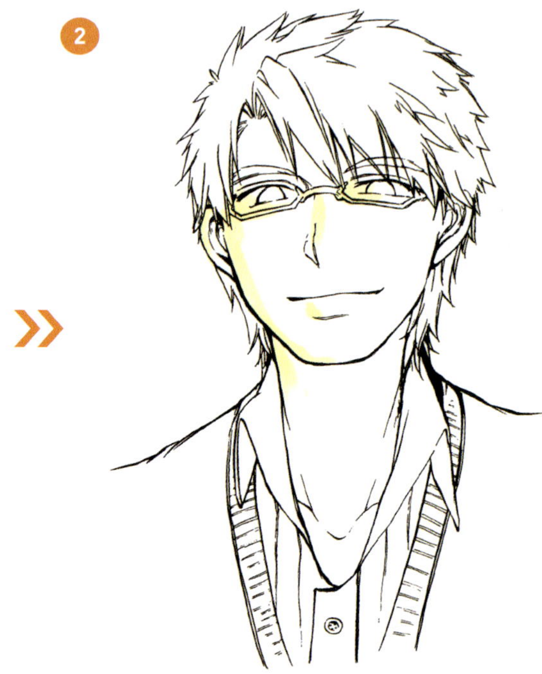

2

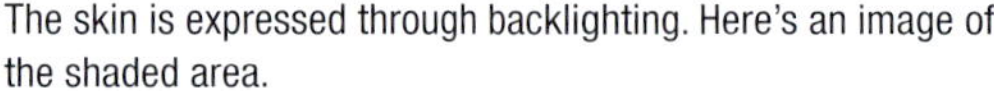
Y11
Pale
Yellow

Use Y11 to add color where the light hits.

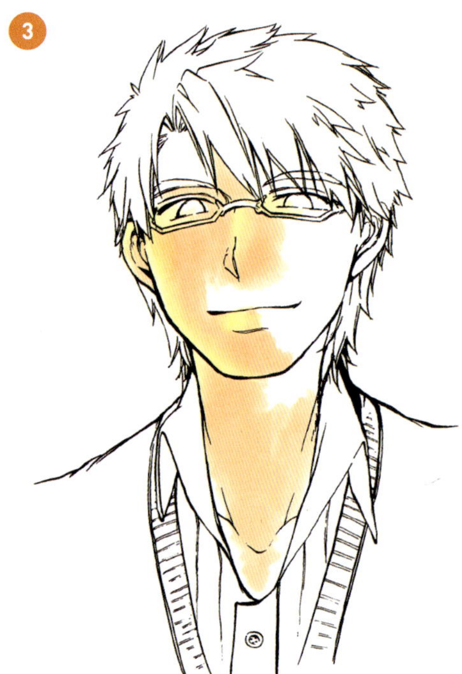

3

YR20
Yellowish
Shade

Connect the Y11 with YR20. This is the original skin color.

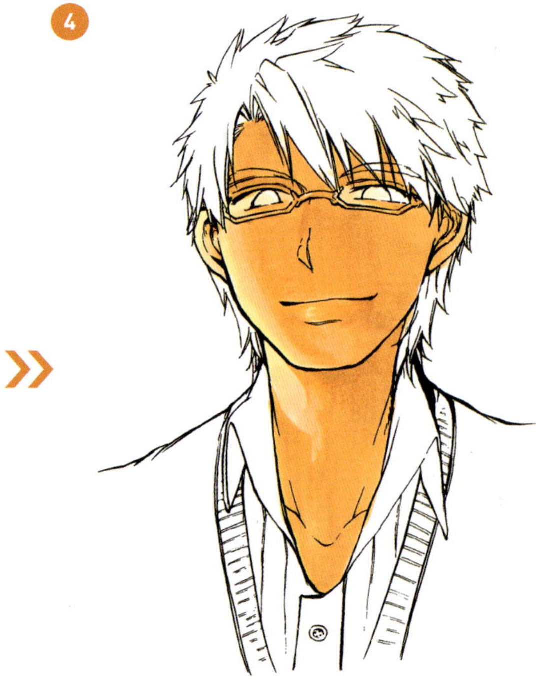

4

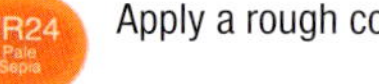
YR24
Pale
Sepia

Apply a rough coat of YR24. Don't worry if it looks darker.

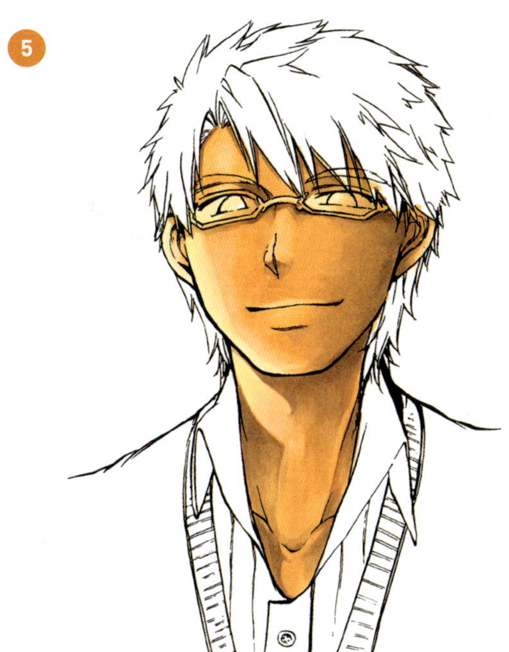

5

EX

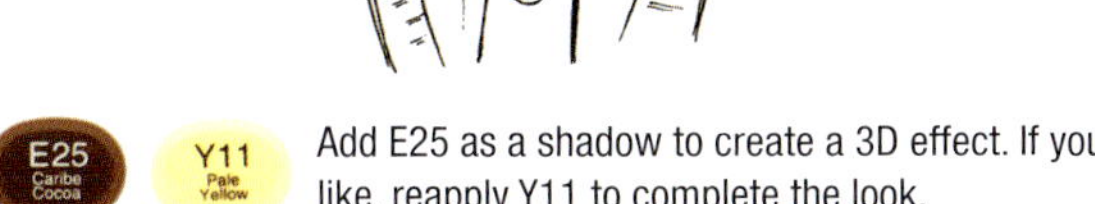

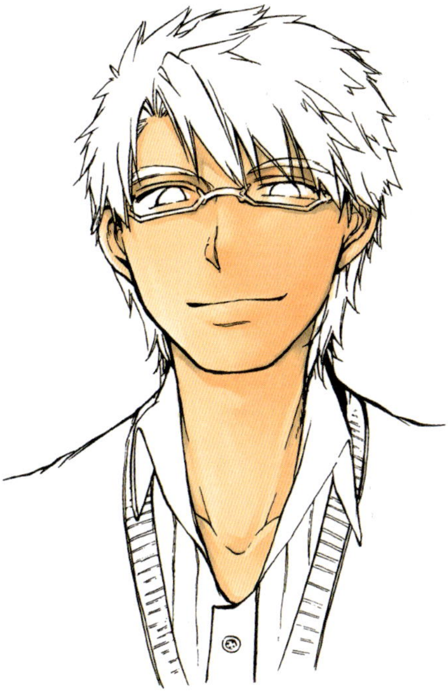

E25 Caribe Cocoa
Y11 Pale Yellow

Add E25 as a shadow to create a 3D effect. If you like, reapply Y11 to complete the look.

An example of direct lighting. This is what it looks like if the light comes from the front.

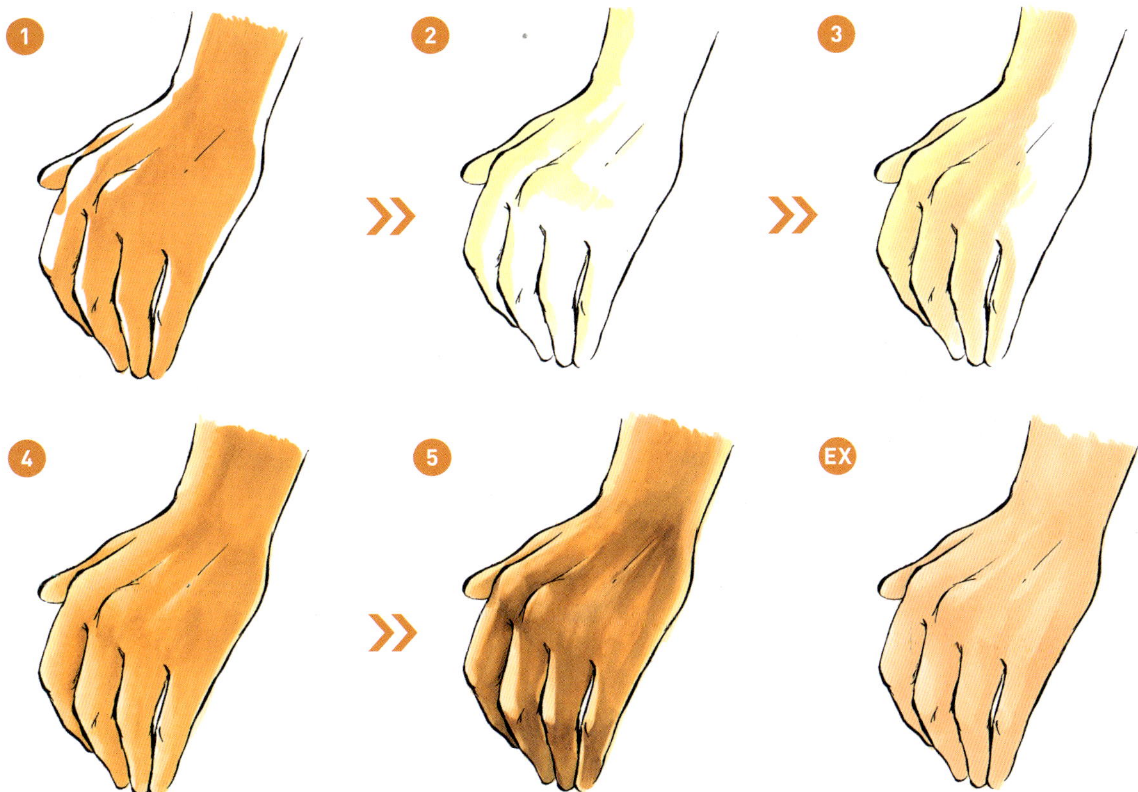

Color the hands exactly the same as you painted the face.

Pants and Shoes

1 We will paint the pants like this.

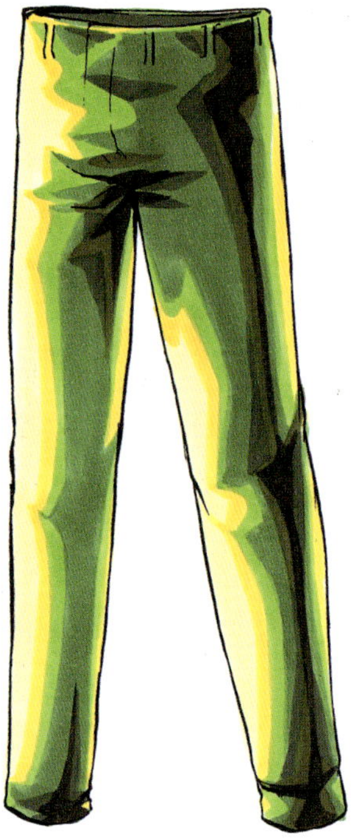

2 **T8** Toner Gray No.8 — First, paint the shadow areas with T8.

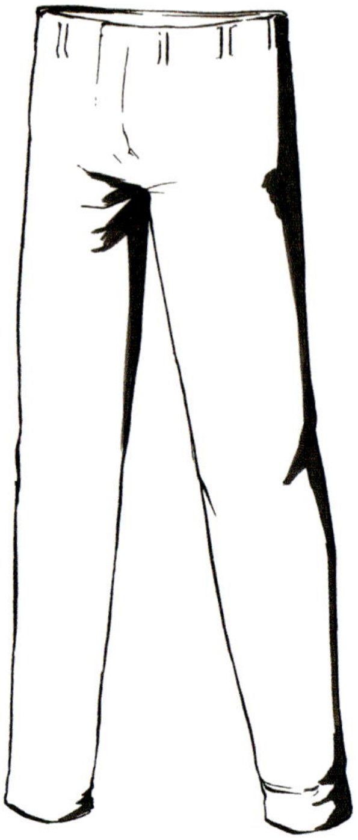

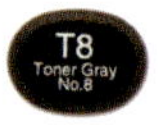

3 **YG97** Spanish Olive · **BG78** Bronze · **YG67** Moss — Blend the area with YG97 > BG78 > YG67.

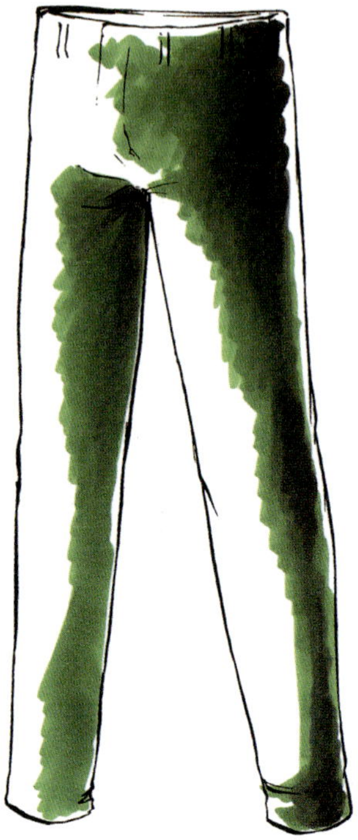

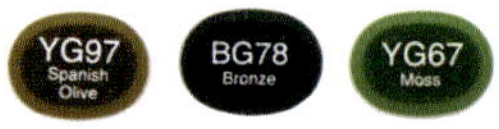

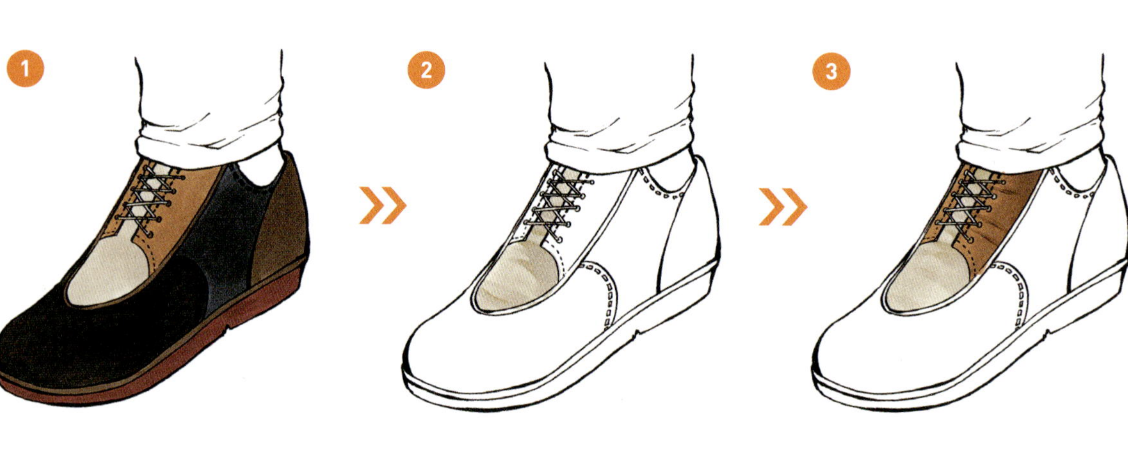

1 The first step is to decide on a general color scheme. We'll paint each part like this.

2 **YG91** Putty · **W2** Warm Gray No.2 — Start with the lightest color (remember, it's light so it's okay if it spreads out to neighboring areas!). After applying W2 as a base, draw in the creases with YG91 and W2.

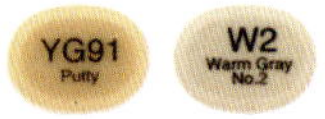

3 **E37** Sepia · **E25** Caribe Cocoa · **E39** Leather — Next is the throat of the shoe. Shade with E37 and blend E25. If you want to add creases, just use E39 and add thin horizontal lines.

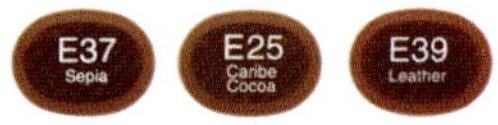

Then apply YG25 > Y08 > Y11, blending as you go. This is the base coat, so it's okay if it's uneven. Paint aggressively!

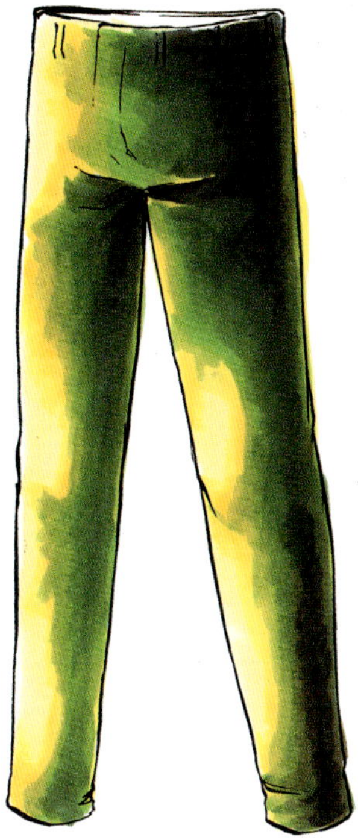

Add fine creases next. Use E79 and E17 in addition to the colors used in **2** to **4**.

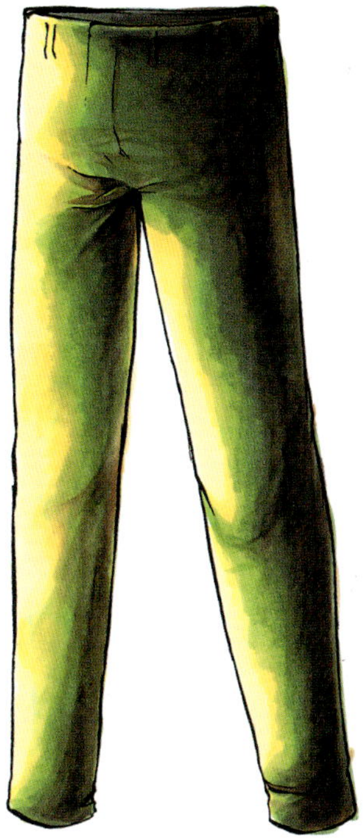

For the layer of light, blend T8 until it becomes pale. You're done!

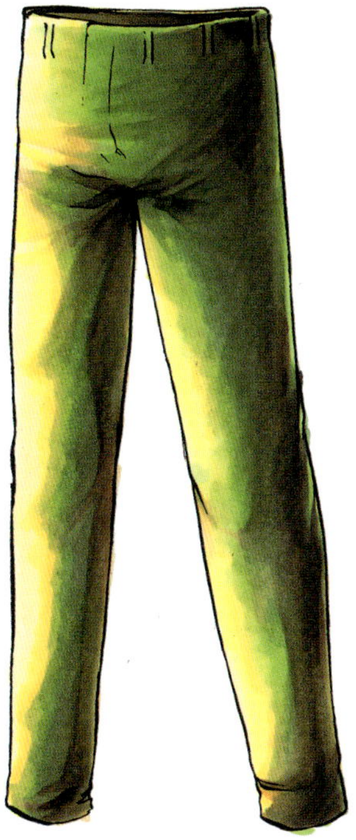

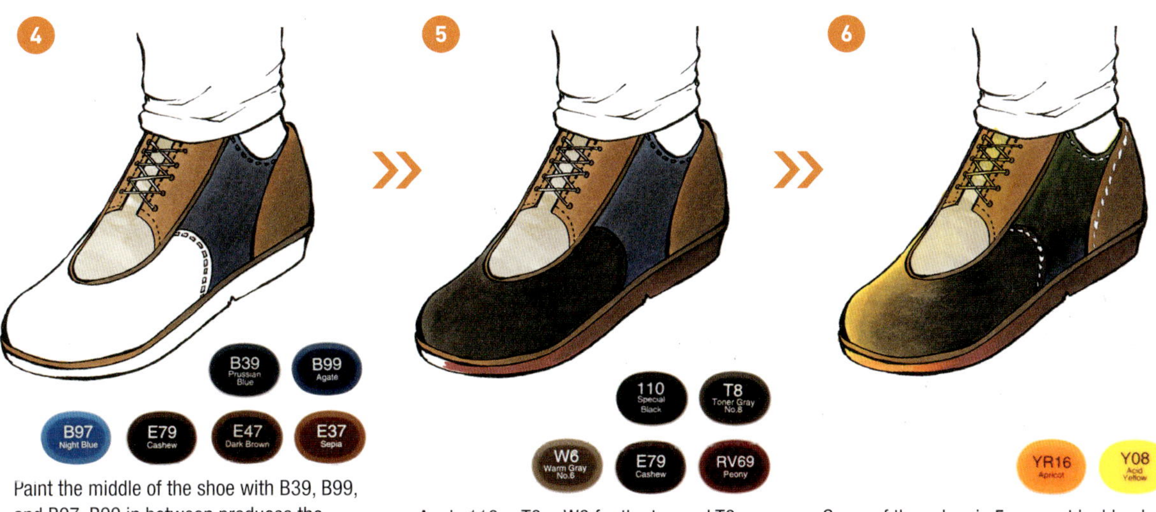

Paint the middle of the shoe with B39, B99, and B97. B99 in between produces the texture of sanded leather. The heel is painted with E79 > E47 > E37, and the border between the heel and the sole is painted in the same way.

Apply 110 > T8 > W6 for the toe and T8 > E79 > RV69 for the sole.

Some of the colors in **5** may not be blended by layering. Feel free to express light by overlaying YR16 and Y08 on top. Finally, add in the thread with white ink and you are done!

Shirt and Jacket

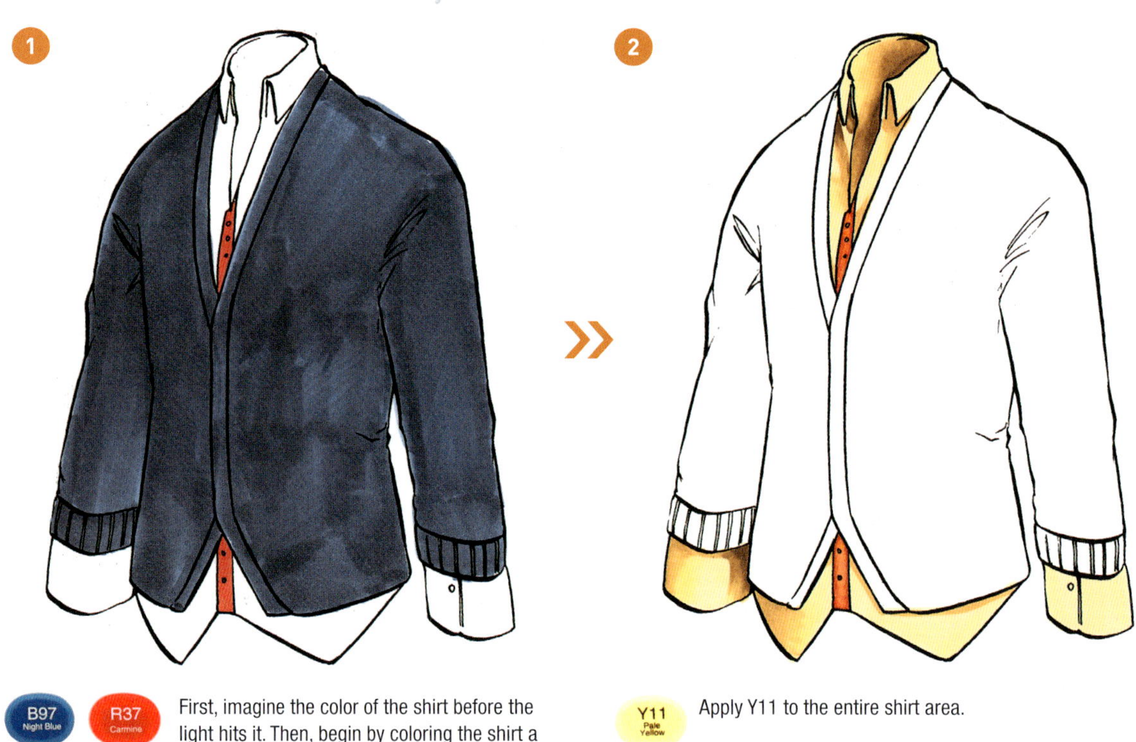

1 B97 Night Blue R37 Carmine

First, imagine the color of the shirt before the light hits it. Then, begin by coloring the shirt a lighter color because the sunset light is hitting it.

2 Y11 Pale Yellow

Apply Y11 to the entire shirt area.

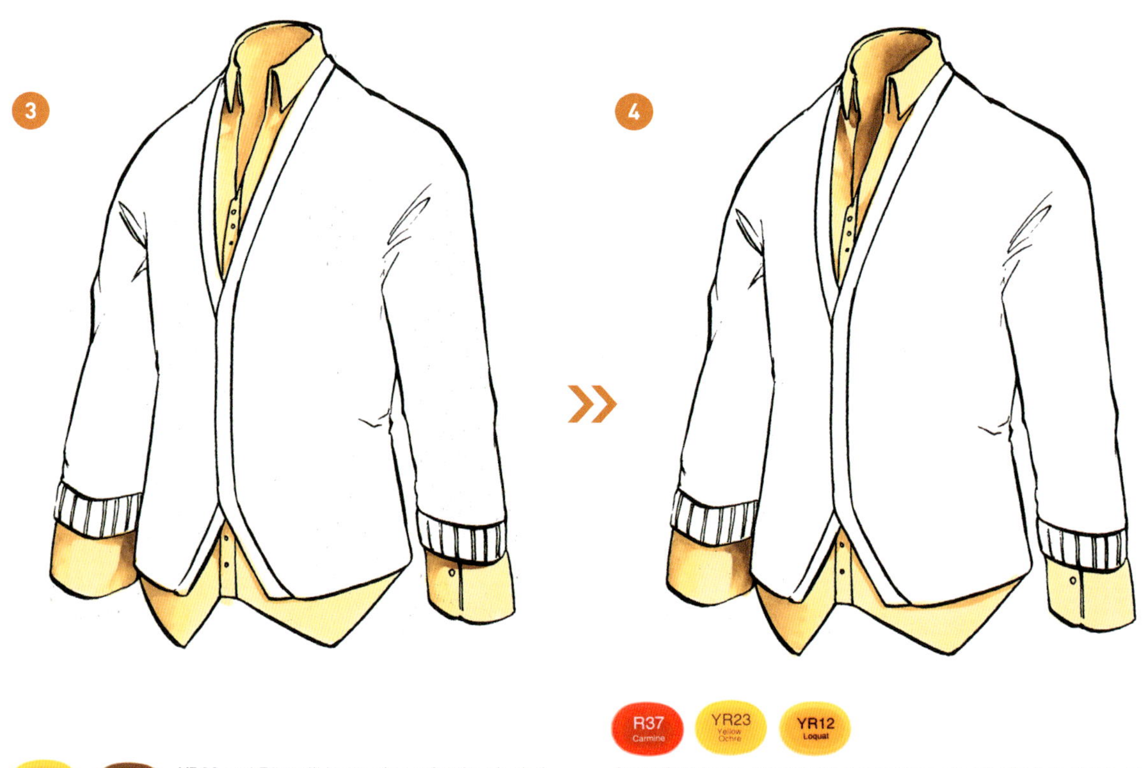

3 YR23 Yellow Ochre E37 Sepia

YR23 and E37 will be used to paint the shaded areas of the shirt.

4 R37 Carmine YR23 Yellow Ochre YR12 Loquat

Apply R37 to the area where the buttons are attached. To finish, blend the E37 with YR23 and YR11 where you see light due the creases.

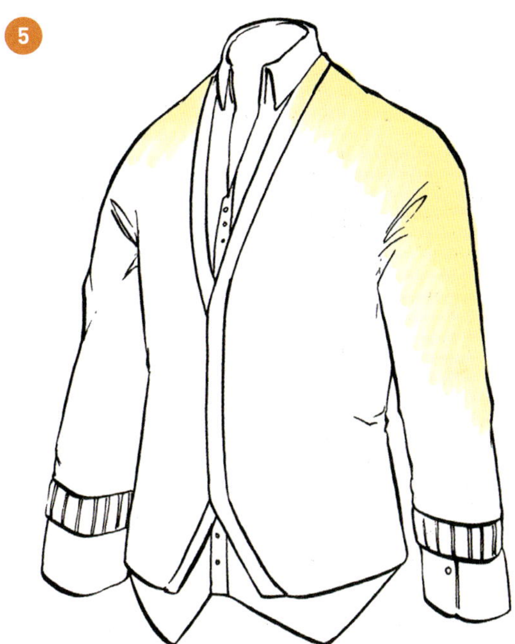

5

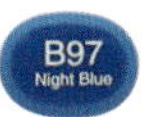
Y11
Pale Yellow

This is the upper part of the jacket. Paint the area where the light will hit with Y11 to secure it (it was bothersome to color while figuring out how wide the light would be).

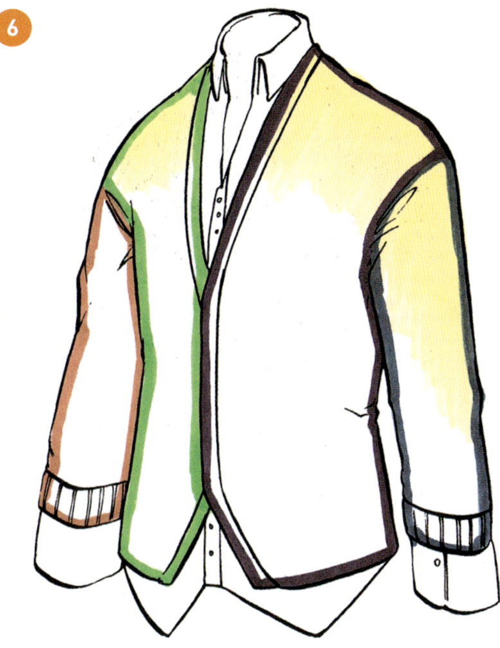

6

Next, think about your strategy. You can start from anywhere, but it is easier to paint if you divide it into blocks in your mind. In this particular case, it looks like this.

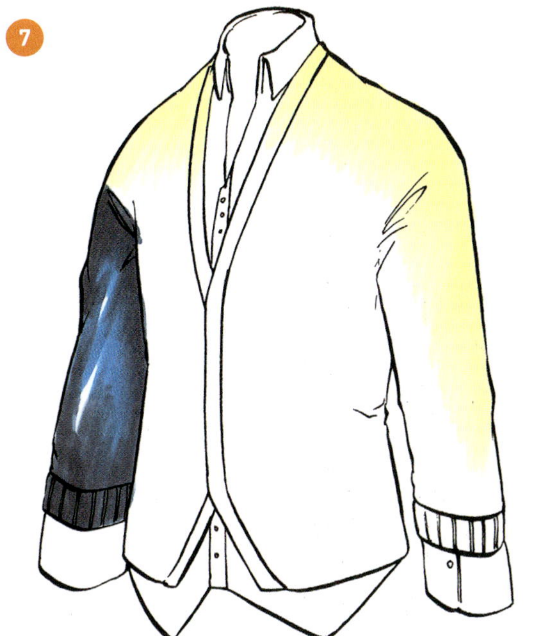

7

B97
Night Blue

B14
Light Blue

In my case, I started with areas of deepest shadow, using B97 as the base color and B14 to blend the creases.

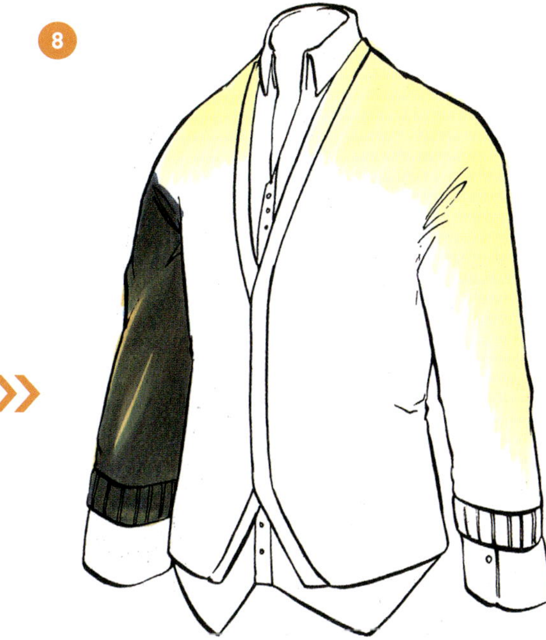

8

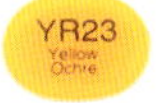
YR23
Yellow Ochre

Overlay YR23 quickly. This completes the base coat. The rest is a repeat of this pattern.

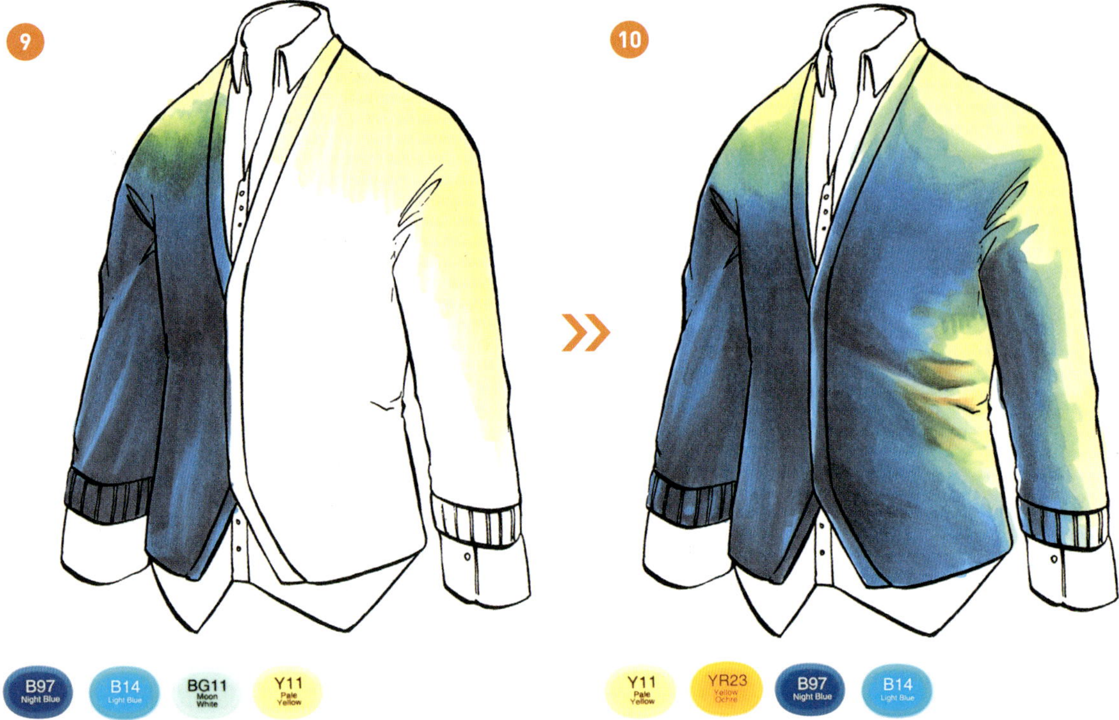

9

B97 — Night Blue B14 — Light Blue BG11 — Moon White Y11 — Pale Yellow

For blocks with light, gradate the lit area using B97 > B14 > BG11 > Y11.

10

Y11 — Pale Yellow YR23 — Yellow Ochre B97 — Night Blue B14 — Light Blue

On the right side, since it is exposed to more light, a few creases should be drawn during the base coat. After drawing the light colored creases with Y11, use YR23 as a connection to B97 and B14.

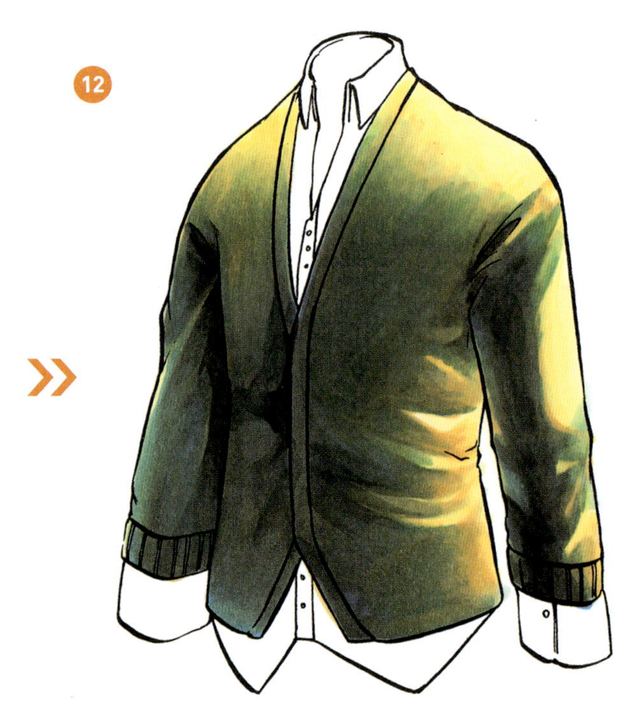

11

Y11 — Pale Yellow YR23 — Yellow Ochre

Paint all areas except for the light part of Y11 with YR23. Then, use YR23 > Y11 to create the gradation for Y11.

12

T8 — Toner Gray No.8

Add creases, etc. with T8 and the colors used so far. You're done!

Strong Light and Hair

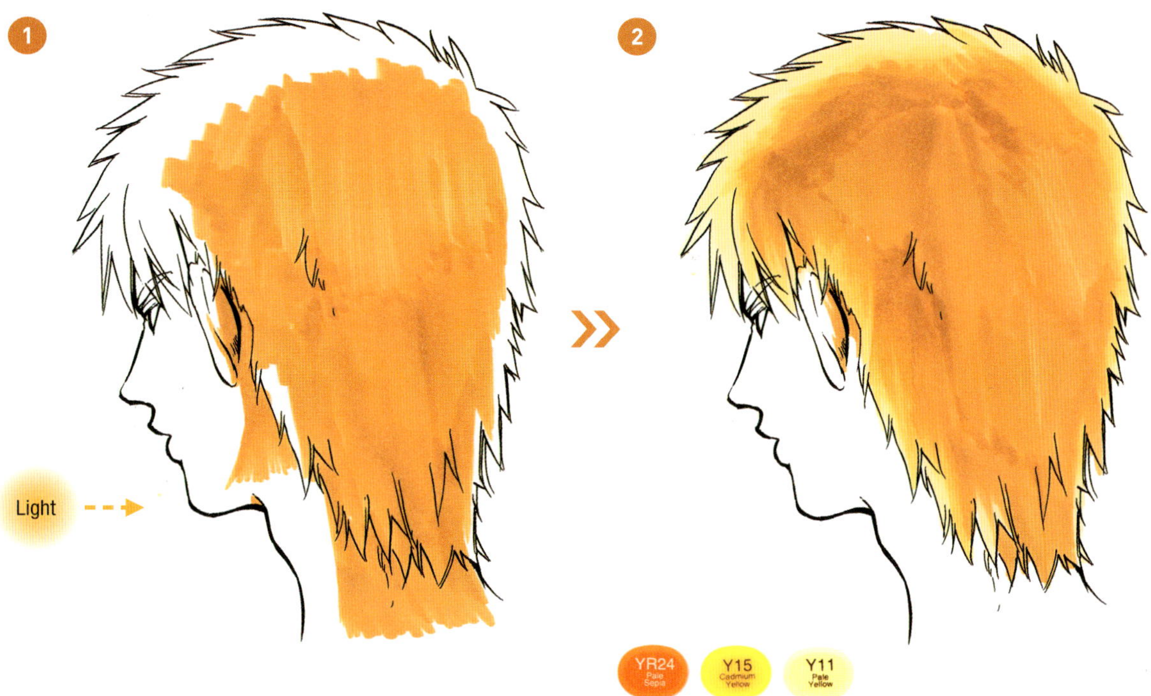

1 — YR24 Pale Sepia

Paint all at once with YR24. The direction the light comes from is broad, and will thus leave a small white space on the shaded area.

2 — Start from the lower edge of where the light hits. Use YR24, Y15, and Y11 to create gradations to the edge. Don't worry about unevenness, as you'll be adding in the hair flow later.

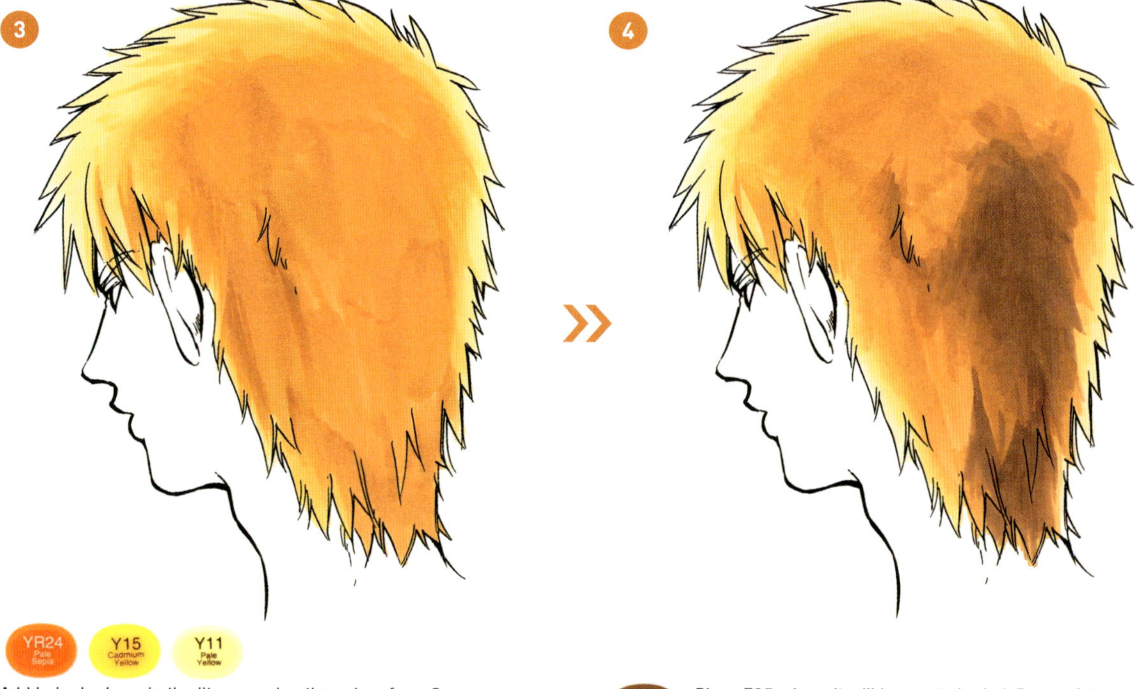

3 — Add hair shadows in the lit area using the colors from **2**.

4 — E25 Caribe Cocoa

Place E25 where it will be most shaded. Be careful not to make it too big!

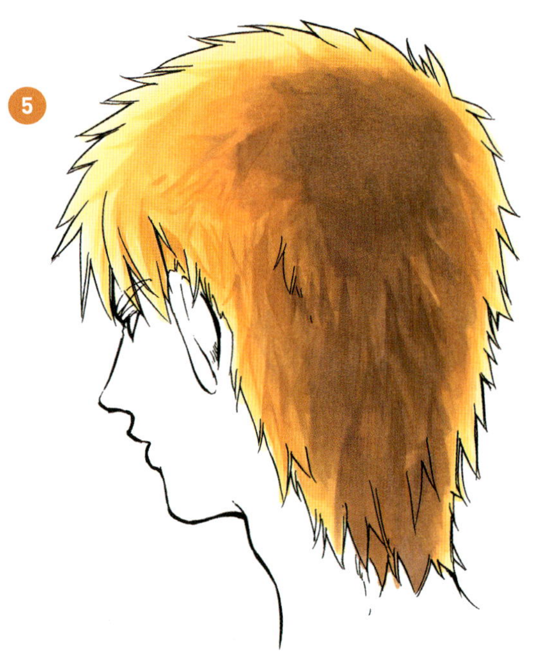

5

E25
Caribe Cocoa

For the shadow side, draw in the flow of the hair and you're done!

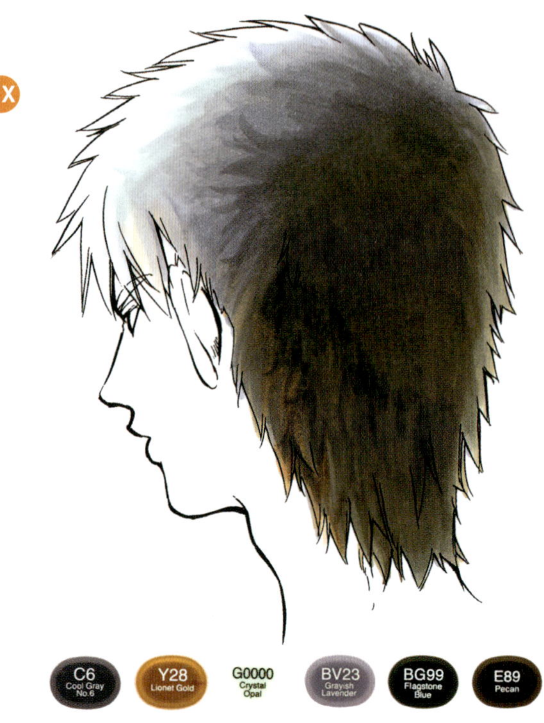

EX

C6
Cool Gray No.6

Y28
Lionet Gold

G0000
Crystal Opal

BV23
Grayish Lavender

BG99
Flagstone Blue

E89
Pecan

As another example, here is what happens when white light hits dark hair.

Transition

1

Differences in the Color of Light Over Time

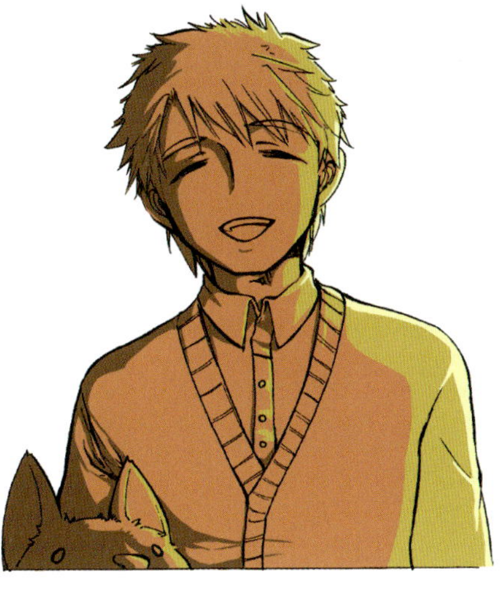

The difference in light can indicate the time of day in an illustration. Here are some of the most obvious examples. These are all backlit environments.

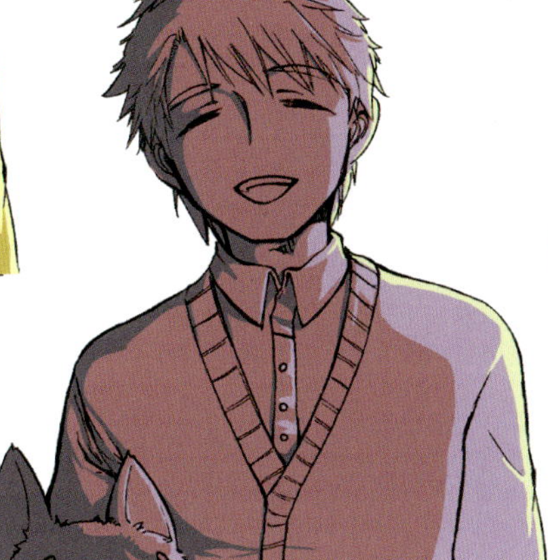

● **At Dusk**
Use red and orange tones.

● **Dawn**
Using blue and purple.

● **Moonlight**
Use a greenish color scheme. The point is to apply the darkest part second.

Next

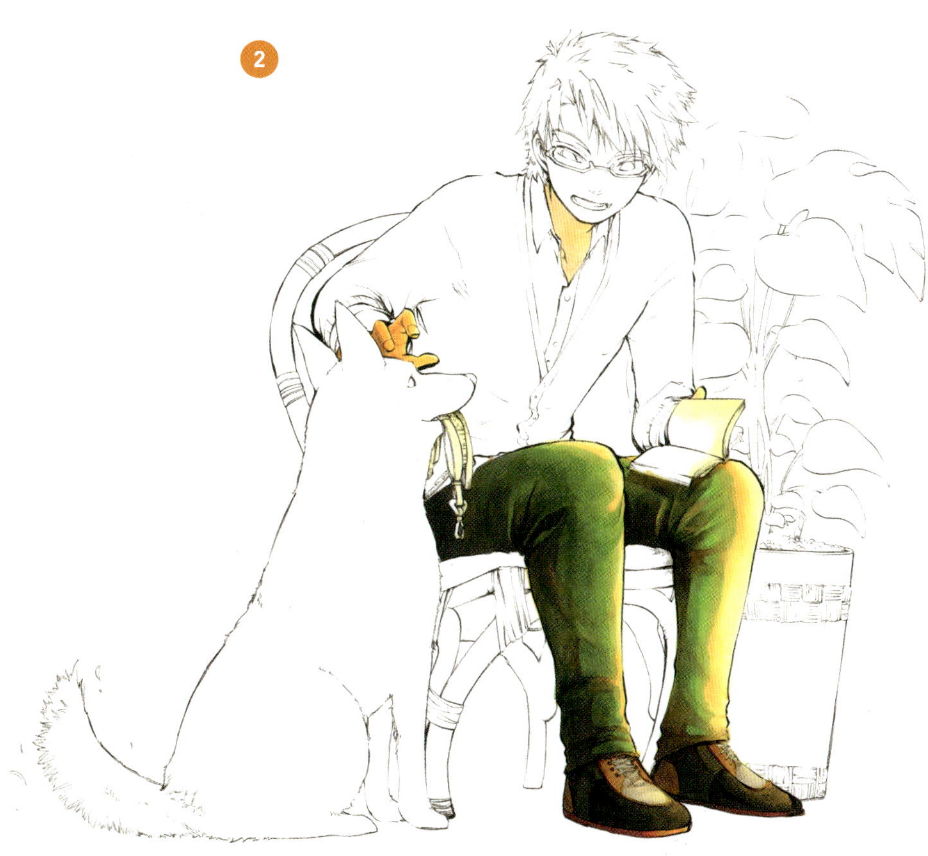

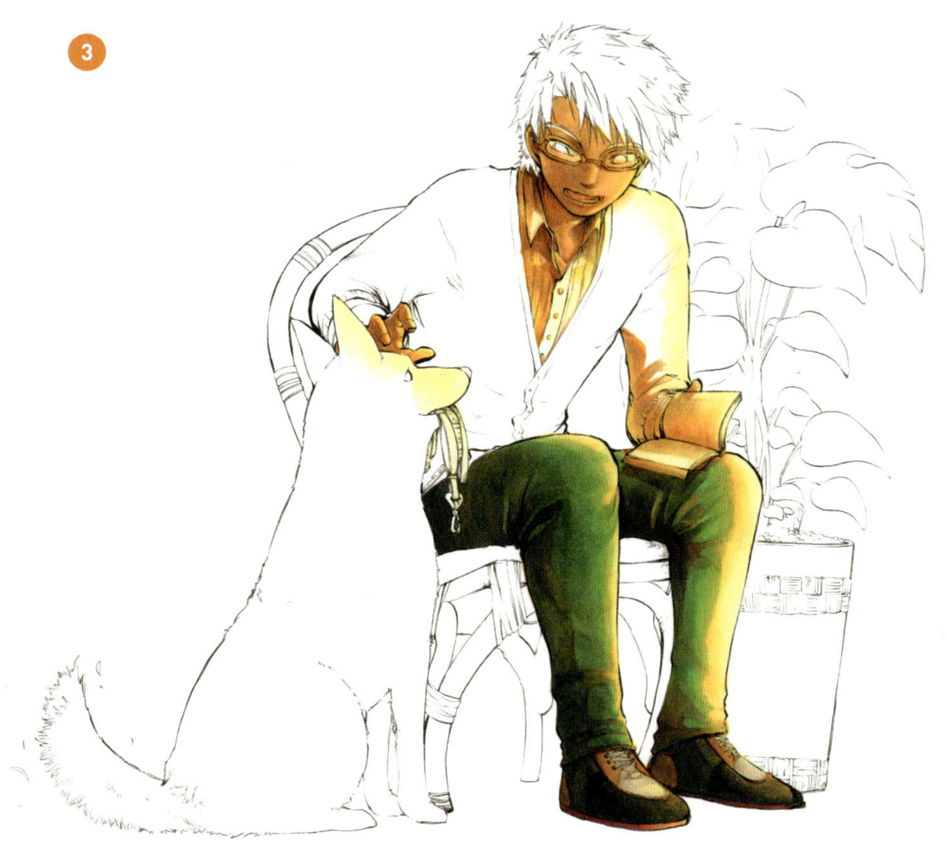

3

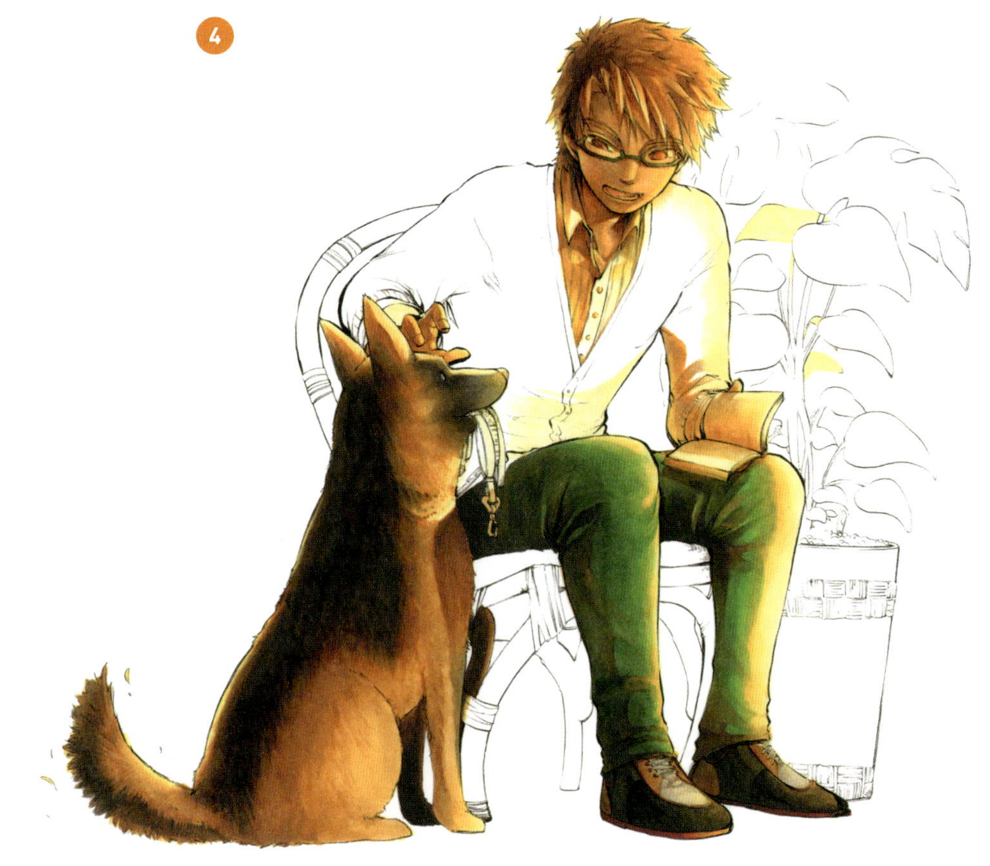

4

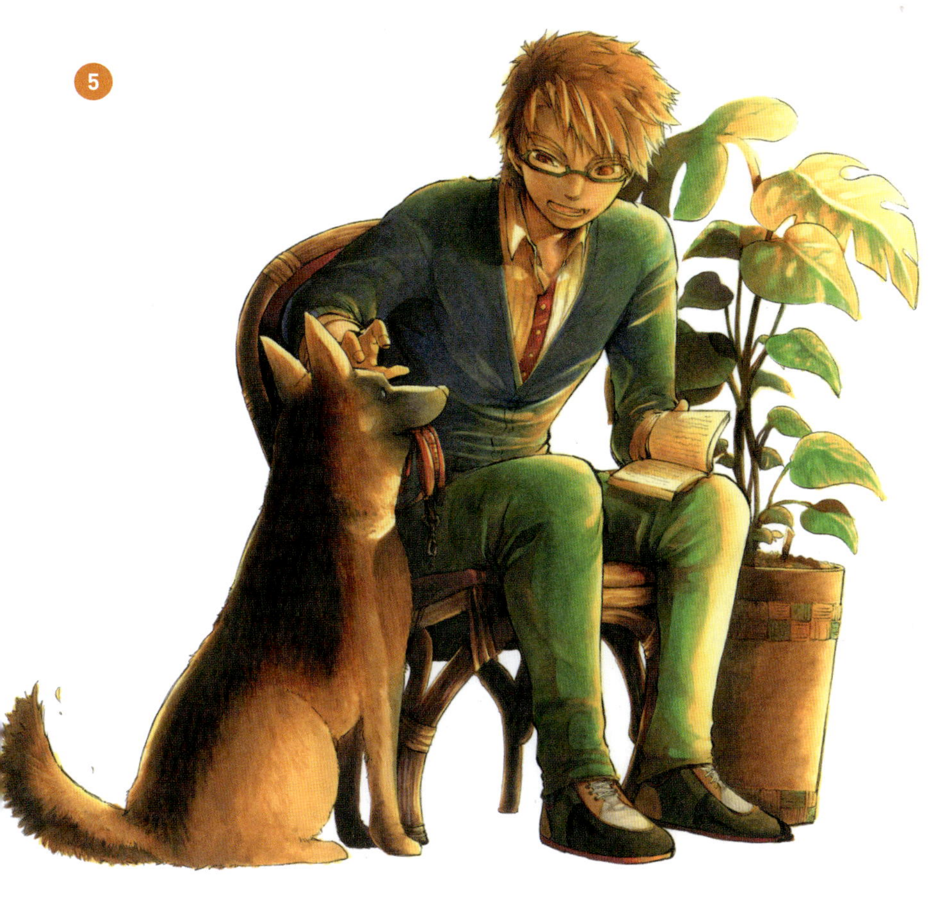

Transition

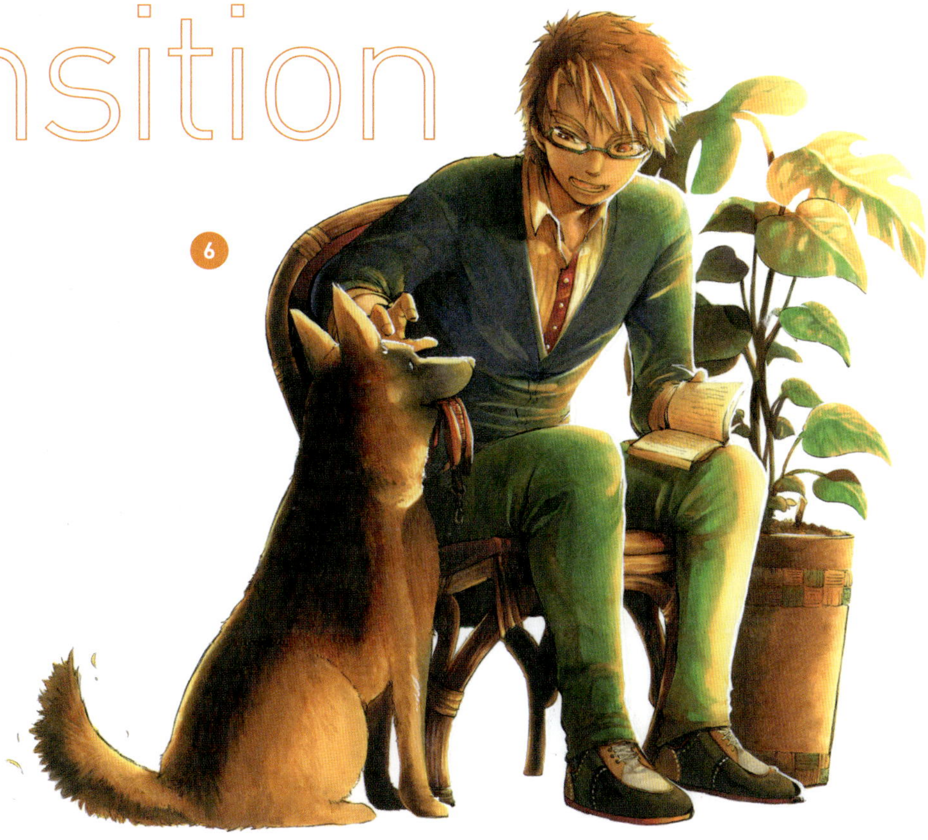

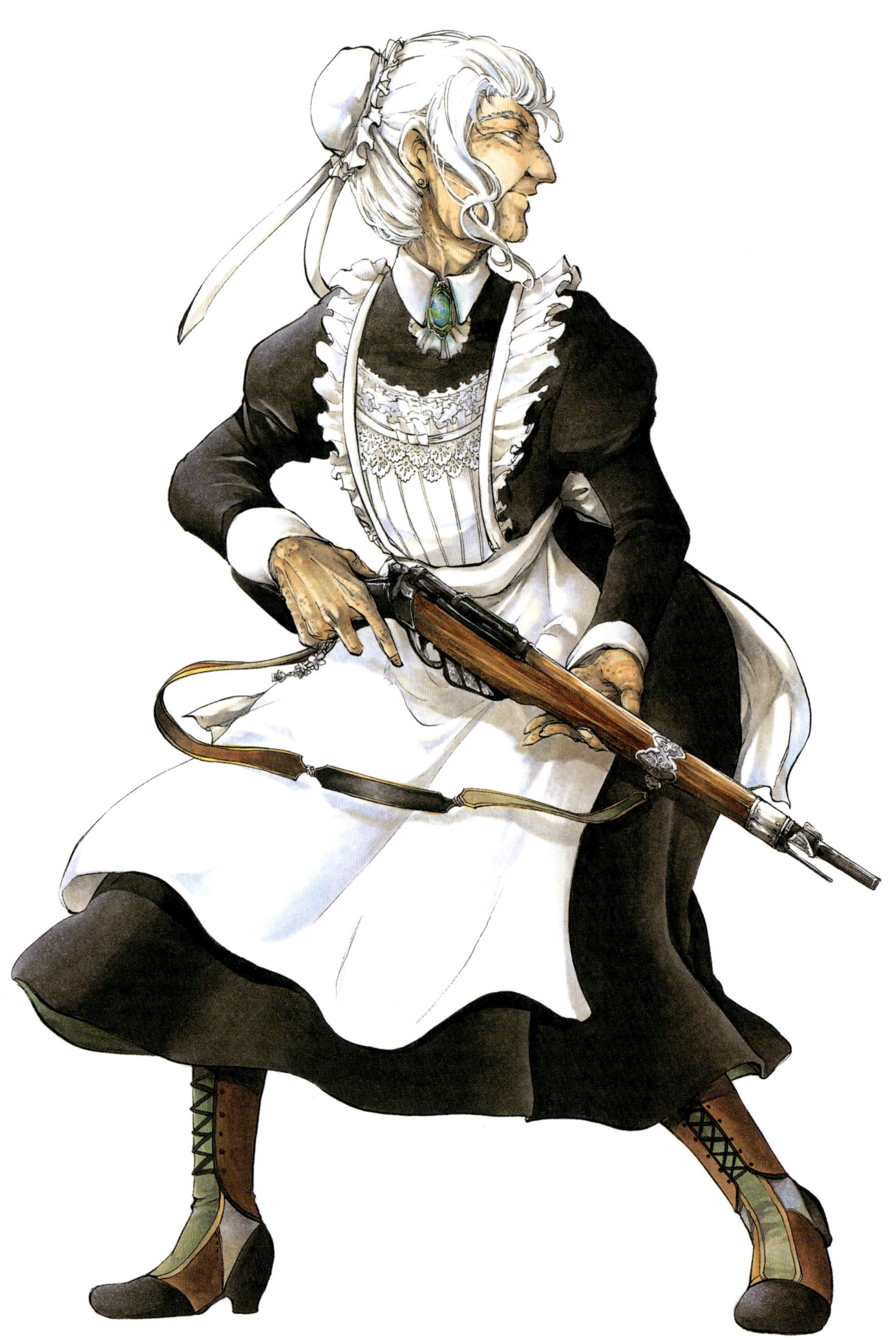

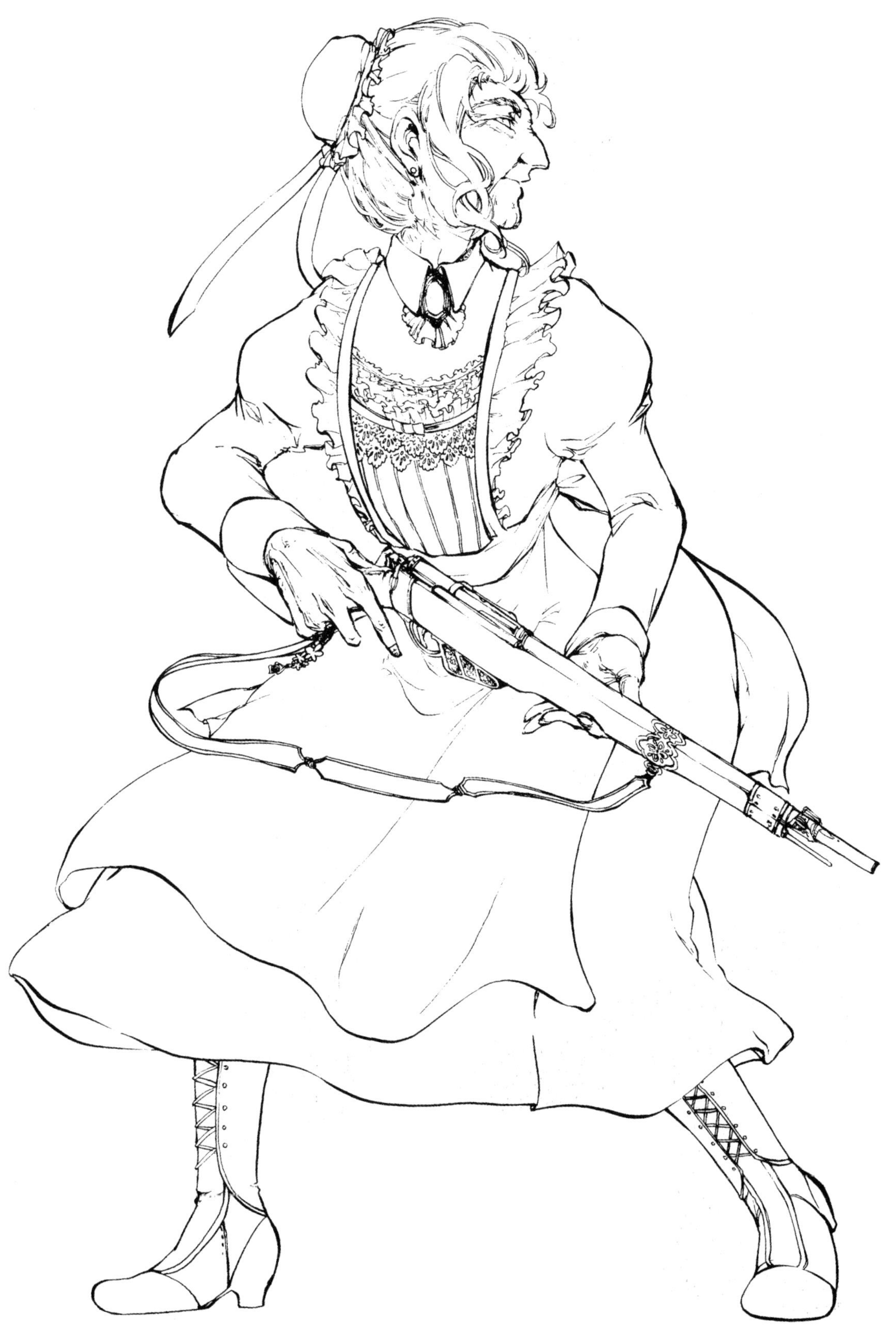

Coloring to Create Heaviness

This is a technique that uses dark colors to create a strong texture. It's easy to shy away from applying dark colors with COPIC markers, but don't be afraid to just go for it.

Selected Ink

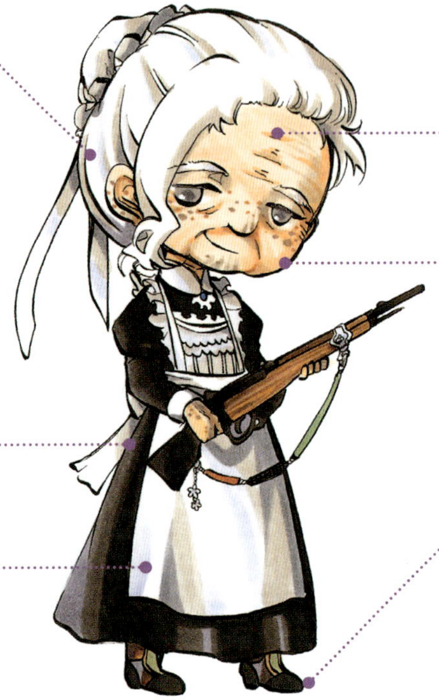

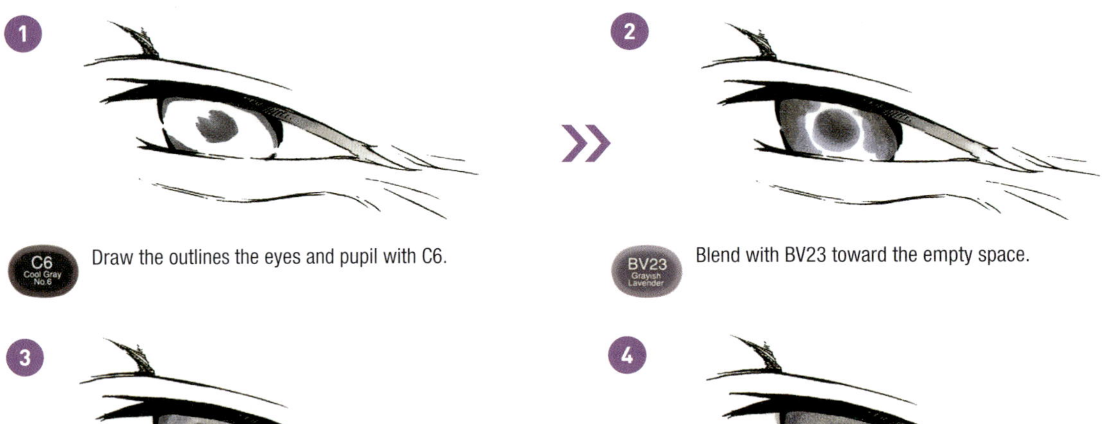

Hair

- BV23 Grayish Lavender
- W2 Warm Gray No.2
- B60 Pale Blue Gray
- C5 Cool Gray No.5

Skirt

- 110 Special Black
- W7 Warm Gray No.7
- BV23 Grayish Lavender

Apron

- C4 Cool Gray No.4
- W2 Warm Gray No.2
- B60 Pale Blue Gray
- 0 Colorless Blender

Wrinkles

- E71 Champagne
- E34 Toast
- W2 Warm Gray No.2

Skin

- YG91 Putty
- E53 Raw Silk
- Y23 Yellowish Beige
- W0 Warm Gray No.0
- YR000 Silk

Shoes

- E18 Copper
- YR24 Pale Sepia
- RV99 Argyle Purple
- BV23 Grayish Lavender
- YG91 Putty
- G99 Olive
- YG93 Grayish Yellow
- T9 Toner Gray No.9

Elderly Eyes

1 C6 Cool Gray No.6 — Draw the outlines the eyes and pupil with C6.

2 BV23 Grayish Lavender — Blend with BV23 toward the empty space.

3 T3 Toner Gray No.3 — Blend C6 and BV23 with T3.

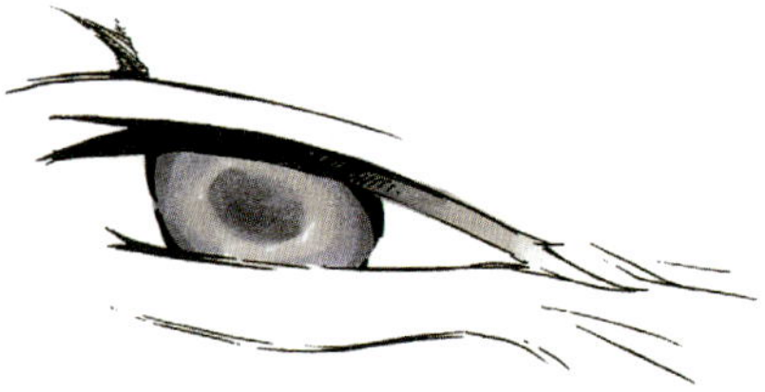

4 BV23 Grayish Lavender, T3 Toner Gray No.3 — Using BV23 and T3, blend alternately.

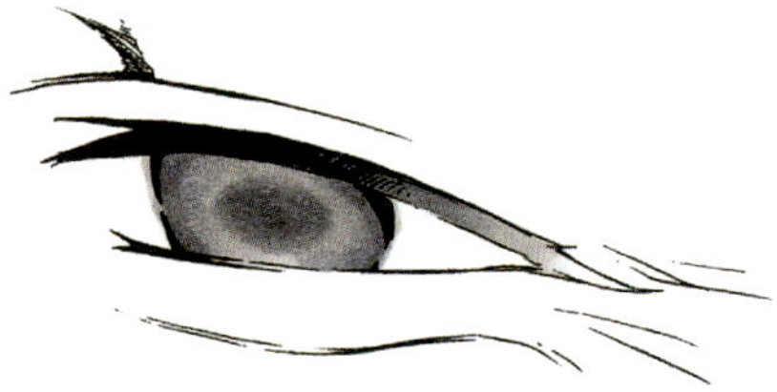

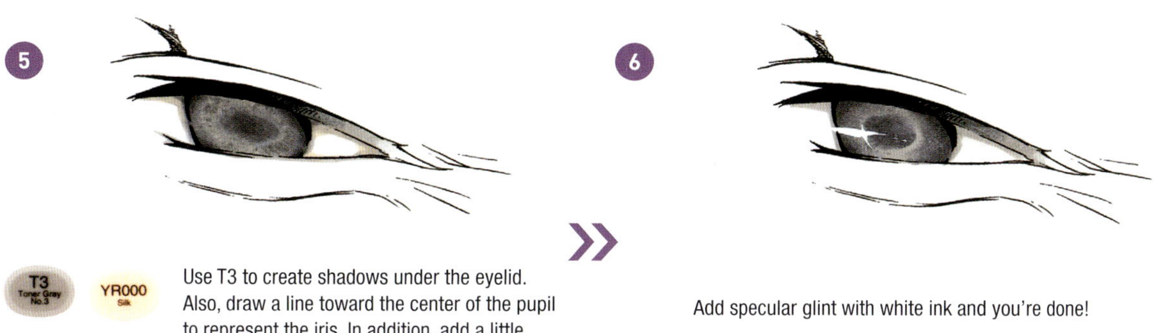

5 Use T3 to create shadows under the eyelid. Also, draw a line toward the center of the pupil to represent the iris. In addition, add a little YR000 to the whites of the eyes.

T3 Toner Gray No.3 | YR000 Silk

6 Add specular glint with white ink and you're done!

Lips with Wrinkles

1 Apply a solid coat of W0.

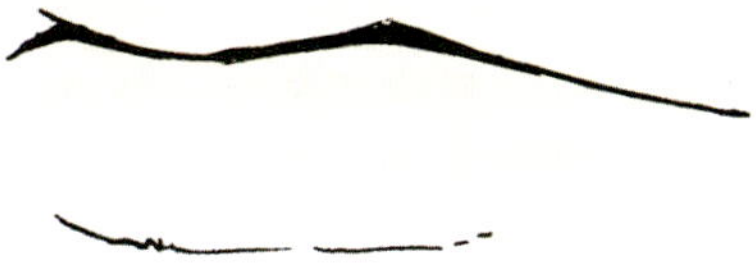

W0 Warm Gray No.0

2 Apply a dab of YR000 between the upper and lower lips.

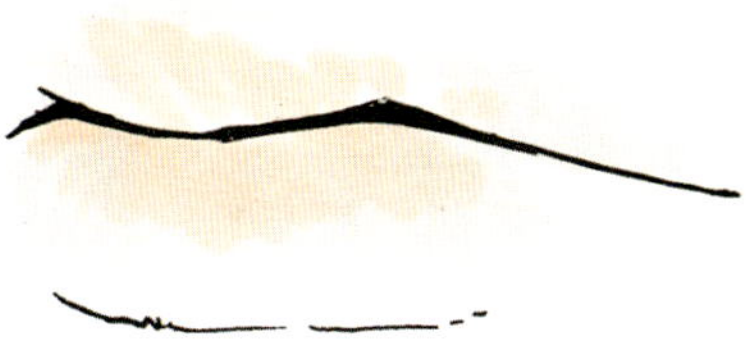

YR000 Silk

3 Apply RV91 to the entire lip area, starting from above.

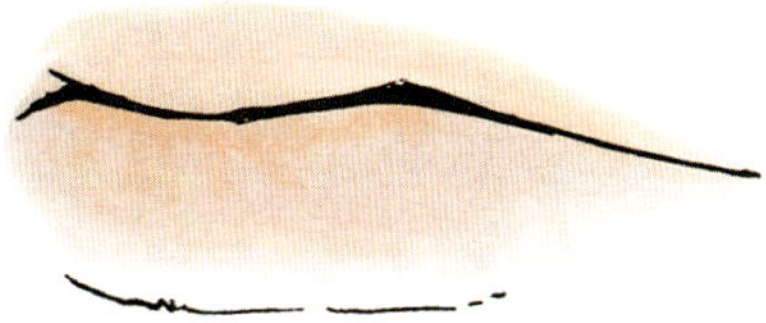

RV91 Grayish Cherry

4 Use E53 and Y000 to draw the lips, and then add in the vertical wrinkles.

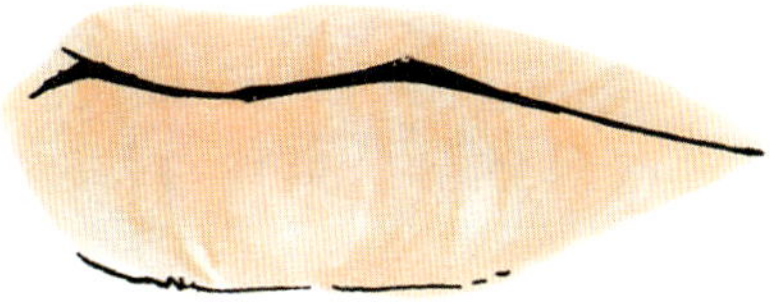

E53 Raw Silk | Y000 Pale Lemon

5 Overlay RV91 and R81. You're done!

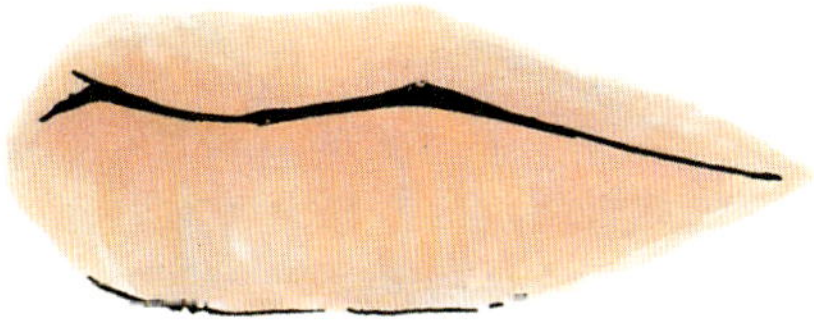

RV91 Grayish Cherry | R81 Rose Pink

6 Put some white ink on your finger and press down to finish. Be careful not to make it too shiny!

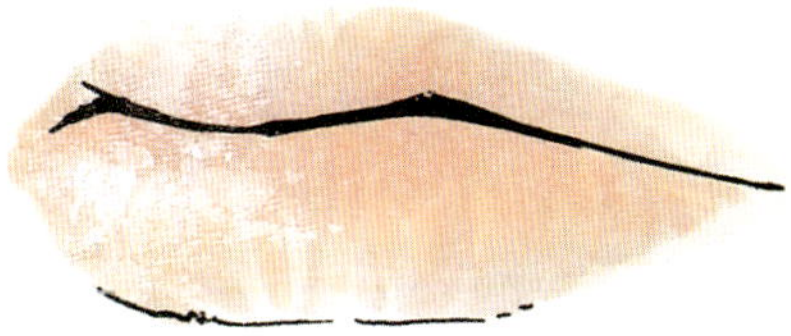

Expressing Elderly Skin

1

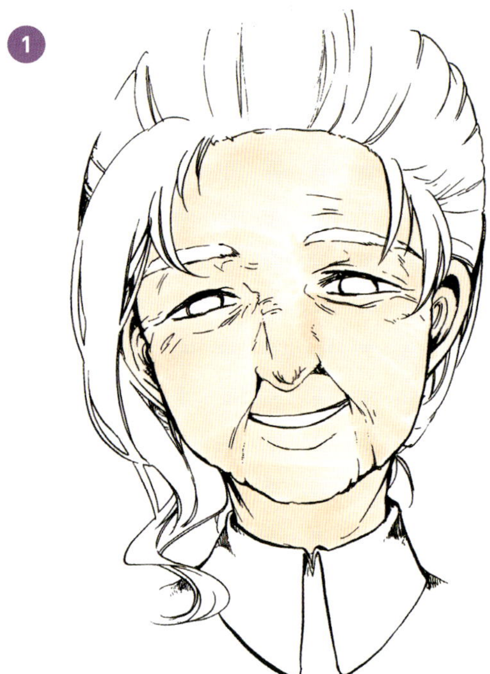

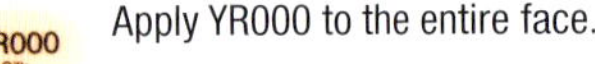

Apply YR000 to the entire face.

2

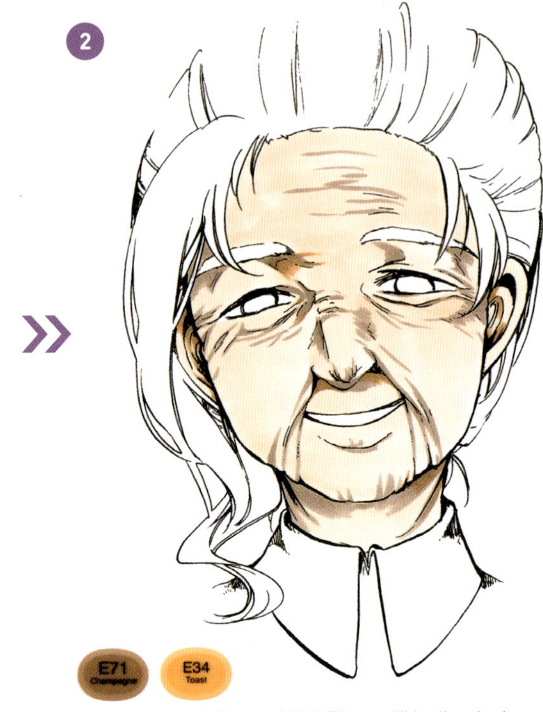

Add wrinkles with E71 and E34. These will be the shadows. If you want to add more wrinkles, put them at the corners of the eyes, chin, forehead, and between the eyebrows. For the bridge of the nose, draw a line toward the forehead.

3

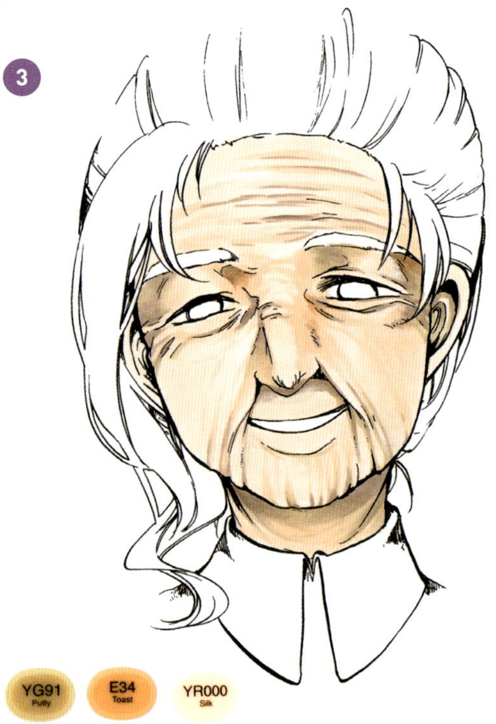

Blend the E71 with YG91, E34 and YR000. Be careful not to erase the sense of shadows in the wrinkles.

4

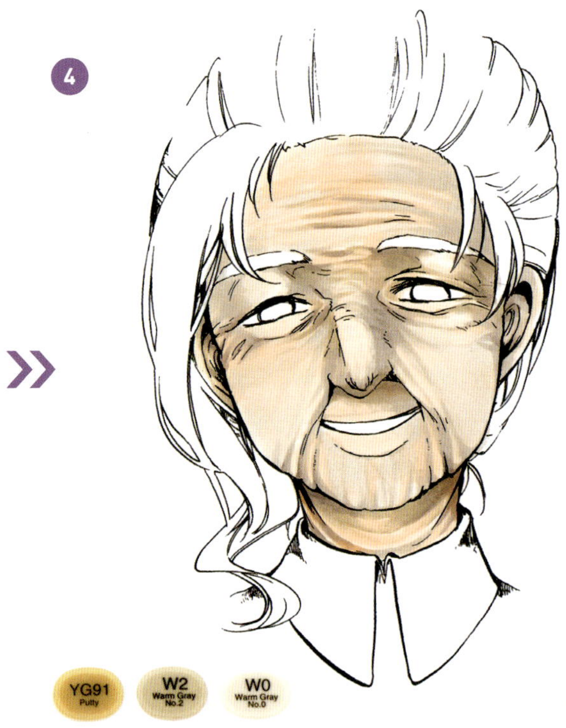

Use YG91 and W2 to create light shadows. Then, apply W0 over the entire face. This is an elderly lady, so the skin will be dull.

5

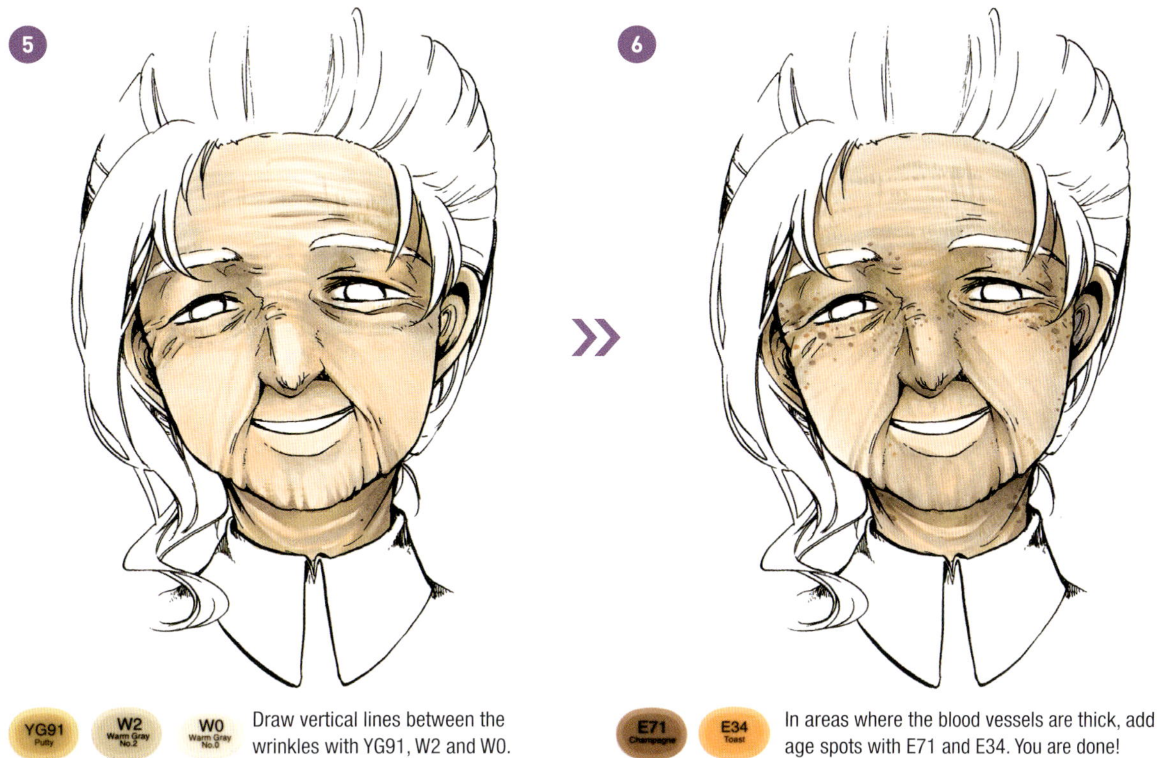

YG91 Putty · W2 Warm Gray No.2 · W0 Warm Gray No.0

Draw vertical lines between the wrinkles with YG91, W2 and W0.

6

E71 Champagne · E34 Toast

In areas where the blood vessels are thick, add age spots with E71 and E34. You are done!

7

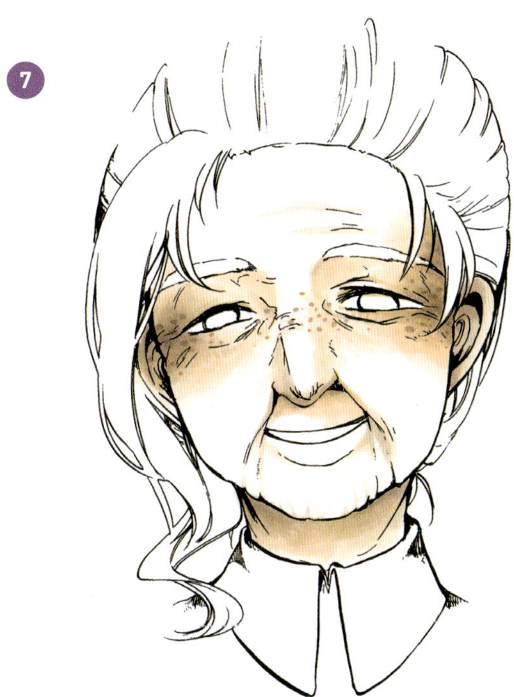

For reference, here is a blended version that is more clear. This will make the character look younger.

Hair Clips and Fabric Bulges

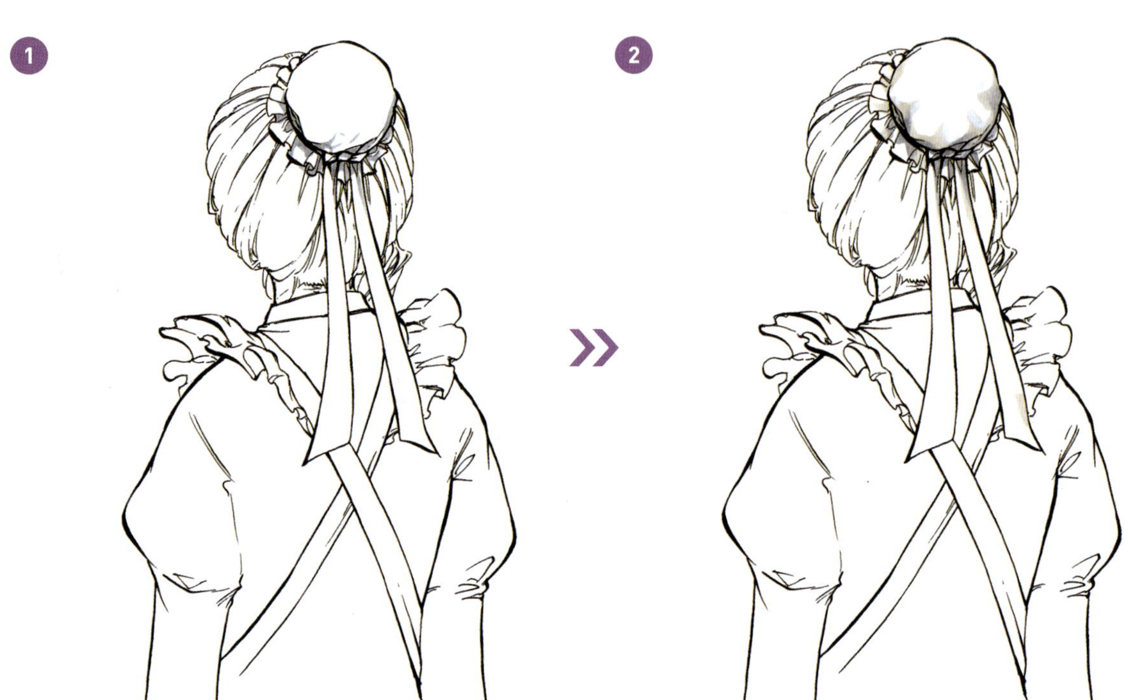

1

C4 — Paint with C4 where you think it's the darkest.

2

W2 — Determine the location of the creases and blend with W2.

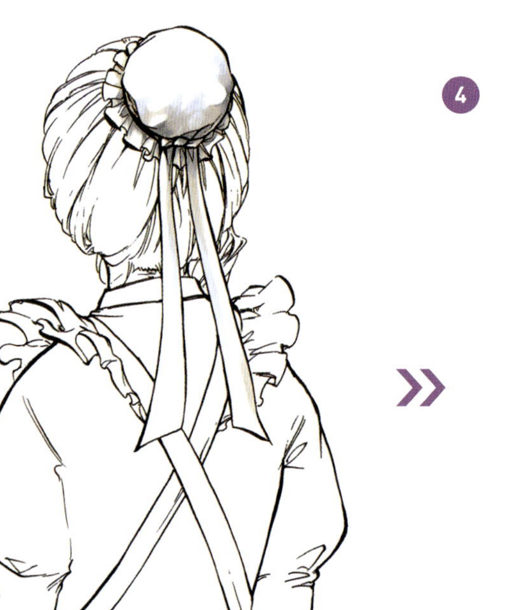

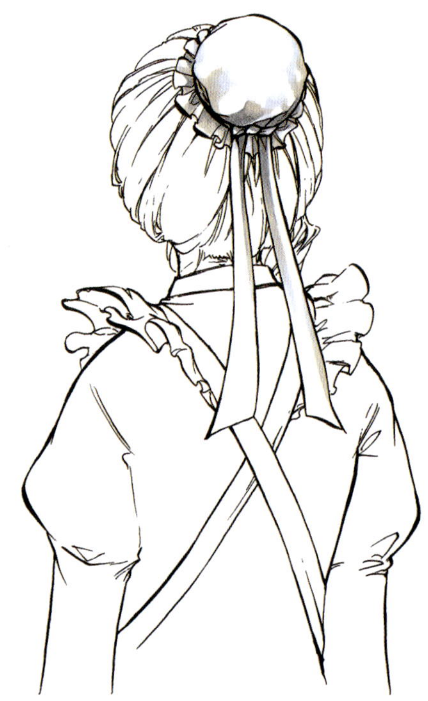

3

B60 — Following **2**, blend further with B60. The point is to blend only partly at the bun because of the creases created by the volume of the bun.

4

0 — Gradate the blended area with #0. If you get a crinkly look, you've succeeded!

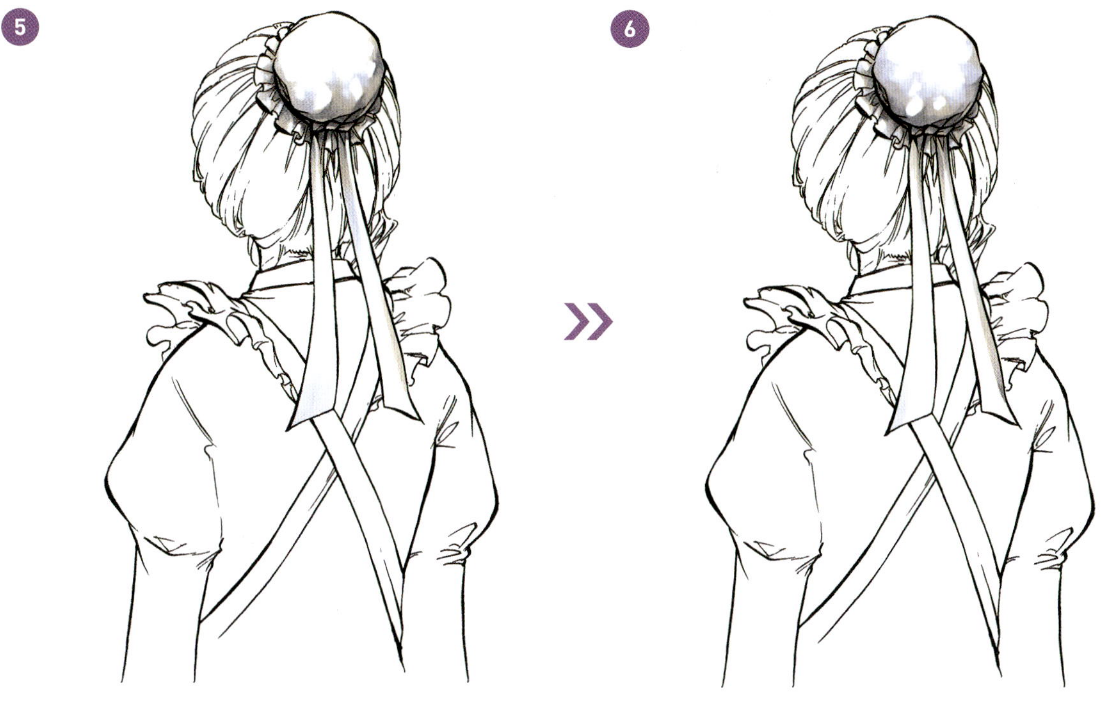

| 5 | | 6 |

C4 Cool Gray No.4 · W2 Warm Gray No.2 · B60 Pale Blue Gray

Use three colors to add creases and for the overlay. This will create texture.

Finally, put some white ink on your finger and press it directly onto the paper.

How to Express Gray Hair 1

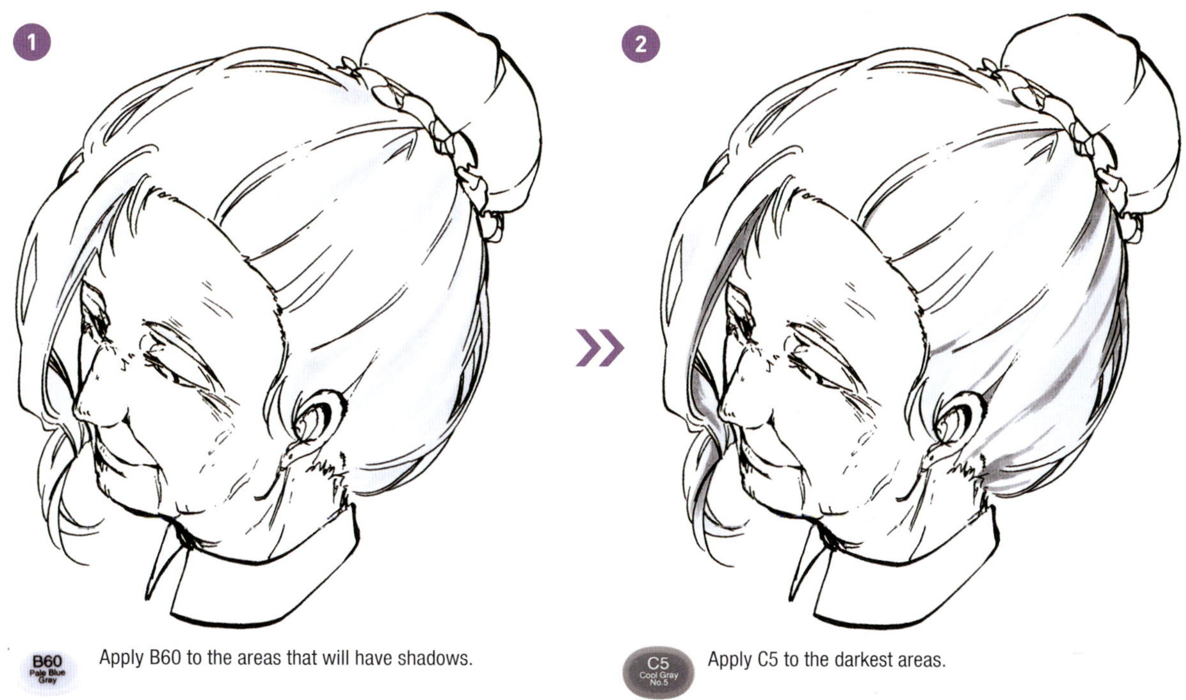

| 1 | | 2 |

B60 Pale Blue Gray — Apply B60 to the areas that will have shadows.

C5 Cool Gray No.5 — Apply C5 to the darkest areas.

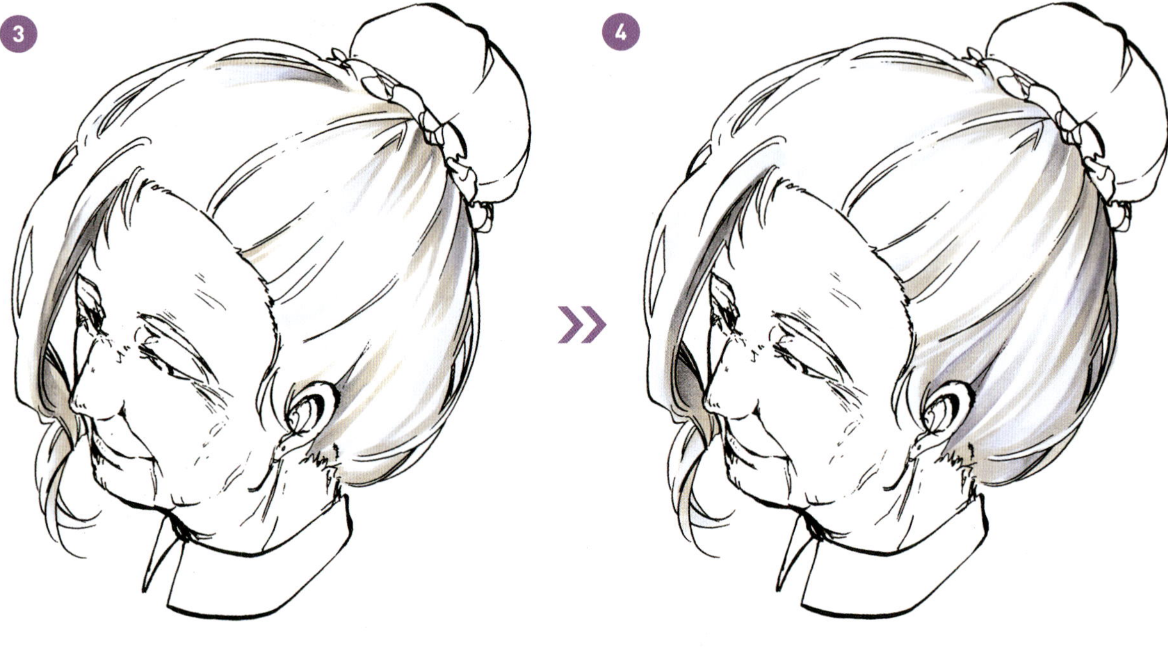

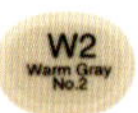  Add W2, blending with B60 each time you add some.

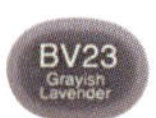 Layer on some BV23 to create depth.

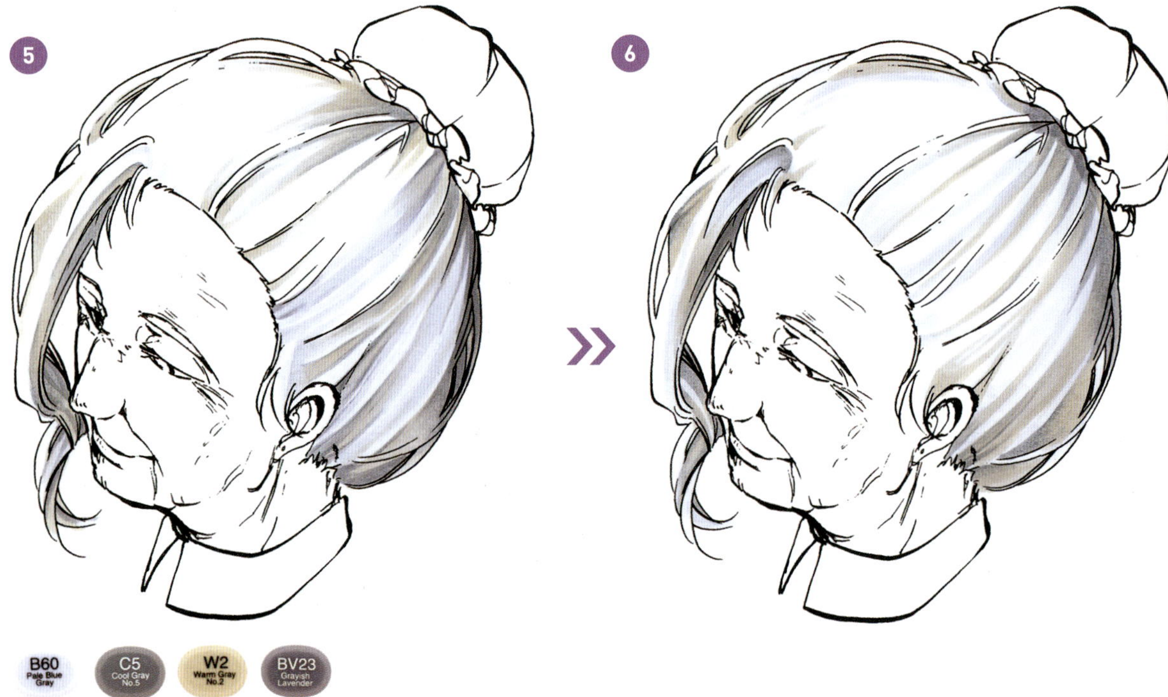

Use B60, C5, W2, and BV23 to draw hair lines moving toward the bun. Adjust colors as you go to achieve your desired look.

Finish by drawing the flow of the hair with white ink.

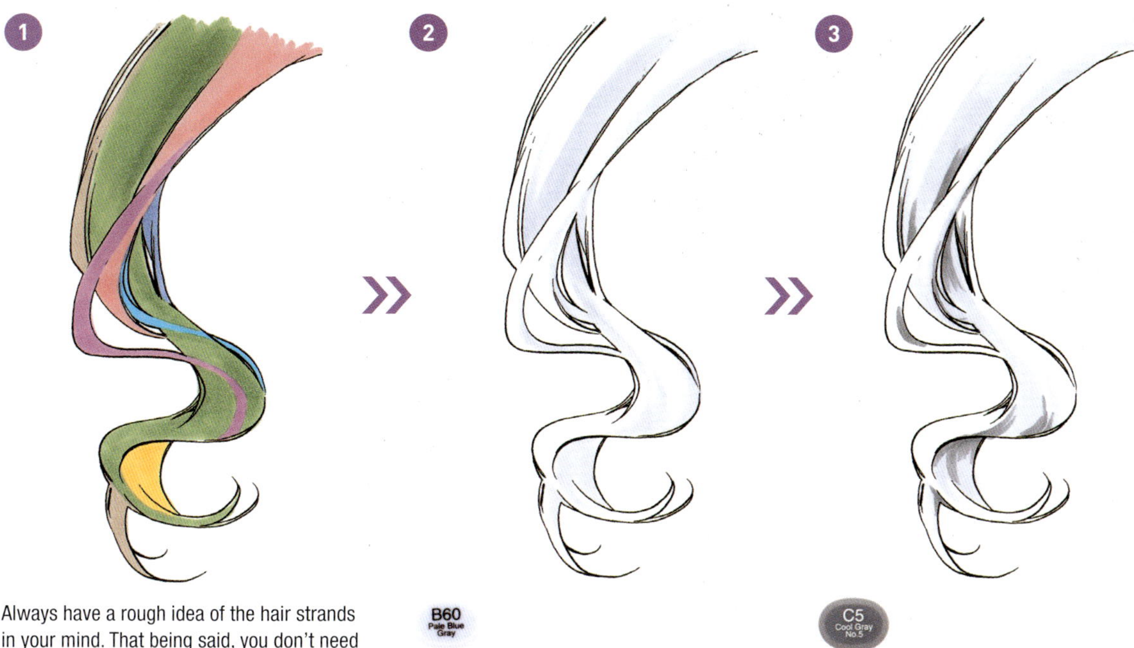

1 Always have a rough idea of the hair strands in your mind. That being said, you don't need to think about them too strictly, as in which strand connects one bunch to the one below. If you see hair that looks like it might be connected nearby, go ahead and connect it, but don't think too much about it.

2 Paint large shadowed areas with B60. This is like a primer coat.

3 Place C5 in the darker areas.

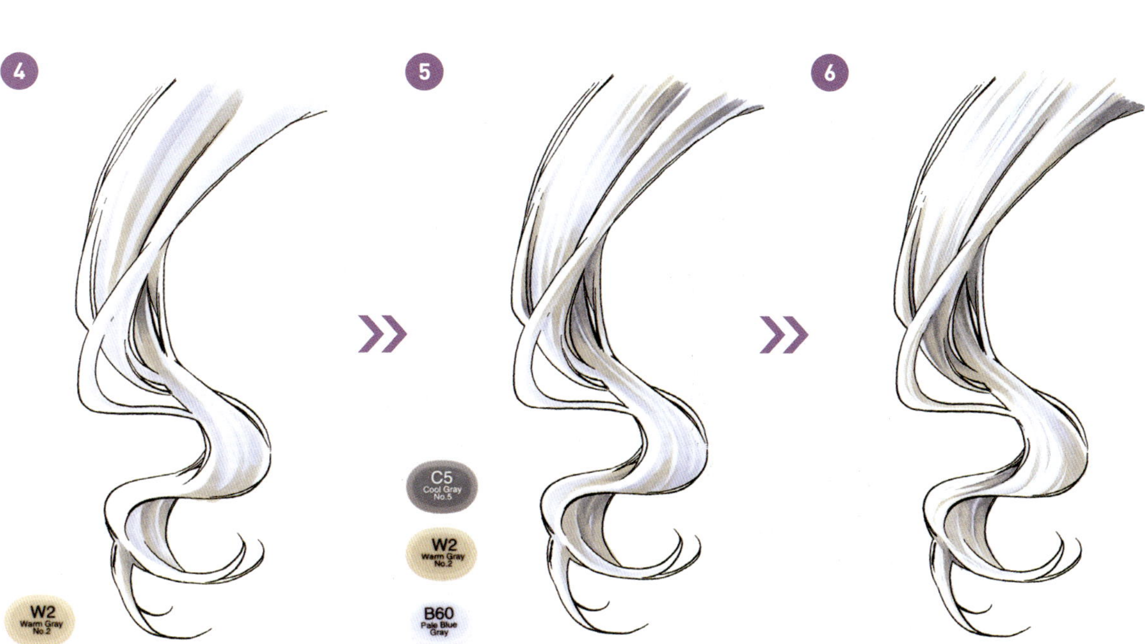

4 Blend the C5 with W2. Be careful not to disrupt the flow of the hair. It's okay to apply in the opposite direction as well, but if it's in a completely different direction, it won't look as smooth and sleek.

5 Use colors 2 to 4 to draw a fine flow of hair, starting with C5 (or BV23) and working up to W2 and then B60 to create a gradation of strands. Even if you paint a lot, it's okay because you can add white ink in 6. However, leave the areas where the light hits.

6 Add white ink. White, gold, and silver hair are very shiny, so I first put some white ink on the ball of my finger, and press it against the paper several times and blend. Then, add in the highlights.

Coloring the White Apron

1

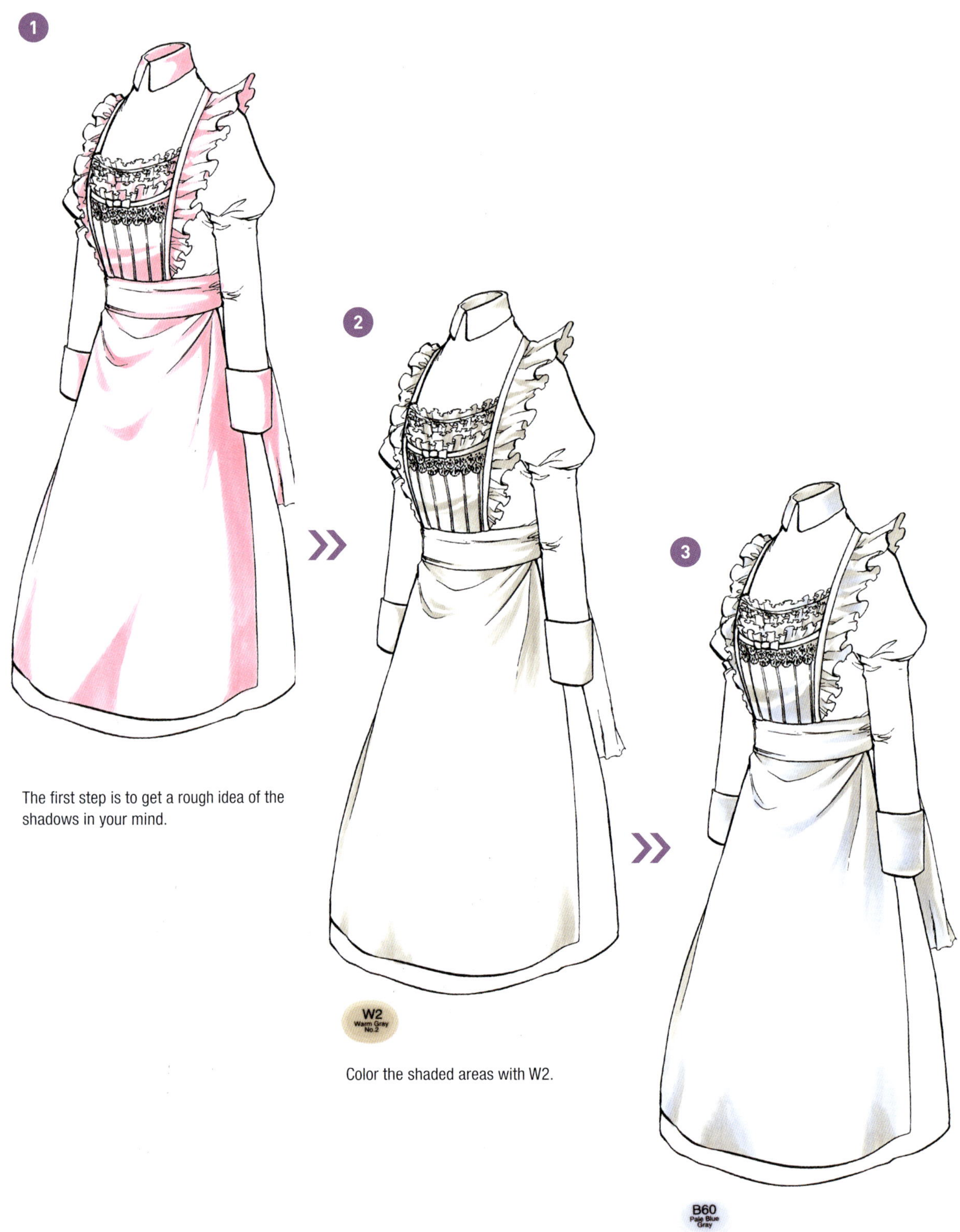

The first step is to get a rough idea of the shadows in your mind.

Color the shaded areas with W2.

First, simply blend B60.

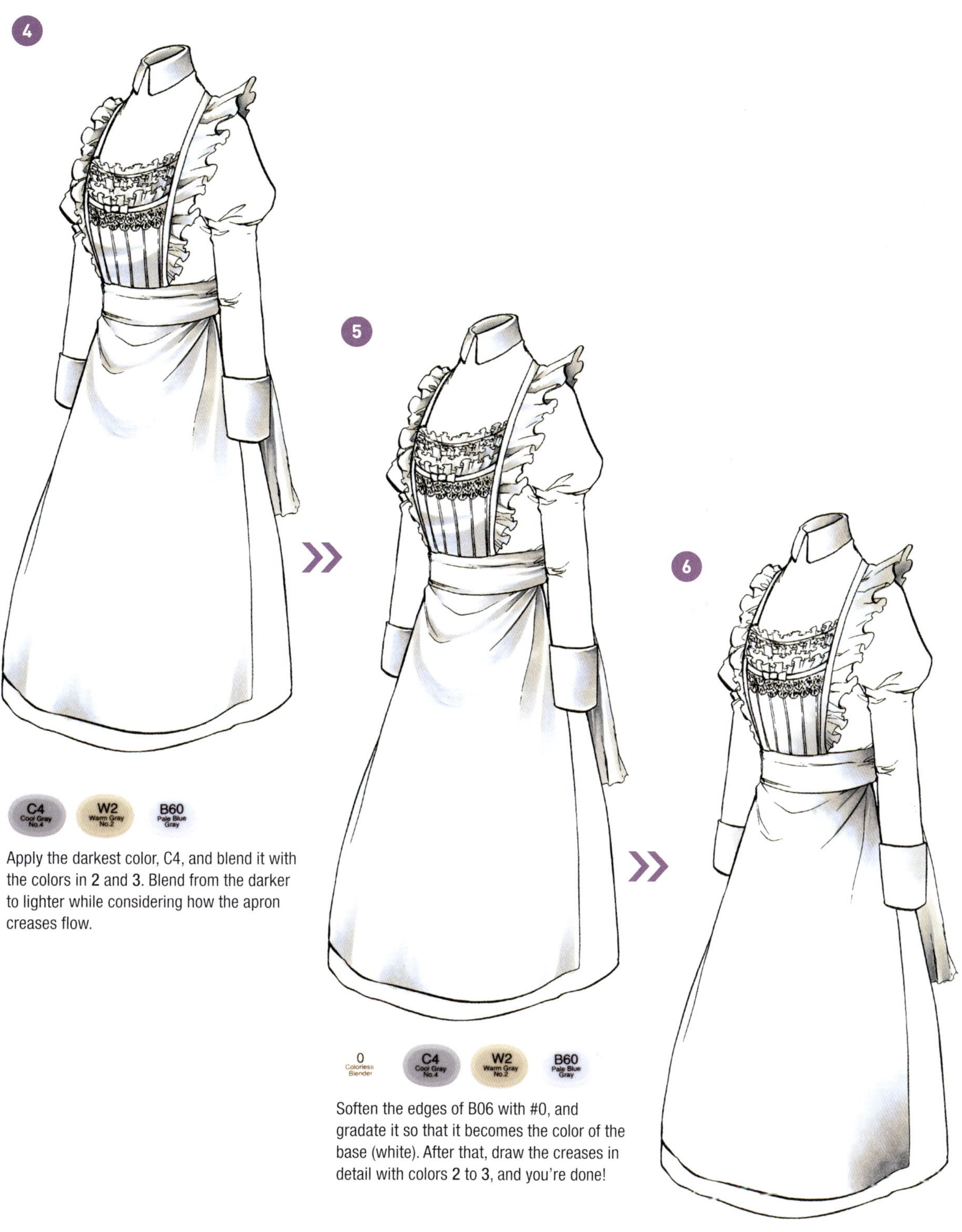

4

C4 — Cool Gray No.4 W2 — Warm Gray No.2 B60 — Pale Blue Gray

Apply the darkest color, C4, and blend it with the colors in **2** and **3**. Blend from the darker to lighter while considering how the apron creases flow.

5

0 — Colorless Blender C4 — Cool Gray No.4 W2 — Warm Gray No.2 B60 — Pale Blue Gray

Soften the edges of B06 with #0, and gradate it so that it becomes the color of the base (white). After that, draw the creases in detail with colors **2** to **3**, and you're done!

6

Similar to the example on p. 88, this coloring style, which makes use of blending and spreading colors over to neighboring areas, will achieve the look above.

Rendering Black Maid's Dress Textures

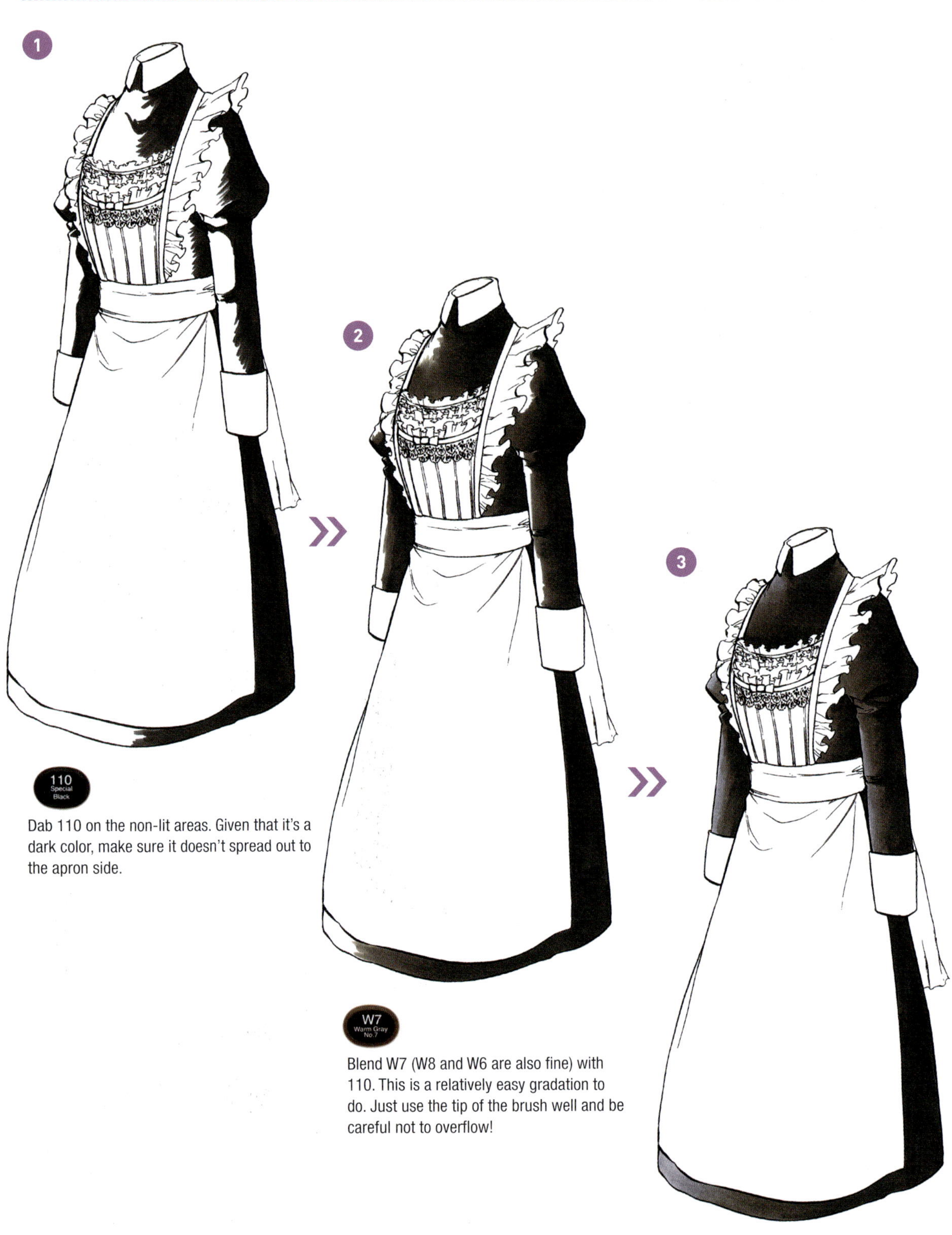

110
Special Black

Dab 110 on the non-lit areas. Given that it's a dark color, make sure it doesn't spread out to the apron side.

W7
Warm Gray No.7

Blend W7 (W8 and W6 are also fine) with 110. This is a relatively easy gradation to do. Just use the tip of the brush well and be careful not to overflow!

BV23
Grayish Lavender

Apply BV23 to the remaining areas. The base coat is now complete.

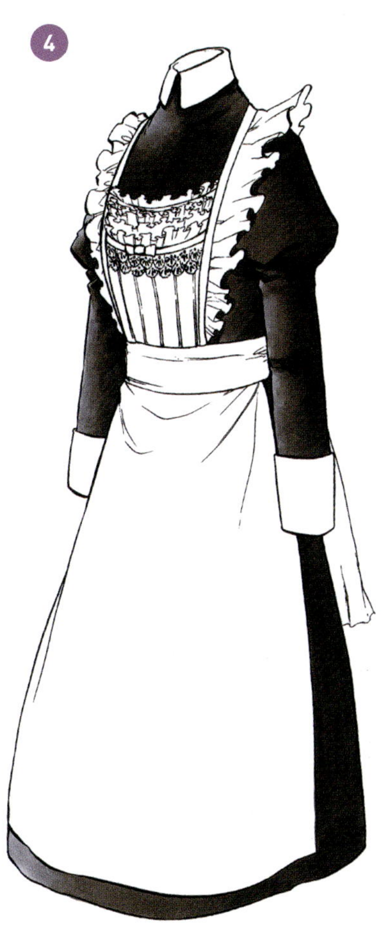

 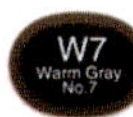 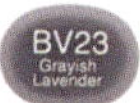

110 Special Black **W7** Warm Gray No.7 **BV23** Grayish Lavender

Then, using the three colors above, draw in the creases and you're done. I know some people are afraid to use dark colors, but dark colors are actually easier to gradate. So, I recommend this one if you want to practice.

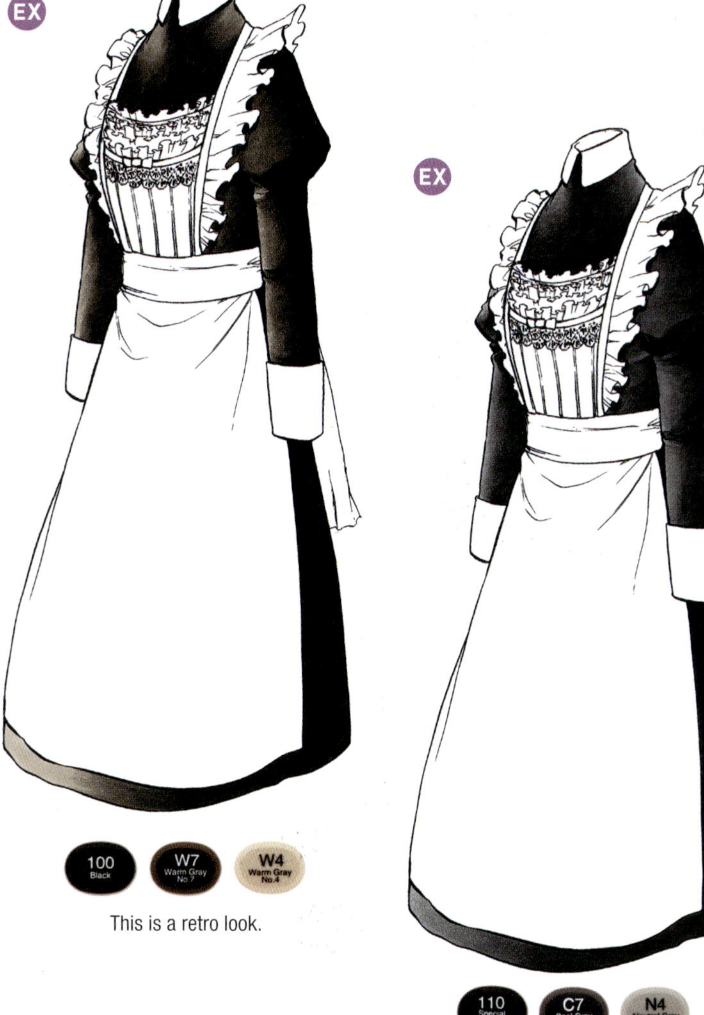

100 Black **W7** Warm Gray No.7 **W4** Warm Gray No.4

This is a retro look.

110 Special Black **C7** Cool Gray No.7 **N4** Neutral Gray No.4

This one has a high blue content and looks really sharp.

I used 110, W7, and BV23. In terms of the type of gray, W is gray with yellow, and N and C are gray moving toward blue. As for black, 100 is more compatible with W than 110. In this picture, the clothes themselves are more yellowish, but I wanted to make the light source more electric than natural light, so I used BV, which is actually even bluer than N and C. I prepared two different versions showing what would have happened if I had matched the colors.

Drawing a Brooch

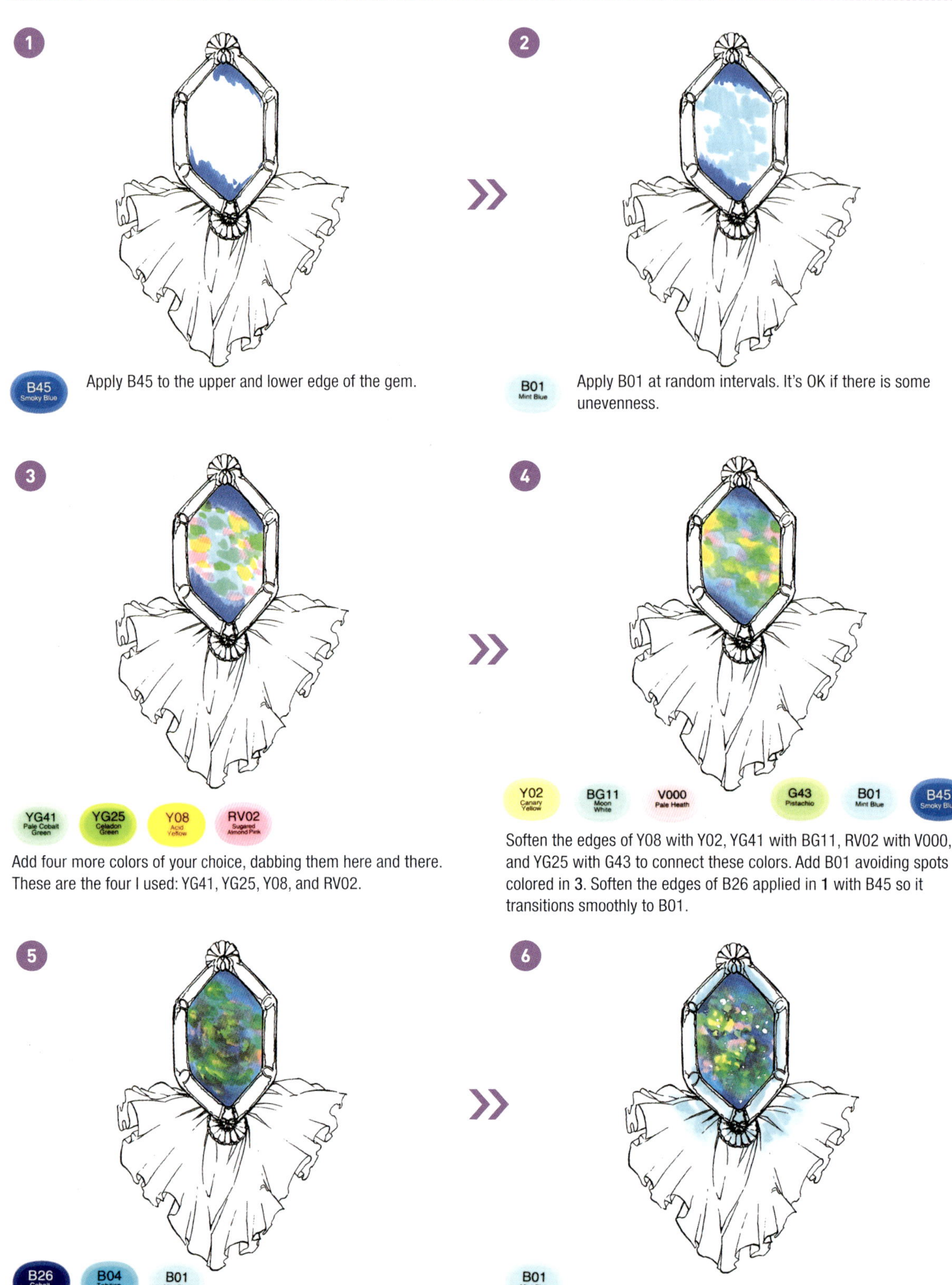

1 Apply B45 to the upper and lower edge of the gem.

B45 Smoky Blue

2 Apply B01 at random intervals. It's OK if there is some unevenness.

B01 Mint Blue

3 Add four more colors of your choice, dabbing them here and there. These are the four I used: YG41, YG25, Y08, and RV02.

YG41 Pale Cobalt Green · YG25 Celadon Green · Y08 Acid Yellow · RV02 Sugared Almond Pink

4 Soften the edges of Y08 with Y02, YG41 with BG11, RV02 with V000, and YG25 with G43 to connect these colors. Add B01 avoiding spots colored in 3. Soften the edges of B26 applied in 1 with B45 so it transitions smoothly to B01.

Y02 Canary Yellow · BG11 Moon White · V000 Pale Heath · G43 Pistachio · B01 Mint Blue · B45 Smoky Blue

5 Overlay B26, B04, and B01 in a way that the colors from 3 remain.

B26 Cobalt Blue · B04 Tahitian Blue · B01 Mint Blue

6 Sprinkle in some white ink and add B01 on the casing of the gem. You're done!

B01 Mint Blue

Transition

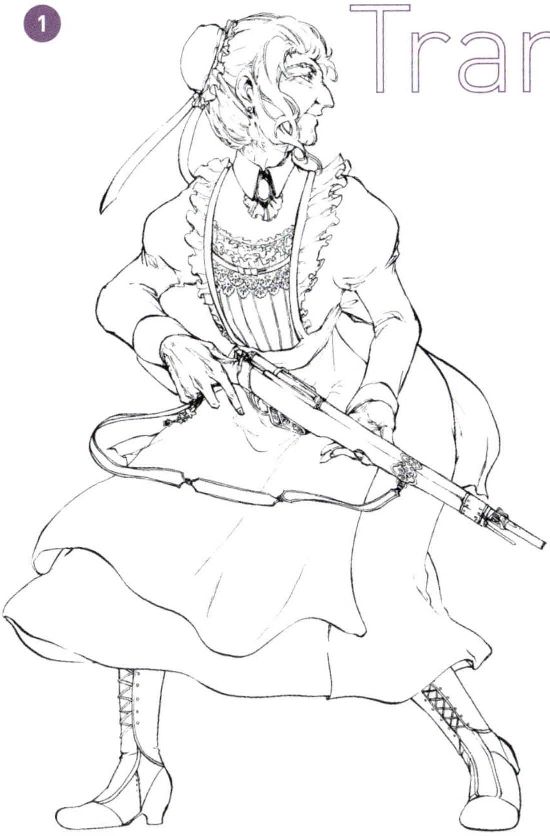

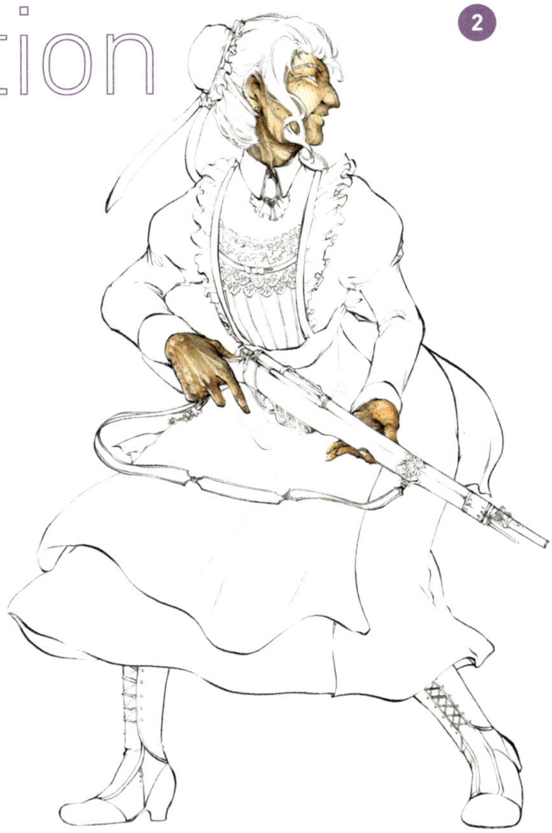

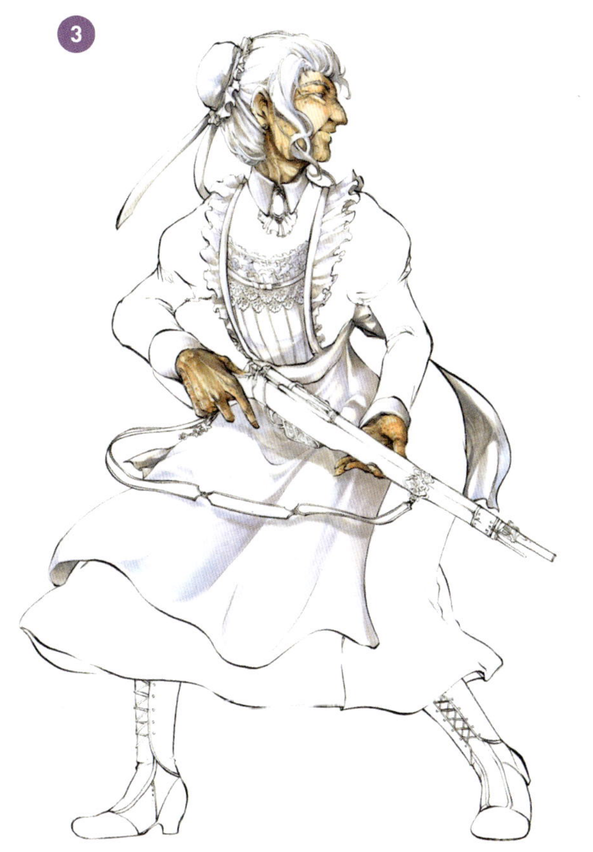

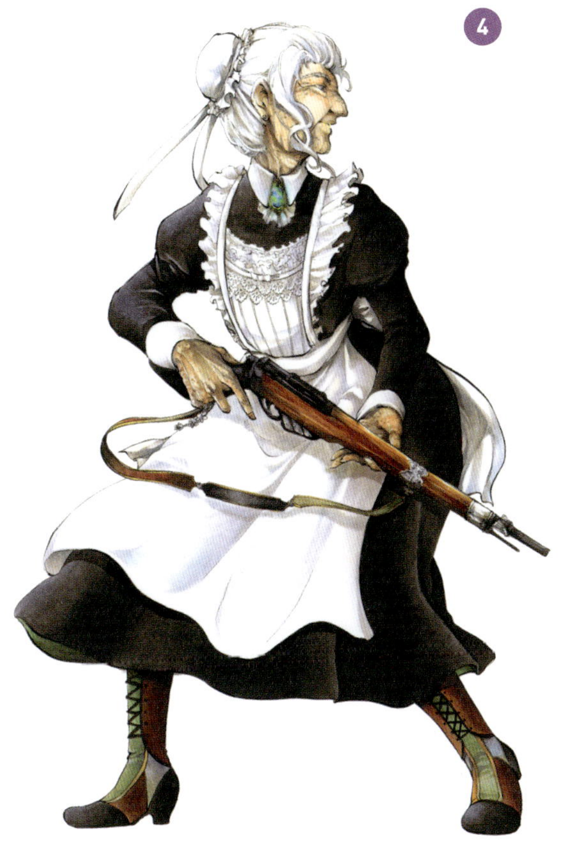

COPIC Sketch and COPIC Ciao

Color Chart on Kent Paper

This chart shows all 358 colors available in COPIC Sketch applied to Kent paper.

When purchasing COPIC markers, most people are at a loss about which colors to choose.

You would think it makes sense to choose a color by looking at the cap of the marker, but it often turns out that the color is not what you thought.

This is because the color may look different depending on the absorbency of the paper.

Having said that, for reference purposes, this section shows colors that are actually applied on paper.

We elected to use Kent paper, which is popularly used for illustrations and manga.

In addition, the color chart shows the colors for single applications and double applications. Note that the second application is painted on after letting the first application dry.

Use the color chart as your reference to find your desired colors.

* Although color reproduction here is as precise as possible, since the color charts are printed, they may not show all colors exactly.

* The maker of COPIC, Too Marker Production Inc., uses PM paper as their standard.

How to Use the Chart

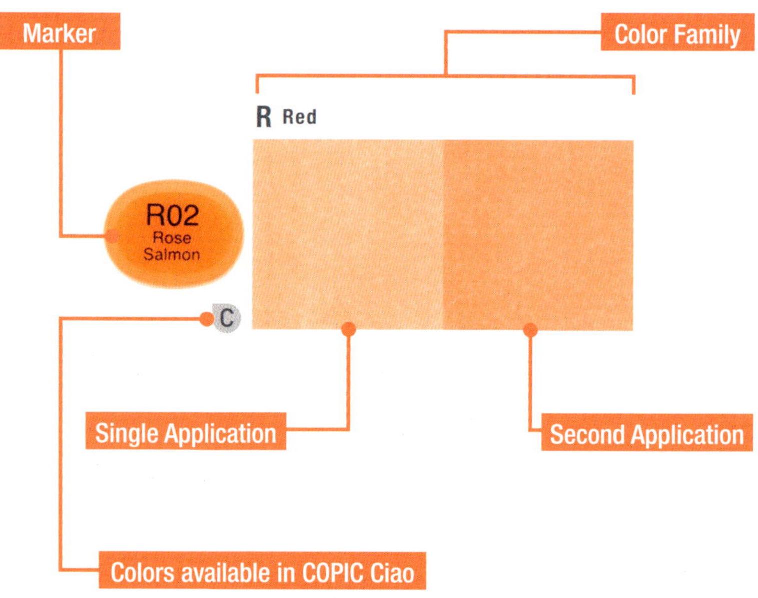

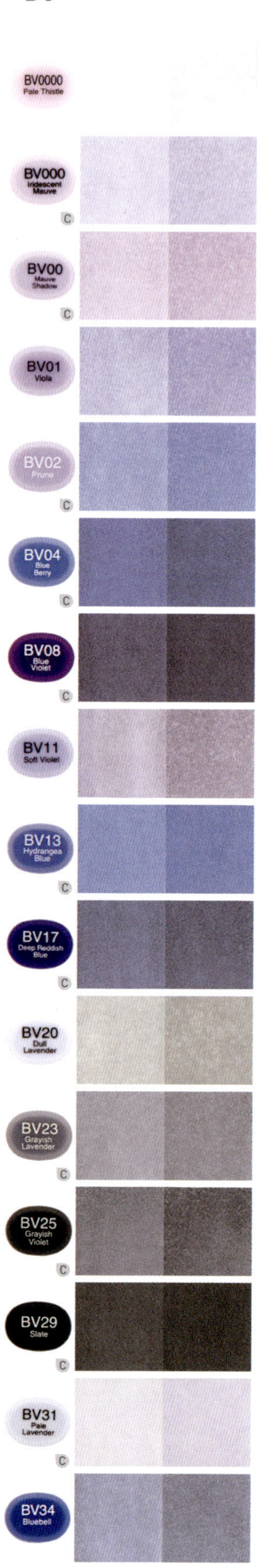

V Violet

Color	Swatch
V0000 Rose Quartz	
V000 Pale Heath	C
V01 Heath	C
V04 Lilac	C
V05 Azalea	
V06 Lavender	C
V09 Violet	C
V12 Pale Lilac	
V15 Mallow	C
V17 Amethyst	C
V20 Wisteria	
V22 Ash Lavender	
V25 Pale Blackberry	
V28 Eggplant	
V91 Pale Grape	C
V93 Early Grape	
V95 Light Grape	C
V99 Aubergine	

RV Red Violet

Color	Swatch
RV0000 Evening Primrose	
RV000 Pale Purple	C
RV00 Water Lily	C
RV02 Sugared Almond Pink	C
RV04 Shock Pink	
RV06 Cerise	C
RV09 Fuchsia	
RV10 Pale Pink	C
RV11 Pink	
RV13 Tender Pink	C
RV14 Begonia Pink	C
RV17 Deep Magenta	
RV19 Red Violet	
RV21 Light Pink	C
RV23 Pure Pink	C
RV25 Dog Rose Flower	
RV29 Crimson	C
RV32 Shadow Pink	
RV34 Dark Pink	C
RV42 Salmon Pink	C
RV52 Cotton Candy	
RV55 Hollyhock	
RV63 Begonia	
RV66 Raspberry	
RV69 Peony	C
RV91 Grayish Cherry	
RV93 Smoky Purple	
RV95 Baby Blossoms	C
RV99 Argyle Purple	

R Red

YR Yellow Red

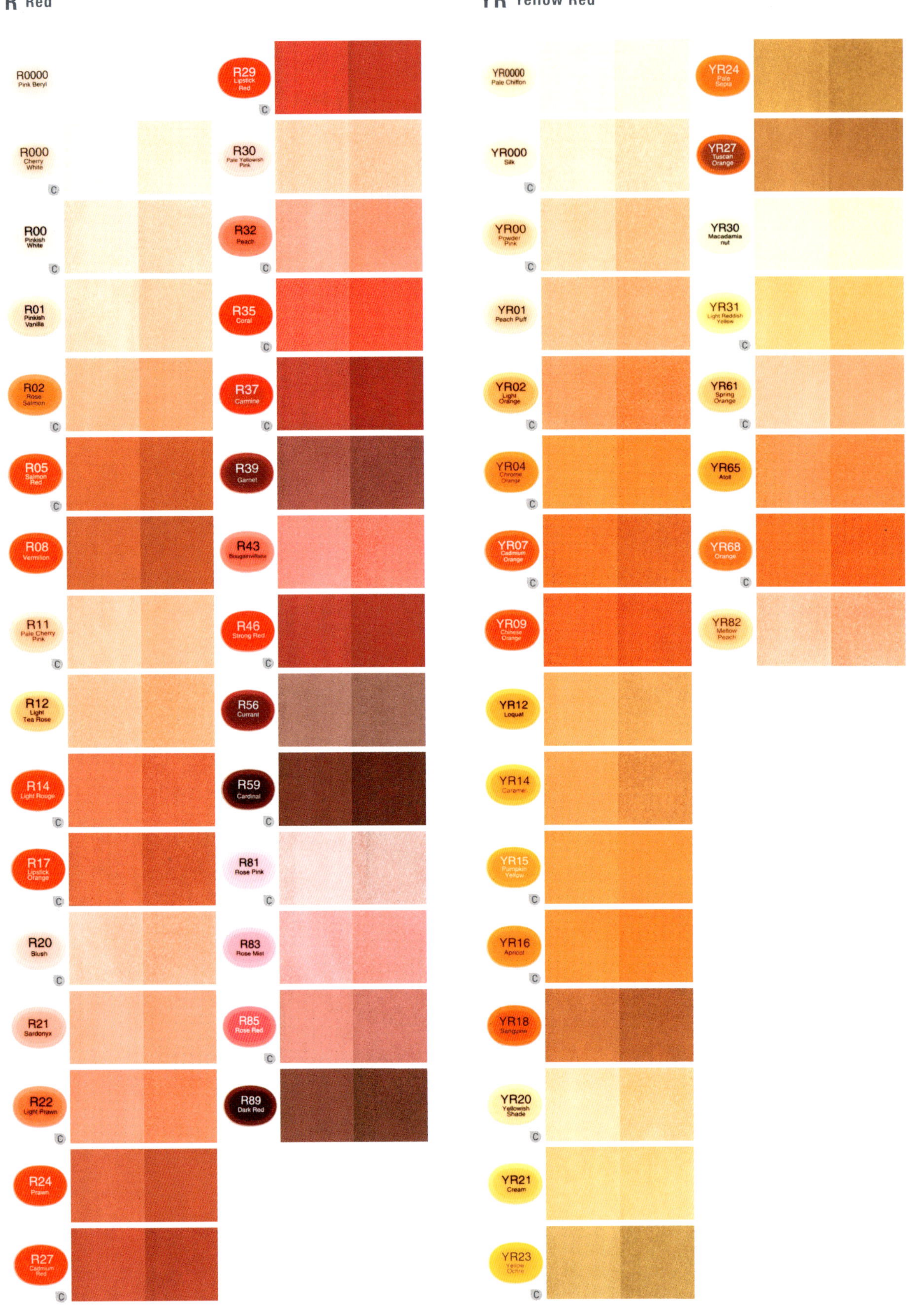

Y Yellow

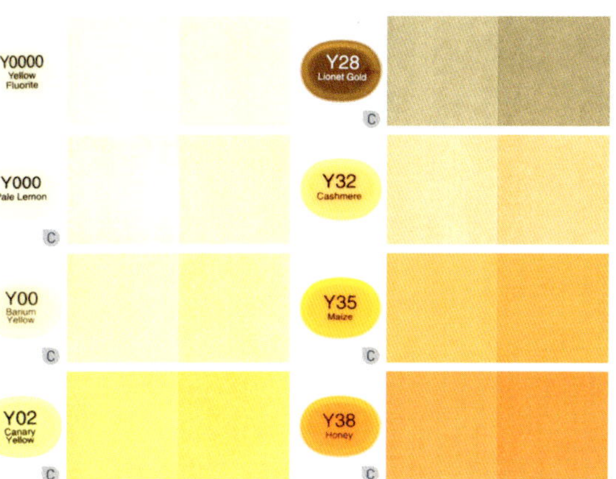

Y0000 Yellow Fluorite	Y28 Lionet Gold
Y000 Pale Lemon	Y32 Cashmere
Y00 Barium Yellow	Y35 Maize
Y02 Canary Yellow	Y38 Honey

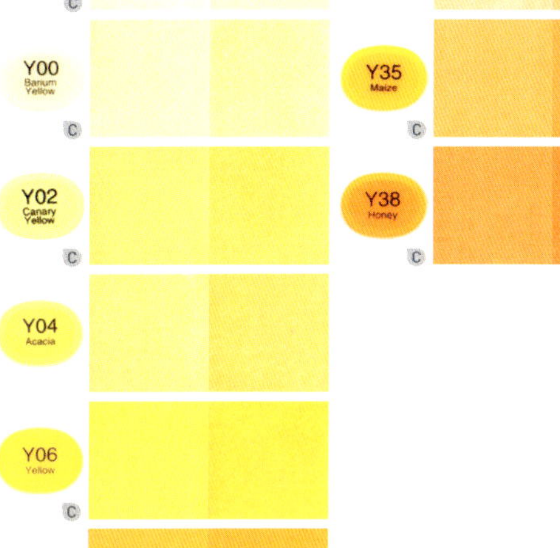

Y04 Acacia

Y06 Yellow

Y08 Acid Yellow

Y11 Pale Yellow

Y13 Lemon Yellow

Y15 Cadmium Yellow

Y17 Golden Yellow

Y18 Lightning Yellow

Y19 Napoli Yellow

Y21 Buttercup Yellow

Y23 Yellowish Beige

Y26 Mustard

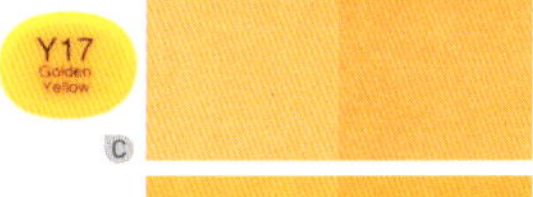

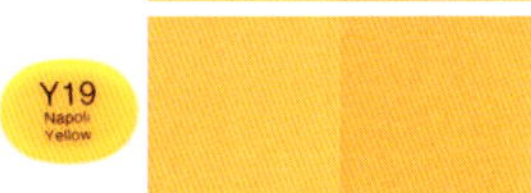

YG Yellow Green

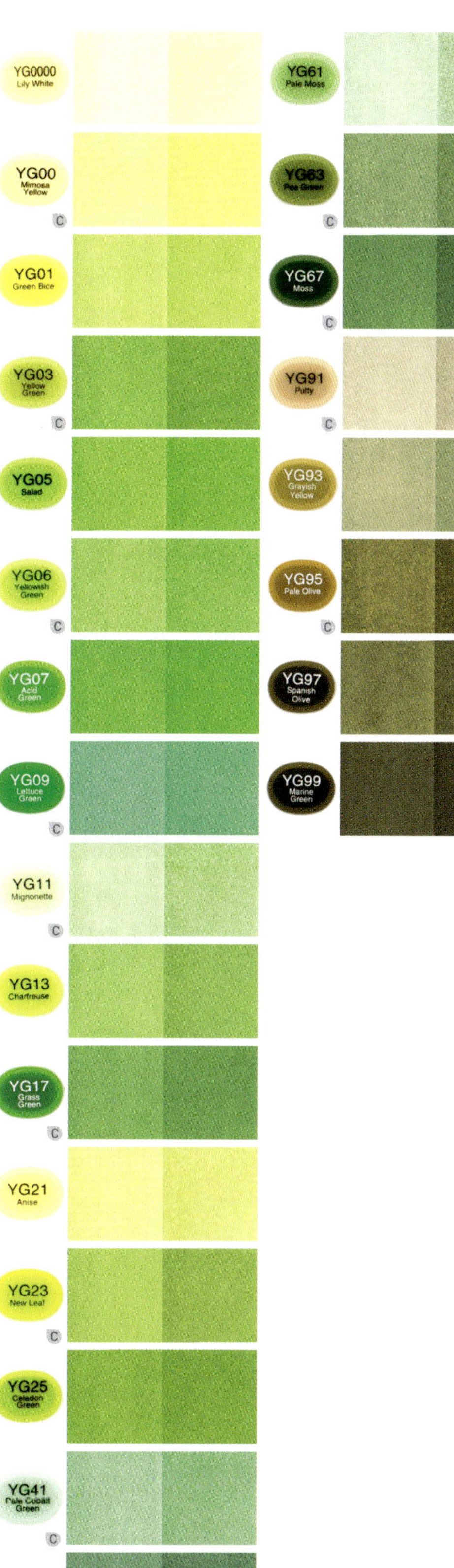

YG0000 Lily White

YG00 Mimosa Yellow

YG01 Green Bice

YG03 Yellow Green

YG05 Salad

YG06 Yellowish Green

YG07 Acid Green

YG09 Lettuce Green

YG11 Mignonette

YG13 Chartreuse

YG17 Grass Green

YG21 Anise

YG23 New Leaf

YG25 Celadon Green

YG41 Pale Cobalt Green

YG45 Cobalt Green

YG61 Pale Moss

YG63 Pea Green

YG67 Moss

YG91 Putty

YG93 Grayish Yellow

YG95 Pale Olive

YG97 Spanish Olive

YG99 Marine Green

G Green

- G0000 Crystal Opal
- G000 Pale Green
- G00 Jade Green
- G02 Spectrum Green
- G03 Meadow Green
- G05 Emerald Green
- G07 Nile Green
- G09 Veronese Green
- G12 Sea Green
- G14 Apple Green
- G16 Malachite
- G17 Forest Green
- G19 Bright Parrot Green
- G20 Wax White
- G21 Lime Green
- G24 Willow
- G28 Ocean Green
- G29 Pine Tree Green
- G40 Dim Green
- G43 Pistachio
- G46 Mistletoe
- G82 Spring Dim Green
- G85 Verdigris
- G94 Grayish Olive
- G99 Olive

BG Blue Green

- BG0000 Snow Green
- BG000 Pale Aqua
- BG01 Aqua Blue
- BG02 New Blue
- BG05 Holiday Blue
- BG07 Petroleum Blue
- BG09 Blue Green
- BG10 Cool Shadow
- BG11 Moon White
- BG13 Mint Green
- BG15 Aqua
- BG18 Teal Blue
- BG23 Coral Sea
- BG32 Aqua Mint
- BG34 Horizon Green
- BG45 Nile Blue
- BG49 Duck Blue
- BG53 Ice Mint
- BG57 Jasper
- BG70 Ocean Mist
- BG72 Ice Ocean
- BG75 Abyss Green
- BG78 Bronze
- BG90 Gray Sky
- BG93 Green Gray
- BG96 Bush
- BG99 Flagstone Blue

358 COLOR CHART

B Blue

B0000 Pale Celestine
C

B000 Pale Porcelain Blue
C

B00 Frost Blue
C

B01 Mint Blue

B02 Robin's Egg Blue
C

B04 Tahitian Blue

B05 Process Blue
C

B06 Peacock Blue

B12 Ice Blue
C

B14 Light Blue

B16 Cyanine Blue

B18 Lapis Lazuli
C

B21 Baby Blue

B23 Phthalo Blue
C

B24 Sky
C

B26 Cobalt Blue

B28 Royal Blue
C

B29 Ultramarine
C

B32 Pale Blue
C

B34 Manganese Blue

B37 Antwerp Blue

B39 Prussian Blue
C

B41 Powder Blue

B45 Smoky Blue
C

B52 Soft Greenish Blue

B60 Pale Blue Gray
C

B63 Light Hydrangea
C

B66 Clematis

B69 Stratospheric Blue

B79 Iris

B91 Pale Grayish Blue

B93 Light Crockery Blue
C

B95 Light Grayish Cobalt
C

B97 Night Blue

B99 Agate

F Fluorescent

FRV1 Fluorescent Pink

FYR1 Fluorescent Orange

FY1 Fluorescent Yellow Orange

FYG1 Fluorescent Yellow

FV2 Fluorescent Dull Violet

FYG2 Fluorescent Dull Y.G.

FBG2 Fluorescent Dull B.G.

FB2 Fluorescent Dull Blue

A Achromatic

0 Colorless Blender
C

100 Black
C

110 Special Black

E0000 Floral White	E23 Hazelnut	E47 Dark Brown	E89 Pecan
E000 Pale Fruit Pink	E25 Caribe Cocoa	E49 Dark Bark	E93 Tea Rose
E00 Cotton Pearl	E27 Milk Chocolate	E50 Egg Shell	E95 Tea Orange
E01 Pink Flamingo	E29 Burnt Umber	E51 Milky White	E97 Deep Orange
E02 Fruit Pink	E30 Bisque	E53 Raw Silk	E99 Baked Clay
E04 Lipstick Natural	E31 Brick Beige	E55 Light Camel	
E07 Light Mahogany	E33 Sand	E57 Light Walnut	
E08 Brown	E34 Toast	E59 Walnut	
E09 Burnt Sienna	E35 Chamois	E70 Ash Rose	
E11 Barley Beige	E37 Sepia	E71 Champagne	
E13 Light Suntan	E39 Leather	E74 Cocoa Brown	
E15 Dark Suntan	E40 Brick White	E77 Maroon	
E17 Reddish Brass	E41 Pearl White	E79 Cashew	
E18 Copper	E42 Sand White	E81 Ivory	
E19 Redwood	E43 Dull Ivory	E84 Khaki	
E21 Soft Sun	E44 Clay	E87 Fig	

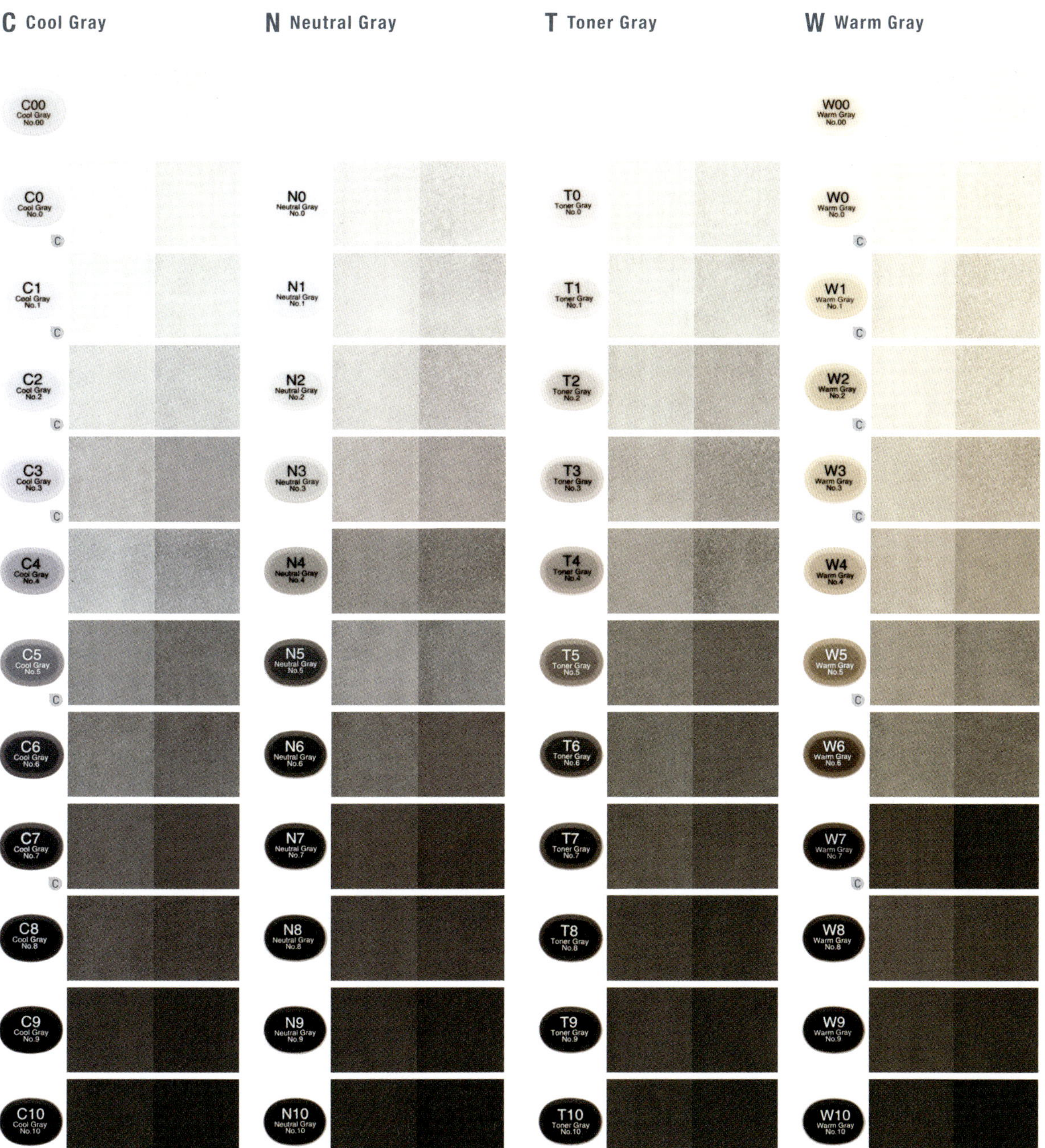

C00
Cool Gray
No.00
C0
Cool Gray
No.0
C1
Cool Gray
No.1
C2
Cool Gray
No.2
C3
Cool Gray
No.3
C4
Cool Gray
No.4
C5
Cool Gray
No.5
C6
Cool Gray
No.6
C7
Cool Gray
No.7
C8
Cool Gray
No.8
C9
Cool Gray
No.9
C10
Cool Gray
No.10
N0
Neutral Gray
No.0
N1
Neutral Gray
No.1
N2
Neutral Gray
No.2
N3
Neutral Gray
No.3
N4
Neutral Gray
No.4
N5
Neutral Gray
No.5
N6
Neutral Gray
No.6
N7
Neutral Gray
No.7
N8
Neutral Gray
No.8
N9
Neutral Gray
No.9
N10
Neutral Gray
No.10
T0
Toner Gray
No.0
T1
Toner Gray
No.1
T2
Toner Gray
No.2
T3
Toner Gray
No.3
T4
Toner Gray
No.4
T5
Toner Gray
No.5
T6
Toner Gray
No.6
T7
Toner Gray
No.7
T8
Toner Gray
No.8
T9
Toner Gray
No.9
T10
Toner Gray
No.10
W00
Warm Gray
No.00
W0
Warm Gray
No.0
W1
Warm Gray
No.1
W2
Warm Gray
No.2
W3
Warm Gray
No.3
W4
Warm Gray
No.4
W5
Warm Gray
No.5
W6
Warm Gray
No.6
W7
Warm Gray
No.7
W8
Warm Gray
No.8
W9
Warm Gray
No.9
W10
Warm Gray
No.10

Manga artist and illustrator **Midorihana**'s techniques
for using COPIC markers are highly regarded. Her
unique worldview manifests itself in her illustrations
and captivates many fans. She uses various pen
names; for example, broccolico and Hidekazu Gomi.
Her work is found in major publications, including
Rock and *Shōnen Sunday Comics*. She is also the
author of *How to Render Eye-Catching Textures with
COPIC Markers*. She lives in Tokyo.

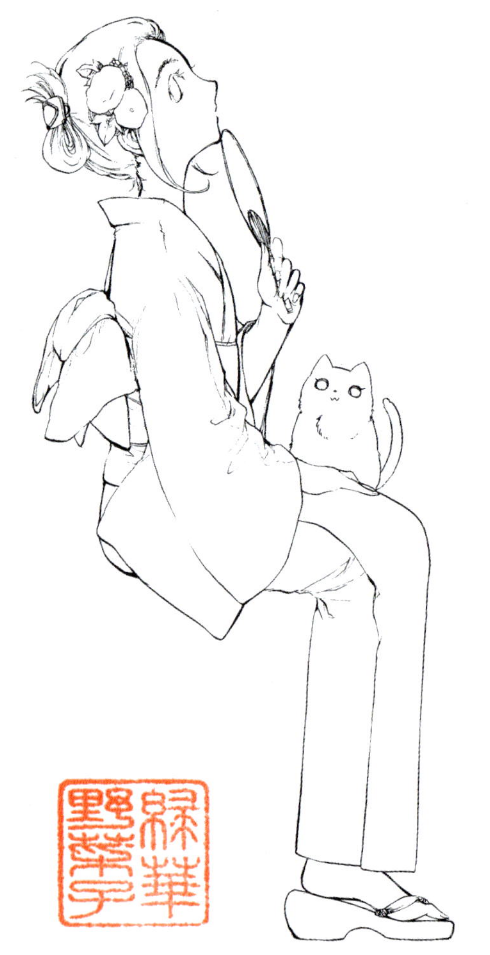